PENGUIN

ARKANA

The Gods of Change

The ancient science of astrology, founded on the correlation between celestial movements and terrestrial events, recognizes the
universe as an indivisible whole in which all parts are interconnected. Mirroring this perception of the unity of life, modern
physics has revealed the web of relationship underlying
everything in existence. Despite the inevitable backlash as old
paradigms expire, we are now entering an age where scientific
explanations and models of the cosmos are in accord with basic
astrological principles and beliefs. In such a climate, astrology is
poised to emerge again as a serious study offering a greater understanding of our true nature. Arkana's *Contemporary Astrology
Series* offers, in readable books written by experts, the insight and
practical wisdom the world is now ready to receive from the
newest vanguard of astrological thought.

Howard Sasportas, an American who lived in London from 1973
until his death in 1992, established a reputation as one of the
world's leading consultant astrologers. In 1979 he was awarded
the Gold Medal for the Faculty of Astrological Studies Diploma
Exam. He was the first series editor of Arkana's Contemporary
Astrology Series and was the author of *The Twelve Houses: An
Introduction to the Houses in Astrological Interpretation* (1985) and
Mercury, Venus and Mars (1992).

D1133925

Other books in Arkana's Contemporary Astrology Series

CONTEMPORARY ASTROLOGY
Series Editor: Erin Sullivan

Howard Sasportas

THE GODS OF CHANGE

*Pain, Crisis and the Transits of
Uranus, Neptune and Pluto*

ARKANA
PENGUIN BOOKS

ARKANA

Published by the Penguin Group
Penguin Books Ltd, 27 Wrights Lane, London W8 5TZ, England
Penguin Books USA Inc., 375 Hudson Street, New York, New York 10014, USA
Penguin Books Australia Ltd, Ringwood, Victoria, Australia
Penguin Books Canada Ltd, 10 Alcorn Avenue, Toronto, Ontario, Canada M4V 3B2
Penguin Books (NZ) Ltd, 182–190 Wairau Road, Auckland 10, New Zealand

Penguin Books Ltd, Registered Offices: Harmondsworth, Middlesex, England

First published 1989
5 7 9 10 8 6 4

Printed in England by Clays Ltd, St Ives plc
Filmset in 10/12 pt Photina

To Rob

Contents

Acknowledgements

My thanks go to Marion Russell and Eileen Campbell for getting the ball rolling, and to my agent Barbara Levy for dealing so skilfully with the complicated contractual issues which arose out of the Neptunian blue. Thanks also go to Dennis Hyde and Robert Walker for seeing me through the more difficult moments and to Liz Greene, Margi Robinson and many other friends who gave me advice and encouragement. Finally, I am especially grateful to Christine Murdock, whose friendship, support and editorial assistance in the later stages helped make writing this book a much happier experience.

Introduction

Your pain is but the breaking of the shell that encloses your understanding.

KAHLIL GIBRAN

Life isn't always easy. It's impossible to live deeply and not to feel pain or go through times of crisis, breakdown or major disruptive change. Although this is clearly inevitable, what is not always obvious is the crucial role pain and crisis play in the process of growth and evolution. While some people fall apart altogether and never make it through difficult times, many others emerge from conflict and turmoil renewed and transformed, indeed, more fully alive. They 'return' to life with a renewed commitment to a neglected potential, with a renewed sense of what we might call the 'sacred' in life, and with a richly enhanced sensitivity to others.

The ancient Chinese had a wise word for crisis: *wei-chi*, a combination of two words, danger (*wei*) and opportunity (*chi*). A crisis can be viewed as a catastrophe, as something terrible to be avoided at all costs, but it also can be understood as a turning point, a critical step or stage in development – as the possibility for something new to happen, an opportunity for letting go and changing. It's quite human to draw away from painful situations, to crave for things to return to the way they were before the crisis occurred. And yet it's also possible that these times can be used as opportunities to develop and grow, to learn more about life and oneself. Something dies, but something new is born. Nothing is left unchanged: the old is taken away, but something different may emerge.

The question is thus not 'how can we avoid pain, crisis or change?' but rather 'how can we understand and use these periods in our lives most creatively?' Roberto Assagioli, the founder of Psychosynthesis called this 'the collaboration with the inevitable'.[1] Living fully means experiencing and accepting both the light and the dark, joy and pain. Inevitably there will be times of disruption, even anguish, in all our lives, but there is nothing to stop us from finding ways to grow and learn from these periods.

I'm often asked 'What brings people to astrologers?' Some of my clients come primarily out of curiosity – a friend of theirs had a reading done and told them about it and now they want to know more about what goes on in an astrology session. Others are motivated by a belief or hope that the chart might cast some light on how they could more fully use their potentials and resources. But in my experience, the majority of people come because they are in some sort of crisis. They pick up the phone and ring an astrologer because they are desperate to know what is going on in their lives; something is happening which they are unable to deal with – their usual ways of trying to resolve their problems aren't working, and they feel as if they've lost control. They're in the middle of relationship turmoils; they're having crises at work; they can't cope with their children; they can't cope with their parents; they're confronting a life-threatening illness or facing the death of someone close to them; they are in the middle of a depression or they have lost the will to live. Some people come to me in the hope that I will work magic, and make everything instantly all better for them. Others see my role as astrologer more realistically, as a counsellor and guide, someone who may be able to help them find meaning and relevance in what they are having to face.

In most cases, times of pain, crisis, breakdown or change correlate with major transits to or from Saturn, Chiron, Uranus, Neptune and Pluto, or progressions involving these planets. Each of these planets brings its own distinctive dilemma, its own particular type of trauma, test or trial. A conflict earmarked by Saturn is different in nature from a crisis involving Uranus; Neptunian confusion doesn't feel the same as Uranian disruption; and pulverizing Pluto works on us in its own unforgettable way, reminding us of the adage that 'life is like a stone – either it grinds you down or polishes you up'. Sometimes two, three, or all of these planets join forces, and touch important points in the chart at nearly the same time, as if the cosmos has decided to 'gang up' on a person. But no matter what specific kinds of conflicts, traumas, paradoxes or dilemmas they bring, these planets all have one thing in common: they don't want to leave us the same way they found us.

Dane Rudhyar once wrote that 'it is not the event which happens to the person, but the person which happens to the event. An individual meets particular events because he needs them in order to become more fully what he is only potentially.'[2] Clearly then, our attitude towards pain and crisis will affect the way we go through such periods: if we believe that a crisis is only something terrible and our main impetus is somehow to turn back the clock and get rid of it as quickly as possible, we are likely to stay caught in the crisis for a longer period of time. However, if we believe, like the ancient Chinese, that a crisis is an opportunity for something new to be born, we increase our capacity to use these periods constructively. Some people are fortunate: even in the midst of great turmoil or despair, they can glimpse the meaning or relevance a crisis has in terms of their growth and development, and this understanding helps them through their difficulties. For others, a longer time passes before they can begin to see any purpose in their misfortune, or the opportunities for new life which it offers. And, sadly, a number of people may never come out of the crisis at all – they remain oriented not to the future but to the past, longing for what life used to be like, and forgoing the chance to live with a new, hard-won wisdom.

Our attitudes towards these phases of life not only affect how we as individuals go through such periods, but also how we as astrologers communicate with our clients. If our tendency is to view these times as wholly negative, how can we help others find meaning in what they are going through? If our pattern is to avoid turmoil or conflict at all costs, we will probably (directly or indirectly) encourage our clients to do the same. We will try to make everything 'all better' and rescue people as quickly as possible – not realizing that in doing so, we are depriving them of the strength or the transformation which facing the crisis could bring.

The purpose of this book is to focus on the kinds of changes and crises associated with the transits of Uranus, Neptune and Pluto, and the potentials for growth and development which they offer.[3] Wherever possible, I have included examples gathered from my astrological practice, and the last chapter explores three case histories in greater depth.[4] This book can be used simply as a guide to interpreting the outer planets by transit; but more than that, I hope it will enable the reader to gain a little more insight into what is needed to turn a crisis into an opportunity.

Howard Sasportas
London, 1988

PART ONE

The Collaboration with the Inevitable

The Search for Meaning

Woe to him who saw no more sense in his life, no aim, no purpose, and therefore no point in carrying on. He was soon lost.

VIKTOR FRANKL

Jung once wrote that 'meaning makes a great deal of things bearable – perhaps everything'. Meaning helps us get through life. We have more chance of dealing constructively with pain or crisis if we can find some sort of meaning, relevance or purpose in what we are going through or having to endure. No better example of this can be found than in Viktor Frankl's book *Man's Search for Meaning*.[1] In this book, Frankl describes the time he spent in a German concentration camp from 1943 to 1945, historical events which, for many, mark a watershed in Western consciousness, radically calling into question our notions of moral and immoral behaviour, or even of good and evil, of the existence of a benevolent deity. From his personal experience, he concludes that (aside from pure chance) the inmates who managed to survive such degradation were those who could attribute some kind of meaning or purpose to what they had to face. Some people found meaning through the belief that God was testing them, while others found a more concrete, personal motive for staying alive: 'I have to survive in order to see my family again.' Frankl's own capacity to endure the horrors of the camp stemmed from a powerful urge to live so that he could tell others about what had actually gone on there. Frankl writes of the day when he felt he could take no more, when the winds were bitterly cold; when, he, sick and starving, was forced to march many miles, his feet already covered in sores. He wanted to die. But then he had a vision, a picture of himself standing on the platform of a comfortable, well-lit lecture room where a captivated audience sat in front of him to hear him deliver a talk on the psychology of the concentration camp. This vision helped to keep him alive – it gave meaning and purpose to what he had to endure. He had to survive in order to tell the world just how horrific it had been. At that moment, Frankl realized something he would never forget and which later became one of the philosophical premises upon which his own form of psychotherapy (logotherapy) was based: 'The prisoner who had lost faith in the future – his future – was doomed. With his loss of belief in the future, he also lost his spiritual hold; he let himself decline and became subject to mental and physical decay ... he simply gave up.'[2] Nietzsche wrote: 'He who has a *why* to live can bear with almost any *how*.' As Frankl discovered through his personal ordeal, if we can find some sort of meaning in a painful event, even if we are only open to the *possibility* of meaning, we may find the resources to face the crisis more honestly, perhaps even courageously. 'Life ultimately means taking the responsibility to find the right answer to its problems and to fulfil the tasks which it constantly sets for each individual.'[3]

The Core Self and the Birthchart

One way I find meaning in life is through the belief that we all have a deeper Self or core Self which guides, unfolds, and regulates our growth and development. Just as an apple seed 'knows' that it is meant to grow into an apple and not a pear, there is a part of us which 'knows' what we are meant to become and the path we need to follow to get there. Concepts such as individuation, self-realization and self-fulfilment describe the process of growing into what we are meant to become. Piero Ferrucci, in *What We May Be*, describes his view of how we unfold according to certain inner designs:

There seems to be a way for things to happen which is intrinsically *right* for them: they become what they were meant to be. Aristotle called the end of this process *entelechy* – the full and perfect realization of what was previously in a potential state. Whether it appears in a butterfly flying out of its cocoon, in a ripe fruit falling from a tree, or in the development of an acorn into an oak, this process clearly evidences qualities of harmony and underlying intelligence ... According to the Eastern doctrine of *dharma*, we are each called upon to achieve a particular life-pattern ... Each of us should try to discover the pattern and cooperate with its realization.[4]

This is where the birthchart is uniquely useful, for it reveals the nature of our seed: it is a map or guide suggesting what the deeper, core Self has in mind for us. The birthchart tells us something about the kind of seed we are – whether, as Liz Greene puts it, we're a lentil or avocado or a brussel sprout. Consultant astrologer Christina Rose compares looking at the birthchart with looking at the picture on the front of a seed packet: you can see from the picture what the seed is meant to grow into and become.

In the introduction to *Planets in Transit*, Robert Hand makes a similar point:

It is my belief, which I cannot 'prove' here, that within each of us is a creative core that actively creates the universe, either by making up each part out of nothing or by agreeing in advance, prior to our physical incarnation, to play a certain game with certain rules. In this scheme your horoscope becomes a symbol of your intentions, not a record of what is going to *happen* to you. As astrologer Zipporah Dobyns likes to say, character is destiny.[5]

The idea that there is a deeper Self guiding our development also is echoed by Liz Greene, although she chooses to call it by another name:

From what I have observed in my analysands and my astrological clients, there is certain something – whether one calls it fate, Providence, natural law, karma or the unconscious – that retaliates when its boundaries are transgressed or when it receives no respect or effort at relationship, and which seems to possess a kind of 'absolute knowledge' not only of what the individual needs, but of what he is *going* to need for his unfolding in life ... I make no pretence of knowing what 'it' is, but I am unashamedly prepared to call it fate.[6]

The Timing of the Seed

The birthchart is a moment frozen in time – a picture of the heaven as it appeared at the time of birth from the place of birth. But the planets don't stop moving at birth: they keep going, and as they keep moving, they do things such as coming back full circle to where they were at birth, or they cross over another planet's natal position, or they make a square (90-degree angle), or an opposition (180-degree angle) or other angles to where they were in the birthchart. *Transits* show where the planets are now in the heaven in relationship to where they were at birth. *Progressions*, another form of updating the chart, symbolically depict how the movements of the planets after birth are affecting the natal chart. The birthchart reveals what kind of seed we are, but the transits and progressions to the chart tell us something about the *timing* of our seed. Is something ready to be sown? Is something new ready to grow? Some seeds may take only weeks to germinate, others may take many months or years to grow.

Each of us is in a continual process of unfoldment, and it is my belief that transits and progressions show what our deeper Self (that part of us which guides and unfolds our development) has in mind for us at any point in our lives. The core Self energizes different aspects of the psyche and the chart according to what new or further growth is to be achieved at any particular phase of development. Transits and progressions reveal what the core Self wants to make happen for us – what the deeper Self intends to bring to our attention to develop or work on. In order to co-operate with our inner growth and unfoldment, we need to listen to what is going on inside us. If we do so, we will experience transits and progressions to our birthcharts as urges and inclinations stemming from within our own psyches.

However, we cannot deny the fact that transits and progressions often *do* correlate with outer events which seem to land on us out of the blue. Even so, I still believe that these events are the synchronous external manifestation of inner changes which are taking place. In other words, the core Self may use outer events to promote the kinds of changes we need to go through in order to grow into what we are meant to become. Earlier I quoted Robert Hand's theory that the birthchart shows the original intentions of our creative core Self. He also makes this point about transits and progressions:

> Both transits and progressions indicate the working out of various phases of this original intention. Although I frequently lapse into causal vocabulary ... I do not believe that the planets 'cause' anything. They are merely signs of the manifestation of the original intention, part of which is experienced as flowing through you as will. This is the intention that you are aware of. Part of the intention is experienced as coming from without; you may call it fate, destiny or circumstances beyond your control. But this, too, comes from within you, and you need only raise your consciousness to know it. Part of the function of astrology is to raise the individual's consciousness in just this way.[7]

If we are not listening to or respecting the growth pattern the core Self has in mind for us, we are more likely to attract outer circumstances into our lives which force us to change or adapt. For instance, when transiting Uranus conjuncts our Venus, the time has arrived for us to alter our existing patterns of relationship. If we are attuned to our inner world, we probably know this and can do what is necessary to respect this next step of development. But if we are frightened or reluctant to accept the Uranian urges which are making themselves felt through our Venus, the transit could manifest as an external event which coerces us to change. In this case, our partner may leave or disrupt the relationship, forcing us to make needed changes in this area of life. In other words, the core Self will often work through events to bring to our awareness the kind of growth it expects from us at any time in our life. Again, I quote Hand, who elaborates on the relationship between the inner psychological significance of transits and the kinds of outer events we attract into our lives:

> It is my contention that ultimately transits signify changes totally within the self – psychological changes, to be sure, but only if you expand what is normally meant by psychological. However, you may experience these inward changes either as psychological

changes in the conventional sense, as social interactions, or as events totally outside of yourself. An 'event' may also be felt as an illness. These are projections through which your inner energies are experienced at various different levels of life. This is an important idea to understand, because if you do not understand how you are involved in causing a particular event, it means that you are operating unconsciously and arc therefore not in control of the circumstances.[8]

Liz Greene, in *The Astrology of Fate*, also attributes an uncanny intelligence to what she calls fate, and to what I am referring to as the core Self:

It appears to make arrangements of the most particular and astonishing kind, bringing a person together with another person or an external situation at precisely the right moment, and it appears to be as much part of the inner man as the outer. It also appears to be both psychic, and physical, personal and collective, 'higher' and 'lower', and can wear the mask of Mephistopheles as readily as it can present itself as God ... And I feel that if we understood this thing better we might be of far greater assistance to our clients, not to mention ourselves.[9]

Finding Meaning in Transits and Progressions

Properly understood, transits and progressions give the astrologer insight into the deeper and more essential meaning of a particular life-experience or phase of development in the client's life. An examination of the chart through these methods reveals in a clear and concise way those parts of a person's nature which are ready to be consciously integrated, explored or transformed. A major part of the work of the psychological astrologer is to somehow align his or her self with the core Self of the client. Through establishing this link or congruence with the client's Self, the astrologer can best guide the person to co-operate with or promote what the Self is wanting to bring forth or make conscious within the personality.

In Psychosynthesis, a branch of transpersonal psychology founded by the Italian psychiatrist Roberto Assagioli, the next step in development which a person has to take is referred to as *purpose*.[10] Purpose reflects the intention of the core Self at any time, and will be related in some way to the client's immediate concerns and life issues. These immediate concerns – or *presenting problems* as they are sometimes called – will also mirror the kinds of transits and progressions occurring in the client's chart. When examining the transits and progressions in a chart, the astrologer can ask him- or herself these three questions in order to help assess what the deeper Self has in mind for a person at any particular time:

1 What is trying to emerge or be born through the presenting problem?
2 What archetypal quality or qualities is the client's Self trying to bring through?
3 What is the next step for this person that the Self is trying to make happen?

Although the French writer and philosopher Pascal asserted that 'the branch cannot hope to know the tree's meaning', Frankl, by contrast, is a little more hopeful about our capacity to fathom the workings of the Self. He asserts that apes used to test polio vaccines had no way of comprehending the purpose for the periodic jabs to which they were subjected, but then argues that human beings are different: our more highly developed brain enables us to stand back and reflect on why something is happening.[11] Through the birthchart and the system of transits and progressions, we have a symbolic mapping which will help us discover meaning in the kinds of experiences – both positive and negative – we create and attract into our lives.

Sometimes it's fairly clear what the deeper Self is up to. At other times, the reasons for the Self putting us through times of pain and crisis are not always that obvious or straightforward. I don't believe that the Self sets up situations which torture us simply for the sadistic fun of it. The Self just doesn't work that way. The purpose of the Self is to oversee and guide our development and full unfoldment; therefore, whatever the Self brings our way – even if this involves times of upheaval, trauma and turmoil – must have some bearing on our growing into what we are meant to become.

The deeper Self may ask that we suffer periods of pain and crisis in order to develop certain qualities or traits which we wouldn't develop if we didn't have these challenging times. In other words, conflict, when viewed from the larger perspective of our overall unfoldment and individual journey, may serve creative and constructive ends. Also, if we have grown away from ourselves, then some degree of pain or conflict might be needed as a way of helping us regain touch with who we really are or as a way of guiding us back to the path we are meant to follow. Pain can be a messenger telling us that things are not as they should be. If over a period of time we have not been true to ourselves – if we persistently neglect fundamental needs or truths of our nature – the resulting disharmony is reflected in illness, tension, and pain. Whether we choose to listen or not, physical symptoms or other life-difficulties are often attempts on the part of the Self to let us know that somewhere along the line something has gone wrong.

Some people seem quite happy to live out or express certain parts of their charts, while ignoring other bits with which, for whatever reasons, they are not comfortable. In a lecture given to the Astrological Association of Great Britain on the use of astrology in psychotherapy, Beata Bishop, a practising astrologer and psychotherapist, underlined the consequences of suppressing or denying parts of our chart or parts of our own nature. One of her clients was a woman with the Sun in Leo, Moon in Aries, Sagittarius midheaven, and Pisces rising. She was able to live out her Neptunian and Piscean side, but had problems coming to terms with her fiery Aries, Leo and Sagittarian urges – that part of her nature which is more extroverted and wilful. In line with her Pisces rising, she constantly put her own needs aside for the sake of other people, centring her life around her husband and family. When transiting Uranus in Sagittarius came to conjunct her midheaven, the denial of the fiery bits of her chart clearly expressed itself in her presenting symptoms – symptoms which included terrible panic attacks, nightmares and fits of anxiety. Beata Bishop's deductions will strike a chord with anyone who has used astrology as a counselling tool: 'It seems to me that when people don't resemble their charts, don't live out their most important chart factors, the resulting conflict is easily translated into physical symptoms. The woman in my previous example got away comparatively lightly with her night terrors and daytime panics. But it can be much worse . . .'[12]

This woman's physical and mental symptoms were a way of letting her know that she was out of touch with much of her true nature. The resulting pain and discomfort led her to seek help, as if the Self had to resort to these ploys in order to communicate to her that something needed to be done about how she was conducting her life. We can't deny that her discomfort must have been great, but it was this very discomfort that was necessary to initiate the self-healing process. In the following chapter, we will look more closely at how stress and crisis serve to transform us, and in particular, the role the transits of Uranus, Neptune and Pluto play in this process.

2

Breaking Down to Break Through

Near is but difficult to grasp the god
But where there is danger
the saving powers also rise.

HÖLDERLIN

Whether we attribute it to fate or to the workings of the deeper Self, the transits of Uranus, Neptune and Pluto challenge and disrupt our existing ego-identity or sense of self, so that we can put ourselves back together again in a new way. However, before we can discuss specific transits of these planets, we need to come to a clearer definition of how I am using the term 'ego'; and we need to understand a little something about how our ego develops in childhood.

Ego is usually defined as that part of the mind which has a sense of individuality. In other words, the ego is our sense of 'I', the feeling of a 'me-in-here'. We are not born with a very clear sense of 'I'. In the womb, we are in an ego-less state and have no awareness of the self as a separate, distinct entity. We think we are everything; we think we are the whole universe.

Being born means 'taking on' a body, and once we become aware we have a body, we also become aware we have a boundary; my body ends somewhere and yours begins somewhere else. This is called a 'body-ego'. Time passes and we develop a 'mental-ego': the sense that we have a mind which is our own, and feelings which are our own. People may sometimes share our thoughts and emotions, but in general, what we are thinking and feeling is not what the whole world is thinking and feeling. The ego, or our sense of being a separate 'I' with our own body, mind and feelings, once established, expands to include more and more attributes.

We come to think of ourselves as pretty, clever, and lovable or as stupid, useless and inadequate. We have many different urges and drives, some of which we feel are acceptable and will allow into our awareness, and others which we are frightened to admit are there – usually because the environment doesn't condone these in us.* So we start off in life thinking we are everything, but gradually, our original global identity narrows down to include certain qualities and traits, and to exclude others. Our ego is a limited edition of the Self, made up of those parts of our nature we are willing to accept.

Our ego-identity is thus like a boundary line: everything inside the boundary we define as ourselves, everything outside the boundary line is 'not-us'. The most common line of demarcation is the skin: what is inside my skin is me, what is outside my skin is not-me. Things outside the boundary line of my skin may belong to me – my car, my family, my house, my job – but they are not me.[1]

However, the skin-boundary is not the only type of dividing line we make. We also draw boundaries inside our own skin. Some of what goes on inside us we are willing to allow into our ego-identity, and other parts we will keep out. We may accept that part of us which is loving and kind, and deny that part of us which is cruel and destructive. Some of us do the reverse: we identify with being cold and harsh, and deny our softer, more sensitive side. So even within the boundary line of the skin, we make further boundaries, further divisions between what is us and what is not-us. Jungians would call this the ego/shadow boundary, or the boundary between what we are conscious of in ourselves and what we are unconscious of in ourselves – the boundary between what we let others see and what we keep dark and hidden.

Astrologically, Saturn is the planet associated with boundaries and represents the skin that separates us from 'other'. Most positively, Saturn helps us to define ourselves and to steady, focus and harness our energy within specific forms and structures – through Saturn, we learn discipline and commitment. Saturn also is the boundary line we draw between those parts of our nature we are willing to admit into our identity, and those parts we want to prohibit entering into our awareness. In this sense, Saturn symbolizes the ego's urge to structure itself – the ego's defence system – a

---

*For a fuller discussion of how we come to deny or repress parts of our nature, see pp. 226–30 and pp. 245–7.

dynamic in us which builds and tries to stabilize and maintain the status quo of our narrowed-down identity. In this capacity, Saturn can express itself negatively by disallowing the new and compelling us to defend ourselves – our thoughts, our feelings, our behaviour – in rigid, outworn ways.

Anyone familiar with military strategy knows that a boundary line is a border, and that borders are potential battle lines. Borders are where wars are fought. As soon as we create boundaries – whether between ourselves and others, or between those facets of our nature we own and express and those facets of ourselves we deny are in us – we also create the possibility of war and conflict between the elements on either side of the border.[2]

Uranus, Neptune and Pluto are inimical to boundaries, and in this sense, they are anti-Saturn. As these planets transit the chart, they threaten our existing ego-identity because their energies destroy the boundaries the ego has built. They will undermine the boundary between ourselves and others and make us aware once more of our essential unity and interconnectedness with all life (Neptune is particularly adept at this). Or, even more significantly, they will destroy the boundary between what we are conscious of in ourselves and what we are unconscious of or are denying, so that we are forced to admit into our awareness those aspects of our psyche we have hitherto banned. Saturn will struggle to maintain the status quo and to keep things the same; but in the end, Saturn will lose. Whether we choose to change or we are made to change, transiting Uranus, Neptune and Pluto challenge our old ways of being, and coerce us to remap the borders of our identity.

The Theory of Dissipative Structures

In 1977, the Nobel Prize for chemistry was awarded to a Belgian physical chemist, Ilya Prigogine, for his *theory of dissipative structures*, and his work scientifically demonstrated what the ancient Chinese knew very well: that stress and crisis play a critical role in the process of transformation. Like *wei-chi*, the Chinese word for crisis, Prigogine's results support the idea that breakdowns and upheavals in our lives are also opportunities for something new to happen.[3]

Prigogine was studying what in physics are called 'open systems'. An open system is any system that is involved in some sort of continuous interchange of energy with the environment. They are characterized by a certain amount of *fluctuation*, that is, they are vulnerable and accessible to different kinds of energies coming into them. Human-made things like towns, cities, groups and organizations also are open systems. A town, for example, is not something isolated and closed off from the rest of life: the town's industries use power and raw materials from neighbouring areas and then recycle this energy in a transformed state back into the environment again. Because you and I can be changed by our interaction with the environment and by the invasion of unconscious contents of our psyche into our existing conscious awareness, our ego-identity is also an open system, and therefore subject to the laws of Prigogine's theory.

According to Prigogine, provided that the fluctuations and disturbances coming into an open system stay within a certain limit, the system's self-regulating properties allow it to maintain its overall function and identity. In other words, the system can cope with a certain amount of disturbance and perturbation and not completely break down. Similarly, inevitable external or internal disruptions may periodically shake up our lives; but providing the disruptions aren't too great, the homoeostatic nature of the ego enables us to adjust to these fluctuations without having to alter to any great degree what is going on in our lives. We make some minor adjustments and remain pretty much the same.

However, if the fluctuations and disturbances coming into an open system increase beyond a certain limit, they will drive the system into a state of 'creative chaos'. What has been there before, and what has previously worked, can no longer continue in the same way. The system is forced to assimilate or accommodate too great a disruptive influence to survive in its old format and a crisis occurs: if the system is going to function at all, some new order of things must be established. In other words, the breakdown of the system makes it possible for it to break through to a whole other way of organizing itself. Such is the dynamic nature of growth and the nature of transformation.

Similarly, when our lives are progressing smoothly, there really is no reason to change. It's usually only when things start going all wrong, when we suffer major set-backs in important spheres of our life, or when circumstances become intolerably difficult, tedious or chaotic, that we seriously begin to think about making changes. Or existing structures in our life collapse so totally that we can no longer maintain our normal or habitual functioning: a relationship which we have been closely identified with breaks up, a partner dies, a child dies, we lose a parent, we are made redundant, a philosophy we dearly believed in fails or we are faced with a life-threatening illness. While not everyone will be affected to the same degree or in the same way, disruptions such as these generally call for significant transformations in our lives. It becomes difficult or impossible to go on in the same manner as before; the upheaval creates or necessitates a process of re-examination and re-evaluation of our life, attitudes, motives and values.

The connections between the theory of dissipative structures to the possible effects of the transits of (or progressions involving) Uranus, Neptune or Pluto are obvious. I have already said that Saturn is associated with form, boundary and structure; and that Uranus, Neptune and Pluto are, in this respect, the enemies of Saturn. They are 'de-structuring principles', undermining existing structures so that something new can take the place of what has been there before. In one sense, Saturn represents the homoeostatic principle of the ego – the desire to maintain and preserve what is. By contrast, Uranus, Neptune and Pluto (each in its own way and style) bring fluctuations and critical perturbations: they break us down so that we can break through to a new way of being.

Sometimes the disturbances they bring are unpleasant: illness, depression, etc. But the disruptions could be of a positive nature as well: getting married, falling in love, buying a home, gaining new knowledge which alters our view of life, sudden success, achieving a promotion or even winning the pools. These outwardly positive events cause nearly as much stress to the existing order of our lives as do negative occurrences. No matter what the exact nature of the disturbing fluctuations, no matter how Uranus, Neptune or Pluto go about it, the kinds of shifts, conflicts, paradoxes, tensions and traumas they bring are all calling out for some sort of change.

Making changes is not always easy. Being human and creatures of habit, much of our energy is invested in trying to avoid pain and crisis. Most of us don't relish the idea of losing anything which we are attached to – even, as Jungian psychologist Sallie Nichols reminds us, our 'decaying teeth or falling hair'.[4] We especially don't like to lose those things from which we are deriving our sense of identity or 'I-ness': relationships, jobs, income, ideals or principles. Outworn parts of our psychic make-up such as old habit patterns, negative self-images, or what Transactional Analysis calls 'scripts', which may really have never helped us that much to begin with, are just as difficult to let go of as possessions or people who have been close to us. Maharishi Mahesh Yogi used to tell the story of a couple who moved from a tiny hut into a magnificent palace, but still mourned for the cosy little hut they knew so well.

In her work with the terminally ill and dying, Elizabeth Kübler-Ross noted five steps or stages that many of her patients had to go through before they could accept their imminent death. Her findings are not dissimilar to the way people often react to difficult transits of Uranus, Neptune or Pluto. Because these planets threaten to tear us down and rebuild us – bringing an 'ego-death' – we may try to resist the effects of these transits in the same way that many of Kübler-Ross's clients resisted the fact they were dying.[5] Most of her patients reacted to the knowledge of their terminal illness with the response: 'No, not me! It can't be true!' So the first stage was *denial*: 'There must be some mistake; my records have been mixed up with those of somebody else.' Similarly, when Uranus, Neptune or Pluto are beginning to make their effects felt and we are sensing a crisis around the corner, we often do whatever we can to avoid acknowledging it. We employ a tactic known as 'selective perception' – we choose not to look where the crisis is. A number of years ago I did the charts of a married couple. I saw them separately, the husband in the morning and the wife in the afternoon. He was a Libran with the Sun in the seventh house and Uranus was transiting over this placement. At the same time, transiting Uranus was squaring his wife's natal Sun in Cancer. During the session with him, I enquired about his marital relationship, and he replied that everything was just fine and couldn't be better. His wife, however, began the afternoon reading with the comment, 'Well I'm sure you know why I'm here – I'm so fed up with the marriage.' Sadly, such selective perception is quite common.

The second phase or reaction Kübler-Ross observed among the patients was that of *anger*. Instead of 'No, not me', the cry became 'Why me? It isn't fair. Why isn't this happening to Joe Bloggs down the road, who smokes forty cigarettes a day and guzzles six pints at the local every night?' They are angry about the fact that their lives are coming to an end. Hopes they had about the future, projects they were in the middle of working on, relationships they were involved in – all these would end. Most displayed a tendency to displace their anger on to the environment, complaining that the doctors were incompetent, the nurses did nothing right, the bed was never comfortable, and so on. People who find themselves on the verge of other kinds of major life crises also may go through a similar phase, becoming angry with any other people involved in the situation, and blaming them for what is happening. Some vent their anger at God, the cosmos, or the planets involved for putting them through such turmoil. There are a number of people walking around right now angry at Pluto for doing such-and-such to them.

After the denial and the anger comes what Kübler-Ross labelled 'the *bargaining* stage', when patients can no longer deny they are seriously ill. They have expressed their anger at God, life, the doctors, the nurses, etc., but nothing has changed, so they now attempt to make a deal with the powers that be. They bargain with their disease or illness: 'If I promise to change my ways right now, eat well for the rest of my life and exercise regularly, can I get better?' Or 'If I can be made well again, I will devote the rest of my life to serving God or the church.' Trying to postpone death is another form of bargaining exhibited by her patients: 'Just let me live until my son's wedding' or 'Don't let me die until I at least have one chance to sing on stage again.' Sometimes, with a significant change of diet or attitude towards life, bargaining may work and the person is healed. But for most of her patients, all this came too late.

Bargaining is an attempt to avert the crisis, to make amends in the hope that the situation can be reversed, or to turn back the clock to before all the trouble happened. We are all familiar with this in children. For instance, what if a fourteen-year-old girl asks permission from her mother to go to the disco that night? The mother is likely to reply that she is too young, at fourteen, to go somewhere like that. In short, mother's answer is a firm 'No'. The young girl may react first with denial: 'I don't care, I'm going anyway.' Mother retorts with a chorus of 'over my dead body', swiftly putting an end to the daughter's attempt at denial. Then the girl gets angry: 'I hate you. You are the worst mother. You never let me do anything!' Not influenced in the least by this anger, the mother still says no. Finally, the girl resorts to bargaining as yet another way of trying to get her way and to avert the crisis: 'Well if I promise to wash the dishes every day this week and not to fight with my brother any more and keep my room clean from now on, then can I go to the disco?'

People who find themselves in the midst of the kind of disruption, pain or turmoil symbolized by the more difficult transits of Uranus, Neptune or Pluto, often try the tactic of bargaining. 'Okay, darling, if I promise from now on to be a faithful and devoted husband and never sleep around again, will you stop the divorce proceedings?' They look for ways to get off the hook. If the ploys or reparations don't work and there is no way the upheaval can be avoided, they may slip back into the anger or denial phase. Or they move on to a fourth stage, that of *depression*.

Kübler-Ross makes a distinction between two kinds of depression that a dying person goes through: *reactive* depression and *preparatory* depression. Reactive depression is the first to set in, and will begin to take hold when patients realize that nothing can be done about their illness. Their symptoms grow worse, and they become increasingly weak and debilitated. What they are left with is a sense of loss. A woman with cervical cancer who has had her uterus removed may feel that she is no longer a woman. A businessman who has worked his whole life to prove his worth as a man by providing for his family, and who has derived much of his sense of identity from his job, grows sicker, thinner and more helpless and must now forfeit this 'identity'. Understanding friends and family can help people through this phase of reactive depression; a woman can be reassured that she is still attractive and worthwhile even after the loss of her womb, and she can learn from other people who have gone through a similar operation and yet still lead full, meaningful lives. A man can be reassured that his self-esteem and self-worth are not based just on how much money he can earn or how well he functions in the world. Social workers can deal with the immediate problems of mother being in hospital and away from home, and find ways of giving assistance to families suffering financial problems as a result of the breadwinner's illness. Reactive depression, which comes about as a result of having to deal with the contingencies surrounding illness, can be helped.

Preparatory depression is quite different: this is the grief people need to undergo in order to prepare for their death and final separa-tion from the world. Preparatory grief involves mourning the future, a deep sadness and regret about all the things the dying person will now not be able to live to do. The patient is about to lose everything and everyone. The time has come to mourn the lost future and grieve for those people the dying person is leaving behind and will never see again. Trying to make a person feel better about their bodies, or reassuring them that their children and families are being looked after in their absence, can help people going through a reactive depression. But reassurances and encouragements to look on the bright side of life are not the way to deal with someone in a preparatory depression. In order to arrive at the possibility of accept-ing death, the dying person needs to have this depression: they need this time to be with their grief and deep sense of loss.

The same applies not only to the situation of an imminent physical death, but also to any crisis in which our old way of life is dying. Blessed are those that mourn. Grieving is part of a process which helps to clear away the old so that room can be made for the new. It prepares us for the next stage of our journey. People having challeng-ing transits of Uranus, Neptune or Pluto, and who are faced with the disruption of their life as they knew it, need time to mourn what is passing away.

Finally, after the sadness and the grief, comes *acceptance*. If dying patients have enough time and are helped through the previously mentioned stages, they often arrive at a point where they reconcile themselves to their imminent death. They have expressed their anger and feelings of injustice, they have grieved for the past and the future, and now they are able quietly to contemplate the inevitability of their death. This phase is not one of hopeless resignation or a 'what's the use' kind of giving up. Yes, the struggle has been let go of, but the feeling is more one of quiet acceptance rather than despair. One of Kübler-Ross's patients compared this phase to 'the final rest before a long journey'. It is not necessarily a happy stage, but it is, on the whole, peaceful. The patient reaches for the doctor's hand and they sit silently together, listening to the song of a bird coming from the outside.

Likewise, those of us experiencing the challenges or disruptions of Uranus, Neptune and Pluto, eventually can reach a stage where we accept the kinds of crises and changes these planets bring with them by transit. When this stage has been reached, the writer and psychoanalyst James Hillman would say that our feelings finally have succeeded in flowing freely into our fate, reconciling us with an event – what he also calls 'that union of love with necessity'.[6] The crisis is accepted, and along with the acceptance, there may, in time, come the recognition that what we have had to go through has been a necessary part of our growth and unfoldment. Bitter tears turn into the salt of wisdom.

Acceptance allows the healing magic to work. I'm not saying that arriving at this point is simple or happens overnight. It's not always easy to trust the workings of Uranus, Neptune or Pluto, or to recognize that pain, breakdown, disruption and change, which feel more like some sort of curse when they are occurring, have something worthwhile to offer. Pain, conflict and tension are, however, 'transformations trying to happen'. By denying them, we cheat ourselves of transformation. By accepting them, the process of transformation begins.[7]

3

Interpreting Transits: Some Practical Guidelines

In actual practice, the entire chart must be examined to assess the effects of any particular transit to it. For this reason, astrological 'cookbooks' on transits have their inherent limitations. However, even within these limits, they still can be used as a guide to stimulate our thinking about the possible expressions of a transit. It is difficult when writing on this topic not to slip into causal language. For instance, I might write that Uranus brings disruption or that Neptune asks us to make adjustments, or that Pluto tears us down in some way. But I don't believe the planets themselves *do* things to us, or *make* us do anything. Transiting planets don't cause events, but they do symbolize psychological energies and forces at work in us which influence what we meet and attract in life. Bearing this in mind, before we examine specific Uranus transits, we need to establish a few practical guidelines for assessing and interpreting these and other outer planet transits.

The Question of Orbs

What orbs should we give transiting aspects? Astrologers will advise differently on this point, but experience has taught me to be generous with orbs in respect to the transits of Uranus, Neptune, and Pluto. In the case of a transiting outer planet conjuncting, squaring or opposing a natal planet, we usually start noticing its influence when it is 5 degrees away from the exact transiting aspect – in some cases, even sooner than that. The stage is being set: if we take the time to attune to what we are feeling inside, we will be aware of certain rumblings, perhaps a growing sense of restlessness, boredom or frustration. Or we are aware of a desire inside ourselves for change, a need for something new to happen. Such feelings mark the prelude to the events which might occur as the transiting aspect becomes more exact. For a transiting trine or sextile, I would reduce the orb of influence slightly, to 3 or 4 degrees before an exact aspect.

I believe we can prepare for an outer planet transit well before it becomes exact. For instance, if we know an important Uranus transit is coming, we can listen to that part of us which wants change, and begin to explore and experiment with bringing new things into our life. We don't have to destroy totally existing structures in our lives, but we need to make room for some new elements to enter. If we anticipate and co-operate with the upcoming transit in this way, its force when exact will not catch us off guard or overwhelm us with its intensity. However, if we are not conscious of the changes that need to be made and are not doing anything to integrate the new, the transiting aspect will gather greater power as it approaches exactitude. The end result is that our desire for change explodes uncontrollably and expresses itself in an extreme way, *or* change is forced upon us via external events and agencies.

Betty Lundsted, in her book *Transits: The Time of Your Life* uses a 10 degree orb in charting upcoming transits, and her rationale makes sense:

> Transits signify periods of growth. If we wish to use the transit period for our growing, we need to begin when the seeds of the transit are planted ... Many students attempt to interpret a transit when it is basically over, for they begin to work with it when the crop is being harvested. The unpleasant crop harvested from a difficult transit occurs when we haven't been aware of the effect of a transit soon enough. I use a ten degree applying orb. In that way the energy can be transformed with knowledge and understanding.[1]

Tracy Marks makes a similar point:

> If we don't want the universe to burn down our houses or destroy our cars or send our spouses or lovers to bed with other people in

order to get us to pay attention to what is happening, we must motivate ourselves to actively live our transit; we must attune ourselves to the energy of the transit as it first approaches, and discover ways to express that energy constructively.[2]

Robert Hand has devised a rather sophisticated system for timing outer planet transits. In part, it involves watching for inner planet transits which trigger the outer planet transit. For instance, if you have transiting Uranus squaring your natal Moon, you will notice the effects of this transit most clearly when an inner planet, such as the Sun or Mars, moves into aspect (by transit or progression) with transiting Uranus or your natal Moon. For a complete explanation of Hand's method for timing transits, the reader is referred to chapter 2 of *Planets in Transit*.[3]

We will normally continue to feel the influence of an outer planet transit until it is two or three degrees past the exact aspect in question. However, judging the passing of a transit is complicated by the incidence of retrogradation, which we cover next.

Retrogradation

The term retrograde denotes the *apparent* backward motion of a planet. The Sun and Moon never appear retrograde, but all the other planets will move forward or *direct*, then seemingly pause for a space of time (in a *stationary* phase), before moving backwards. After going backwards for a while, a planet will eventually pause or appear stationary once more, and then turn direct again.

The direct, stationary, and retrograde movements of Uranus, Neptune or Pluto need to be taken into consideration when interpreting their transits. When one of these transiting planets makes an exact aspect to a natal one, we usually register the need to make changes in relation to the facet of life associated with that natal planet. However, when the transiting planet stops going direct and moves backward, our efforts to make alterations or adjustments may be hindered or blocked – our desire or need to change also may recede for the time being as well. When it turns around again and begins to move forward to the exact aspect, the blockage will pass, and the changes can occur more readily. When a transiting outer planet changes direction, it makes what is called a *station*, and for a while it hardly appears to be moving at all. If that station is within one degree of an exact aspect to a planet in the natal chart, we will feel the effects of the transiting planet very strongly.

The Nature of the Transiting Aspect

In discussing the transits of Uranus, Neptune and Pluto to the planets, I have grouped trines and sextiles together and called them *soft* or harmonious transits, and have grouped conjunctions and the major *hard* angles – squares and oppositions – into the category of difficult or stressful transits. I do, however, encourage the reader to be flexible with these groupings. A transiting Uranus trine to a planet could, in some instances, activate problematic natal configurations and therefore feel quite stressful. Conversely, some transiting Uranus conjunctions, squares and oppositions may not be that difficult to handle – in certain cases they even may be enjoyable, while transiting trines of Neptune and Pluto can sometimes be as testing as the transiting conjunction, square or opposition of these planets.

To judge the effects of a transiting outer planet *conjuncting* a natal one, it is necessary to consider how that natal planet is aspected in the birthchart. If, for example, transiting Uranus conjuncts a natal Mars squared by Jupiter and opposing Saturn, the transit is likely to stir a great deal of conflict; but should transiting Uranus conjunct a natal Mars which is trine Jupiter and sextile natal Uranus, the transiting conjunction usually will be less stressful.

On an inner psychological level, a transiting square or opposition from an outer planet are similar. However, we are more likely to experience the opposition in terms of outside forces which either coerce us into change, or block our attempts to change. The following general points are worth noting when interpreting transiting squares and oppositions made by outer planets.

1 The area of experience associated with the planet being transited is in a process of change or renewal.

2   The need for change is felt more intensely and often will be accompanied by more upheaval than in the case of the transiting trine or sextile.

3   There may be an internal conflict between those parts of us which require change and another part of us which is resisting it. In the case of the transiting opposition (and sometimes in the case of the transiting conjunction and square), the resistance may appear to come from external agents, but these can be understood as reflections of our internal uncertainty or ambivalence. The reverse is also true. In the case of the transiting opposition (and sometimes in the case of the transiting conjunction and square), external contingencies apparently force change or disruption on us. However, I would argue that these external factors reflect an inner need to change which we are not aware of.

Although I have not discussed the transiting inconjunct (quincunx), semi-square or sesquiquadrate, I would interpret these along the lines of the transiting conjunction, square and opposition. Their effects may not always be felt so strongly or clearly, but they can have an important influence – especially in the case of the inconjunct. The same applies to the transiting semi-sextile and quintile, which can be grouped with the transiting trine and sextile.

The triggering of Natal Aspects

An outer planet transiting in aspect to a natal planet will activate any natal aspects to that planet. Remember this when using the cookbook sections of this book. For instance, if you are born with Mars in 7 degrees of Aries in square to Saturn in 13 degrees of Cancer, when transiting Uranus comes to square Mars it also will start to have an effect on Saturn – even though transiting Uranus is still 6 degrees wide of an exact opposition to Saturn. Transiting Uranus will bring out the natal Mars–Saturn square. In this case, the interpretation of the Uranus–Mars transit will need to take the natal Saturn square to Mars into account, as well as the upcoming influence of transiting Uranus opposing Saturn. Because of Saturn's natal connection to Mars, the freeing of assertive energy usually associated with a Uranus–Mars transit is likely to be more difficult to deal with and accept. The effects of the transit will last until Uranus finishes squaring Mars and opposing Saturn.

Midpoint Transits and Transits to Progressions

Outer planet transits to midpoints in the natal chart are important, and often do coincide with major events and times of crisis and change. If the Sun is natally conjunct the midpoint of Mars and Pluto, a planet transiting over the Sun will activate the principles of Mars and Pluto as well. Midpoints to squares and oppositions in the chart are particularly influential. When a transiting planet crosses such a midpoint, the natal square or opposition will be brought to the fore. Transits occurring at the midpoint of two planets not in natal aspect also are worth noting. For example, if 5 degrees of Libra is the midpoint of Venus and Saturn, a planet transiting over that degree of Libra (whether or not there is a natal planet there) will stimulate Venus and Saturn.[4]

Similarly, the impact outer planet transits to progressions have on our lives should not be underestimated. In the cookbook sections, I discuss outer planet transits to natal planets, although there is no reason why these interpretations cannot be used to amplify the significance of outer planet transits to progressed planets as well.

Transits and Houses

Uranus, Neptune or Pluto transiting through a house signifies change, disruption, breakthrough and crisis in relation to the affairs of that house. An outer planet spends many years moving through a house, but this doesn't mean we will be experiencing dramatic shifts and upheaval for the entire period it is there. Besides having an obvious effect when it crosses into a house, its influence will be most apparent when it conjuncts a planet in that house, forms a transiting aspect from that house to any other planet in the chart, or when another transiting planet in the heaven aspects it. In the case of the transiting outer planet aspecting a natal planet, the house (or houses) which the natal planet rules in the chart will be affected. For instance, if transiting Uranus opposes Saturn, the house (or houses) with Capricorn on the cusp or contained within it, will be involved in the kinds of issues raised by the transit. Obviously, the house transiting Uranus is passing through, and the house Saturn is in, are also essential to consider. I do not always repeat these general guidelines in the sections of this book dealing with the specific transits of Uranus, Neptune and Pluto, so please bear them in mind.

PART TWO

Uranus Transits

4

Uranian Crises

Where are you making for? It takes
So many thousand years to wake,
But will you wake for pity's sake?
CHRISTOPHER FRY

It seems as if ideas choose the time when they're going to be born. The French astronomer Pierre Lemonnier (1715–99) had sighted Uranus on at least 12 different occasions, and yet he never suspected that this tiny flickering light could be a planet. Perhaps he found it impossible to conceive that the neat arrangement of the solar system, with its seven heavenly bodies revolving around the Sun, could be any other way. Little did he know that disrupting existing systems was exactly what Uranus would come to symbolize. The actual discovery of Uranus is attributed to William Herschel (1738–1822), who reported his findings to the Royal Society of Astronomers on 26 April 1781. How fitting for Uranus – the planet associated with eccentricity and surprise – that its discoverer was not at the time a professional astronomer, but a musician who had taken up stargazing as a hobby.

Uranus is twice as far from the Sun as Saturn, and its recognition as a planet doubled the size of the solar system in one go. The existence of Uranus also accounted for certain inexplicable eccentricities in the orbits of the known planets, a mystery that had been bothering astronomers for some time. Right from the start, Uranus was a rule-breaker, with little regard for the traditional cosmological scheme. And, as synchronicity would have it, Uranus timed its entrance with flair, to coincide with three major social revolutions also intent on disrupting the established order of things. In the American and French revolutions, those oppressed rose up to challenge the status quo and existing authority. And along with Uranus came the advent of the Industrial Revolution: the emergence of major new breakthroughs in science, technology and communication, which would drastically change the pattern of life on earth.

On a personal level, a Uranus transit is associated with change and disruption, and a phase in our lives when something new – something 'eccentric' – needs to break through into conscious awareness. It's a time to be curious and experimental, a period when new things can be tried, and there are risks to be taken. Sometimes we consciously choose to make these changes; at other times they seem to be forced on us by external events. In any case, Uranus is intent on putting us in touch with unexplored parts of our nature. Where, for the sake of safety or security, we have become set in our ways, Uranus signals that we are ready to break out of routines and patterns which are too rigid or limiting. Uranus, whether we like it or not, is the alarm which jolts us out of our sleep and wakes us up to a new day. Some people leap out of bed eager to embark on what's ahead; others pull the covers back over their heads and just don't want to know.

Uranus in Mythology

Not a great deal is written about Ouranus in mythology, but the main myth concerning this deity helps to clarify the workings of Uranus by transit. For the Greeks, Ouranus played a key role in the saga of creation. In the beginning there was Chaos, out of which came Gaia or Mother Earth. Gaia then gave birth to Ouranus, and although he was her son, he also became her mate and lover. Gaia had control over the earth, while Ouranus, the first sky-god, ruled the starry heavens and vast limitless space. Already we can see that Ouranus was not an earthy principle: he was married to one, but he himself was associated with the airy realm of visions and ideals, not with the mundane practicalities of everyday existence. Every night the starry heavens (Ouranus) came to lie on the earth (Gaia), and as a result, they produced a rather odd assortment of children. First there were the Titans, a race of giants believed to be the progenitors of the human race. Then there came the Cyclopses and various other monsters, some with a hundred arms and fifty heads.

Ouranus was not pleased with the children he produced, finding them ugly, gross and deformed – not at all what he had hoped for his offspring. Rather than allow them to exist, he pushed each one back into Gaia's womb, a poetic way of saying that he banished them to the underworld of the unconscious and disallowed them expressive life (something we all do with parts of ourselves we dislike).

In his mind, Ouranus had an ideal vision or picture of what his children should be like; but once they came into being, they didn't live up to his expectations. Similarly, when people born with a strong Uranian element in their chart try to turn a vision into a concrete reality, they're often disappointed with the result. They might have an image, for instance, of what their ideal relationship would be like, but when they manage to establish a union, the reality falls far short of their hopes. Somehow the relationship doesn't match the concept they had in their minds, so they destroy it and try again in a continual search for one that meets their ideal. Or the Uranian person might conceive of a perfect political system which, when put into practice, none the less lets them down, so they abandon that one and turn to another. Strongly Uranian types leave a wake of half-finished projects behind them, and a parallel situation sometimes occurs wherever Uranus is transiting in our charts: we grow discontented or restless with the affairs of the house or sphere of life affected by Uranus. We want to disrupt or revamp that area of our existence, and we will be tempted by anything that comes along promising something better than what we have already.

Mother Earth, not surprisingly, wasn't overjoyed when Ouranus kept forcing their children back into her womb, and retaliated by forming a sickle out of steel and imploring one of her offspring to castrate their father. Her youngest, Cronus or Saturn, already exhibiting his characteristic sense of responsibility, volunteered for the task. Ouranus descended as usual that night, and just as he was about to lie on Gaia, Cronus cut off his father's phallus, and threw it into the sea.

As Cronus castrated Ouranus, so astrologically does Saturn cut off the creative impulse and potency of Uranus. This image encapsulates a basic war that exists in all our psyches: a Saturnian urge for maintenance and preservation conflicts with our Uranian urge for disruption, variety and change. One part of us prefers to keep things as they are (the principle of homoeostasis) while another part wants new growth and development. Saturn builds, conserves, and honours what is known and tried; Uranus, in the name of progress, wants to tear down and make room for something new.

The Saturn/Uranus Dilemma

A myth is something which never happened but is always happening. Psychologically, Saturn castrates Uranus every time forces of resistance (sometimes external, sometimes internal, and sometimes both) inhibit our taking some new action or direction. We could block Uranus for a whole range of reasons. It might be a sense of duty, commitment and responsibility which keeps Uranus at bay; or it could be a basic need for security coupled with a fear of the unknown which overrules any disruptive inclinations. Paying homage to Saturn, we stop and stay put, but the Uranian need for change is still there, hiding underground.

The consequences of Cronus castrating Ouranos are clearly portrayed in the myth. Some of the blood from the dismembered phallus fell on to the ground (Gaia's womb) and gave birth to the Furies, whose names translate into envious anger, retaliation and never-endingness. If we block or repress the changes called for by Uranus, the Furies are born inside us. Outwardly we keep the lid on things, but inside we boil with resentment towards those we feel are holding us back – we seethe with envy towards those who are free to progress while we remain stuck. And, whether we know it or not, we are probably angry with ourselves as well. Uranus demands that we take some action, but in not allowing this to happen, the energy which would have been used to make changes in our lives now has nowhere to go. It turns back on itself, attacking the body in the guise of illness. Or it dangerously festers in the psyche until it erupts, sometimes in the form of a nervous breakdown. Or so much of our energy is used to keep Uranus down that we have very little left over with which to live life. No wonder we end up tired, apathetic and depressed. Transits of Uranus are not usually associated with depression, sickness or fatigue; but should such states occur under major Uranus transits, they are signs that some needed movement or expression is being blocked.

However, let's say we do decide to obey our Uranian impulses, and disrupt existing structures in our lives for the sake of something new. In other words, what happens if Saturn is not totally successful at the job? He takes a swipe at Uranus and misses; perhaps a few drops of blood are spilled, but Uranus remains intact, proceeding happily on his way. Now Uranus is still in one piece, but it is Saturn who is angry. If, in true Uranian spirit, we challenge the status quo or established order of things, we may find that the Furies are hurled at us by those who are threatened by our 'rebellious' actions. We have taken the step and carried out our Uranian urges, so its energy is not left to fester within. The Furies are not born inside us, but instead come at us from the outside.

Such a reversal is not uncommon in cases such as the break-up of a relationship. I did the chart for a woman who had been in a relationship with a man for a number of years, but as Uranus inched its way closer to her Venus, she became increasingly discontented. Both in obvious and in subtle ways, her partner made her feel inadequate, and at the same time wouldn't support any of her attempts at self-development. He objected to her attending evening classes in astrology, through which she hoped not only to discover more about herself but also to learn skills she could ultimately use in a professional capacity. Even when Uranus went over her Venus and then moved backwards again on to it, she kept her anger towards him in check, although she admitted to a growing frustration with the relationship. The Furies were building up inside her. She tried to discuss the problem with him, and he would at first make some small efforts to change his attitude, but eventually slip back into his old patterns. When Uranus turned direct and was coming to pass over her Venus for the third time, she could no longer tolerate the limitations of their relationship, and finally moved out of the flat they shared.

Her immediate reaction was one of relief. She felt a little sad about the ending of the relationship, but with all the new possibilities opening before her, she had few regrets. Her life felt so exciting now; she was sure she had done the right thing. It was her boyfriend who suffered: he was furious with her. The Furies no longer seethed inside her, but for weeks and months after she had left, the Furies badgered her through the post and taunted her over the phone in the form of angry and threatening letters and calls from the man she had left behind. It is obvious from this story that the Furies are as alive and well as they were in ancient Greece, and are kept incredibly busy not only in divorce courts around the world, but also in various government offices where they are set in motion against dissenters and rebels who threaten the state.

Families, too, form systems or structures which organize and determine how its members interact. Unwritten rules and repeated transactions create patterns and boundaries regulating what kind of behaviour is allowed in the family – who can do or say what to whom. Should one family member begin to act in ways that threaten the maintenance of the established system, the Furies are likely to be released on that person. This was the case of a young man I counselled on a weekly basis for a number of years. Originally it was his mother who brought him along. She desperately wanted him to train as an accountant, which had been her late father's profession. The boy in question, however, had the Sun in Pisces in the fifth house and the Moon in Leo in the tenth, and showed no interest in maths or business. He dreamed of being an actor. His mother hoped therapy would 'straighten him out', that through it he would be brought to his senses, stop being so impractical, and agree to follow her wishes. As our work together progressed, transiting Uranus passed over his Scorpio ascendant, and then moved into Sagittarius, squaring his Sun in the early degrees of Pisces and trining his Moon in Leo. Rather than adjusting himself to her will, he became increasingly determined to pursue his acting ambitions.

Gradually his mother realized things weren't going the way she had planned. She and the rest of the household (which included an aunt and an older sister) colluded in an expertly choreographed attempt to unleash the Furies on him, and to sabotage his sessions with me. The family system did not allow room for his own individuality; and they were all reaping dubious psychological benefits from keeping him in his place. About three-quarters of an hour before our scheduled appointment time, his mother, aunt, or sister would present him with some urgent task they needed done immediately, designed to ensure his not being able to get to our meeting on time, if at all. 'You must run to the chemist and pick up this prescription for me right now,' or 'You have to go and collect your nephew from school.' Transiting Uranus was squaring his Sun and part of him desperately wanted to free himself from the bondage of his family. The more he listened to his urges to change and grow into a person in his own right, the more the family contrived ways to keep him within the boundaries of the existing family structure. He was caught in a vice between Uranus and the Furies. If he didn't follow his own Uranian need to break out and pursue the path he wanted to follow, the Furies seethed inside him. He became increasingly depressed and angry. But whenever he tried to assert his individuality, the Furies were directed at him by his family, who quickly gathered forces and closed ranks around him. In the end Uranus won out, and he enrolled in drama school.

The Birth of Venus

Fortunately, the Furies are not the only things born out of the conflict between Uranus (change) and Saturn (the desire to maintain or preserve). According to the myth, Cronus throws Ouranus' dismembered phallus into the sea, where it merges with the foam and gives birth to Aphrodite or Venus. What does this mean?

This part of the myth suggests that Venus – the principle of love, beauty, harmony, diplomacy and balance – can be born from the tension between Saturnian forces of homoeostasis and Uranian forces of disruption and change. The birth of Venus indicates the possibility of presenting new ideas and alternatives in a way that is tactful and diplomatic, and will not be so threatening to the existing order of things. Unrestrained, the Uranian tendency is to do away with Saturn altogether, or to smash it to pieces. Saturn's response to this attack is to dig his heels in and do everything possible to suppress any change. However, if Uranus evolves a more Venusian style, it may be possible to coax Saturn into a stance of greater flexibility. Tempered by Venus, Uranus could plead his case: 'Let's keep the best of the old, but make room in it for something new.' Or, 'I've been around for a while, Saturn, and have been observing your way of doing things; a lot of what you do makes sense, but I've been thinking that maybe we should try altering certain things slightly to see if they wouldn't work better in a new way.' Helped by Venus, Uranus could more gently and thoughtfully prepare Saturn for something new.

For example, let's say that we are in work which we don't like. Rather than just quitting the job and leaving ourselves without anything, we could hold on to the job but use our free time to study or train at something else. If possible, we might be able to cut down on the number of hours we are working at our present employment in order to create more time to pursue our new interests. Eventually, we could progress far enough along with the new study or training to find some work in that line. In this way, we have gradually made room within the old for something new to happen. We have made the transition from Saturn to Uranus, but in a diplomatic, Venusian fashion.

Or let's say that we have just begun a new job. We come in and see all sorts of aspects of the work that could be improved. The chances are, however, that if we rush up to our boss with a list of all the things we're sure should be changed, he or she will look at us and think, 'Who is this upstart? You've been here a week and you think you know it all!' In other words, if we challenge the existing authority too quickly, it normally resists our efforts. However, if we keep our view under our hat for a while and first concentrate on establishing ourselves in the work and proving we can do it by the old rules, we will be in a better position later to voice our opinions and ideas for change. In this way we establish some credibility, and there is a greater chance those in authority will respect some of the changes we would like to see implemented.

If diplomacy and tact should fail and the existing system refuses to give, we may have no alternative other than to challenge the status quo directly and face the consequences. Sometimes we may have no choice but to disrupt facets of our lives in order to get back on a path which is more right or true for us. In addition to her role as the goddess of love and beauty, Venus also served as a redresser of imbalance or injustice. If we are involved in a relationship, for instance, which blocks our growing into what we could become, we may have to disrupt or abandon that partnership in the name of bringing our life more in line with what the core Self has in mind for us. In this way, through conflict and turmoil, we remove an aspect of our existence which is not in accord with the deeper truth of our nature.

Choice or Coercion

If, under a Uranus transit, we are involved in something we have outgrown or which is incongruous with what the deeper Self feels we need, and if we are not altering this situation, disruption may be forced on us by external events and contingencies. In other words, we will meet the effects of a Uranus transit by *choice* or by *coercion*. When a job or relationship we are in is blocking our evolution or some further growth which the core Self requires of us, but we are avoiding making any changes or facing what needs to be done, the Self somehow will organize circumstances which compel us to change. The other person in the relationship might walk out, or we may find ourselves made redundant and forced to reconsider our work. When this happens, our first reaction may be to blame other people for what has happened to us. It may be true that our partner turned out to be disloyal or that our boss treated us unfairly; and yet, when viewed in terms of the core Self's intention to awaken us to new ways of being, we can find meaning and relevance in these apparently unfortunate events.

I tried to make this point to a French woman who came for a reading a number of years ago. She had a funnel-shaped chart with Saturn in Aquarius as the handle. Saturn, a singleton by hemisphere, also squared her Sun–Venus conjunction in Taurus. Altogether she had six planets in earth. Usually, the people who have the most difficulty with Uranus transits are those with an emphasis on earth in their charts or those with a prominent Saturn. Saturn and earth placements show the need for order, consolidation, security and structure, and a strong desire to maintain and preserve the status quo. Earthy types are more likely to deny or resist their own Uranian urges to make changes in their lives. Frightened of the unknown, they don't enjoy taking risks, even if it offers the possibility of finding something better than they have already. They don't have the same faith in life which fiery people possess, the conviction that, come what may, life will somehow look after them. This woman was no exception to the rule.

At the time of our meeting, I didn't need a chart to tell me that she was distressed. She had been married to her husband for 25 years, and he had suddenly run off with a younger woman. The transits of Uranus for that year (1978) revealed the whole story. Moving slowly through the middle of Scorpio, Uranus had been stationary in a close opposition to her Sun in 13° of Taurus (the Sun is often associated with males in a woman's chart). When Uranus finally moved forward, it immediately squared her Saturn in 15 Aquarius and opposed her Venus in 17 Taurus. Poor woman, I thought, Uranus bringing all this upheaval into her life. And that horrible husband to do such a thing after all those years of marriage.

However, as we discussed her situation, additional factors came to light. Yes, she had been a faithful wife for so many years, but she confessed that for most of the time she had detested the marriage. It was a marriage in name only, 'a loveless match', to use her words. She was honest enough to admit maintaining the marriage out of a sense of duty, and also because of her fear of losing the security it offered. She dreaded the unknown, and was terrified of loneliness. Who would she be if she wasn't this man's wife? What else could she do? So she stayed with it. That is, until Uranus transiting through Scorpio disrupted the marriage for her.

She had been unwilling to rectify the lie of her marriage, but by the time Uranus reached mid-Scorpio, it was not prepared to let the masquerade go on any longer. Uranus can't tolerate non-truth, and when it finally came to oppose her Sun and Venus and square her Saturn, her husband was the one to act on its urge to disrupt the old, false and outworn. In denying her own Uranian impulses and refusing to abandon her unfulfilled marriage, she had helped to create a situation in which external forces had to do the job for her. In other words, she was forced to come to terms with Uranus, not by choice, but by coercion.

If you were in a job you couldn't stand and wanted to leave, but were afraid to take that step, your frustration with the work could surface in various forms. You might repeatedly turn up late or find reasons to be nasty to the boss. It will be only a matter of time before your employer won't be able to tolerate your misdemeanours any longer, and lo and behold you are fired. And then you think: 'Look what that so-and-so did to me', when in actual fact you have unconsciously provoked your boss to do something which you could not bring yourself to do – namely, change your situation. I couldn't help speculating that something similar had occurred in the case of this woman's marriage. Her underlying unhappiness, her dislike of her husband and their relationship, must have been manifested in a hundred different ways, despite her attempts to be the dutiful wife and make everything look all right. In the end, he acted out something she couldn't bring herself to do. Astrologically, all this happened under a transiting Uranus opposition – it looked as if Uranus were coming at her from the outside, but really she had just met her own denied Uranian urges through the agency of another person.

I tried to explain some of this way of thinking to her, but she couldn't hear it. Still too caught up in the anger phase of crisis, she wasn't ready to see that all those years of suppressing her own desire to end the relationship had a connection with her husband's leaving. Rather than understanding the dissolution of the marriage as a release from a bad situation and as the possibility for her life to open up to new or better relationships, she spent most of the session complaining about her husband ('How could he do such a thing to me?'), and sharing with me the most elaborate schemes of how she would take her revenge and make life miserable for him. It became obvious that what she needed most at that point in time was simply the space to moan and complain. Later in the session, I attempted to discuss with her what she might do with her life now, ways she could find her own sense of self-worth and security independently of the marriage. Despite some glimmers of emerging from the crisis reborn, she was still too eaten up with rage (the Furies produced by her castration of Uranus all those years) to be receptive to very much of my explanations or suggestions. She couldn't see how the break-up of the bad marriage ultimately could help to make her life more harmonious or truthful. Aphrodite had not yet risen out of the foam.

Prometheus and the Uranian Backlash

If we repress Uranian urges within ourselves, the Furies are born inside us. However, if we act on our Uranian urges, there is a good chance that those we are threatening or disrupting will unleash the Furies at us. One way or another, we have to pay the consequences. Even if we're sure we have done the right and noble thing, challenging the existing authority invites guilt and punishment. The story of Prometheus illustrates this point.

Prometheus was one of the Titans, whose name meant foresight, the ability to see before an event. When Zeus was engaged in battle against the Titans, Prometheus foresaw him as the victor, and decided to side with Zeus against his own race. In the beginning, he and Zeus were firm allies, and they performed various favours for one another. Prometheus assisted at the birth of Athene, who was born from the head of Zeus; Athene, in return, offered to teach Prometheus astronomy, mathematics, medicine, architecture and other valuable subjects. As a result, Prometheus grew very wise.

But trouble was brewing. As time passed, Prometheus became increasingly agitated at the injustice he perceived around him: why should the gods have had a monopoly on knowledge and all the good things in life? In an effort to improve the condition of ordinary mortals, he passed on his learning to the race of humans. Zeus, angered by Prometheus' attempt to make the gods and humans more equal, punished these transgressions by denying humans the gift of fire, at which point Prometheus, a rebel with a cause, stole fire from the gods on Olympus and offered it to humankind. Zeus retaliated by having Prometheus chained to a rock on Mount Caucus, where a vulture came every day to eat and tear at his liver.

Prometheus represents the Uranian urge in all of us to progress and advance, to change our existing situation for the sake of something better. Prometheus stands for that part of us which wants to rise above our animal origins and purely instinctive natures, and become something more than we already are. Zeus, in this story, symbolizes that part of the psyche which resists change, and which exacts a price for our growth and development. Zeus doesn't want his secrets and privileges given away, and punishes Prometheus for trying to do so.

This dynamic applies to Uranus transits as well. Under a Uranus transit, we may have a breakthrough in our awareness, a revelation which changes the way we view ourselves or our life. However, the immediate results of that revelation are not always pleasant: for example, if you have always thought of yourself as kind and caring, you could suddenly realize that beneath your positive disposition you actually feel envious and resentful towards close friends who seem happier or more successful than you are. The realization that you are not the nice person you thought you were can come as a disturbing shock, a kind of punishment for the awareness you have gained.

Or you may suddenly see clearly how a hitherto unconscious negative image you have had of yourself has hindered your enjoyment of life. You realize that for many years you have been walking around with an unconscious belief that you are inferior to others, and may now have to confront the pointless self-denial and missed opportunities, the wasted years, as a result; or the many times your low self-esteem interfered with or compromised your development. Undeniably, becoming conscious of your negative self-image is a good thing, since this awareness ultimately enables you to change destructive patterns. But what about the fact that, had you come to this insight sooner, your life might have been much happier and more successful all along? Even a joyous breakthrough to a new level of awareness may be accompanied by remorse, shame, guilt or embarrassment about the way we have been before. Change has its costs.

Whether or not others attack us for Uranian changes we make in our lives, we still have to deal with our own *inner* guilt, and with that part of us which expects to be punished for breaking with established patterns. A woman came to me for a reading when transiting Uranus was crossing her seventh house cusp. She decided to end her present relationship for the sake of starting one with another person she had recently met. Even though she was quite certain that this was the right action to take, she still felt guilty about what she was doing, and expected to suffer in some way as a result. She was worried that the man she was abandoning would have a breakdown, become ill or even commit suicide because of her actions. She imagined that the new relationship would not work, and in the end she would be left totally on her own.

Sometimes our guilt and fear of punishment are unconscious – we are not even aware that we expect reprisals. Unfortunately, whatever we are unaware of has a way of sneaking up on us. Without realizing what we are doing, we unwittingly set up or attract what we unconsciously anticipate. For instance, if you disrupt an existing relationship for a new one, your own unconscious belief that you should suffer for what you have done can contribute to your acting in ways which endanger the new relationship. However, if you are conscious of that part of you which expects retribution for your Uranian transgressions against the established order, then you can keep an eye on yourself. You can examine and explore the guilt or shame you feel. You can watch more closely to see that you are not unconsciously setting yourself up to be punished for your Uranian actions.

The Divine Mind

We all have a core Self which guides, regulates, and oversees our development. The Self sets up the kinds of situations and circumstances we need for our growth and unfoldment, but most of the time we are unconscious of this part of us. It does its job without our necessarily knowing what it is up to. However, under a Uranus transit, it is possible to glimpse the workings of the Self. A veil is lifted and a bigger picture of our life comes into view. With this perspective, we catch sight of the true meaning behind what is happening in our lives at any time, and the direction in which the Self intends for us to go. A Uranian vision clarifies what steps we need to take, or what action we need to perform in order to co-operate with what the core Self has in mind for us. Even in the midst of crises and difficulties, if Uranus is involved by transit, we are often better able to understand why we are attracting such occurrences and what these are meant to show or teach us.

For example, a man came to me for a reading when transiting Uranus was conjuncting his Jupiter in the tenth house of career. The company he was working for had just gone bankrupt, and he was made redundant. And yet he clearly felt that his redundancy was serving a definite purpose: he hadn't been very happy or fulfilled by his job, and now he was forced to face this situation and look for work which would be more in line with what he wanted. He was experiencing the disruption often associated with Uranus, but at the same time he could understand why it had to happen. Similarly, an actor came for a reading when transiting Uranus in the eighth was squaring his fifth house Sun. Previously he had enjoyed many years of success and regular employment, but his 'luck' seemed to change under this transit. He just couldn't land any acting work. However, rather than sinking into a bitter depression, he told me that he knew why this was happening to him. He had always wanted to try his hand at writing, and this reversal of fortune gave him the opportunity to do so. Like the man who had been made redundant, the actor was going through what many would call a rough patch, and yet he was able to perceive these difficulties as serving some greater purpose. By contrast, when we are undergoing crises which primarily correspond to the transits of Neptune or Pluto, we may experience more difficulty perceiving the relevance or purpose of what we are having to face.

Not only do we have a deeper or core Self which regulates our development, but many astrologers and philosophers believe that the entire cosmos also unfolds according to a certain grand plan or design. In other words, there exists a higher organizing centre of creative intelligence which guides and oversees the evolution of all life. Along these lines, Dane Rudhyar equated Uranus with 'the power of the universal mind'. By transit, Uranus sometimes connects our awareness to the workings of this higher intelligence, enabling us to glimpse its purpose and intentions, and giving us insight into what some call the mind of God. Under the influence of Uranus, we think we know the Truth with a capital 'T'. Accordingly, we may undertake actions which we believe are in line with the will of God or the will of the cosmos. We feel that it's not just our personal will that insists we follow a particular path or plan: it is God's will which demands we act in a certain way. Or as Rudhyar states, 'the trans-figured individual has become a focal center for the release of the power of the Universal Mind'.[1]

Obviously, in some cases the belief that we are acting on behalf of some all-knowing higher authority contributes to arrogance, hubris and ego-inflation at the very least, and psychotic behaviour at the very worst. History records numerous atrocities and injustices perpetrated by blindly self-righteous individuals and nations claiming to be the agents of divine will. None the less, we shouldn't dismiss altogether the concept of a universal mind. Mystics and mentors from a diversity of civilizations and epochs have repeatedly claimed the existence of a higher unifying element which pervades all life. And, as recent research shows, many scientists wouldn't argue with this point. The twentieth-century physicist Fritjof Capra (an Aquarius born with Uranus in Taurus in the twelfth conjunct the Ascendant) has this to say about the interconnectivity of all life:

> modern physics reveals the basic oneness of the universe. It shows that we cannot decompose the world into independently existing smallest units. As we penetrate into matter, nature does not show us any isolated basic building blocks, but rather appears as a complicated web of relations between the various parts of a unified whole. As Heisenberg expresses it, 'The world thus appears as a complicated tissue of events, in which connections of different kinds alternate or overlap or combine and thereby determine the texture of the whole.'[2]

Capra's statement gives credence to the mystical concept of a universal mind which links the entire universe together in a complex network of relationship. Nothing can be understood in isolation, but only by its relationship to other things. On some deep level we are all connected to one another; the minds and beings of everything in existence are inextricably interwoven.

If our minds are linked together, it is not hard to appreciate an idea put forth by the Jesuit priest and philosopher Pierre Teilhard de Chardin: 'A truth once seen, even by a single mind, always ends up imposing itself on the totality of human consciousness.'[3] Rupert Sheldrake, a British scientist, proposes something quite similar.

He believes there are invisible organizing fields (what he calls 'morphogenetic fields') which connect members of a species to one another. Whenever one member of a species learns something, the morphogenetic field for that species changes, making it possible for others of that class to follow suit.[4] Again, we arrive at the concept of a group mind.

Uranus transits can activate our ability to connect with and understand the workings of the universal mind, allowing us to glimpse its intention and direction. When this happens, we may become the channel or agency through which some new idea or trend circulating in the collective psyche can manifest. Obviously, not everyone will be affected by Uranus in this way, but my case files show a number of people who, while under a significant transit of this type, have served as mediums through which new ideas are disseminated. Two examples immediately come to mind. One is a film director born with Venus in Libra trine Uranus in Gemini. Transiting Uranus came to oppose his natal Uranus, and he began to experiment with new techniques in music videos. Not only did he win acclaim for his technical ingenuity, but he initiated a whole new trend in this medium. Another example is that of a woman born with Mercury conjunct Mars in Pisces squaring natal Uranus in Gemini. When transiting Uranus in Sagittarius squared her Mercury–Mars conjunction, she introduced certain new concepts into the educational establishment which have since been taken up and developed on a large scale.

Whether or not we believe in the concept of a universal mind or group mind, there is no doubt that Uranus transits often stimulate greater political consciousness. Certain individuals under important Uranus transits envisage new systems or concepts which they believe will alter or improve the existing order of things; or they find causes and ideals to promote which challenge rigid and obsolete structures in society. In this way, Uranus instigates not just personal or internal growth and change, but also evolution on a social scale.

Having established some guidelines for interpreting Uranus transits, we can now look more closely at specific transits of Uranus to the planets and through the houses.

5

The Transits of Uranus to the Planets and Through the Houses

Uranus–Sun

In itself, the transiting trine or sextile of Uranus to the Sun usually is not felt as an especially overpowering transit. None the less, it does suggest a time when we are in accord with our own inner need to develop and expand the self in ways we haven't done before. There is a part of us which is in the mood to open up, explore and experiment with life, and we can take advantage of harmonious Uranus–Sun transits by following these urges. Opportunities to change could come through people we meet, a new job, or a new course of study. Transiting Uranus' house, the house the Sun is in, and the house with Leo on the cusp or contained within it, will be the areas through which expansion is possible. As with any Uranus–Sun transit, some of the existing structures in our life may have to go in order to make room for new things. How much disruption this entails depends to a large degree on how our natal Sun was aspected at birth. Provided the Sun doesn't have too many stressful natal aspects to Saturn or the outer planets, the process of integrating change in our lives under harmonious Uranus–Sun transits shouldn't be too difficult.

However, transiting Uranus conjuncting, squaring or opposing the Sun often brings more upheaval. If we are the kind of person who enjoys the excitement of change, these transits will be easier to handle. But if we fear the unknown or untried – if we would do everything possible to maintain an existing situation even if we are unhappy with it – then the hard transits of Uranus to the Sun will not feel very comfortable.

Feelings of restlessness usually accompany these transits. We might feel bored or trapped by circumstances in our life. We may want to blame others for our dissatisfaction: 'If my husband/wife/ boss/parents were different, then I wouldn't feel this way.' To some extent this might be true, but it is not necessarily the people around us who have to change, but ourselves. We need to pay attention to that part of us which is restless and dissatisfied, and make room in our lives for new things to happen. The core Self wants us to change at this time, and if we deny these inclinations, we are more likely to attract disruption from the outside which forces us into it. Or, because we are using so much of our energy to hold back that part of us which needs to make some changes, we could end up feeling tired, ill or depressed. Difficult Uranus–Sun transits do not require overthrowing every structure in our lives, but we will probably have to make some important adjustments or alterations in order to respect the new growth these transits signal. Again, the house placements involved will provide clues to the areas of our life in which this needs to happen.

The Sun is also a symbol of father, and Uranus–Sun transits sometimes indicate changes in our relationship with him. Again, much depends on how the Sun is aspected natally: if the Sun has stressful natal aspects, a transiting Uranus trine or sextile can provide the opportunity for a positive breakthrough with the father. Communications improve, and previous negative patterns of relating make way for new understanding and openness. However, transiting Uranus conjunct, square or opposing a difficulty aspected natal Sun tends to expose the inherent problems between our father and ourselves. Some of my clients with these transits felt the need to take a stand against the father, challenging his authority over them or his expectations of them; the time had come to separate from him, and to find out who they were in their own right.

Transiting Uranus aspecting the Sun is also symbolic of finding 'the father inside us' – that is, the ability to take charge and direct our own lives. This is a period when it will be difficult to adapt easily to what other people want, especially if it is not in line with what we feel we need for ourselves. Rather than adjusting to others, we may find ourselves demanding that others adjust to us.

Uranus–Sun transits awaken us to our own power, and this could manifest itself in fights with authority figures, and our standing up to people whom we previously allowed control and influence over us.

If a woman has not already contacted her own power or developed her assertive side, this is the time to do so. Besides using this transit to strengthen her own identity and expression, she also may experience its effects through the men she knows or meets during this period. For instance, she might encounter a man with Uranus strong in his natal chart, or someone who is undergoing a major Uranus transit himself. He may be bold and dynamic, and bring a whole new energy into her life, or a new perspective on the world. In this way, she imports Uranus into her sphere via his influence on her. In some cases, a woman may find that a man she is involved with goes through major changes or disruption when Uranus is transiting her Sun. As a result of what is happening to him, her own life alters.

Regardless of gender, under the more difficult transits of Uranus to the Sun, we may not be the most peaceful person to live with. We are excitable, 'wired', unpredictable and restless. We want to remove what we feel is stifling, and break free of the restrictions of tradition or past conditioning. We are 'buzzing' with new ideas and ways of looking at life. If we can accept this new influx of energy, and make necessary changes as diplomatically as possible, these transits – while not the easiest – signify a major step forward in self-unfoldment.

Uranus–Moon

While the Sun points to how we express our individuality and power, the Moon is concerned with our emotions and feelings – the manner in which we instinctively respond or react to others. The Moon also describes something about the conditions of our home life, anything related to mother or mothering, and our relationship to women in general. When transiting Uranus comes to make an aspect with the natal Moon, it is in these areas that Uranus signals change or disruption.

With transiting Uranus trine or sextile the Moon, we usually find it easier to deal with the kinds of changes associated with Uranus, that is, our feelings may be aroused or heightened, and we are receptive to new experiences of an emotional nature. Both men and women have the opportunity during this time to experience a wider range of emotional responses within themselves. For men, this sometimes happens through meeting a woman who awakens them in this way. In a woman's chart, the harmonious transits of Uranus to the Moon indicate a further unfolding of her identity as a woman. For instance, in a number of cases I have seen, women become mothers for the first time when Uranus was trining or sextiling their Moon.

Likewise, if we move home while transiting Uranus is making a harmonious aspect to our Moon, the change is likely for the better, even if at first the move seems disruptive and uncomfortable. The trine or sextile also could manifest as a positive breakthrough in terms of our relationship to our mother. The ability to understand one another improves, and we find we can be with her without feeling invaded or overwhelmed. We are better able to detach and separate ourselves from her, and therefore see her more clearly. However, with the difficult transits of Uranus to the Moon, we might experience problems with mother. If our identity has been too enmeshed with hers, we now may have to stand up against her in order to establish a clearer separate identity. Transiting Uranus conjunct, square or opposing the Moon also could describe a time when our mother is experiencing a disruption or change in her own life.

Some young mothers under difficult Uranus–Moon transits could feel frustrated with the confinements and limitations of mothering, and they may benefit by seeking outlets through which they can express other aspects of themselves. For older women, these transits sometimes correspond to menopausal changes, signifying a time to explore new ways of expressing the lunar urge to care for or nurture others. Men with Uranus–Moon transits may attract women of a Uranian nature who alter their experience or view of life, or they may be in close contact with a woman who is going through a major change or self-reappraisal which directly affects their own lives. Children with Uranus–Moon transits will normally experience its influence in terms of their relationship with their mother, who may be having a challenging or disruptive time herself.

With the transiting conjunction, square or opposition of Uranus to the Moon, we are likely to be experiencing some fairly jarring or disturbing emotional states. If you have been the kind of person who never cried easily, you suddenly may find yourself breaking down and weeping at the slightest provocation. You not only surprise others, but you surprise yourself with the feelings you have at this time. Some people with difficult Uranus–Moon transits are so distressed by the kinds of emotions which surface that they fear they're having a nervous breakdown, or that they are losing all control over themselves. Feelings previously kept in check erupt into consciousness and shatter the hold they have had on themselves. If transiting Uranus contacts a difficultly aspected natal Moon, it might be necessary to seek some advice or counselling during this period – someone with whom we can explore such volatile feelings. For instance, a woman came to see me with transiting Uranus conjuncting her Moon, which natally was in square to Pluto. She had recently given birth to her second child, and found herself suffering from severe post-natal depression. The natal Moon square Pluto is an aspect which describes feelings of a dark or intense nature, which transiting Uranus to the Moon had activated. She felt guilty about the destructive fantasies she was having, both towards herself and the new baby, but talking through these feelings helped her towards gaining a greater understanding and objectivity about what she was going through.

The Moon reveals a great deal about our early experience of mother and the environment, and when Uranus transits the Moon, some of these patterns could resurface in the guise of a current situation. A man came to see me for a reading when transiting Uranus was bringing out a natal Moon square Saturn aspect in his chart. He had been brought up by a strict, conventional mother who didn't find it easy to respond to his emotional needs, and, when transiting Uranus triggered this aspect, he found himself again in a relationship with a woman whom he felt didn't understand and relate to him in the way he needed. Through the present partnership,

Uranus exposed the earlier problems which had begun in childhood. The time had come for him to explore not only his immediate feelings with his current partner, but also the unresolved emotional issues he had with his mother.

When Uranus makes a difficult transit to the Moon, we are likely to feel restless and uneasy in the area or areas of life shown by the houses involved (the natal Moon's house placement, the house position of transiting Uranus, and the house with Cancer on the cusp or contained within it). We may want to break out of whatever circumstances we believe are limiting or constricting us. While it is appropriate to examine our feelings of frustration and discontent, it may not always be wise to act too quickly on these urges – especially if our past pattern has been one of readily disrupting the status quo whenever we feel trapped or ill at ease. Before making any major changes, we need to take time to examine our desire to run away from or destroy existing relationships and structures in our life. If our evolution or growth truly is blocked by the circumstances we are in, we may have to act on our Uranian urges and break free. However, we may discover that the external situation isn't really what is deterring us; we may discover that the block is an internal one, and that we have projected on to the environment our own inner fears or apprehensions about moving forward in our lives. We accuse others of restricting us, when in actual fact we are hesitant or frightened about developing ourself in new ways. In this case, it isn't the outer circumstances which are at fault and need to be altered; it is our inner resistance which has to be faced. Urges to disrupt the status quo at this time also could arise from a deep fear of commitment, which in itself is something that deserves close examination.

We might experience a difficult Uranus–Moon transit through outer events, apparently out of our control, which shake up our world or threaten our security. A relationship could suddenly end, or we may be forced to move homes, or both. Again, even if these appear to be totally the work of fate, we should take time to assess whether feelings we have been having prior to this disruption are connected in any way with what we have attracted into our life. Our own unacknowledged desires for change, projected outwardly and coming back to us through an external agency, could have some-thing to do with the upheaval we find happening around us. Should we examine the situation and still find no relation between these events and concealed urges in ourselves, it is likely that the core Self deems the upheaval necessary in order for us to develop certain qualities which we wouldn't have developed if life had remained the same.

Uranus–Mercury

If we are hoping for a time of mental calm and serenity, transiting Uranus aspecting Mercury is not it; even with transiting Uranus trine or sextile Mercury, our thinking is meant to change. Our minds will be more receptive to new ideas coming our way. Learning or studying new subjects is a good use of these transits. Old modes of thinking and habitual thought-patterns are replaced by fresh atti-tudes, insights, and the ability to look at life from a different perspec-tive than before. Intuition works well under this transit and we may find inspired solutions to certain problems or difficulties which have stifled or dogged us for a long time. Answers and resolutions 'pop' into our head in unexpected ways and at unexpected moments.

When Uranus trines or sextiles Mercury, we will benefit from exploring the city, town or country in which we live. In the process, we are likely to discover people, places, groups, societies and activities which stimulate our mind and interest. We may be attracted to 'Uranian' subjects at this time – anything from astrology, meta-physics and ecological concerns to science and computer technology. We are open to new ideas and trends circulating in the atmosphere, and could act as a spokesperson to promote and spread these. The environment is ready to receive what we have to say, and these are favourable transits for launching new schemes, proposals or cam-paigns. If we are involved in writing, or any form of public speaking or teaching at this time, our mind will be working well, alive with insights and new ideas.

Transiting Uranus conjunct or in difficult aspect to Mercury is a period of mental stimulation, but can bring more problems than the trine or sextile. Our mind could be hyperactive or erratic during this period; we feel nervous and restless, unable to settle easily into any situation. If we have been placid and well organized, accustomed to plodding along at a comfortable pace, the difficult transits of Uranus to Mercury could cause us some concern. Without our normal mental poise and stability, we feel as if we have lost control of ourselves: some people even develop twitches, convulsions or nervous ailments under these transits. It will be helpful to find a constructive outlet for heightened mental energy – something into which to channel the increased tempo of our mind. A sensible programme of physical exercise, sports, or yoga could also siphon off excess mental activity and help us to relax.

Ideas and insights come with such power and force that there is a danger we will be knocked off-balance by them, and although some of these ideas may be quite valid, we may also be carried away with them; caution and restraint is therefore needed, as may be discussing our thoughts and feelings with someone we trust to help us sort out what is useful in our way of thinking from what is extreme or imbalanced. Even so, some of us with these transits may latch on to and become obsessed by notions and beliefs of an overpowering and uncontrollable force. We believe we have glimpsed the Truth and must act on it. Later, after the transit passes, we may look back and wonder what exactly got into us, what 'possessed' us. Sometimes we learn only by making 'mistakes'.

Some of our thinking may be of a radical or unconventional nature. These ideas could be inspired and worthwhile, but it is the intensity with which they are felt and acted upon that needs to be examined and sometimes checked. Provided that we proceed with some caution and common sense, we will be able to fight hard and well during this period for any cause or principle we believe in.

Our thoughts and how we express them are not meant to stay the same during these transits. When Uranus trines or sextiles Mercury, we are ready to receive new ideas; and the environment, in turn, is generally open to our new insights and ideas. This may not be the case, however, when transiting Uranus squares, opposes or conjuncts a difficultly aspected natal Mercury: in these instances, other people or external forces appear determined to challenge or change what we think or believe at a time when we don't feel ready or able to make such adjustments. Especially with the opposition, we feel as if Uranus is coming at us from the outside, trying to disrupt frameworks and structures in our life. However, if we are attracting this kind of situation under these transits, it is likely that the core Self is working through other people and external agencies to shake us up in some way which is needed for further growth and development. Conversely, this could be a period when we have many original insights and intuitions which other people do not understand or accept. They may find our ideas too controversial, impractical, odd, or ahead of the times.

Mercury is associated with brothers and sisters and our relationship with relatives in general. When transiting Uranus trines or sextiles Mercury, a positive change or influence could come to us through siblings or relatives. A new interest, project or study in which they have become involved might be something that arouses or excites us as well. However, when transiting Uranus forms a difficult aspect to Mercury, arguments, disruptions and partings could occur. Some form of compromise or adjustment is asked for, although it may take a while before either side is ready to be more flexible. If we have been too closely identified with a sibling or relative at the expense of developing our own thinking and view of life, a break or struggle with them may be necessary to help us separate our identity from theirs.

Any contact between transiting Uranus and Mercury indicates a time when our mind and thinking is more powerful than usual, and can exert a strong influence both on our self and others. During this period, we can use our mental powers and imagination constructively by forming positive images rather than negative ones. An old adage says that energy follows thought. It's true.

Uranus–Venus

Transiting Uranus aspecting Venus brings change or disruption in the area of love, relationships and creativity. Our values could shift: what we find beautiful, attractive or desirable is not likely to remain the same as before. The way in which we express ourselves creatively also could alter or open up during this period.

When transiting Uranus trines or sextiles Venus, these changes usually occur in a more gentle or flowing fashion. This is a good time to revitalize existing relationships which have become boring or repetitive. Break up your old routines, go to new places with your partner, try things you haven't done before. If we have been too dependent on someone else, we could use this transit to find out who we are in our own right, making the time to explore and develop our own interests and identity separate from the relationship. Whether we are already attached or not, we might meet another person we find stimulating and exciting, someone who introduces us to new ideas and interests, and a new way of looking at life. The new relationship may be a sexual one, although when Uranus is involved it's possible to enjoy a meeting of two minds, which does not necessarily need sexual expression; physical attraction might be there, but extenuating circumstances could inhibit exploring the relationship on that level.

In my experience, any Uranus–Venus transit favours creative expression. If we haven't been in touch with our creativity, these transits mark a good time to explore this side of ourselves. If we are already involved in some kind of artistic activity, this is a period to experiment with new techniques, media or avenues of expression. However, with the hard transits, it's possible that our creative endeavours may be considered too shocking, extreme, unconventional or ahead of their time.

The conjunction, square, or opposition of transiting Uranus to Venus can be just as exciting as the trine or sextile, but they also tend to be more disruptive, jarring or challenging. If we have been sitting on feelings of restlessness and frustration within an existing relationship, and have done little or nothing to improve the situation, the difficult transits could signify a separation or parting of the ways. As the transit takes effect, pressure builds up to such a point that we finally voice or act on our growing frustration. If we don't do something to change the situation, external circumstances probably will do the job for us, and it may be our partner who disrupts or ends the relationship. We tend to associate Uranus with unexpected events which come out of the blue; and yet I believe that, although transiting Uranus may correlate with an apparently sudden ending to a relationship, it is likely there have been unresolved problems and difficulties brewing under the surface for a number of years which then manifest themselves in dramatic or decisive actions when Uranus eventually 'hits' the Venus.

All this sounds messy and unpleasant, and it often is. However, it is also possible to understand and deal with these transits in a more constructive and creative way. When frustration comes to the surface and seriously challenges an existing relationship, Uranus provides the opportunity to examine what isn't working properly or isn't being expressed in the present situation, and may act as a spur to explore other ways of relating which breathe new life into the partnership. If we or our partner have been living in each other's pocket, Uranus doesn't necessarily want the relationship to end, but it does ask that one or both of us establish greater separateness and independence.

Uranus flips us over. If we've been too dependent, it asks we become more autonomous. However, if our pattern has been to avoid commitment, depth or fidelity in a relationship, a Uranus–Venus could mark a time when we discover a need and desire in us for monogamy. Uranus encourages us to try what we haven't yet tried, and to learn how to relate to others in new ways.

Even given the best will and intention, the difficult transits of Uranus to Venus could mean the end of a relationship. In many cases I've seen, when endings occur under these transits, one or both of the parties involved have registered the 'rightness' or necessity of the separation. We deeply sense that the partnership needs to finish or change in order to open our life in a way which couldn't happen if the relationship stayed as it is. We will still need to mourn what is passing, but Uranus helps the adjustment because it activates that part of our psyche which can 'see' the necessity of one phase ending so that another can begin. I did the chart for a couple who had been together for seven years. The man had transiting Uranus opposing his natal Venus, and the woman had transiting Uranus square her natal Venus at the same time. Tension had been building for a number of years, and the Uranus transit brought their joint restlessness and frustration to the surface. They had tried various ways to breathe new life into the relationship and keep it going, but none of these attempts succeeded. One day in the middle of their respective Uranus transits, they looked at each other and said 'Well, it's time to part.' The Uranus transit to Venus in both their charts signified a time when they were able to acknowledge the need to separate. Neither of them knew where they were going next, and they were both aware they would have to mourn and grieve for what they were leaving behind, and yet there were no doubts about what had to be done.

Of course, it isn't always the case that both parties are under a Uranus–Venus transit at the same time. The person having the transit may want to end or change the relationship, but his or her partner may not feel the same way. It may even happen in reverse: you are having a Uranus–Venus transit, but it is your partner who leaves or demands changes in the relationship. Should this be the case, if you honestly examine yourself, you may find that your partner has acted on the frustration or restlessness you have been denying or suppressing over a long period of time. The disruption these transits bring may only be temporary. You or your partner has an affair or wants to be independent, perhaps even solitary, for a while; but when the transit passes, these feelings pass, and you reunite to re-establish the relationship on a new footing.

Transiting Uranus in hard aspect to Venus doesn't always mean the end of a relationship. If you have not been involved for a while, this transit could signify a relationship coming into your life, although given the 'unpredictability' of the Uranian influence, whether it lasts beyond the duration of the transit is not always assured.

Uranus–Mars

Uranus arouses and intensifies whatever planet it touches by transit, and when it trines or sextiles Mars, we can expect a period in which we feel more alive or energetic than usual. This is not a time just to sit around and watch television. Go out and find constructive outlets and projects into which you can channel your increased energy and life-force. Take up an exercise routine, look for a cause to fight for, enrol in a course which interests you, or find a mountain to climb, for by challenging or stretching yourself you can use these harmonious Uranus–Mars transits to your greatest advantage.

When Uranus conjuncts Mars by transit, or makes a square, inconjunct or opposition aspect to it, the increased energy and excitement could be more difficult to handle. We may be more restless, anxious, angrier and more impatient than usual, and little things we normally let pass become the focus for battles and confrontation. We are more inclined to stand up for ourselves, and fervently resent others intruding into or blocking what we are doing. Anger is related to blocked movement: if we want to move forward in our life, but something from the outside stops us, or something from within holds us back, we become angry. This dynamic will be operating powerfully during these transits. If we need to be asserting ourselves and moving ahead in our life and we are not respecting these urges, Mars turns back on itself and attacks the body in the form of illness or physical dysfunctions. Also, if most of our energy is invested in holding back changes or moves we need to make, there will be less energy available with which to direct our life. If we suffer from depression during a Uranus–Mars transit, it may be that we are reluctant to begin something we need to be getting on with and doing.

We need something to be obsessed with during this period – a project or outlet which grips and excites us, and into which we can siphon our excess Mars energy. Mars represents the desire to assert the self. When Uranus activates Mars, the need to make an impact on life is increased. Provided that we can find ways to direct Mars into constructive or creative outlets, even the most difficult Uranus–Mars transits will indicate a time when our growth and unfoldment speeds up and takes a major step forward.

Hard Uranus–Mars transits have been linked with accidents and mishaps, and there are a variety of reasons why this might be true. The combination of Uranus and Mars can be quite impulsive or rash: we rush into things with too much force and wind up tripping over our own feet in the process. And if we are hauling around a load of anger, anxiety and frustration, we attract more accidents than when we are truly calm and tranquil. We may be able to avoid certain mishaps if we take the time to confront and examine our angry feelings before they build up to a dangerous degree.

A wide variety of feelings and moods accompany the difficult transits of Uranus to Mars. On the positive side, we will be overflowing with excitement and enthusiasm for life. Negatively, we could feel angry much of the time, or ill, off-balance and depressed. Most likely we'll fluctuate between these two extremes. However, these transits do offer the opportunity to contact more of our will, authority, power and vitality. The house placement of transiting Uranus, the house position of natal Mars, and the house or houses with Aries or Scorpio on the cusp or contained within them, will show the areas of life where we could come alive in a new way.

Uranus–Jupiter

Our view of the world and our philosophy in life are not likely to remain the same while Uranus transits in aspect to Jupiter. We feel new possibilities, and an exciting sense of what the future could hold in store for us. Some of these visions might come true, and others may prove unrealistic or too pie-in-the-sky. And yet, by the time a Uranus–Jupiter transit finishes, our perspective on life is bound to have changed considerably.

Transiting Uranus trine or sextile to natal Jupiter often denotes a phase of growth and expansion, with new opportunities or breakthroughs coming our way. Good fortune comes in the form of sudden monetary windfalls, excellent work or business offers, beneficial new friendships, and the discovery of interests or philosophies which give greater meaning to our life. Travel can be exciting and worthwhile during this period as well. The whole chart would need to be considered, but whether we stay close to home or roam farther afield, these harmonious Uranus–Jupiter transits often signal the right time to try new ventures, take a few risks, follow our hunches, and stretch ourselves beyond our normal boundaries. We can use these transits constructively by reaching for the best and highest in ourselves, and by believing in what we are capable of accomplishing. We waste the possibilities of transiting Uranus trine or sextile Jupiter if we sell ourselves too short, or doubt our ability to achieve what is actually within our reach.

Transiting Uranus conjunct or in difficult aspect to natal Jupiter also indicates the possibility of change and expansion, but there could be more problems and hitches than with the trine or sextile. Intellectual restlessness is not uncommon at this time, and we may feel the need to challenge or break free of any restrictive or limiting philosophies we believe are holding us back. This is a most iconoclastic aspect, and, if in such a state of mind, we might be ready to jump into anything which promises instant riches or fulfilment or to give our allegiance to anything which we think holds the key to the meaning of existence. Uranus activates the Jupiterian urge to expand and reach for more in life, but the difficult transits bring opportunities which may be too extreme, unreliable or dubious. Someone offers you an exciting new proposition, and it falls through a few weeks later, but even before you have a chance to get depressed about this, another new, perhaps equally dubious, venture comes your way. Without taking the entire chart into consideration, it is not easy to predict the outcome of these transits.

However, we should be wary of rushing into something too rashly or impulsively. We might formulate a new plan or business venture we believe will change our life and give us everything we've ever dreamed of. There probably are some worthwhile elements in this vision, but somehow we go too far with it. We overshoot or aim too high too quickly. While not totally stifling our faith and imagination during this period, we will benefit from taking the time to listen to the advice or suggestions of trusted friends who could help us gain a more balanced or clearer perspective.

As with transiting Uranus trine or sextile Jupiter, our philosophy in life could change radically under the transiting conjunction, square or opposition. In general, it is a good time to undertake a course of study which would broaden and enrich us in some way. However, with the hard transits, we could be drawn to extreme religious sects or unusual cults which take over our entire existence. It's difficult to do anything by halves when transiting Uranus is aspecting Jupiter: we give up everything and take off for India, or we go overboard and believe that we now have the answer to everything for everybody. Some of our new ideas and beliefs could be valid, but again we go too far with them. The intense way we pursue or promote our beliefs could put other people off, and they naturally back away, worried that we have lost our balance altogether. If possible, the force of these transits should be tempered by restraint and common sense; if not, we may discover that our enthusiasm has been misguided and our dedication misplaced.

We might be drawn to travelling when Uranus conjuncts, squares or opposes Jupiter, although we shouldn't expect a prearranged timetable to work out as planned: an exciting time could be in store for us, but anything could happen. Travel during this period will inspire us, or we may be drawn to unusual places 'off the beaten track'; either way, we won't come back the same person – if we come back at all.

Uranus–Saturn

When transiting Uranus aspects Saturn, the new and the old meet, and the nature of the aspect suggests how friendly or fraught the meeting will be. Transiting Uranus trine or sextile Saturn generally indicates that we are ready and prepared to integrate new things into our life. We can keep the best of the old, but gradually and gently make room for new ideas, beliefs, goals, objectives, people and interests, and although we may try to keep change at bay, we would only be cheating ourselves of the growth and unfoldment that is meant for us during this period. What is old and established is open to change, and the time is right to coerce authority figures into new ways of thinking. We could act as a bridge between entrenched conventional attitudes and original, new or untried approaches to any situation.

Transiting Uranus conjunct, square or opposing Saturn also suggests a time when the new meets the old, but in a way that usually proves more problematic and disruptive, possibly even explosive (especially if Mars is involved). In many cases, we will feel so restless and fed up with certain spheres of our life that we have little choice but to make drastic changes in these areas. If we've stayed in a relationship or a job for Saturnian reasons, that is, for the sake of security, loyalty, a sense of duty or a need for status, we will be swayed by – or pushed by – the force of Uranus to alter these circumstances. Our allegiance switches from the old to the new, and we are willing to take risks and disrupt what is known in order to explore different possibilities in our life.

Even if the old structures in our life have not been that wonderful or satisfying, some of us may still find it difficult under hard Uranus–Saturn transits to chance letting go of what is familiar and established. We cling to the known and existing, even though another part of us wants to break loose. In the end, however, transiting Uranus in hard angle to Saturn won't let us get away with keeping everything the same, and we can only try to avert total disruption by maintaining the best of the old while making space for the new, or we can try to salvage what has been spoiled, and improve unsatisfactory situations. But should we fail at these attempts to make things better, we may have no choice but to clear away what is old and stifling in order to create room for the kinds of changes Uranus wants to bring.

A Uranus transit can feel particularly cruel if Saturn is involved, because it threatens those aspects of our existence which provide us with our greatest sense of security or safety. This happens most frequently with transiting Uranus opposing Saturn, but it can also occur under the conjunction or the square. Like an earthquake, the structures in our life collapse and the very ground under our feet gives way. We may be a true victim of fate. Something from the outside happens to us which we couldn't have avoided and which, apparently at least, we have had no part in attracting. However, if we understand Uranus to be an agent of the core Self, the upheaval must have occurred for a reason. Even if we don't believe in the concept of a deeper Self guiding our unfoldment, we can deal with the situation more creatively and successfully if we find some sort of meaning in it. Eventually we may discover that a difficult Uranus–Saturn transit was the catalyst for our developing ourselves in ways which we would not have done otherwise.

In a majority of cases, honest self-analysis will reveal the role we played in inviting a disaster or upheaval into our life. If transiting Uranus hitting Saturn does bring these kinds of external disturbances, we may benefit from taking time to examine what really was going on in our mind during the years leading up to the event. If we have been bored, restless and frustrated, but haven't acknowledged these feelings or done anything to act on them, we unconsciously may have prompted a disruption our way. We would love to blame others for what has happened to us, but we will use these transits most constructively if we can eventually understand what part we have played in setting up facets of our life falling apart.

Uranus–Saturn transits challenge areas in which we are too defended, rigid and restrained. I did the chart of a man with natal Saturn in the eleventh house of groups who had been terrified all his life of speaking up in any group situation. He would have things to say, but he would just sit there and hold himself back. Transiting Uranus conjuncted his eleventh house Saturn, and he finally gained the nerve to break out of his old pattern and stand up in front of a group he was attending. In like manner, we can use these transits constructively by exploring new ways of being in different situations. If in the past we've been the kind of person who has always said 'No', then we can try saying 'Yes'. If our pattern always has been to say 'Yes', then we can try saying 'No' and see what happens. With Uranus, however, we can't always predict which we'll say.

As Uranus moves closer to making a conjunction, square or opposition to natal Saturn, we could find ourselves engaged in some kind of battle with an authority figure (father, mother, teacher, boss or governmental official). Our vision of how things should be will differ from theirs, and we will have more difficulty than usual keeping our opinions to ourselves or standing by and allowing to continue something with which we disagree or don't approve. However, confronting others too directly at this time may not be the wisest way to handle the situation – they are likely to defend their position with a staunch determination equal to our own.

The battle between Ouranus and Cronus (Saturn) led to the birth of Aphrodite (Venus). With difficult Uranus–Saturn transits, we may need to find ways to communicate our ideas and beliefs in a manner that doesn't threaten or put off those we are trying to convince. It could help to bring in a little Venus – some diplomacy and tact – when challenging authority figures at this time. Should we do so and the situation still doesn't improve, we may resort to ultimatums, since we feel our principles very strongly under hard Uranus–Saturn transits and are disinclined to make allowances. If diplomacy doesn't work, and our ultimata fail to produce the desired result, we may have no choice but to take the more drastic step of packing our bags and going elsewhere.

Uranus–Uranus

In considering Uranus aspecting itself by transit, we are looking at what is known as 'the Uranus cycle'. Uranus takes approximately 84 years to circle back to its natal position, and during this period it will form various aspects to its natal placement. As it moves towards the opposition, it will make, among other aspects, a sextile, square and trine to its natal position; after transiting Uranus opposes natal Uranus, it will then trine, square, and sextile natal Uranus once again before returning to its original degree and sign.

The Uranus cycle symbolizes patterns of development which all people go through around certain ages or phases in their lives – what Gail Sheehy, in her book *Passages*, calls 'the predictable crises of adult life'.[1] Beginning with the transiting sextile and ending with the transiting conjunction, we will examine the kinds of challenges and crises associated with the major transits of Uranus to its own place. In all cases, the areas of life most directly affected will be shown by the house position of natal Uranus, the house position of transiting Uranus, and the house or houses with Aquarius on the cusp or contained within it.

Transiting Uranus sextile natal Uranus

Transiting Uranus sextiles its own place twice: first around the age of 14, and then again near the age of 70. We'll start with a discussion of the first occurrence, which also coincides with the first opposition of Saturn to its own place. Both these transits come at the onset of adolescence, the phase of life when we emerge out of the womb of the family into a larger social sphere.

Adolescence is akin to another birth. One dies as a child eventually to be reborn a young adult. In accord with natal Uranus touching off its own place, striking physical and psychological changes hail the arrival of puberty. In girls, menstruation has begun or is about to begin, the pelvic area enlarges, pubic hair shows, and the breasts enlarge. In boys, the presence of sperm can be traced in the urine, the shoulders broaden, hair grows on the face and pubic region, the testes and scrotum descend, the penis enlarges in size, and the voice gets lower.

Puberty is marked not only by a physical transformation, but also by changes in one's social and cultural roles. The time is coming when we will have to stand on our own feet in the world, when our support system shifts from parents to peers, and we explore different ways of behaving with others. In search of an identity, we might gaze for hours at ourselves in the mirror, and try to figure out who we are *and* what we are to be. We may see ourselves as the wave of the future, challenging the values and morals of an older authority. And yet we are caught in that uncomfortable gap between physiological maturity and social immaturity. Our body can now perform the functions of an adult, but very few people really would consider us ready to play a complete productive part in society.

The freeing and liberating effects of transiting Uranus sextiling its own place is reflected in the possibilities adolescence gives us to work through negative patterns from childhood. During adolescence, old issues come to the surface again. For instance, if in the formative years just after birth we weren't provided with a sense of safety and trust in life, these deep fears and insecurities will come to the foreground in adolescence, when we begin to venture out into the world on our own. But now that we are older, we have a chance to come to terms with patterns left over from infancy. Forming a positive bond with a teacher who extends to us the kind of understanding and care we didn't receive as a child may be exactly what is needed to help heal developmental wounds, making up for what we missed or weren't allowed earlier in life. As we grow older we acquire more skills and abilities which enable us to feel the kind of power and faith in ourselves which parents, inadvertently or not, might have quashed in us during childhood.

Transiting Uranus sextiles natal Uranus again around the age of 70. Gail Sheehy calls this era 'The Thoughtful Seventies'; and according to her studies, the most happy and healthy septuagenarians share two basic similarities, both of which reflect a positive use of the Uranus transit which occurs at this time: (1) they are engaged in activities and outlets which they can pursue independently of others and yet which entail some sort of work or involvement with the community; and (2) they are still planning for the future, at least five years ahead.[2] The first condition is Uranian in that it involves being part of a group in which each member, while still a person in their own right, has his or her own particular function to serve. The second finding is in accord with the sense of vision and possibility that attends most of the flowing aspects Uranus makes by transit. Even at 70, we can still change.

Old age is a time to do what we *want* to do, rather than what we or others think we *should* be doing. We have probably spent much of our life focusing on outer or external achievements, but now we have a chance to pause and take stock. Through evaluating, reflecting on and digesting what we have accomplished or not accomplished so far, we will be able to reassess and reformulate the values, goals and objectives which are important to us now. Our obligations and commitments to the world no longer paramount, this is an appropriate time in our lives to reconsider what is personally meaningful to us. What are our own individual needs and desires? What is the purpose of our existence? What do we *want* to do with the years we have left? With transiting Uranus sextile its own place, even as a septuagenarian, it is possible for us to clear the old to make way for the new.

Transiting Uranus square natal Uranus

This transit also occurs twice in life: first in our early twenties and then again in our early sixties. And true to the nature of Uranus and the square aspect, these are times of major changes in orientation and values.

The first transit of Uranus in sextile to natal Uranus heralds the beginning of adolescence; but the *first square* of Uranus to its own place marks the end of adolescence and the full entry into young adulthood. Around 14 and the time of the Uranus sextile, we felt the urge for greater autonomy, but there was only so much we could do about it. We might have confronted and challenged our parents, but chances are we still went on living with them. When Uranus squares Uranus in our early twenties, we also feel (consciously or unconsciously) a drive towards autonomy, but now we can take it a step further.

Probably the most common manifestation of this transit is what

Sheehy calls 'pulling up roots', or leaving the parental home.[3] The task of separating from the family and finding out who we are in our own right (which began in early adolescence) becomes more pressing and urgent. Even if we aren't wildly rebellious during this period, it is still a time of significant growth and rapid change. More than ever before, we are expected to locate ourselves in a peer group, to establish a clear sexual identity, and to find some sort of work or occupation which will serve to define us. In short, we are expected to be more responsible for ourselves than ever before.

Uranus is associated with ideologies and '-isms', and when it squares our natal Uranus in our early twenties, the desire to find something to believe in is also activated. At this time many of us look for a group or cause to attach ourselves to, something to give meaning and direction to our life. Uranus stimulates an urge to greater independence and autonomy, and the particular attraction of one group or another may be the fact that its ideals or values differ significantly from those of our parents. Finding a world view which differs from that of our family is part and parcel of finding our own identity.

Some of us might not rebel or strike out on our own in this way at all. We may go along with our parents' values and expectations, and slot into the kind of lifestyle they have had in mind for us. The positive thing about passively accepting our parents' view of the world is that we avoid a crisis; the negative thing is that we forgo an opportunity to explore our own identity and find out who we are independently of them. But more likely than not, the crisis we have managed to elude at this stage will erupt later in our life, probably between the ages of thirty-five and forty-two, when Uranus comes to oppose its own place. Just as well, because sooner or later we'll have to confront the fact that going through an identity crisis of this sort is a prerequisite to self-discovery.

The *second* Uranus square occurs in our early sixties, not far from the second Saturn return. The obvious concern is ageing. Some people give up growing around this time, nail their coffin lid down and slip into an 'is that all there is?' state of mind, obsessed with the past, with loss, and with opportunities they have missed. Fortunately, however, not everyone reacts this way. Studies show that many people who were worried about getting older in their mid-forties and fifties stop worrying so much about it in their sixties.⁴ They accept the fact they *are* older, and get on with the task at hand, making the most of the time they have left.

In the early twenties, the *first* Uranus–Uranus square entailed separating from one's family and discovering one's self in one's own right. In the early sixties, the *second* Uranus–Uranus square is also about separation, but of a different sort. The task at hand is to separate what really matters to us from what doesn't. We may begin to feel detached from (or not so bothered about) issues or concerns which previously meant a great deal to us, but this doesn't mean we are slipping into a state of indifference where nothing matters. On the contrary, those things we still find important become even more important. Having discriminated between what is of significance to us and what isn't, we can now find ourselves feeling even more intensely about and revitalized by those things we deem worthwhile to focus on.

For most people at this time, disengaging from what mattered in the past takes its most obvious form in retirement from full-time employment. Issues to do with career and personal success in the world are no longer so primary. For many of us, stopping or slowing down work leaves a frightening gap, and we are forced to confront one of the main existential fears in life – the loss of structure. Faced with hours of free time and less responsibility than ever before, we are left with the task of giving new meaning to our life.

Those people who cope best with retirement are the ones who have rehearsed and planned for it well before the actual time. Even while we are still employed, we can use our spare time to develop a skill, craft or resource which will later help to fill the gap retirement creates. Women and men in their early sixties need to find something that *engages* them. We are more likely to use the second Uranus–Uranus square most constructively if we plan ahead for it. We don't have to wait until Uranus squares our Uranus to start looking for interesting activities and projects outside our line of work or separate from the domestic sphere. If we anticipate the gap left by retirement or a fully grown-up family, we can prepare ourselves for it.

In accord with the Uranian nature of this period, those outlets which could prove most rewarding are ones that we can pursue independently of other people, and yet which serve the community in some way. We can find things to do that we want to do. What's more, these don't necessarily need to involve our spouse. Social or humanitarian clubs and organizations, or anything from bird-watching groups to the church and politics, can provide the kind of fulfilment and involvement which were previously the domain of family or career.

Transiting Uranus trine natal Uranus

This transit happens twice in our life: first around the age of 28 (coinciding with the first Saturn return) and then again near the age of 56. At the time of the *first* Uranus–Uranus trine, we have a chance to reappraise and reconsider choices we have made up to now. What we've built and established may have been appropriate for earlier stages of our development, but is it in accord with our present state of mind? If we feel too restricted by our lifestyle or by decisions we have made in the past, this is the time to make necessary adjustments. Usually this stage is accompanied by a feeling of wanting to be something more than we already are, a sense that we have outgrown what is there in front of us. For many people, this means taking an entirely new direction in life; for others, the changes will not be so drastic, but there will still be the need to renew or deepen one's commitment to earlier choices.

The combined effects of transiting Uranus trine natal Uranus, along with the Saturn return around this age, show up clearly in clients coming for readings. Married people are having doubts about whether the marriage is really what they want. Single people decide they no longer wish to go solo, and their main concern is whether the chart indicates a marriage coming up. Women without children start thinking about having them. Mothers who have already spent years looking after children feel the itch to make something of themselves in other ways – going back to college or finding a career. Men have doubts about their professional choice and want to know what other kinds of jobs the chart suggests.

When transiting Uranus squared natal Uranus in our early

twenties, we may have rebelled *in toto* against our parents' values and expectations. Now, however, as transiting Uranus trines our natal Uranus at the same time as our Saturn return, and we turn the corner into 30, our view of the world may be changing. To our surprise and possible dismay, we could find that some of our parents' beliefs about what was worthy or good for us actually make a bit more sense now. Could it be that in the process of separating from our family background, we threw away too much? Maybe they weren't *totally* wrong after all? The process of sorting out what to keep from our parental inheritance and what to discard and replace with our own truths, is undertaken again in earnest at this stage. We start to look at aspects of ourselves which we have never wanted to admit to before – aspects which uncannily resemble qualities we have identified previously in our mother or father, but certainly not in us!

Such questioning and soul-searching can yield fruitful results. We are more in touch with ourselves than ever before, and the choices and adjustments we make now in our life are likely to be more enduring and lasting as a result. But if we somehow let things ride during this period, and shun the kind of inner probing the Saturn and Uranus transits are prompting us to do, we won't be let off the hook, for very long at least. A number of years later we'll be hit even harder by the kinds of issues Uranus stirs when it comes to oppose its own place in our birthchart.

The *second* transiting Uranus–Uranus trine occurs around the age of 56. Ideally, this is the time to give ourselves permission to be who we are – to do what we want to do, not just what we think we *should* be doing. And if we have successfully managed to pass through some of the dangers of early mid-life, this period could be one of the happiest we know. In keeping with the promise of freedom and expansion symbolized by Uranus trining its own place, this transit may coincide with certain positive changes in outlook and character. We feel freer to say what we think. Men are more able easily to express their needs and admit to their feelings. Women are more confident about owning their power and asserting themselves. We all generally have more time and space for ourselves, having been around long enough to learn quite a bit about who we actually are, what we need and want, and how to go about getting it.

Just sticking in one place, trying to derive identity and satisfaction from a single well-worn track, is not the most creative way to use this transit: it's time to diverge, experiment and expand. If you're an older woman still trying to play mother to a grown-up family, you're not diverging; you're staying in the same place working at a situation that has outlived much of its truth and usefulness.

Men and women in careers need to wake up to the fact that eventually they will retire. Prepare for that time under this transit – start developing buried or neglected resources and talents, look around for interests and activities which will be there to replace the vacuum created by retirement. It's up to you to make the most of this passage. If you find yourself falling into a hole of passive resignation, you can at least try to stop and dig yourself out, for your life is far from over – that is, if you are prepared to take a few risks and make a leap or two into the unknown. Don't be afraid to try those things you've been wanting to do, but haven't had the courage. If for years you've been toying with the idea of starting your own small business, this may be your last chance to do so. If you're bored with where you are, but your inclination is to stay within the same career, you could look into the possibility of moving into a new department or finding another aspect of the work which interests you more. Uranus also opens us up to concerns extending beyond those of personal advancement, and we may find our greatest sense of well-being and purpose working for the community, engaged in activities which serve others. The second Uranus–Uranus trine, like the first, is much more than just a passive period of reflection: it may be time to look back and review life, but it's a time to plan ahead as well.

Transiting Uranus opposing natal Uranus

Transiting Uranus opposes its own place any time from age 38 to 45. People born in the 1930s, 40s or 50s will have this transit at the earlier end of the scale, between the ages of 38 and 41. People born in the first two decades of the 1900s and in the 1960s, 70s and 80s will experience it a little later, between the ages of 41 and 45. Saturn also comes to oppose its own place around the age of 42. This means that both Uranus and Saturn are activated during this period. And in some cases, these transits also coincide with transiting Neptune in square to natal Neptune, and transiting Pluto squaring its own place! No wonder this period is considered one of the most crucial turning-points in life.

This phase of life has been dubbed 'the mid-life crisis'. Besides providing the theme for numerous television stories and film scripts, the mid-life crisis has been covered fairly extensively in some astrological texts, as well as in academic and popular psychology books. In a nutshell, it's a time for disassembling ourselves and then putting the pieces back together again, but in a different way. Parts of our nature we haven't integrated yet into our conscious awareness, and which we have been ignoring or not looking at, demand to be acknowledged and examined. Facing the conflicts and crisis of this period increases the likelihood of a fulfilling second half of life. Avoiding the kind of self-examination asked for during this phase spells trouble later on. The problems don't go away: they hide and wait for other Uranus or Saturn transits and then resurface. It's generally easier to have your mid-life crisis at 42 than at 56 or 60.

A wide spectrum of psychological issues occur during this stage. The stark realization that we're not getting any younger sets us thinking about what we have or haven't achieved so far. In our late teens and early twenties (at the time of our first Uranus–Uranus square) we probably had a vision of what we hoped we would be like as a fully mature adult. Now we have the chance to compare this vision with what we have actually achieved. If our current reality falls short of what we imagined it would be, we could find ourselves on the downhill slide into a depression. If there is a discrepancy between our earlier hopes and ideals and our present reality, it is a signal that the time has come to adjust our goals and make them more realistic. Maybe we won't make it to the top of a large corporation, as we might have hoped. Maybe our dreams need to be scaled down. Even so, this transit is an opportunity to find our second wind, and to get on with doing the most we can with the resources we have.

Even if we have manifested our early life vision and ideals, we may now be asking ourselves 'So what?' The happiness and fulfilment we thought would be ours has somehow eluded us all the same. The time has come to review our situation and make some changes. Our success frees us to take up other interests or endeavours which we have had to put aside to arrive where we are now. We can throw ourselves into new projects or outlets which will fulfil parts of us that our present achievements, no matter how great, don't satisfy.

Our youth is over, our physical prowess isn't what it was when we were 21. Regardless of whether we've fulfilled or failed to achieve our dreams, we're still left feeling incomplete and aware that something is missing. This situation could drive us into an intense and restless search for anything that will fill the gap. Perhaps losing ourselves in a new relationship, or an affair with someone younger, will pull us out of the pit? Maybe if we keep as busy as possible, we won't have time to feel the pain or emptiness that's there? Maybe jogging three more miles a day will do the trick? These ploys may help, but only for a while. If we try to run away from what we are feeling now, these same feelings will just come back again at a later time, and hit us even harder. If we avoid the necessary changes called for by any stage or passage of development, we create psychic congestion: we end up stuck on the same track, cramped with old, rigidly defined borders. Having affairs or cramming our life with things to do may temporarily delay or deter 'the mid-life blues', but such tactics alone won't resolve anything. A more creative solution to the crisis involves going down into it – facing the pain and the darkness. Let go: let the crisis happen and see where it leads.

As with any transition, phase one is to grieve for the old you that is dying, for the identities and roles that have taken you this far, but which must be shed so that a new you can develop. The next step is to look at those parts of yourself which you have not been in touch with – those aspects of your nature you have denied or kept hidden.

We may have to look at emotions and qualities in ourselves which we don't like very much – our jealousy, envy, greed or the side of us which is fearful, dependent or competitive. Owning these parts of our nature means expanding our existing self-definition to include more of what is actually there. Instead of believing in an edited edition of the self, cut to fit into conventional norms and acceptable standards, we look at the full version of who we are, complete with the good parts as well as the bad. This does not mean unleashing our 'darker side' out on to the world, but it does mean reconnecting to more of what is there in us, and becoming more whole and authentic in the process.

Looking into ourselves will also put us in touch with positive aspects of our nature which have yet to be developed and integrated into our conscious personality. If previously we have lived in a very one-sided way, it is during the mid-life passage that those parts of us which we have ignored or neglected have a chance to be explored and worked on. For instance, if you have lived the first half of your life in a very down-to-earth manner, concerned primarily with practical issues of earning a living or establishing yourself in the world, the mid-life crisis could open you to values of a more spiritual or esoteric nature. Conversely, if you have spent your twenties and thirties meditating all day in an effort to achieve *nirvana* or spiritual enlightenment, you could find that transiting Uranus opposing natal Uranus awakens in you an interest in earning money and making something of yourself in the material sphere of life. In short, those parts of our nature we haven't favoured or encouraged – those parts which haven't been a major source of motivation – are the very areas which become important, and form the focus of our new aspirations. Although the process of expanding our identity to include previously undeveloped qualities can begin in earnest now, this task is not over when Uranus finishes opposing its own place. Becoming more whole and authentic is the work ahead for the entire duration of the second half of life.

Personality changes which take place in middle age generally involve what are known in psychology as 'cross-sex' issues. This means that men start exploring qualities in themselves which are traditionally associated with 'feminine' urges; and women turn to spheres and issues which are more conventionally classed under 'masculine' drives. Exactly what this entails is worth exploring in a little more detail.

Men who have devoted the first half of their lives to achieving in the outer world may begin to question the amount of time and energy they're investing in that direction. Focusing on external deeds and worldly accomplishments usually means that the inner world of feelings, and the need for real intimacy, closeness and fulfilment in relationships, have been relegated to second place. Taking a greater interest in his marriage, and spending more time with his children, is one way a man can further develop his capacity for relationship and intimacy. However, the obvious course of turning towards his wife and family is not always the way he first chooses to awaken his feeling side. Sometimes, it takes the external agency of a mistress to draw his attention to the realm of passion and feeling. Or his wife is the one to run off or have an affair, and in this way he is shocked into examining and questioning his ability to form relationships.

During the mid-life crisis (or *middlescence* as it is sometimes called), a man's attention also could turn inward to the creative and imaginative realms of the psyche. He may realize that the job or work which takes up so much of his time is not fully satisfying his need for creativity and self-expression. One solution to this problem is to look for another kind of work altogether, or to try adjusting his schedule so that he has more space and energy to devote to the development of new interests and forms of creative expression.

A woman may experience her mid-life crisis in a diametrically opposed way. If her attention has been focused primarily on relationships and the needs of her partner and children, she is stirred by new drives and urges which involve fulfilling herself in her own right, in a way not related only to attending to the well-being of those close to her. What about her own need to assert her power in the world and achieve recognition in a concrete way? What about her own development and growth? Her child-bearing days are drawing to a close; her children are getting older and won't need her so much in the future . . . where does that leave her? It's at this juncture that she could take important steps which will alter the rest of her life. What about going back to college to develop her mind or skills further? What about the possibility of re-entering the job market and seeing what she could do there? Neither of these steps may be easy, or executed without strain. But rather than running away from these issues, if she faces herself and others now and risks making some changes in her life, she has a much greater chance of happiness and fulfilment in her later years. And in doing so, she becomes what Gail Sheehy calls a *pathfinder*. Of course, the choice (apparently at least) may not be hers, but it may be forced on to her if her marriage or relationship falls apart, and she may have no alternative but to become a more complete and autonomous person in her own right. By contrast, other women may have accomplished a great deal in the world during their twenties and thirties; for them, the mid-life crisis may mean refocusing their attention away from career and achievement, and making more time in their lives for relationships and intimacy.

Whatever one's specific circumstances are, transiting Uranus opposing its own place signals the need to pause and consider how we have organized our life so far. If we've veered too much in one direction at the expense of other avenues of expression or fulfilment, now is the time to make some changes and restore the balance.

Transiting Uranus conjuncting natal Uranus

It's possible for transiting Uranus to conjunct natal Uranus shortly after birth. If we were born with Uranus retrograde, for instance, then within a number of months it will turn direct and pass over where it was at birth. Or we may have been born with Uranus direct, and then it moved backward over our natal Uranus and forward over it once more within the first year of our life. In either case, this early conjunction of Uranus to its own place could signify some sort of disruption or upheaval which makes an impression deep within our psyche. We are left with an underlying belief that life is unpredictable; or somewhere buried inside us is the expectation that whenever we settle into something – a job, a relationship, a home, etc. – disruption is just around the corner. Early experiences cut very deeply, and even though we don't remember consciously what happens in the first few months or years of life, what occurs then contributes to the formation of beliefs and patterns we carry around inside us far into adulthood.

However, when astrologers refer to Uranus conjuncting natal Uranus, they usually mean what is known as *the Uranus return*, which occurs roughly around the age of 84 and marks a complete cycle of Uranus around the chart. Hopefully our health and state of mind still allow us to experience some of the most positive changes symbolized by this transit. The full circle of Uranus means that a major cycle or phase of our life is completed and something new can begin. We've met most of our responsibilities to society, we've worked for and served the collective in some way; perhaps we've raised a family, or passed on some of our knowledge and experience to later generations. In any case, we are no longer expected to be doing any of these kinds of tasks. If anything, this is *our* time to be looked after. Friends, family or the government will help tend to our daily needs and mundane concerns, leaving us free for other things.

But free for what? This is a good time to ponder both the meaning of our existence and the meaning of life in general. In other words, it is partly a period of contemplation. What have we learned? How would we have done it differently? What's wrong with the world today? And of course, there is the subject of death to think about. What lies beyond? Will we go on living in some other form? Death requires not only thought and speculation, but also preparation. If we haven't prepared properly for our death, this is the time to put our life in order so that we can die in peace. This doesn't necessarily mean we are going to die tomorrow. We may have a number of good years left and we can be planning for these as well. After all, we are under a major Uranus transit – there is still time to try a few more things. Johann von Goethe, the German literary genius, continued writing into his eighties as transiting Uranus was approaching his third house Uranus in Aquarius; Michelangelo was working on St Peter's during his Uranus return in Scorpio in his tenth house; and socialite Alice Roosevelt Longworth was still at the hub of Washington society at the time transiting Uranus conjuncted its natal placement in Virgo in her eleventh house.

Uranus–Neptune

Because Neptune spends around 14 years in each sign, large numbers of people will experience Uranus–Neptune transits at roughly the same time. For example, Neptune was in Libra during 1942–56, and everyone born then has that placement. In 1968 Uranus moved into Libra and, by transit, a seven-year period began during which Uranus eventually would conjunct Neptune in the charts of all those people born with it in Libra. The placement of Neptune in the Venusian sign of Libra describes a tendency to idealize love, and to view the Libran qualities of peace, justice and harmony as something numinous or divine. Uranus' awakening effect on Neptune in Libra was obvious: a wave of idealism spread throughout the world – a vision of life on earth inspired by the Neptune in Libra principles of peace and love. Aided by such Neptunian accoutrements as drugs and music, Uranus activated Neptune in Libra on a collective scale. Uranus also politicized Neptune, elevating an emotional yearning for peace and love into an ideology. By 1974, Uranus completed its transit of Libra, and the love and peace movement began to lose its initial force. (In the meantime Pluto had entered Libra and, by transit, began conjuncting Neptune in the charts of everyone with it there; the ideals and dreams of the Neptune in Libra generation were about to be affected in yet another way.)

Uranus–Neptune transits relate quite clearly to trends taking place on a collective scale, which influence large numbers of people. However, these transits also affect each of us personally, especially if we are sensitive to the new movements and fashions that periodically pervade the atmosphere. The house position of transiting Uranus, the house placement of natal Neptune, and the house with Pisces on the cusp or contained within it, show the areas of life where we will be most affected.

Any Uranus–Neptune transit will arouse and enliven what Neptune symbolizes. Since Neptune can operate on so many different levels, the exact way in which it is stimulated will vary from person to person. For some, Uranus–Neptune transits trigger creative inspiration and spiritual awakening, and gives rise to new and vivifying dreams and aspirations. For others, these transits signify the onset of strange and inexplicable illnesses, various degrees of experimentation with drugs, and an irresistible fascination for magic, the occult, or any 'way-out' notions and beliefs. Which way it will go depends not only on how Neptune is aspected in the natal chart, but also on the individual's level of consciousness and psychological maturity. In general transiting Uranus trine or sextile Neptune is easier to handle and more gentle than the conjunction, square or opposition.

Neptune has the capacity to alter our ordinary perception of everyday reality and expose us to other dimensions of experience. When transiting Uranus aspects Neptune, this capacity is activated. Uranus–Neptune transits can coincide with 'peak experiences', times when our usual ego-boundaries dissolve, and we feel a unity and empathy with those around us or with all of creation. Our heart opens up and love pours out. This is a positive experience in itself, but there is the danger of being swept away by Neptune and losing a healthy sense of one's individuality or personal boundaries. In extreme cases, we might believe we are God's chosen messenger, here to redeem the world. In such an inflated state, we make choices or decisions which later we realize were extreme or misguided.

Transiting Uranus conjunct, square or opposition Neptune can activate Neptune with such force that we are taken over by powerful emotional yearnings. Physical exercises will help ground us during this period, and enable the body to contain and direct Neptunian upsurges of feeling, but before committing ourselves to any drastic actions or changes in life, it might be wise to discuss our plans with friends and associates (preferably of another generation) whose guidance we trust.

By nature, Uranus jolts us into awareness, shifting us quickly from one state of mind to another. Under Uranus–Neptune transits, some people may turn to drugs as a means of escape from ordinary life, or as a way of gaining entry to elevated states of consciousness. When transiting Uranus conjuncted Neptune in Libra in the late 1960s and early 70s, experimentation with drugs increased. Under the influence of Uranus, we stand adamantly for what we believe regardless of established conventions and mores, and some members of this generation openly defied the law, and proclaimed the positive value of psychedelic drugs: they were going to do it their way. In many cases, the nervous system was not sufficiently strong to withstand the kinds of physiological and psychological changes produced by such drugs, and some people simply ended up with their minds 'blown' as a result.

The result of that era still stands today as a reminder to anyone undergoing a Uranus transit to Neptune: certain drugs (be they psychedelics, heroin, cocaine, or valium) may be a quick and apparently easy way to escape from where we are and to alter our state of awareness, but in the long term it's safer to find more natural ways of doing this. Meditation, therapy or other forms of self-exploration and self-development are more effective agencies for change and growth during Uranus–Neptune transits.

Also, under these transits, we may be gripped by an urge to escape from what is dull, routine and ordinary. Creative people may experience a change from their usual form of artistic expression. Uranus activates the Neptunian compulsion to be swept away by something, whether an intense love which transports us to new heights of ecstasy, a sudden upsurge of religious or mystical feeling, or an overwhelming attraction to a new idea or philosophy which promises to open heaven's door. Some people become fascinated by magic or the occult during this period. Again, some discrimination and common sense is needed to use these transits most constructively. Falling in love can be wonderful, but we will be disappointed if we expect our beloved to give us *everything* we need for total fulfilment in life. The exploration of religious, spiritual and mystical urges is a natural part of life, but we need to make sure that the groups and philosophies we become involved with are sound. It is also worth remembering that under this Uranian influence such feelings may also 'turn off', and in general there can be an unpredictable and agitated urgency to many of our emotional responses.

However, standing back and being objective in the middle of a hard Uranus–Neptune transit is much easier said than done: our feelings may be too overwhelming to allow room for much detachment or self-observation. In such cases, we might have no choice but to go fully into the experience, giving ourselves to the new love which is going to make our life happy-ever-after, absolutely believing in that philosophy or technique which promises enlightenment within a year, or delving into magic and the supernatural. In the end, we may find ourselves disillusioned, let down, imbalanced or even psychotic, and yet, properly assimilated, it's possible for these kinds of experiences to teach us something we wouldn't have learned if we had acted safely and sensibly all along.

Uranus–Pluto

Pluto moves very slowly through the heavens; therefore those people born in the same year (or two or three years before or after) will experience Uranus transits to Pluto at roughly the same time. When this happens, friends and people around us will be facing similar kinds of issues and challenges as those we ourselves are going through.

When a planet as powerful as Uranus touches off Pluto, change in some form is inevitable. If we insist on clinging to the old, and refuse to acknowledge what needs to be altered in our life during this period, Uranus–Pluto transits have a way of forcing us to change regardless of our conscious desires. The house position of transiting Uranus, the natal house of Pluto, and the house with Scorpio on the cusp or contained within it, will show the areas of life most clearly affected. Transiting Uranus trine or sextile Pluto generally is more gentle and easier to handle than the transiting conjunction, square or opposition. However, in order to assess Uranus–Pluto transits, the natal aspects to Pluto need to be considered carefully. When Uranus contacts Pluto by transit, it will activate any natal configurations involving Pluto.

Uranus–Pluto transits also signify social, economic or political forces that affect our life and from which we cannot escape. We can try to fight the effects of these transits, but chances are we won't have too much success. Some sort of change of our social and economic status or our political beliefs needs to happen, although a number of years may pass before we honestly can admit there was anything valuable or positive about what we went through at the time.

In the case of the transiting opposition and square, we may feel that external forces are provoking such change: people we meet or ideas we come across disrupt and disturb the status quo. However, Uranus–Pluto transits are felt not only through outside influences. Uranus is a planet which brings insight and illumination, and when it interacts with Pluto – the planet of renewal and transformation – we may be overtaken from within by a sudden urge to move forward in life: obstacles which hold us back from further growth and development are seen for what they are and can be cleared away. We have probably been sensing the need to confront certain issues in our lives and to make some changes for some time now. Uranus acts as a catalyst to bring these feelings to the surface and translate them into action.

This illuminating quality of Uranus also serves to make us aware of personality traits and deep-seated inner complexes that trap us in negative, repetitive patterns. Pluto is associated with emotional complexes left over from childhood, those which still affect us deeply; for instance, if your mother abandoned you at an early age, you may form a belief or expectation that anyone you become close to or dependent upon will also leave. Life has a way of obliging deep-seated beliefs: later on you may find yourself unconsciously drawn to people who fulfil your negative expectations. You might repeatedly choose the kind of person who does eventually end up walking out or abandoning you. Or you could be so frightened of someone leaving you (like mother did) that you attempt to control or manipulate the relationship in a manner which ultimately drives that person away. When Uranus transits Pluto, we have an opportunity to discover and to explore more fully some of the inner images and patterns we have harboured since childhood. Uranus–Pluto transits thus give us new insight into our own unconscious.

Pluto can also be linked to anger and destructive rage, often stemming from childhood. In infancy, our life depends on other people looking after us and providing for our needs; should they fail to do this adequately, we not only feel depressed and frightened about our survival, we also feel angry at those who are letting us down. We may suppress these feelings at the time, but they remain buried within us. When Uranus transits Pluto (especially with the conjunction, square or opposition), the earlier infantile rage is reactivated and could be unleashed on anyone around who is not giving us exactly what we want. Although it isn't very pleasant to feel such emotions, under this transit we are being provided with an opportunity to rediscover parts of the self we have previously denied. When we cut off from our early anger and rage, we also alienate ourselves from reserves of energy and power inside us. Reowning buried infantile anger is a way of reconnecting to the energy contained within those feelings.* In doing so, we can free the energy that has been trapped in suppressed infantile emotions and reintegrate it back into the psyche. It can be more constructively directed into our life, and as a result, we will not only feel more whole, but also more vital and alive. Uranus–Pluto transits can also lead to the discovery of buried treasure inside us – the reclaiming of unexpressed positive traits and resources.

Transiting Uranus aspecting Pluto not only stirs unconscious patterns, early wounds and anger, but it can sometimes manifest in the body in the form of illness. A disease or ailment which has hitherto been hidden or 'under the surface' could manifest itself during these transits, or an illness we have had in the past which hasn't been completely resolved might reappear. Although this may seem a very unwelcome occurrence, it is only when a malady or weakness is apparent that something can be done to heal it. Under this transit, too, we may discover 'inspired' cures, remedies or solutions to a chronic complaint.

Uranus–Pluto transits can affect our sexual expression, and if we have been repressing feelings or desires, Uranus could arouse passions in us which we never knew existed. We may feel overwhelmed by such eruptions, and yet Uranus is doing nothing more than revealing what has been buried in us all along. On the other hand, if we have been very sexually active, these transits could have the effect of transmuting or sublimating our sexual drive into other outlets.

Finally, we should remember that in Greek mythology Pluto was the god of death. Whenever Pluto is activated by transit, we may have to face death in some form: someone we know may die, or we might have a near-death experience.† Such events are not pleasant in themselves, but they may provoke us to think more seriously

---

*For a further discussion of dealing with infantile complexes, see pp. 226–33 and pp. 242–5.
†See Suggested Reading (p. 386) for a list of books dealing with death and the grieving process.

about the meaning of existence, and precisely what it is that we are doing with our life. Whether we like it or not, any Uranus–Pluto transit offers the opportunity to go deeper into ourselves. By taking the plunge, we use these periods most constructively.

Transiting Uranus Through the Houses

First House

The ascendant is the point in the chart associated with birth and new beginnings, and when Uranus crosses the ascendant and moves into the first house it's almost like being born again. One's whole approach to life – sometimes even one's physical appearance or style of dress – can change. If we have not been in touch with the qualities of our rising sign, Uranus will bring these aspects of our nature to the surface now. If we have already been expressing our ascendant, Uranus asks that we explore other possible manifestations of that sign; a man with Sagittarius rising, for instance, who has travelled a great deal and expressed his ascendant in that way, could discover other facets associated with Sagittarius such as writing or studying philosophy.

At this time, parts of the self which have been suppressed or undeveloped insist on inclusion into conscious awareness. Shy people discover a confidence they never knew they had, while previously down-to-earth and practically minded individuals awaken to values and aspirations of a very different nature: they are willing (or forced by external events) to forgo their need for security and stability, and branch out in new directions. People who have been predominantly 'thinking-types' suddenly discover a vast new realm of feeling, while those who have been dominated by emotions and sentiment find themselves better able to stand back and be more objective and detached. Whatever sign is on the ascendant, this transit often reverses our sense of self, and gives us the opportunity to explore new ways of meeting life.

When aspects of the self which have been held in check or ignored for a long time eventually erupt into consciousness, they may at first be unleashed in a rather awkward, imbalanced or uncontrollable manner. For example, if your tendency in the past has always been to put yourself aside for the sake of others, you could swing too far the opposite way when Uranus crosses the ascendant. No longer willing to take a back seat in life, you temporarily go wild with your new-found assertiveness: it's your turn to call the shots, and no one is going to stop you. You cast off anything which you find restricting or limiting, and demand that everyone else adjust to you. Gradually, however, as Uranus moves away from the ascendant and further into the first house, you calm down, and begin to learn how to use your assertive energy more wisely and skilfully. Equally, if you have been a pragmatic, cautious person, you might throw caution and practicality to the winds during this transit, as you discover an inner, spiritual dimension to life, and give up your job in order to meditate 20 hours a day. It may take a little time before you can begin to integrate the qualities Uranus brings to the fore with other aspects of your being.

This transit brings out restlessness and impatience, no matter what sign is on the ascendant. We wake up in the middle of the night 'buzzing' with ideas and revelations; bolts of energy hit us out of the blue; we feel 'wired', excited, changeable and frenetic. We act in ways that surprise us as well as others. Obviously, this degree of intensity doesn't last the entire transit, but comes in spurts, first when Uranus crosses the ascendant, and then whenever, in its movement through the first, it makes an aspect to another planet in the chart. We will also clearly feel its effects when another transiting planet in the heaven (or a progressed planet or angle) makes an aspect to transiting Uranus: for example, transiting Mars conjuncting, squaring or opposing transiting Uranus will act as a trigger releasing the impact of the Uranus transit. We also will notice a sudden resurgence of Uranian energy just as it is about to leave the first and enter the second, as if Uranus is determined to have one last chance to change our personality and our way of meeting life before moving on to influence a new domain of our chart.

When interpreting this transit, as with all transits, we must take age into consideration: a young child, for example, with Uranus transiting the first is more likely to experience the effects of Uranus from the outside, usually via the actions of his parents who may move house, get divorced, or produce another child – all of which serve to disrupt existing structures and routines. Older children and teenagers might display even more than the usual degree of wilful rebellion and obstinacy under the influence of this transit. Young adults often face major junctures at this time: they leave home, start or finish college, get married, have children, or discover a new philosophy or political system which revolutionizes their life. Later in life, this transit could correlate with divorce, changing jobs, or the awakening of undiscovered aspects of the personality or those traits uniquely 'ours'. For elderly people, Uranus crossing the ascendant and moving into the first house will help them break free from old patterns of thought or behaviour. In some cases it augurs death – the release from an old form into a new dimension of being – although other transits in the chart would have to support this interpretation as well. At any age, this transit could indicate an external or collective influence which dramatically alters the course of life, such as the outbreak of war or a change of government. Whatever the time or phase of life at which we experience this transit, one thing is certain: we see the world and relate to it in a radically different way afterwards.

Second House

The most obvious effect of this transit is to change our financial situation and the way we relate to the world of money and matter in general. In other words, our values change. There could be an increase in income, a sudden windfall, or money coming to us through unexpected sources. Sometimes the reversal of fortune works the other way, and our income takes a drop. A number of people who have come to me for readings while transiting Uranus was moving through their second house had left jobs they didn't find interesting or meaningful in order to begin something new which promised greater stimulation and satisfaction – even if this shift had meant a lower salary. How we earn a living is likely to change at this time. Many people become dissatisfied working for others, and start their own business. Or they are fed up with the nine-to-five routine and go freelance, or take up employment with unusual hours. If we have been financially dependent on another person, this transit often activates a desire to earn money and support ourselves in our own right.

In whatever house it transits, we experience Uranus by choice or by coercion. In the second house, although consciously we may want to maintain the status quo, something external can come along to undermine our financial security or compel us to change jobs. Of course this is not always easy to accept, especially if we derive our sense of self-worth and security from our job and financial position; disruptions in this sphere will then activate much fear and anxiety. And yet something positive can be born out of these upheavals. Perhaps our core Self is asking that we grow and develop in new ways through this area of life: we may begin to see that there are other ways of feeling self-esteem that are not related to our earning capacity, or we may be forced to develop new skills and abilities which we wouldn't have bothered to explore if there hadn't been a crisis. Take the case of a woman who was raised in a wealthy family and later married a successful businessman: when Uranus transited her second house, her husband's business ran into severe difficulties and she was compelled to find work for the first time in her life. In the end, she not only re-evaluated her previous attitude towards money and status, but she also gained a new sense of her own identity and value in the process.

If we have never bothered too much about money, security or possessions, we may now find ourselves wanting these things. Conversely, if we have lived our life in the pursuit of financial security and well-being, this transit may coincide with the emergence of a different value system, one in which money and security are not the prime focus. We base our lives on what we value. If we value security, we make choices for security. If we value freedom, we make choices for freedom. Up to its usual tricks, Uranus moves through the second house and disrupts one value system for another, altering our whole basis for making choices.

The second house also describes innate skills and resources. When Uranus enters the second, it is a time to take stock of our potential talents and abilities, to see if there are any we have neglected or previously put aside, which now might be worth exploring or developing further. We might feel restless or bored with the work we have been doing, and look for more interesting ways to make money. However, in any house, through which Uranus is transiting, we are inclined to make dramatic or extravagant gestures and sweeping changes, and when it moves through the second we may find ourselves so frustrated with our work or the way the office or firm is run that we impulsively give notice there and then. On the whole, I would usually advise restraint – at least at first. Before picking up and leaving, look for ways to make an existing job more interesting or exciting. Obviously, if this can't be done, it may be necessary to make a clean break and to search for a new line of work, either within the same field or in another one. None the less it makes sense to hold on to an old job, if possible, until another is found, rather than putting ourselves in the position of being without any work at all. Also, we should remember that every case of Uranus transiting the second is slightly different, and before advising or passing judgement in this respect, the whole chart must be taken into consideration.

Third House

Uranus brings new experiences to whatever house it transits, and in the third this means new learning and knowledge. What we learn or study during this period will have a profound effect on us. A lecture we hear, a book we read, a conversation with a friend or associate, not only could suddenly and radically alter our views on particular issues, but could end up changing our life as well.

We will be receptive to new ideas, trends or currents circulating in the environment. We wake up in the middle of the night, our head reeling with new insights and revelations. Or at any time of day, sudden intuitions or flashes of understanding come to us. Some of these may be valid and useful, while others will need further reflection and analysis. There are a few pitfalls to watch out for with Uranus moving through the third. Our thinking might be too radical, ahead of its time, or (especially) out of touch with practical reality.

Uranus enables us to glimpse things which other people cannot or are not ready to see; we may try to explain our new concepts or insights to friends, teachers, parents or associates only to receive back blank stares, while others may be shocked or feel threatened by what we have to say. If we take time to shift through or to write down and refine our ideas, we may be more successful in imparting them to others. Younger people with this transit could experience some disruption to their education – for instance, they might change schools and have to adjust to new classmates and new surroundings. Or they may feel unusually restless and rebellious with the educational system or with conventional forms of learning. Children or adolescents having these kinds of difficulties often benefit from discussing and sharing what they are experiencing with an older person whom they trust.

Because Uranus can make us rather obstinate, during this transit we might think we have discovered the truth about someone or something. Absolutely certain that the way we are seeing it is the only right way, we don't leave much room for compromise, and adamantly defend our views, no matter how many people disagree with us. However, Uranus makes us not only obstinate, but also unpredictable and erratic: a few weeks later we wake up in the middle of the night with a new realization that drastically alters or reverses our previous standpoint, and we will now passionately defend this new point of view, until Uranus revolutionizes our thinking again.

This transit alters our perception of life around us. We might grow bored or dissatisfied with where we are living, and believe that moving to a different part of town, or moving to another area of the country, or even a different country, will resolve our restlessness. Before uprooting, however, it makes sense to try to make better use of our present environment – to search out aspects of it we haven't yet taken advantage of or explored, to make an effort to meet new people or expand our existing circle of friends, groups or interests in the present location. If this doesn't prove possible or satisfactory, a change of environment could be exactly in line with what Uranus transiting the third house has in mind for us. In some cases, however, this kind of move is not undertaken by choice, but by coercion: our family moves and we have to go with them, or we have to move because of our work, or our spouse changes employment or is transferred. If such a situation occurs under this transit, it may mean that a disruption of this sort is needed for our next stage of growth or development, or that some experiences await us in a new environment that couldn't transpire where we are now. Alternatively, Uranus may be asking that we take a stand, and refuse to be forced into a move. The kinds of aspects transiting Uranus is making to other planets in the chart may help to clarify the best way to handle the situation.

In a number of charts I have seen, Uranus transiting the third coincides with a phase when relatives, siblings or neighbours are experiencing significant changes or upheaval in their lives, and something they are going through at this time may directly affect us.

Fourth House

We might experience Uranus crossing the IC and moving into the fourth house as a bolt of energy emanating from the depths of our being, or as an inner explosion of energy which releases hidden or repressed aspects of our personality. Changes of a deep nature are occurring. This is not a time to inhibit or sacrifice our own inner needs and desires for the sake of keeping the peace or making other people happy. We need to listen to and respect what is happening inside us, make space for ourselves, and wake up to who we are.

Other people may not like this, especially if they have grown accustomed to our behaving in set or predictable patterns, but there is no way around the fact that during this transit we need room to grow and change. I have done many charts for people with Uranus transiting in this position, and in most cases they have expressed a powerful need to act on what they were feeling. One person even compared the transit to internal fireworks. Inner urges exert such a strong pressure now that we may have no option but to respond to them. Those people with this transit who didn't feel or respect this inner pressure did not escape untouched, but were those who had change thrust upon them. Although they didn't chose to recognize or act on their own urges to alter facets of their life or behaviour, external influences chose this time to invoke disruption.

The fourth house is associated with our home base. Uranus transiting this house doesn't want to leave these aspects of our life the same. In its most simplistic expression, Uranus here could indicate the time to redecorate our home – to change the colour scheme, rearrange the furniture, replace old, familiar fittings with new ones, etc. We could even take this a step further and consider a move to a new home altogether. Most people are quite happy to change residences when Uranus is transiting this area of the chart, since they feel restless and bored with the known, or they have outgrown existing circumstances. The present home is too small or too big or not in the right area, and moving is the obvious thing to do. However, there are some instances where Uranus might force a move. If this is the case, we will need to grieve for the loss of what we have known. Given time, we will come to see that the change was necessary to bring out qualities in ourselves which would have remained undeveloped in the old situation.

With Uranus in the fourth, domestic disruption can come in other forms: someone new is born or brought into the home, a grown-up child leaves the nest, a flatmate goes through a major change or upheaval, the family breaks up, etc. Compared with the transits of Neptune and Pluto, we are usually able to discern more readily a deeper meaning or purpose in negative events under Uranus transits: Uranus may bring upheaval, but it also stimulates the intuition and that part of the brain which can perceive relevance in what we have to face or endure. Whereas Neptune or Pluto transiting the fourth sometimes coincides with experiences which can be quite devastating, we normally are able to adjust to Uranian changes more quickly. After the necessary period of mourning, the intuitive resourcefulness naturally associated with Uranus helps us to pick up the pieces and to build a new life for ourselves.

The fourth house shows the influence of our family of origin on us, our early childhood conditioning and our inborn predisposition. From these factors, we form 'scripts', patterns or beliefs about what kind of person we are and what to expect in life. For instance, natal Saturn in the fourth could indicate unhappiness, pain or difficulty in the growing-up years which leaves a psychic wound or scar; because of these early experiences, we form the opinion that we are not good enough to be loved, or we harbour a conscious or unconscious fear that our later life will bear the same bitter fruits. When Uranus transits the fourth, these old scripts and patterns are activated: we attract situations which bring them to the surface, and we catch ourselves reliving childhood issues in our present home situation. At the very least, Uranus transiting the fourth marks the time to begin to work more constructively with issues from childhood. The intuitive insights attending a Uranus transit enable us to look more objectively at our patterns and scripts – we can better understand how they were formed and how they have been influencing us. Uranus can liberate us from the bondage of repetition. Bringing these patterns to light and exploring their origins are the first steps towards sorting through them and ultimately gaining a greater degree of freedom from their less pleasant ramifications.

The fourth house also describes our experience of mother or father, depending on which parent 'fits' best with the placements in this house.[5] If we take the fourth to indicate father, Uranus transits to this area of the chart could show a change in his circumstances or situation, or we may find that, at this time, we are able to perceive or to interact with him in a new way, breaking through old patterns or boundaries that have previously defined our relationship to him.

Transiting Uranus in the fourth house is an opportunity to find the power from within ourselves to direct our own lives. We discover an inner strength, an inner sense of independence which may have been missing in our personality up to now, and then gain a new sense of direction or purpose. This transit has the potential to rock the foundations of our being in a way no other transit can.

Fifth House

When Uranus moves through the fourth, the place 'where we are coming from' changes. Now, as Uranus enters and transits the fifth, our newly freed spirit has the chance to reveal itself more fully. The underlying impulse behind the fifth house is to express that part of us which is unique and individual. Transiting Uranus steps up the tempo of this house, making this a time to explore our new sense of self. If we are too cautious or too held back during this period, we will miss opportunities to discover more about who we are and what we are capable of doing.

Uranus hates boredom, and its transit of our fifth house kindles our enthusiasm and involvement in life. During this period, we discover or gravitate towards new hobbies or interests which excite us, and, in general, I would encourage people to follow any impulses they have to become involved in spare-time or recreational pursuits while under this transit. These outlets not only stimulate our enjoyment of life, but also provide the medium through which our inner nature can express itself. However, should we become too obsessed with a hobby or interest, we may need to exercise some restraint: staying up all night playing with a new computer or avidly reading about astrology can be both stimulating and fulfilling, but what about the job we have to go to the next morning? Are we so engaged in a hobby or recreation that those around us are beginning to feel neglected? And, above all, is the hobby safe? I wouldn't feel too comfortable encouraging (beyond a certain point) a new-found interest in gambling or fast cars. As usual with Uranus, discretion and caution are needed.

Those of us already involved in artistic activities could experience breakthroughs in this area. Or we may wake up to previously undeveloped creative potential. If we are bored with the kinds of creative outlets in which we normally engage, we might want to experiment with different media and techniques. Some of these attempts could fail miserably, while others could open new avenues of expression we never thought possible. We won't know unless we try.

Romance comes under the umbrella of the fifth house, and if we are restless or dissatisfied with an existing liaison, Uranus will bring these feelings to the surface. Unless we can find some way of breathing new life into our old relationships, we are in the right frame of mind to be receptive to something else coming along. We may meet someone who serves as a catalyst to reawaken our emotional or sexual life, or who introduces us to things we've never tried before, marking a new chapter in our life. Under a transit of Uranus, however, whether the new relationship lasts is a moot point; it may pull us out of a rut, but once this purpose has been achieved, it could disappear from the scene.

We might become involved with someone different from the kind of person we have been attracted to in the past, or there may be something unusual or unconventional about the relationship itself. Wherever Uranus is transiting, there we find ourselves acting in ways not in accord with conventional values, or not in line with how we have behaved in the past. We surprise not only others, but ourselves as well.

The fifth house – the house of creative self-expression – describes something about our offspring and our relationships with them. When Uranus transits here, our lives could be changed by becoming a parent for the first time. (This can sometimes happen unexpectedly, so precautions will need to be taken if we don't wish to become a parent at this time.) The existing relationships between ourselves and our children could alter in some way, and a child may leave home or go through an unusually rebellious or disruptive phase. Uranus may be asking us to relinquish the hold we have tried to maintain on our children, so that they can be free to find their own identities. The challenge is to find the right balance between allowing them greater autonomy, while still being there for them and setting the limits they need.

Sixth House

Uranus moving through this house can bring change or disruption in the areas of work and health. If our present employment is boring or doesn't challenge us enough, Uranus will want to alter these circumstances. This does not necessarily mean changing our line of work altogether. We can first look for ways to enliven our present job by introducing new projects, schemes or incentives, or by moving to another department or branch of the same place of employment. If innovations of this kind are not possible, then it probably is the appropriate time to seek work somewhere else.

In some cases, Uranus moving through the 6th corresponds to pursuing an entirely new vocation, which intrigues or interests us. This is a good time to undertake any training which would equip us with fresh skills. Wherever Uranus is transiting, we are meant to be adventurous and willing to experiment, although it may be wise to keep our old job until we find something with which to replace it, or until we have sufficient training to embark on new ventures. We might undertake work considered unusual by conventional standards, or a job of a 'Uranian' nature, such as a career in science, technology or the field of computers. Some people become involved in ventures which are communal or co-operative. Whatever the job, we need to be free to express our own style and originality.

We might be forced into a change of work when Uranus is transiting the sixth house: we may be fired or made redundant, or the company that employs us could go bankrupt or through a major reshuffle. Should this be the case, there is likely to be some hidden meaning or purpose in these occurrences. If we have been finding our work dull and uninteresting, but haven't bothered to do anything to alter these circumstances, it may be that we have attracted this external disruption (through the promptings of the core Self) in order to confront needed changes. If we have been too attached to or identified with our work, and have neglected other areas of our life as a result, the disruption could serve to redress this imbalance. While long-term unemployment can turn into a gruelling ordeal, a period off work could give us a chance to reassess our priorities and reconsider what kind of job would best suit our nature.

Uranus transiting the sixth can affect our health and the relationship we have to our own body. We are motivated to change our diet, take up an exercise routine, or to try some form of healing or therapy which would enhance our physical or psychological well-being. I've met a number of people with transiting Uranus in the sixth who developed – some for the first time in their lives – an interest in health and healing. Also, because this house describes the connection between body and mind, emotional problems and psychological distress can manifest themselves in illness and disease; obviously, the state of our health will also affect our mind and feelings. If we fall ill during this time, it may be a sign that our body is trying to tell us of adjustments we need to make in the way we are leading our lives.

Seventh House

Uranus transiting the seventh signals change in the area of relationships and, most obviously, we may want to disrupt an existing partnership. An urge like this doesn't just appear overnight – it has probably been gaining momentum for a while. When Uranus crosses the descendant and moves into the seventh, we can no longer easily contain our grumblings and frustrations with an unsatisfying relationship, and, more than likely, these feelings erupt and compel us to act. We might want to end the relationship entirely, hoping or knowing that there is something better 'out there' for us. Or we feel that being on our own would be preferable to keeping to the status quo. One way or another, we believe our relationship is no longer what is meant for us. That part of us which is willing to act for change takes the upper hand, gaining supremacy over our desire to maintain and preserve what we already have and know.

In some cases, it may be possible to stay with our partner and work on improving the relationship. This will take a certain amount of courage: we will have to stand up to the other person and voice our restlessness or frustration. If we have been doing most of the adjusting and compromising, now is the time for the other person to adapt to us for a change. However, if we always have been the one in control, Uranus may be asking that we allow a partner more power, and learn how to be more co-operative and flexible.

With transiting Uranus in the seventh, we may need more space and freedom to explore who we are independently of an existing relationship. This transit could bring a new person into our lives who excites or arouses our passions; there is something powerful about the meeting, as if we have 'known' that person before. If we are already in a relatively happy relationship, this new attraction will present a dilemma. Do we keep what we have or risk giving it up in order to pursue this new relationship? If we are in a relationship which is unstable and unfulfilling, the new person will seem like the answer to our dreams, and serve as a catalyst to bring about needed changes.

As with a Uranus–Venus transit or a transit of Uranus through the fifth house, whether this new relationship will last is debatable: its purpose may be solely to provoke us out of a rut and to 'inspire' us to find new ways of relating to others. There is no precise way to determine the outcome, although we may glean some clues through examining the nature of the aspects transiting Uranus will be making in the coming years. Let's say that Uranus crosses your seventh house cusp and you break up your existing relationship for the sake of something new. If, in three or four years' time, Uranus will be making a square to your natal Venus in the fourth, the new relationship may not survive that transit. However, if Uranus doesn't make too many stressful aspects in its journey through the seventh, any new relationship formed during that period may have a better chance of enduring.

On the whole, what's been discussed so far makes it sound as if transiting Uranus in the seventh is likely to destroy any relationship we are already in. This is not necessarily the case, but Uranus does demand that we re-examine existing partnerships and work on what needs to be improved. Uranus doesn't want us to stay in something solely from a sense of duty or obligation, or from a fear of the unknown. Uranus wants truth, not pretence. If, with Uranus transiting this house, we want to preserve an unfulfilled or floundering relationship, we had better find some way of breathing new life into it. However, if we aren't in a relationship, this transit could bring one to us. People we meet now can have the effect of changing our lives dramatically, and this is a good time to circulate and go to places we've never been to before.

Sometimes under this transit another person leaves or walks out on us. In other words, change is forced on us through this area of life. It would be wise to examine what role we might have played in bringing this about. Have we been feeling restless and unhappy for some time, but not doing anything about it? Have we unconsciously provoked the other person to leave in order to gain the freedom or space we want for ourselves? If one part of us was feeling imprisoned or trapped by the relationship and we haven't been attending to these feelings, it's possible our core Self provoked the other person to carry out what we have been afraid or unwilling to do. We may need to experience this kind of disruption in order to develop parts of ourselves we would have neglected otherwise. We still need to mourn the loss of the existing relationship, and accept the reactions of anger and betrayal caused by the other person leaving, but in time we will probably be able to find meaning or relevance in what we have had to go through.

The descendant suggests aspects of our nature to which we are blind. As a result, we usually identify more readily with the ascendant, and attract the descendant through others. For instance, if we have Aries rising and Libra on the seventh house cusp, we will probably be more in touch with our need for independence, assertion and power (Aries), and less at home with that part of ourselves which must learn to compromise, blend and balance with others (Libra). We often attract a partner who in some way reflects our descendant sign: in this case, we look for someone with obvious Libran traits, rather than expressing these in ourselves. However, Uranus crossing the descendant can awaken the qualities of our descendant in us. Developing the characteristics associated with this sign will help to balance out any tendency we have had to go overboard in the expression of our ascendant, and we thus become more whole and complete in ourselves.

The seventh house also describes how we relate to the public and society in general. When Uranus is moving through this area of the chart, we can act as an agent of change for other people, introducing them to new ideas or new ways of looking at life. In some cases, our activities may be considered shocking or condemned as too radical by the more conventional elements of society.

Eighth House

The urge for closeness and intimacy with another person is one of our primary drives. As a child, our lives depend on another person loving, feeding and looking after us. Later, as an adult, we can probably survive on our own, but we still seek fulfilment through love and relationships. The seventh house describes quite a bit about what we meet in partnership, but the eighth house goes a step further and depicts what we are like in situations of intimacy – what happens behind closed doors. The eighth indicates the kinds of exchanges that go on between ourselves and another: what we give and receive in a relationship. This can mean money, joint finances and resources, but it can also mean the kinds of emotions and feelings that pass between ourselves and those with whom we are closely involved. When Uranus transits the eighth, we will experience change and disruption in this sphere of life.

Our partner's financial situation could alter under this transit. His or her business might suddenly take off, or she or he could receive an unexpected windfall in the post, but equally our partner might suffer financial setbacks, and our own security could be shaken in the process. Which way it goes would depend not only on the kind of aspects transiting Uranus in the eighth makes to other planets in our chart, but also on what was happening in our partner's chart as well.

This transit could also indicate our embarking on a new business partnership, or changes within existing business relationships (again, the aspects of transiting Uranus will have to be taken into consideration). If Uranus is making harmonious aspects to other planets in our chart, changes in our business relationships are probably favourable. But if transiting Uranus makes difficult aspects to the chart, changes which occur at this time could be more fraught and disturbing, and the positive consequences less certain.

Money and material resources, however, are not the only things shared between people. Under this transit, our lives can be affected strongly by emotional and psychological changes which we or a partner are experiencing. A woman came to me for a reading when Uranus was moving through her eighth house. During this period, her actor husband faced a long spell out of work, and consequently spent much more time at home than was usual. He grew increasingly restless, moody, depressed and more difficult to live with – qualities she had never experienced in him before. Uranus transiting her eighth reflected changes in her husband's situation, and stirred issues which challenged and tested their relationship.

Reminiscent of Uranus transiting the fourth, transiting Uranus in the eighth also asks that we examine hidden sides of ourselves. Problems that arise between us and others at this time reveal deep patterns and complexes rooted in childhood (or from past lives, if you believe in the theory of karma and reincarnation). If, as a child, your mother repeatedly pushed you away when you reached out for her, you will form certain opinions of beliefs about life and yourself. You might think you are unlovable and unworthy. You might form the opinion that whenever you ask for something you need, you will be rejected. At the time, you might have tried to cushion the pain of rejection by telling yourself that you didn't really need anyone anyway. But later in life you throw a childish tantrum whenever another person can't meet a demand. Uranus transiting the eighth works to expose these kinds of deep-seated complexes, scripts or life-statements.

The eighth house is the area of the chart in which we learn how to merge more closely with another person – where we die as an 'I' to be reborn as 'we'. The sexual act is the physical expression and the closest approximation of two people coming together and uniting. When Uranus transits the eighth, we have a chance to open to others in ways we have never done before. If, for example, we've had difficulty expressing ourselves sexually or fully letting go with an-other person, this could be a time of breakthrough. Married people may be able to breathe new life into their sexual relationship. Whatever our situation, married or single, we might meet someone new who expands our sexual horizons.

The eighth is concerned not only with other people's values, but also with death, and our mortality might become an issue for us when Uranus moves through this house. In some cases, we might experience the death (perhaps sudden or unexpected) of someone close to us, and this could awaken an awareness of our own finitude, or of the precious brevity of lilfe.* Our attention may turn to a study of death or the philosophy of karma and reincarnation. Or, motivated by a desire to understand the hidden laws and forces operating in life, our interest could move in more unconventional directions towards the occult or magic, but, as always with Uranus, anything extreme or eccentric should be guarded against. It's also possible that during this transit we suddenly come into money via an inheri-tance.

Ninth House

The ninth house is where we look for guidelines and goals which will help us steer the course of our lives. It describes our quest for

---

*See Suggested Reading (p. 396) for a list of books dealing with death and the grieving process.

meaning, and the search for ideals and precepts upon which we can base the choices we have to make in daily existence. When Uranus transits this house, our world view and perspective on life isn't meant to stay the same, and our philosophy in life and our religious attitudes and beliefs could alter radically under this transit. Devout Christians might begin to question some of the basic doctrines of their religion, experiencing a crisis of faith for the first time, which may manifest itself as Uranian 'rebelliousness', an inability to accept the authority of the Church any more. Staunch atheists could discover God, or experience sudden mystical revelations or illuminating insights about the meaning of life. One way or another, our prevailing belief system will be challenged by new ideas and concepts which don't fit comfortably into the old framework. It may all happen suddenly: we wake up in the middle of the night with a vision, or attend a lecture or read a book which revolutionizes our thinking, or more precisely, our faith. A chance encounter or meeting with a wise person leaves us reeling, and although we may not see the world the same way as before, we may (as Blake said) 'see the world in a grain of sand'. Changes in one's philosophy are not to be taken lightly. When our belief system alters, our values also change. And when our values change, the kinds of choices we make about how to lead our life will not remain the same. For this reason, with Uranus moving through the ninth, the direction we have been taking in life could radically alter.

Consonant with these interests is higher education, another ninth-house concern. I've met a number of clients who altered their course of study during this transit: some changed from the sciences to the arts, others from the arts to the sciences. We could start out as a philosophy student and end up with a degree in computer science. Under this transit, we may choose to pursue our education in unconventional ways, or undertake a course of study which is unusual in some respect. We could become the campus rebel, fighting for changes in the educational or political system of our university or college. We may have new ideas, concepts and insights to contribute to our chosen branch of knowledge or to the field of education itself.

Travel also comes under the ninth house, and a Uranus transit could bring unexpected or unusual experiences on long journeys. We visit a country intending to stay for a week, and end up living there, or we meet people or encounter situations while travelling that dramatically change our lives. Travel plans could be disrupted: we head for one destination and wind up in another, or the places we visit may themselves be unusual or out of the way. In any event, we don't come back the same person as when we left.

Because the influence of Uranus is unpredictable and generates erratic behaviour, when it transits this house our plans for the future 'chop and change': we start out with certain goals but finish up with entirely different ones. At any moment, we could receive an intuitive flash – a picture or insight that tells us what we are 'meant' to be doing with our lives, and the direction we need to take to arrive there. Some of these inspirations or visions may be useful and profound, but others may prove misguided or off the mark. The aspects transiting Uranus in the ninth makes to the rest of the chart could help clarify how reliable our revelations are. If transiting Uranus is forming a difficult aspect to Mercury, Jupiter or Neptune, it may be wise to reflect very carefully on ideas which come to us 'out of the blue'. However, under this transit, our convictions and beliefs often are felt so strongly that nobody will be able to talk us out of them. It's worth remembering that there are many different ways of finding truth and of giving meaning to life, each contributing to the good of the collective. Should we turn our own particular view of the truth into an absolute, we box ourselves into a very tight corner. Fortunately, with Uranus around, we are unlikely to be allowed to remain fixed in one belief system for very long before something happens that seriously challenges our rigid position. Don't forget – Uranus may be stubborn, but it's also changeable.

Tenth House

While Uranus moves through the ninth, our overall world view and the way we find meaning in life alter significantly. When Uranus enters the tenth, the consequences of these changes become out-wardly apparent, especially in terms of our social role. Because the ways we give meaning or value to our lives have changed, we may not want to remain in the same line of work as before. We feel a 'calling', a need for a 'vocation', and are motivated to find work which will be in accord with our current interests.

Some people with this transit will set up businesses of their own at this time, while others may become involved with unusual careers and enterprises. Sometimes an offer of new work comes unexpectedly, and it is too intriguing or inviting to turn down. Generally, if clients with Uranus transiting the tenth speak about their desire to change professions, I wouldn't argue with them. Uranus is a forceful planet, and the time probably is appropriate to make a change. However, I will explore with them the possibility of staying in their work, but making room within it for something new to happen. Could they introduce new projects or incentives which would enliven their existing duties? Could they convince a boss to give them the freedom to pursue their work in a way which would be more satisfying? Perhaps extra responsibilities, as well as greater freedom and autonomy (the Uranian watchwords) to act upon them, would assuage our professional restlessness.

If we haven't acknowledged our need for some sort of change in our work situation at this time, we may be forced into changing. In some cases, this transit coincides with redundancy or the folding of a business, but through these contingencies we are coerced into another direction or into a new field. Or we may be restless and bored with our job, but hesitant to do anything concrete about these feelings: we grow increasingly intolerant towards those in charge, and increasingly resentful of being told what to do. Pressure builds until a confrontation is inevitable, and we either hand in our notice and storm out of the office, or we are fired.

In whatever house Uranus is transiting, we want to break free of restrictions and old, outworn patterns. In the tenth house of social conventions and norms, this could express itself in a desire to act in ways which challenge the existing values and expectations of society. We don't mind shocking others during this period. We could end up fighting the establishment, or battling against outdated or unfair laws and mores, or we may be the agent or catalyst for helping to bring new ideas or trends to the collective.

Parental issues also arise with Uranus transiting the tenth.

Whether the tenth is associated with mother or father, Uranus transiting here usually manifests as an urge to break free of their domination or influence. We might stand up to them in a way we've never dared to before, rebelling against their views, and following our own inclinations whether they like it or not. In order to separate our own identity from others, we may have to challenge the image and expectations they have of us. We also could have breakthroughs in how we relate to a parent. We may have had difficulty communicating or connecting with our mother, for instance, but under this transit we see her in a new light, and the relationship improves. Finally, in some cases, Uranus through the tenth is synchronous with one or both of the parents experiencing a major change or disruption – positive or negative – which somehow directly affects our own life.

Eleventh House

Our goals and objectives in life (especially those concerning our sense of belonging to or contributing to society and something larger than ourselves) are likely to change significantly under this transit. Our former goals no longer seem relevant or feel too limited and restricting, and we find ourselves with aims and ambitions we never believed would be important to us. People who haven't thought much about money or security look for ways to increase their material well-being, while those who have always been predominantly practical or down-to-earth may suddenly discover an interest in other, less tangible dimensions of life.

As with Uranus transiting the ninth, we discover new ideologies and belief systems which challenge or expand our usual ways of looking at life. This may coincide (in true eleventh-house fashion) with the discovery of groups or organizations that previously didn't interest us, or we knew nothing about. This is usually a good time for involvement with groups, and I would generally encourage a person with Uranus transiting the eleventh to explore different group activities. We might align ourselves with 'Uranian' groups: humanitarian or political organizations which promote changes in society. In the past we may not have given much thought to social issues, but now we ardently feel the need to be involved in these matters. However, groups which are too radical or extreme in their views or purpose could lead us into some difficulties under this transit – especially if transiting Uranus in the eleventh is making stressful aspects to other planets in the chart.

With Uranus moving through the eleventh, the initial enthusiasm and excitement we feel when we first discover a new organization or direction in life is bound to ebb slightly away after a while. We may think we have discovered a group, cause or formula which will be the answer to everything, but if our expectations are too high, 'inflated' or unrealistic, we will eventually be disappointed. On the other hand, if we are already involved with a group when this transit first begins, we could become disenchanted with how it is run or find ourselves increasingly at odds with the aims it espouses. Other group members may find us too refractory, too challenging, and we end up battling with them over certain principles – possibly to the point where we feel the need to break with the group altogether.

Uranus brings disruption wherever it transits, and in the eleventh this occurs not only in the area of goals and groups, but also in the sphere of friendship. During this period, we replace some of our old friends with new ones, whose thinking and ways of life are more in accord with our present way of seeing things. A friend may be the vehicle or catalyst for bringing to us new ideas or insights that alter our life. Provided that we aren't being wildly unrealistic or extreme in our behaviour, attitude or choice of groups and friends at this time, we can generally trust the kinds of changes, insights and revelations Uranus brings at this time.

Twelfth House

Traditionally, the twelfth house describes patterns, drives, urges and compulsions which operate unconsciously and yet significantly influence our choices, attitudes and directions in life. What the conscious mind isn't in touch with or doesn't choose to acknowledge is 'stored' – even 'imprisoned' – in the twelfth. Uranus transiting here has the effect of forcing some of these unconscious complexes and compulsions into conscious awareness. For instance, if you have an unconscious fear of being rejected, when Uranus transits the twelfth, you somehow attract situations which compel you to confront and learn about that fear. In short, during this period, Uranus changes us by exposing more of what is hidden or lurking in the recesses of our psyche.

Some of what we discover about ourselves when Uranus transits the twelfth may be frightening and disconcerting, but this transit can also serve to connect us to parts of ourselves which are positive and beneficial. The unconscious, as shown by the twelfth house, is not just the storehouse of negative patterns or feelings from the past: it is also the reservoir of untapped positive potential we have yet to develop. This is a good period to undertake some inner psychological exploration, some 'deep diving' in this watery house, either through psychotherapy or other related avenues and techniques. In this way, we co-operate with Uranus in its effort to reveal and illuminate what previously has been undifferentiated or inaccessible in us.

Under this transit – often in unexpected and unusual ways – people and circumstances from our past (and this may mean past lives) will reappear, giving us an opportunity to resolve unfinished issues with them. They might literally turn up on our doorstep, or they come to us more indirectly in our dreams or fantasies. In any case, our past returns to greet or haunt us. There may be unfinished business to resolve, or the joy of rediscovering someone we once knew and loved. Meeting the past and settling old scores can be both cleansing and healing, preparing the way for the rebirth which will occur when Uranus crosses over our ascendant and into our first house.

When Uranus moves through the twelfth, the ordinary boundaries between ourselves and others break down. This could mark a period of psychic insights and revelations, a time when we are unusually attuned to the feelings of others. A friend might be a thousand miles away, but somehow we sense accurately what he or she is going through. Or we dream about someone and that person rings up or knocks on our door the next day. Some of our psychic insights might be disturbing; others could be of a more positive or revelatory nature. How much these should be trusted is hard to say, although (once again) some indication of their validity or truth could be gleaned by analysing the kinds of aspects transiting Uranus in the twelfth is making to other planets in our chart. We will also be more sensitive to collective trends or currents in the atmosphere. We may have sudden precognitions about what trouble spots in the world will flare up next, or uncanny foresight into what new styles, fashions or movements are about to burst on to the scene. Some of us may serve as channels to bring change and new ideas to the collective.

The twelfth house is associated with institutions – hospitals, prisons, museums, libraries or organizations of a charitable nature. If we have been aligned with an institution for some time, Uranus transiting the twelfth could indicate a phase of feeling dissatisfied with our role there, or increasingly unhappy about how the place is run. We may want to promote change or reform within an institution, and it's possible we will run into conflicts with authority figures in this respect. If institutions have not played much of a part in our life, this could change with Uranus in the twelfth, and we may want to devote some of our time to serving or caring for others less fortunate than ourselves.

Many people describe Uranus in the twelfth as a time when they both feel more restless and more hamstrung than usual: they want to make changes in their lives, and yet they are not yet able to carry these out, or they can't quite put their finger on how or where to start. Change is brewing, to be sure, but it may not be ready to take shape fully until Uranus finally crosses the ascendant and moves into the first house. In the meantime, we can prepare the groundwork by tying up the loose ends of the phase of life which is about to finish.

PART THREE

Neptune Transits

6

Neptunian Crises

*Our destiny, our being's heart and home
Is with infinitude, and only there.*

WORDSWORTH

These words, written by a great English Romantic poet, encapsulate the essence of Neptune: the desire to go beyond the sense of being a separate self and to merge with something greater. Although we often speak of 'finding ourselves', that is, of discovering our unique identity or defining ourselves through self-chosen attributes and achievements, Neptune is the opposite: it is the urge to *lose ourselves*, to dissolve or transcend the boundaries of the isolated ego. But before we can fully comprehend what dissolving or transcending the ego means or entails, we should first recall what is meant by *ego*.

Briefly defined, ego is the sense of ourselves as a separate individual: in other words, our sense of 'I'. Being an 'I' means we can define ourselves: we are this but not that, we end somewhere and other people begin somewhere else. However, we are not born with an ego or sense of 'I', and in the womb, we are unaware of ourselves as separate: we are at one with mother, and mother is the whole world to us. Therefore, we think we are the whole world; we think we are everything, and experience what Freud called an 'oceanic' sense of reality. Gradually after birth, however, we begin to differentiate and distinguish ourselves not only from mother, but also from the environment as well. We grow to recognize that we are distinct or separate from other people and things around us. There is self and there is not-self.

Not only do we distinguish ourselves from other people, but we also come to identify ourselves with certain parts of our personality and nature, at the same time as denying or splitting off from other parts of our own psyche. In other words, in addition to the self/others split, a boundary or division also exists between our ego (our sense of who we are) and other facets of our nature which we won't acknowledge as belonging to ourselves or which we don't even know are there. For instance, we might identify with that part of us which is kind and loving, and deny or repress that part which is negative and destructive. In this way, the I/not-I split involves not only drawing a line between ourselves and others; it is also dividing our own wholeness into two parts – what we are conscious of and willing to identify as being in us versus what we are unconscious of or unwilling to admit as part of us.

Neptune is a boundary-dissolver, and by transit, Neptune blurs or dissolves the boundary between ourselves and others. Neptune transiting the Sun, for instance, could be a time when we 'lose' ourselves in another person, or have experiences of our oneness with all life. But Neptune also breaks down the internal boundary between conscious and unconscious, flooding or overwhelming our existing ego-identity with contents from our conscious. If we have mainly identified ourselves as strong, confident and capable, then under a Neptune transit to our Sun, we could discover a confused, weak or helpless side to our nature. Neptune is like a solvent, diluting the strength of a previously concentrated energy, whether this is a carefully structured career plan or relationship, or a tenaciously held conviction or an inner attitude towards ourselves or the world. Neptune undermines boundaries, whether those between ourselves and others, or those between our ego and unconscious.

Oneness and Separateness

The boundary-eroding effect of transiting Neptune can enhance our awareness of the oneness of all life, and increase our empathy and feeling of connectedness to everything else in existence. Grasping the concept of the essential unity of all life is not easy. It's even more difficult for those of us in Western society who have been thoroughly inculcated to believe that 'I' end in one place and 'You' begin somewhere else – what Alan Watts called the 'me-in-here' versus 'you-out-there' reality.[1] However, both Eastern and Western mystics have always spoken of another dimension of reality in which nothing exists in isolation. The Buddhists have a saying, 'All in one and one in All', an idea echoed by Meister Eckhart, a thirteenth-century Christian mystic who wrote: 'All that man has here externally in multiplicity is intrinsically One.' Although on the surface 'I' may appear different from 'You', and a table is not the same thing as a chair, at our deepest levels we all share the same basic Beingness or Is-ness. Neptune symbolizes the urge to dissolve a rigid sense of individuality and separateness in order to rediscover and reconnect to the underlying unity of all life.

Some twentieth-century physicists have come to the conclusion that such mystical revelations about the essential oneness of life are not devoid of scientific truth. Nineteenth-century physicists viewed the universe as a collection of different parts, each part separate and isolated in space and time from other parts. On this assumption, they then proceeded to measure, define and number all the various bits and pieces that together made up the universe. Everything could be labelled and put in its proper place. But with the advent of more advanced scientific methods and equipment, it was only a matter of time before physicists ran into problems with the old Newtonian concept of the world as a mechanism or machine with separate parts reducible to pieces like a clock.

The trouble started when scientists began to investigate the nature of subatomic particles, the ultra-microscopic particles which constitute the atom. To their astonishment, they found that the electron couldn't be located specifically in time or space. If the particles which comprise the atom refused to be pinned down to one place, how could the atom be said to be concrete or measurable? And if the atom was not behaving like a discrete entity, how could people or objects who are made up of atoms be defined as separate or isolated from one another?

What was considered to be a single, isolated particle now appeared to be more like a wave pattern spreading out infinitely across the universe in all directions. A British physicist, Richard Prosser, believes that these waves cancel each other out except in one very small region, in which is found the particle. 'Everything is in a sense everywhere, but only appears, or manifests, at one particular point.'[2] Another British scientist, David Bohm, theorizes that the universe must be understood as 'a single undivided whole in which separate and independent parts have no fundamental status'.[3]

The transpersonal psychologist Ken Wilber succinctly sums up the results of major developments in twentieth-century physics:

> In short quantum physicists discovered that reality could no longer be viewed as a complex of distinct things and boundaries. Rather, what we once thought to be bounded 'things' turned out to be interwoven aspects of each other. For some strange reason, every thing and every other thing and event in the universe seemed to be interconnected with every other thing and event in the universe. The world, the real territory, began to look not like a collection of billiard balls but more like a single, giant, universal field, which Whitehead called the 'seamless coat of the universe'.[4]

Even physics, then, is reaffirming an insight previously ascribed only to mystics and artists: that at the deepest level of our existence we are all interconnected.

Neptune represents that part of us which yearns, in the heart of our being, to dissolve those boundaries and divisions that prevent us experiencing our essential oneness with the rest of life. In order to do this, we have, to some degree, to let go of our ego – our separate-self sense. Transiting Neptune can bring the kind of spiritual or peak experiences in which we temporarily transcend our normal 'me-in-here versus you-out-there' reality and glimpse that part of us which is universal and unbounded. When Neptune is active in our chart, these breakthroughs in consciousness could happen spontaneously, anywhere and at any time, although they are often associated with certain feelings or activities – quiet moments communing with nature, listening to a particular piece of music, meditating on our own or with a group of people, etc.

The desire to expand and grow spiritually is always there within us, but will be activated more strongly during certain periods of our life. Under Neptune transits, the religious or mystical urge could be triggered by a growing dissatisfaction or unhappiness with our present life and accomplishments: we might have succeeded admirably on a material or external level, and yet we are left thinking 'So what? Is that all there is?' Unfulfilled by our search for happiness in outer things and by our external accomplishments, we may find that our attention turns inward, and we now look for meaning and fulfilment in the inner world of spirit. Gurus or religious groups can guide us on this inward journey, but as the poet Kabir reminds us, even these can be a trap if we are not careful:

I laugh when I hear that the fish in the water is thirsty.
You don't grasp the fact that what is most alive of all is inside your own house;
And so you walk from one holy city to the next with a confused look.
Kabir will tell we the truth: go wherever you like, to Calcutta or Tibet;
If you can't find where your soul is hidden, for you the world will never be real![5]

Losing the Self

The dissolution of the ego doesn't automatically mean an ecstatic experience of our infinite and unbounded nature. Losing our existing ego-boundaries can sometimes feel like coming apart at the seams: we lose control over what is allowed into conscious awareness and what is kept out, and as a result, our existing identity is likely to be invaded by parts of ourselves we previously have managed to keep at bay. Confused about who we really are, we no longer know what we want in life. Neptune's yearning to return to a state of primal bliss can also lead to escapism, suicidal urges and the temptation to lose the self in drugs, alcohol, or in anything or anyone that comes along.

The defeat of the ego is a humbling experience. As Neptune makes important transits to our chart, we often find ourselves in situations we don't want to be in but can do nothing about. We might get angry at God for bringing such troubles on us, or we might pray to him for help. Some of us may blame the existing government as the source of our problems. But, whether we vilify the government or appeal to the Lord, Neptune transits often compel us to acknowledge forces 'out there' which are greater and more powerful than we are. We discover that our ego isn't really running the show at all, and that it sometimes has to bow to a higher will.

Neptune transits often ask that we sacrifice or let go of aspects of our life and identify which have been important to us. There may be people or things we desperately want or feel we need, but the cosmos, fate or our 'higher Self' – however we wish to call it – isn't willing to provide us with what we so urgently desire. Learning to let go is a Neptunian lesson. Under certain Neptune transits, we could find our world crumbling. The rug is taken out from beneath us: structures and supports we relied on or took for granted fall apart or are taken away. We feel powerless and at the mercy of life. While this is happening, it's hard to imagine anything positive could come out of the dissolution we are experiencing. It feels more like a curse than some higher force at work serving our life or furthering our growth. We want to hold on, to turn back the clock and keep things the way they were. And yet no matter how hard we try, our attempts to maintain the status quo fail. *It is only when we finally do give up and let go that we create the possibility for something to come along to help us through our difficulties and into our next step or phase of life.* The Greek hero Orpheus had to learn this lesson, and the story of his love for Eurydice is an example of what can happen when Neptune makes important transits to our chart.

The Plight of Orpheus

Orpheus is a Neptunian hero, a musician and a poet, whose beautiful songs make trees weep and rocks melt. Through his music, he uplifts others, expands their awareness, and opens them to feelings and emotions of a universal or eternal nature. His myth begins on his wedding day, the day he has married Eurydice, the woman of his dreams. By rights, he should be overflowing with bliss – but an accident has occurred: after taking the wedding vows, Eurydice went for a walk with some friends, stepped on a snake, was bitten and died. What should have been a time of great joy suddenly turned into a tragedy. People under Neptune transits may recognize this kind of experience; for what promises to be wonderful may turn into a disaster, while what looks to be awful could reveal itself as a blessing in disguise. Neptune is a boundary-dissolver, and under its influence even the distinction between ecstasy and pain can become blurred.

Unable to accept his tragic situation, Orpheus denies the finality of his beloved's death and employs the tactic of bargaining to try to win her back. Like most people whose lives are disrupted by a tragic fate, he wants to turn back the clock, to have things the way they were before the tragedy happened. By playing a song which puts Cerberus (the dog who guards the gates to the underworld) to sleep, he manages to enter the domain of Pluto and Persephone and pleads with them to allow Eurydice to return with him to the upper world again. Pluto and Persephone are tough administrators – whoever dies and goes to the underworld is not usually allowed out again. But Orpheus, with his poignant words and songs, pleads his case so convincingly that he manages to influence the king and queen of the underworld to bend their rules – another example of the way the force of Neptune can melt rigidity and hardness.

Pluto and Persephone give Orpheus permission to take Eurydice back to the land of the living, with the stipulation that he doesn't turn around to look at her until she has arrived in the upper world again. His hand in hers, he leads Eurydice out of the underworld, but just as they are about to step into the light of the upper world, Orpheus can't resist looking back at her. He turns around to gaze into the eyes of his beloved and she dissolves, along with his hopes for happiness and fulfilment, into thin air. What promised redemption and renewal disappears before his very eyes, and what promised fulfilment is tragically lost.

What made Orpheus look back? He was duly warned not to, and he was so close to achieving his heart's desire. Perhaps he had a moment of mistrust: 'what if they are fooling me and this isn't Eurydice behind me, but someone else they have put in her place?' He doesn't trust; he starts to question and analyse the situation and this leads him into trouble. Very often, under Neptune transits, we have an urge or inclination to pursue a certain path: we begin to move that way, then something stops us and we interrupt the process. We may want sure-fire guarantees about where the direction we are taking will ultimately lead, but Neptune offers no such guarantees, requiring what we give of ourselves without knowing what we will get back in return.

Orpheus is alone again. His bargaining tactic has failed, and he can no longer deny Eurydice's death. Having exhausted whatever resources he had to deal with her demise, all that is left to him is to accept the inevitability of what has happened. Now he has no choice but to do what he so far has not given himself the chance to do – to sit down and properly mourn her loss. He has been so busy trying to fight the situation, he hasn't yet fully surrendered himself to his sadness and pain.

It happens that he chooses to do his mourning in the vicinity of a Dionysian orgy, which is just getting into full swing. Here again, we are faced with the two extremes of Neptune – the bliss and ecstasy of the revellers compared to the deep grief of Orpheus. The party-makers, seeing Orpheus sitting there so depressed, implore him to join the fun. We often do the same with our depressed friends, urging them to come out of the state they're in, inviting them to come to this or that party, meet some new people, etc. 'It will do you good,' we say; 'It will help you get out of yourself.' Seeing them so unhappy makes us uncomfortable, partly because it reminds us of the pain we feel for things we have lost in our lives. But Orpheus refuses to join the party. He wants to stay where he is, not only physically, but psychologically. The revellers get angry – they're trying to enjoy themselves and they certainly don't want to listen to his moaning and to be reminded of all the suffering in the world. So they decide to kill him. One by one, they hurl their spears towards him, but the songs and laments he is singing are so mournful and touching that the javelins stop before actually hitting him. Finally, the revellers realize that if they scream as loudly as possible the javelins won't hear his music and be halted in their path. They do this; the spears hit their mark and Orpheus dies.

And we think: 'Poor Orpheus, what a fate!' But what looks, in this case, to be such a terrible fate is actually the reverse. His death means that he will be reunited in the underworld with his lost Eurydice. They can roam hand in hand through the fields of Hades, and gaze into each other's eyes as much as they want. Orpheus' sacrificial death, which at first appears to be yet another tragedy in his life, turns out to be a blessing in disguise. Bliss turns into pain, but pain turns into bliss. Under the influence of Neptune, such dissimulation confounds the certainty of our judgements.

Orpheus' death can be taken literally, but it also can be understood as symbolic of a major personality change. Fighting to regain Eurydice got him nowhere, but letting go and accepting her loss, even though it was not what he wanted, brought about a transformation which enabled him to find peace and reconciliation. In the process, Orpheus learned one of the lessons that Neptune teaches by transit: a solution to a problem can sometimes only be found by giving up trying to find an answer. Likewise, there are times when the ego exhausts its own resources, and our normal ways of dealing with problems don't work. But it is only then that a situation is created which allows us to discover new ways of resolving or coming to terms with our difficulties – ways we never would have considered unless our usual tactics had failed. Jung had this to say about such times in our lives:

> the unconscious always tries to produce an impossible situation in order to force the individual to bring out his very best. Otherwise one stops short of one's best, one is not complete, one does not realize oneself. What is needed is an impossible situation where one has to renounce one's own will and one's own wit and do nothing but trust to the impersonal power of growth and developments.[6]

Only when the ego has no more power – when our normal ways of trying to make things better fail – can something else appear to redeem us. Under a Neptune transit, we may have to remain stuck for a while in an unpleasant situation until a solution or answer comes. Our old tricks don't work. We just have to wait:

> The faith and the love and the hope are all in the waiting . . .
> So the darkness shall be the light and the stillness the dancing.[7]

An Orphean Client

Acting, a suitably Neptunian profession, was the career choice of a Pisces man who came to see me for a reading a number of years ago. At the time of our meeting transiting Neptune was in Sagittarius and had just finished making its final square to his natal Sun. His story typifies one way slippery Neptune operates by transit.

Because of the slow, direct and retrograde motion of the outer planets, a Neptune transit can last a number of years – it moves forward, backward and then forward again while making an aspect to a natal planet. In the case of Joe, the first time transiting Neptune squared his Pisces Sun, things went rather well. He wasn't long out of drama school when a prestigious director took him under his wing, offering him good parts in productions which received a great deal of public attention. Joe's considerable talent was obvious, and when transiting Neptune first squared his Sun he won a number of acting awards. It looked as if his career was made, but, as Joe discovered, we can't be too sure of anything under a Neptune transit.

Neptune retrograded to square his Sun again, and for no apparent reason his career went dead on him. Months went by without the offer of a good part. Even when he found a role he wanted to play, situations and events beyond his control seemed to collude to thwart his ambitions and rob him of what looked like reliable opportunities. (Neptune often undermines our conscious goals and directions through the agency of mysterious external circumstances.) The first square of transiting Neptune to his Sun offered a taste of success and recognition; the retrograding second square took it away. It's hard to keep a secure hold on anything when Neptune is around.

Retrograding Neptune turned around and began to move forward to make the third square to his Sun, and he landed an important television role. Soon his name was in the air again, and his picture appeared on the front of various media magazines. Later, however, when Neptune turned around once more and retrograded nearly back to the degree of his Sun, he found himself in yet another empty patch.

Like the fate of *The Hanged Man* in the Tarot, Neptune kept Joe dangling, settling on neither success nor failure. If he was hoping to derive his identity, value or self-worth (the Sun) from the outside world at this time, he was out of luck. Neptune was teaching him that he couldn't rely on anything external to give him his sense of identity: if he was to find it at all, it would have to be from within himself.

In fact, the whole experience had the effect of turning his attention inward, rather than outward, in his search for fulfilment. Synchronously Joe met a guru who helped open this kind of awareness for him through meditation and other spiritual practices. During the periods when he was out of work, Joe took on the job of his guru's chauffeur, and generally served him in any way he could. Meditation, gurus, service, opening to the inner world – these are all the hallmarks of Neptune. Even though the transit of this planet was causing chaos in the area of career, in other spheres of his life, Joe was discovering dimensions of his being he never knew existed. Then, near the end of the duration of this transit, Joe learned that his guru, the man who had guided him to these new heights of consciousness and spiritual growth, suffered from a severe drink problem!

Like Orpheus, Joe's fortunes went up and down, from promise to betrayal and back again. He couldn't rely on his public or even his guru, and yet through it all he managed to forge an inner sense of his own worth and identity. His story is reminiscent of the initiation rites of certain primitive tribes: the initiate is forced to spend a night alone in a dark cave or wood with nothing from the outside to support him. He has to face the terrible loneliness of being forsaken. But if he survives the experience, he discovers what supports him when everything else he thought supported him isn't there anymore. Outer things can be taken away, but what you find from within is yours to keep: this was Neptune's gift to Joe.

The Rites of Dionysus

Transiting Neptune can feel 'Dionysian'. Dionysus, the Greek god of wine and poetry, would gather together a group of followers and get them drunk. The intoxicating and loosening effects of wine made it easy for them to abandon themselves – swept away by rapturous feelings, by ecstasy, they let go of the boundaries and rules that marked the parameters of their more sober selves. They didn't stop to think whether their cars were parked on a yellow line or if they had to be home at a certain time to cook dinner. Neptune, the boundary-dissolver, loosens the tight hold we have over ourselves, allowing parts of the psyche into conscious awareness which have previously been kept underground. In this sense, Neptune is the antithesis to Saturn because it disintegrates the boundaries which Saturn creates. Those people with a strong Saturn or Capricorn element in their charts are usually the ones most frightened of Neptune: they don't like to relinquish what is known, safe or established, and are afraid that if they let go, they won't be able to put themselves back together again.

Pentheus, the rational, conservative king of Thebes who wanted above all to maintain law and order in his domain, couldn't see that Dionysus was a god. To him, Dionysus looked like a wild man in animal skins with a bunch of raving women chasing after him, certainly not the image of divinity. Under stressful Neptunian transits, we may find our world falling apart – structures, props and supports we used to anchor our sense of self slip away. And, like Pentheus, we may find it hard to recognize this kind of dissolution as serving the aims of our deeper, core Self, or ultimately acting in favour of our evolution. It feels more like a curse than something positive at work.

Dionysus himself suffered dismemberment when he was torn to pieces by the Titans, the race to which Saturn belonged. In one version of the story, his sister Athene rescues his dismembered heart and gives it to Zeus. Zeus swallows the heart, mates with mortal Semele, and Dionysus is born again. (Interestingly, in this mythologem Athene, the goddess of rational wisdom – as distinct from Dionysian rapturous wisdom – is the god's sister, suggesting a profound link between them, a necessary complement). Like Dionysus, the twice-born, we die and are reborn many times in our life. Under difficult Neptune transits, we too may fall to pieces and lose those things that give us a sense of identity, and yet our heart – our essence – remains. As long as our essence remains, we can be born again. Falling apart means dying as we know ourselves, but it also creates the possibility of putting ourselves back together again in a new way.

The Blurring of Boundaries: Pros and Cons

Neptune transits loosen the hold we have over what comes into consciousness and what stays out. Negatively, this means our imagination might run wild – we start to see things that are not really there, and we believe events are happening which actually aren't. We could become lost in daydreams and fantasies, out of touch with concrete reality. Our ability to concentrate or focus suffers, and consequently we become less efficient at activities which we once executed with great ease. We can also lose all sense of proportion with regard to the planet Neptune is contacting by transit. For instance, when transiting Neptune aspects the Moon, our feelings might run amok and get us into trouble; when Neptune triggers Mars, we could act in reckless and foolhardy ways.

Deception and dishonesty are other Neptunian problems, spawned by Neptune's tendency to blur distinctions and confuse definition. Under a Neptune transit, we could be the one deceiving others. A woman with Neptune transiting her Venus entered a marriage of convenience with a man in order to emigrate to his country. To the immigration authorities, the marriage looked real – in actuality, it was a façade. A man with transiting Neptune aspecting his Mercury made it appear as if he worked for a certain company run by a friend in order to persuade the bank to give him a mortgage. However, a Neptune transit (especially the opposition) could mean we are the victim of someone else's fraud or dishonesty. A woman with Neptune opposing her Sun discovered that her fiancé had been lying to her about his status at work. A man with Neptune opposing his Moon had no idea his wife was having an affair with a neighbour.

More positively, Neptune's tendency to diffuse existing ego-boundaries also has the effect of stimulating our creative imagination. We become more receptive to what is known as the 'imaginal realm' or 'mythic realm', the plane of existence on which archetypal and universal images, ideas and feelings circulate. Through some kind of creative outlet, we could become the medium through which these images are communicated to others. Mystics and modern-day prophets also tap into this realm, and receive 'messages' or visions which they impart to the world. Under a Neptune transit, the reliability of these messages does depend on how 'pure' a channel the medium is. Personal biases and unresolved emotional complexes (such as an infantile desire for omnipotence) could obscure or distort the truth of what supposedly is being channelled.

Neptune softens the ego and dissolves separateness, which means we are more sensitive to what other people are feeling. Our heightened empathy could incline us towards work or activities which involve caring for others less fortunate than ourselves. This can be a constructive use of a Neptune transit, but we also should be aware of the personal gains we might be accruing through service of an apparently 'selfless' nature. Similarly, under a Neptune transit, we may be asked to put our needs aside for the sake of what others want or require. While this kind of giving and compromising can be the hallmark of maturity, it sometimes indicates a weakness in character, and could be used to manipulate others covertly. Many supposed 'martyrs' carry a great deal of hidden resentment around with them. The psychological benefits and dangers of selfless behaviour and of Neptune transits in general are discussed in the next chapter, in which we examine specific Neptune transits to the planets and through the houses.

7

The Transits of Neptune to the Planets and Through the Houses

Neptune–Sun

The Sun represents the sense we have of ourselves as a separate individual. When Neptune transits in aspect to the Sun, it dissolves the borders of our ego-identity, and asks us to give up or let go of our existing sense of self in order to make room for something new. The transiting trine or sextile usually does this in a gentle way, offering us a new version of ourselves which is more loving, expansive or creative than before. Under these transits, however, we should be cautious of false optimism: if we start believing that we have discovered a sense of peace and happiness which no one or nothing could ever shatter, we will be in for a rude awakening when, sooner or later, that bubble bursts.

Transiting Neptune conjunct, square or opposing the Sun could bring similar delusions, but they more often denote a period of confusion and self-doubt. Previously we might have confidently marched into life and action, but now we aren't so sure about our power, worth or identity. External events could trigger off these feelings – someone else getting a promotion we hoped for, or the loss of a job or relationship that meant a great deal to us. Illness or other circumstances could force us to give up work, or rob us of our normal level of energy. In many cases, however, nothing obvious or external seems to be the cause of our psychological malaise, but inside ourselves we feel lost and unable to carry on as usual.

Health problems could be difficult to analyse under hard Neptune–Sun transits: we feel bone tired, anaemic, listless and down, and yet doctors cannot find anything medically wrong to account for our state. It might help to rest more, to take more vitamins, or increase the amount we exercise. But no matter what we do to try to make ourselves feel better, we still may not be able to avoid falling apart during this period. Hard Neptune–Sun transits undermine our confidence, clarity and strength and can paralyse our old self and our normal ways of being. And yet Neptune is doing this for a purpose – in order that we can eventually rebuild ourselves in a new way. Something has to die for something new to be born. Understanding this may not alleviate the pain, frustration and disillusionment we feel at this time, but looking at these transits in this way can help us find meaning in what we are going through. If we can find meaning in our suffering, we are more likely to find ways to make constructive use of it.

All this is easier said than done, especially so because one of the manifestations of stressful Neptune–Sun transits can be the loss of hope – we don't believe we can pull ourselves through and we lose our faith that life will look after us. The intellectual understanding that faith and hope sometimes evaporate under these transits could help us achieve some degree of objectivity about what we are going through. In other words, accepting that we might fall apart when transiting Neptune aspects our Sun – accepting that we might lose our belief in life and ourselves at this time – is one way to work with this transit. We see it for what it is. It may last for a number of years, but it won't last forever. Co-operating with Neptune's dissolving effect also entails allowing ourselves to die as we have known ourselves, so that we can re-emerge with a new sense of who we are. Obviously this isn't easy or pleasant. It will help if we take time to grieve for the old self that is dying. Eventually the transit will pass and we will come out of it a changed person.

Any significant Neptune transit can arouse feelings of 'divine homesickness' – the desire to return to the blissful state we experienced before birth, where there was no sense of isolation, separateness or fragmentation. When Neptune transits the Sun, such longings can be very strong. Drugs or alcohol might tempt us at this time as a means of transcending the isolated self, and escaping from our pain, frustration, and the harsh realities and limitations of life in the physical body. Under Neptune transits, there is always the danger of abusing these substances, and caution should be exercised.

Confusion, uncertainty and self-destructive urges are not the only effects of Neptune transiting in aspect to the Sun. Because we are not so rigidly encased in the shell of our own ego, this transit increases our empathy for others and enhances our openness to any environment we are in. Negatively, this means we could be over-whelmed or 'taken over' by feelings and emotions which are not even our own. (This also applies to the physical level of our being. During a Neptune–Sun transit, we are more susceptible to germs or disease in the atmosphere, and more sensitive to alcohol or drugs – even prescribed medicine could have a stronger effect than usual.) Our heightened empathy could prompt us to take up a work, cause or activity that involves helping people who are going through difficulties or who are less fortunate than ourselves. Serving or caring for others can be a positive way to use this transit, but we should be conscious of what kind of personal gains we are accruing through supposedly 'selfless' behaviour. Is being needed a way of getting others to love us? Are we unconsciously seeking power by trying to help other people?

Even if our motives are mixed, this transit often does enable us to put our own ego-needs aside in order to attend or adjust to what others require. In fact, we may feel we have little choice but to adapt to the needs or wants of others now, even if this entails doing or accepting things which are contrary to how we personally would like them to be. In order to avoid falling into the trap of martyrdom, we should acknowledge those parts of ourselves which are angry at being coerced into relinquishing our personal wants. We need to recognize our resentment and frustration. If we aren't honest about that part of us which really doesn't want to adjust or make sacrifices, we will harbour rage and resentment towards the situation or the other people involved, and over the years this could turn to bitterness and give rise to problems of a physical or emotional nature.

Two examples will help to clarify what I mean. When transiting Neptune in the twelfth house came to square Clara's ninth-house Sun, her husband was offered a job abroad. Accepting the new post meant they would have to leave London, where Clara had built up a successful career as a freelance designer. As usual with Neptune, something had to be sacrificed. In order to move abroad with her husband, Clara would have to give up her career in London. Or she could sacrifice being with her husband and stay in England to continue her work. The other alternative was her husband turning down the new job, which would mean he would be the one doing the sacrificing. She spent weeks agonizing over the different possibilities. The marriage was good and she wanted to be with him, but why should she have to sacrifice her career for his sake? In the end, she decided to give up her work in England for the sake of her husband's promotion. She openly acknowledged the part of her which felt resentful towards him because of what she had to give up, and yet she still decided to make the move. Hers was a conscious sacrifice with the aim of preserving her marriage.

Was she acting like a martyr? To some degree, yes. But she made the choice consciously, well aware of her anger and resentment. Had she just agreed to go without fully examining her reluctance, her unresolved feelings of wrath would have accumulated and sooner or later found some sort of destructive expression. Compare Clara's case with that of Emma. Transiting Neptune in the fourth was squaring Emma's first house Sun. She loved living in London, but her husband wanted to move back to where he came from in Scotland to be closer to his family. She immediately decided that her place was with her husband, and although she wasn't happy about moving, she quickly dismissed her negative feelings without fully analysing them. Emma didn't feel right about causing any trouble or going against her husband's wishes. Six months after they moved, her anger and resentment were expressed in physical exhaustion, accompanied by a severe emotional depression. When transiting Neptune transits our Sun we may be asked to sacrifice our own needs and wants for the sake of other people or the larger situation we are in. It may be 'right' at this time in our lives to do so, but we also ought to recognize and work through that part of us which resents giving up what we personally desire.

Neptune–Sun transits affect the expression of the 'masculine' or 'animus' side of our nature (our will and assertiveness). We might feel inert, disoriented and more apathetic than normal. One reason for this is that our libido or life-force has turned inward, and is being used by the unconscious to promote needed psychological changes. Therefore, even though we have little energy at our disposal to function as productively as usual in the outer world, our dream or fantasy life could be very active now. To facilitate inner changes that need to take place, we should allow ourselves time for meditation or other contemplative pursuits. It is also a good period for psychotherapy or any form of psychological self-exploration.

Since the Sun is a 'masculine principle', this transit is sometimes experienced in relation to men in our lives. We may be asked to make sacrifices or adjustments for the sake of a husband, boyfriend, son, or male boss. Men we are close to may be going through some kind of Neptunian phase – problems with alcohol or drugs, a debilitating illness, or a feeling of being lost in life. Without becoming a martyr or a doormat, we probably need to be unusually sensitive to what they are experiencing. In some cases these transits could coincide with the loss (the giving up) of a male close to us – a husband or son who leaves home, or a father who dies.* Or we may meet men at this time who have Neptune or Pisces strongly emphasized in their charts.

Neptune transits to the Sun also coincide with periods of heightened inspiration of a creative, emotional or spiritual nature, although such experiences could have a manic quality to them. Because this transit works to dissolve ego-boundaries, we may find it quite easy to 'let go' of ourselves and serve as a channel through which creative expression can flow. Musicians, dancers, actors, writers and other artists could actually feel more inspired or creative than usual.

There is something paradoxical about Neptune–Sun transits. Some of us, as explained earlier, lose all hope and faith in life while under these transits, and feel devoid of any meaning or purpose (this is often the case with transiting Neptune in hard angle to the Sun).

*See p. 261 for more on issues raised by the death of a parent. See also Suggested Reading (p. 386) for a list of books dealing with death and the grieving process.

And yet others under either the hard or easy aspects of transiting Neptune to the Sun, actually become more susceptible to any kind of inspiration coming from a supposedly 'higher' force. Again, this has to do with the softening of our ego-boundaries. Transiting Neptune to the Sun makes us less rigid and tight – we loosen up and are therefore more easily swept away by powerful emotions and feelings, especially those which have a 'divinely inspired' feel to them. Religious inspiration is not uncommon under these transits, where, sometimes for the first time, a person discovers a connection to God or a sense of unity with the rest of creation. Such peak experiences can be very positive and transformative, dramatically altering our way of being in the world.

However, there is a danger of being too gullible and open to other people's influence, and if possible we should be wary of encounters with any extreme cults, sects or individuals who promise us the keys to heaven if we follow them. I have met many people who have been swept away under these transits by the teachings of a charismatic figure, only to find themselves let down or disappointed later. Some spiritual growth may come from these involvements, but in a number of cases, more harm than good is done. Doctrine and beliefs we swallow whole at this time may have to be regurgitated or unlearned at a later date.

Under these transits (and this applies to the hard angles as well as the trine or sextile of transiting Neptune to the Sun), we also should be cautious about believing we have some sort of divine mission or message to impart to the world. When Neptune aspects the Sun we are prone to psychological or spiritual inflation, what some people call 'higher side-tracking'. We need to be careful not to allow our personal ego-identity (the Sun) to be swamped or totally overtaken by qualities that rightfully belong to the transpersonal or superconscious levels of existence. During these transits, we may feel more love, compassion or 'higher' understanding flowing through us, but it is psychologically dangerous and immature actually to believe that we personally are the living embodiment of Love or Truth. As a channel of superconscious qualities, we may have a lot to give to others at this time – but we shouldn't forget we're still human. There is nothing wrong in enjoying the higher inspiration we receive now.

Indeed, others would benefit through what we have to give or teach. But if we don't keep our feet on the ground, we are setting ourselves up for a mighty crash. Should this happen, hopefully we can pick ourselves up again, having learned a thing or two in the process.

Neptune–Moon

The Moon and Neptune both symbolize the urge to blend, unite and fuse with those around us. When transiting Neptune makes any aspect to the Moon, these planets combine to heighten our receptivity to the environment and those around us. We feel what others are going through, and this enhances our ability to be caring or comforting. People in pain or conflict, sensing our capacity for compassion and understanding, find their way to our doorsteps. As a result, we are in danger of being drained by the demands people make on us at this time. While Neptune transiting the Moon may be asking that we learn to put our needs aside for the sake of others, we also need to set limits and learn to say 'no' now and then, rather than always bending over backwards to please. If we persist in playing the martyr, we run the risk of unconsciously storing up a great deal of resentment. Drawing our boundaries when appropriate will help to avert this.

It's advisable to examine why we are attracted to the role of martyr or saviour at the time of these transits. We may be motivated by a true compassion for our fellow human beings, but it also is possible we are accruing what psychologists call 'secondary gains' in the process. If we are honest with ourselves now, we may come to see that serving others is partially a way of winning love and compensating for our own narcissistic wounds, or we might have to admit to enjoying the sense of power which saving others gives us. Acknowledging how we are personally benefiting from our supposedly 'selfless' behaviour doesn't necessarily negate the value of what we are doing. In the end, recognizing what we are gaining from these kinds of relationships will enable us to care for others in a more honest fashion.

The role of saviour or martyr is not the only one we might assume under these transits. We also could play the victim. Landing ourselves in problems and dramatizing our plight is a way of getting people to notice us, or it could be an underhanded attempt to manipulate others. Emotional honesty is probably not the first thing one associates with a Neptune–Moon transit, and yet being as truthful as possible with ourselves and others during these periods is the best antidote to their negative manifestations.

Neptune always benefits from a little Saturn. Because we are more open than usual to other people, they could easily take advantage of us unless we exercise greater caution and discrimination. However, exercising discrimination is easier said than done under a Neptune transit. Down-to-earth friends whose opinions we usually trust may try to warn us that somebody else is taking advantage of us, but we are so swept away by our feelings that we don't listen to their admonitions. It is only after we've been deceived or betrayed that we realize our friends were right all along. Under Neptune transits, we may have to learn our lessons the hard way.

When Neptune transits the Moon, we are ready to embrace any of the qualities associated with Neptune, especially the notion of romantic love. We will probably fare better in these matters when transiting Neptune is making a trine or sextile to the Moon; there are more problems with the transiting conjunction, square or opposition. Neptune intensifies the Moon's urge to blend and merge with others, at the same time as it opens us to deception – the ideal recipe for complex and difficult relationships. With Neptune influencing our emotions, we see what we want to see, not what is actually there. So we fall in love with someone who later turns out to be not at all as we first imagined. In time, we will have to face the fact we have deceived ourselves. Or we might discover that the other person has been the one doing the deceiving, lying to us about his or her background, marital status or true motives. After we realize this 'divine' human being isn't as perfect as we thought, the Neptunian backlash of pain, disillusionment and outrage sets in. And yet it is only when our beloved has fallen off his or her pedestal that we can begin the slow task of rebuilding the relationship with the 'real' person, rather than with our projected image or fantasy of who that person is.

Under Neptune–Moon transits, we could unconsciously set up

situations in which we are asked to make major adjustments or sacrifices for the sake of others. We might fall in love with someone who is already married, or who cannot, for whatever reason, love us back in the way we would like. The keynote of Neptune–Moon transits is one of sacrifice and acceptance – pushing the other person to get divorced or to change his or her nature will probably not succeed. If the relationship is going to exist at all, we will have to adapt to and accept its various limitations and conditions. Such sacrifices and adjustments could be interpreted as a noble display of selfless love. It could also be described as a masochistic denial of our own needs. With Neptune transits, it may be hard to tell which is which. Don't we think we are worthy enough to have our needs fulfilled? Are we so attached to suffering that we persist in staying in an unsatisfying or incomplete relationship? What do we gain by being in love with someone who isn't free to love us back? Is the pain worth it because of the sympathy it attracts from others? Would we really want to sit across from her every morning at breakfast, or have to be the one to wash his dirty socks? Asking ourselves these kinds of questions under a Neptune–Moon transit will help clarify the part we have played in attracting a difficult or complicated relationship into our lives.

The Moon relates not only to our own 'anima' or feeling nature, but also to women in our lives – wives, girlfriends, mothers, daughters, etc. Women we meet or know at this time may be going through a Neptunian phase, or have a strong Pisces, Neptune or twelfth-house emphasis in their natal charts. They may be undergoing emotional or physical troubles, or drug and alcohol problems. Or they might be experiencing a time of enhanced creative, religious or spiritual inspiration. We may have to make sacrifices or adjustments for women now – looking after an ailing mother or standing by a wife in the middle of a breakdown. One man with transiting Neptune squaring his Moon was in agony because he was powerless to stop his daughter embarking on a romantic encounter which he thought was doomed to end in disaster. He had to stand back and let her go through a painful experience – but one which would ultimately contribute to her psychological growth.

The Moon is associated with our home environment, and sacrifices or adjustments may need to be made within this area as well. People we live with may be experiencing problems of a 'Neptunian' nature when we are under these transits. Or we may be compelled to move house or give up a home we love, and in such cases we will need to grieve and mourn for what we are leaving behind. Disappointments and setbacks could plague us if we are trying to buy a house at the time of a difficult Neptune–Moon transit. These transits also describe the kind of confusion that takes place when we are redecorating or restoring our home in order to make it closer to our ideal.

Issues around mothering could arise with any Neptune–Moon transit. It may describe having to let go of our children – they grow old enough to leave home or they get married, and we need to find other ways to express our nurturing urges. For some women, it relates to the menopause, a time to relinquish their child-bearing capacity. Women who have any Neptune–Moon transit approaching are advised to go for regular medical check-ups to ensure nothing is surreptitiously growing in the breast or womb. When Neptune is around, things sneak up on us without our knowing, and it makes sense to take precautions and look for any potential problems before it is too late and drastic measures have to be taken. Also for both men and women under these transits, the nervous system is more susceptible than usual to prescribed medicine, recreational drugs and alcohol. We could be attracted to such substances now as a way of escaping from difficulties we are going through, and there is the danger of addiction at this time.

Hard Neptune–Moon transits can play havoc with our emotions: we are soaring one day, and down in the pit the next. Meditation, music and any chance to commune with nature will have a restorative effect on the soul buffeted by the vagaries of life at this time. Even with the most difficult transits between these two planets, many people discover depths of feeling, and a capacity for compassion, understanding and forgiveness they never knew existed in them.

Neptune–Mercury

When transiting Neptune aspects Mercury, the way we think,

reason, communicate and gather information from the environment will be affected by the qualities of Neptune. Neptune feels, Mercury thinks: transiting Neptune trine or sextile Mercury helps us to integrate or marry rational left-brain processes with the intuitive and feeling right brain. Our imagination is active but doesn't interfere with our ability to think clearly and logically as well. What we 'feel' about people and events will often turn out to be uncannily accurate. There may be something 'inspired' about many of the ideas, thoughts and feelings we are having at this time, and we will be able to communicate these in a way which makes sense to other people. Any Neptune–Mercury transit may ask that we 'use' our Mercury for the sake of other people, perhaps taking on the role of spokesperson for those unable, for whatever reasons, to communicate their needs for themselves. Harmonious as well as hard Neptune–Mercury transits increase our capacity to register and take in subtleties and undercurrents in our immediate environment which previously we might not have noticed; with the transiting square or opposition, however, there may be more danger that our psychic receptivity is contaminated or distorted by our own projections and fantasies. Because we are receptive to thoughts and feelings circulating in the atmosphere, psychic flashes are not uncommon. We think of someone we haven't seen in years, and that person turns up the next day. Our dreams during this time will provide our conscious mind with information that will help us in the course of our everyday lives.

The harmonious transits of Neptune to Mercury allow us easier and more constant access than usual to the wisdom of our unconscious mind – to the 'wise person' inside each of us. We can make good use of these transits if we take time each day to be still and reflective. During these periods of introspection, we can ask our unconscious (or our inner 'wise person') to give us the kinds of answers or guidance we need to better understand or resolve any problems we are having, or have had, in our lives. Helpful information or insights might dawn immediately. But even if we receive nothing at first, if we continue to commune with the unconscious in this way, answers will eventually come – sometimes in roundabout ways through things we happen to read or something we see on television.

Under the harmonious transits of Neptune to Mercury, creativity and practicality work well together. The inspiration of Neptune could be channelled into artistic outlets: writing, painting, music, dance, acting and photography are just some of the avenues that benefit from the transiting trine or sextile. Endeavours other than artistic ones can be helped as well. Scientists intent on advancing knowledge in their chosen fields, or stockbrokers gambling in the City or on Wall Street, also will be aided by the kinds of 'flashes', insights and intuitions that accompany the transit of Neptune in trine or sextile to Mercury.

The hard transits of Neptune to Mercury, while intermittently or sporadically giving some of the advantages mentioned so far, are usually much more troublesome and far more difficult to handle wisely. With transiting Neptune conjunct, square or opposing Mercury, the conscious and unconscious minds are again brought together, but in a way which can be quite disturbing. Fear, doubt and confusion can take over the mind, and severely retard our ability to function as well as usual in the world. We have more trouble organizing ourselves and our daily lives – activities that have previously come easily may be more difficult to execute. We may find ourselves wishing we are somewhere else rather than where we happen to be at a particular time. We can be with people or involved in some job or task and yet we are not really 'present' or 'all there' – we are physically present, but our minds are somewhere else. If we're the kind of person who is normally fairly vague, disorganized and without direction, we might not even notice the disorientating effects of this transit. However, if we have always been fairly disciplined and orderly, the hard transits of Neptune to Mercury can be very upsetting.

This was the case with Mark, a freelance writer who, up to the time of this transit, had few problems disciplining himself, structuring his day and accomplishing a great deal. He would wake up by seven, do his morning exercise routine, shower, shave, serve himself a healthy breakfast of orange juice, muesli and fruit, and punctually turn on his word processor by nine to begin his work. Transiting Neptune in Capricorn came to square his Mercury in Aries and he began to experience a kind of lethargy and lack of interest in his work and life which he had never felt before. He didn't feel like getting out of bed at all; he was no longer motivated to keep up with his exercises; he started going to a local restaurant for a breakfast of egg, sausage and chips; and he was lucky if he made it to his desk by noon. He lost touch with his resolve and his direction in life. The conflict between what he thought he should do and what he actually felt like doing created a terrible tension. At first he tried to maintain his old routine, but his feelings of restlessness and lethargy were so strong that he eventually had no choice but to give in to them. Although he was frightened to do so and worried about his ability to keep up with his workload and pay his bills, he gave himself permission to lie in bed, and allowed himself the luxury of doing no work all morning if that was how he felt. He decided not to force himself to write, but to do so only when the urge took over. By mid-afternoon, hours after he would normally have begun to work, he finally wandered over to his word processor. He worked for as long as he felt like writing, and finished when he felt like finishing. In other words he stopped *making* himself do things, but learned to accept and flow with his moods and inclinations. In the end, he found he accomplished as much this way as he had done before.

Although anyone who is not self-employed won't be able to indulge his or her feelings and moods in the same way as Mark, there is still a lesson for us in the way he dealt with this transit. It was only after giving in to his lethargy that he was able to find the energy to attend to his work and daily tasks. Under difficult Neptune–Mercury transits, we may have to let go of our old ways of ordering our life and day-to-day routines, and let ourselves be lost for a while, until the psyche works out a solution. For many people, this is a scary prospect – it feels as if we have relinquished our grip on life – and yet under any significant Neptune transit, it is sometimes only by losing ourselves that we can find ourselves again.

Hard Neptune–Mercury transits cloud the conscious mind: our rational thought processes (as symbolized by Mercury) are taken over by moods and emotional complexes which bubble up from the unconscious or from the depths of our being (Neptune). Any means of escaping from everyday life might tempt us now – overdoing drugs or alcohol, losing ourselves in television or the movies, reading mystery novels all day, or becoming absorbed by our own daydreams and fantasies. Our memory will be less reliable, and we could have more difficulty than usual remembering or retaining information. Phone numbers and addresses are taken down incorrectly – we think we have our facts right, but we don't. When Neptune adversely transits Mercury, communication could also suffer: mail gets lost in the post, and people misquote us or don't clearly hear what we are trying to say. We may not be able to find the words to express accurately what we are going through, or we could purposely try to hide or colour the truth in some way. (One author wrote two books under a pseudonym during this period; another used a ghost writer.) Interactions or business dealings with others may not be totally clear at this time: we might be deceiving certain people or doing things behind their backs, or others might try to fool or deceive us (especially in the case of transiting Neptune opposition Mercury). People inaccurately interpret our motives, or we misread theirs. Most astrology books caution us to examine carefully the fine print of any contracts we sign at this time.

With Neptune conjunct, square or opposing Mercury, our perception of reality could be distorted out of proportion by our feelings and unconscious projections. Taken over by irrational fears, we might imagine other people are thinking or saying things about us which they actually aren't. Whereas transiting Neptune trine or sextile Mercury gives rise to intuitive insights and inspirational dreams, the hard Neptune–Mercury transits often coincide with mental instability, forgetfulness, delusions, bad omens and nightmares. Those of us who do not already have some familiarity with the workings of the unconscious could be thrown badly off balance. Since the unconscious is so actively determined to reveal itself to our conscious minds during this period, these transits indicate a good time for some form of psychotherapy or self-exploration, but we should ensure this is undertaken with experienced and well-qualified practitioners. We are too susceptible now to other people's thoughts and ideas to risk putting our psyche into the hands of charlatans or quacks.

Under any Neptune–Mercury transit, we might experience moments of heightened awareness and vision, during which we glimpse intangible dimensions of being – people's auras become visible to us, or we can perceive disembodied entities or various coloured 'thought-forms' floating in the atmosphere. With the hard transits, however, these experiences could be unpleasant: demons, rather than angels, come to visit. Or we hear voices which tell us to do strange things; in fact, these voices are probably denied and split-off aspects of our own psyche coming back to us supposedly through outside sources. Again, an experienced and supportive counsellor could help us through some of the more difficult manifestations of these transits.

Neptune–Mercury transits (especially the hard angles) sometimes indicate complications with brothers, sisters, other relatives or neighbours. We might be called upon to make adjustments or sacrifices on behalf of a relative or neighbour, and we may need to be extra understanding of what they are going through at this time. They could be experiencing mental or emotional confusion, problems relating to drugs or alcohol, or even a period of spiritual or creative inspiration. Again, as with any Neptune transit, how far we should bend over backwards for other people is called into question. It may be right to adjust to their needs or take on their problems to some degree, but we should also know where to draw the line.

In his book *Planets in Transit*, Robert Hand points out that the stressful transits of Neptune to Mercury could coincide with periods of high anxiety and peculiar nervous ailments.[1] These problems are likely to be emotional in origin. However, these transits may coincide with disorders of the nervous system which are organic at base, so if we are unable to surmise a clear psychological cause of our physical problems at this time, it might be wise to consult a neurologist.

Neptune–Venus

Under these transits, we will meet Neptune in the arena of love and relationships, in issues to do with creative expression, and through changes that occur to our value-system. It is very difficult to cover adequately all the different ways Neptune–Venus transits affect the sphere of relationships, but a general summary of how certain clients experienced these periods will give a good idea of what to expect.

Neptune dissolves separateness: when it contacts Venus by any transiting angle, the urge to lose ourselves in another person is very strong. Whether or not we are already in a relationship, we could fall madly in love at this time. Our new beloved may appear to be the answer to all our romantic dreams – he or she sweeps us off our feet and promises the keys to heaven. But transiting Neptune also brings a tendency to over-idealize and not see clearly whatever it is touching. In the case of Venus, there is a good chance we are not seeing others realistically: we are so enchanted by their good points and the wonderful way they make us feel that we overlook or play down other qualities in them which are more problematic for us. We may marry or form a relationship under any Neptune–Venus transit, believing we will live happily ever after, but soon discover that all is not what it first appeared. Although coming down to earth in this way is never pleasant, at least now we can perceive more clearly the real issues which need to be faced in order to make the relationship work. Even if he isn't really Prince Charming or she isn't the goddess we first thought she was, perhaps we will still see enough worth in the other person to make an effort to establish the relationship on more solid ground.

However, as the transit passes, we may find that the situation is impossible: it was all a dream and destined to fade away. We might even learn something from the experience (besides just remembering to be more careful next time). The potential lesson is a deep one, and involves our letting go of the notion that there is somebody out there who will come along and be the perfect mother or father we once had, or didn't have, as a child. Neptune–Venus transits compel us to seek our lost wholeness (the uroboric or oceanic oneness we felt in the womb and in the first months of life) through romantic love; but these transits also demonstrate that in the end our lost primal paradise cannot be regained through the external agency of another person. No matter how wonderful our beloved is, he or she will not always 'fit' us perfectly, and inevitably we will be let down in some ways. The heights we ascend and the depths we fall to under these transits ultimately teach us a very profound truth: the wholeness we all yearn for can only be found from within ourselves. And from what I have seen in my astrological practice, this applies not just to the hard angles of transiting Neptune to Venus but to the trine and sextile as well.

One way or another, these transits ask that we make sacrifices and adjustments in love which often involve putting our own needs aside for the sake of other people. The following brief case histories illustrate the different ways this can happen. Laura, a single woman of 25, fell in love with her boss when transiting Neptune conjuncted her Venus. The attraction was very powerful – she felt he understood her better than anyone else had ever done. The feeling was mutual: he apparently received the kind of love and understanding from her that his wife was unable to give him. However, he had a young family and was not prepared to upset his home life and risk separation from his children in order to give himself entirely to his relationship with Laura. So Neptune was asking that something be sacrificed: she could forgo her desires for a stable, conventional marriage and carry on with the clandestine, part-time affair, or she could end the relationship altogether. Either way, she had to let go of something. Laura eventually broke off with her boss and left the job.

Tom ran into a similar problem when Neptune squared his Venus. He had been married for ten years and had two children he adored. Under this transit, he fell in love with a woman he met through a friend. As a result, he faced three choices, all of which characterize Neptune's effect on Venus. He could keep the affair secret and carry on behind his wife's back (Neptune transits to Venus sometimes involve one partner deceiving or being deceived by the other). He could end the marriage in order to pursue his new relationship more openly and fully, or he could finish the affair. Tom chose to carry on with the affair but keep it secret. Just after his Neptune–Venus transit finished, his girlfriend met another man whom she ended up marrying.

In love, Venus expects something back in return: 'I'll love you if you love me' or 'I'll love you if you do what I want.' Neptune is a more selfless love – 'I'll love you even if you can't always love me back in the way I need.' When transiting Neptune aspects Venus, we may find ourselves in situations where we are asked to love somebody even if he or she can't always give us precisely what we would like. Diane's story illustrates this kind of Neptunian situation. She and her husband Eric appeared to have an ideal marriage – two beautiful children, an idyllic home in the country, and no financial worries. And yet, when transiting Neptune in Capricorn came to oppose her Venus in Cancer, Eric began to voice his restlessness. He felt trapped; life had become too known and settled, and he yearned for more freedom. Diane's first reaction was outrage – it was all very well for him to talk about his desire to take off and travel around the world, when she would have to be the one stuck at home looking after their children. She complained of his unfairness, but the more she tried to tie him down, the more he wanted to break loose. Eventually she gave up holding him back – although she admitted her anger and resentment, she told him that if he really needed time away, he was free to take it. She loved him enough to give him room to do what he felt he needed. Eric's reaction was interesting. As soon as he had her permission to do what he wanted, his feelings changed and his restlessness subsided. Neptune was teaching Diane how to be more selfless – to love her husband even if what he felt he had to do wasn't what she personally wanted. When Neptune aspects our Venus, we are usually the one who has to make the adjustments to what a partner needs.

Under any Neptune–Venus transit, we might fall for Neptunian types (anyone with Pisces, Neptune or the twelfth house strong in the natal chart, or who is going through important Neptune transits). We could find ourselves attracted to 'losers' or victims, people who just can't seem to get their lives together and look to us for emotional or financial support. Or we play the needy, weak one – the ailing hero or the damsel in distress – and look for a saviour to rescue us. And we are especially susceptible to partners of a dreamy, poetic or artistic sensibility – who inspire us with their vision and imagination, but may not have much to offer in the way of material security. In each of these situations, there is something unequal or imbalanced about the relationship. We are strong and they are weak, or the opposite way around. We need to ask ourselves why we have attracted these kinds of relationship at this time – what is the lesson in it for us? What does rescuing another person do for us? Why do we have such a low opinion of ourselves that we put up with people who treat us badly? If we are looking for a saviour, what unfulfilled early-life longing are we playing out? People are usually dealt into our lives for a reason; if we are drawn to dreamy, poetic types now, it must be saying something about qualities we need to integrate into our awareness in order to become more complete.

Also, as in the case of Laura mentioned above, we might have an irresistible attraction for people who are unattainable or unable to love us back in the way we need. Why is this? There are no set answers, but I would certainly explore the possibility of an un-resolved Oedipal dilemma: are we still trying to steal father away from mother or vice versa? Or is there some quasi-religious drive in us that equates making personal sacrifices with the path of spiritual redemption and salvation? What is it about being tragic that is so appealing? Or is there a part of us that is actually terrified of a committed relationship, so we keep going for people with whom we can't form that kind of union? Loving someone who is unattainable means we can fantasize how wonderful it would be if *only* we could always be with that person, which is very different from the reality of domestic life. In some cases, transiting Neptune aspecting Venus (both the trine and sextile as well as the hard angles) does coincide with the loss or giving up of a loved one – through divorce, death or some other form of separation. If this does occur, we need to take the time to mourn over what has been lost.

More generally, these transits (especially the trine, sextile and some well-aspected conjunctions) indicate a time when our ability to appreciate the world around us is heightened. Our heart expands and is full of love not just for one person, but for all of humanity and the rest of creation. We are easily touched by beauty, and feel more tender and caring towards others. Creative expression can reach an all-time high, along with an increased appreciation of any of the arts. When Neptune transits Venus we are attracted to anything that takes us beyond the boundaries of our separate self, and this accounts for the enhanced religious, spiritual or mystical longings some people feel at this time. However, the transiting square and opposition (and a difficultly aspected transiting conjunction) can 'make' us more gushy or sentimental than usual; we are so desperate for love and affection that we seek it anywhere we can find it, a situation which could give rise to promiscuity or a lack of discrimination in our choice of partners. The urge to transcend the mundane realities of everyday life can also manifest itself in an inordinate amount of pleasure-seeking, and frequently an over-indulgence in drugs and alcohol.

As with any transit of an outer planet to Venus, we may experience a shift or change in our value-system – in what we find beautiful or hope to gain in life. If we have always placed our faith in money or material success as the ultimate goal of existence, we will probably discover that there are other less tangible assets or qualities we need for real fulfilment. There is something paradoxical about the way Neptune–Venus transits work. Sometimes these transits don't give us what we want, so we are forced to look for our happiness in some other way. Sometimes these transits give us precisely what the heart desires, but we then find out it was not all we thought it would be. Ned's case is a good example. When transiting Neptune conjuncted his eighth-house Venus, he came into a lot of money through an inheritance. He had looked forward to this legacy for some time, believing it would solve all his problems in life. It didn't – he still felt an inner emptiness and sadness which all the money in the world couldn't compensate for. When this happens we have to rethink our value-system and look elsewhere for the kind of fulfilment we seek.

Neptune–Mars

Mars represents the impulse to affirm our individuality by asserting who we are – its vital drive enables us to go after what we want in life and make our mark on the world. If we are not in touch with our Mars energy, we are weak and ineffectual; but when Mars is distorted or undisciplined, we can be overbearing, violent and aggressive, wanting our way regardless of how others feel. Any transit of Neptune to Mars will alter the manner in which we assert ourselves.

Transiting Neptune trine or sextile natal Mars usually is much easier to handle and a more obviously positive experience than the transiting conjunction, square or opposition. Mars by itself is rather self-centred and impulsive – it acts because it wants to, and doesn't always stop to take other people's feelings into consideration. With the harmonious transits, Neptune can have a softening or refining effect on Mars. We act less selfishly, not just to affirm our own individual egos, but out of concern for others. At times our actions may feel inspired, as if we instinctively know the right path to take. Under these transits we might use our energy and drive to promote a cause which will benefit others rather than just ourselves. We will be more thoughtful about the way in which we assert ourselves, and try to do so in a manner that respects other people's needs and wishes. We are still asserting our will, but we are more sensitive about the effects of our actions, and unlikely to harm or ride rough-shod over others in the process.

The hard transits of Neptune to Mars (including transiting Neptune conjuncting a difficultly aspected natal Mars) are more complex and problematic. In these cases, Neptune has a dissolving or clouding effect on Mars. We are confused about how to direct our energy or drive; we feel lethargic and listless or unsure of what direction to take. Even if we have a sense of what it is we want to do, we could have great difficulty motivating ourselves and actually getting started. Or we undertake projects which for reasons seemingly beyond our control could end in failure. For instance, one man with transiting Neptune in Sagittarius squaring his natal Mars in Pisces attempted to open a new restaurant in the Brixton area of London. The date for its official opening turned out to be the first night of a whole summer of rioting in that area. Another example is a woman with transiting Neptune conjuncting her second-house Mars. She purchased shares in a newly privatized company, and three days later the stock market took a drastic fall. Neptune demands sacrifices in connection to the principle represented by whatever planet it transits. In the case of Mars, Neptune interferes with our ability to succeed in what we would like to achieve for ourselves. Transiting Neptune in hard angle to Mars works insidiously to find ways to render our personal will and drive impotent, and any new enterprise begun under these transits is likely to run into troubles and difficulties we haven't expected or accounted for.

For those of us who are used to being dynamic and successful, these transits are very uncomfortable. We feel we have lost our drive and power, and our ability to be effective. We don't know ourselves any more. It may be some reassurance to learn that the transit won't last forever, and yet it will still span a period of three to five years. Some astrologers would advise us not to embark on new projects during this period – especially ventures of a speculative or high-risk nature – and this may be wise advice. But in addition to learning to be more careful about when to initiate projects, there are other ways we can grow under difficult Neptune–Mars transits. If we have been too identified with an image of ourselves as powerful and potent, these transits teach us that there are forces out there that are greater than us – forces that supersede the will of the individual ego. If we have been too arrogant and identified with winning, we will have to alter our self-image. We are not a god: we are human. We realize, maybe for the first time, what it feels like to be adrift and unable to get our lives together or achieve our desired goals. We learn what it feels like to lose, and this can make us more sensitive and understanding of other people who have met failure in their lives.

Provided we take the time to try to figure out why we haven't succeeded, failing at something we would like to achieve could also prove a blessing in disguise in another way. By looking more deeply into our own psyches, we may be able to discover hidden assumptions we have about life or about ourselves which are standing in the way of making the most of our potential. Do we unconsciously believe we are weak and inadequate, and therefore compensate by taking on too much in an attempt to prove our effectiveness to the world? Does our sense of inadequacy stem from being put down or rejected as a child? Are we afraid to succeed, because we fear invoking the wrath and envy of others, especially a parent who might be ambivalent about our being more successful than him or her? Or is there a part of us which wants to stay small and weak so that we can manipulate others into taking care of us? In other words, what do we gain by failing? It may be hard to face these kinds of issues in ourselves, and yet difficult Neptune–Mars transits do serve to bring them to the surface.

Neptune works against separateness. When Neptune transits Mars, if we are acting too much for our own sake – to affirm our individual power or to enhance our egos – we are likely to fail. However, if we are using our drive and energy to promote something which will not only benefit us, but which will serve others in some way, then these transits do not have to yield such disastrous consequences. Neptune wants us to relinquish using our Mars just for our own ends. In a sense, we are being asked to give away our power, and to employ it to help others rather than just ourselves. In this way we have raised Mars to a 'higher' level, because we are exercising our personal will for the good of others. However, even though we may be doing something which is designed to aid and help the world, we should be careful about being too identified with the results of our actions. If our egos have too much invested in succeeding (no matter how much others will benefit from our actions), we are more likely to run into trouble when Neptune is transiting Mars. These transits, recalling the precepts of Vedic philosophy, are trying to teach us how to act without being overly attached to the fruits of our action. This concept is so contrary to the way most of us are brought up in our goal-oriented Western society that it is hard to understand, let alone learn.

Even with the best intentions, we should be careful under these transits not to give ourselves over to misguided or extreme causes. And we should be especially wary to avoid being carried away by an image of ourselves as some kind of divine channel through which a higher or greater purpose is being served. A messiah or saviour complex is always a danger when Neptune makes any important transit to our chart. We may be an agent through which some positive changes are effected, but if our own ego assumes too much of the credit, Neptune will make sure that we end up with egg on our face sooner or later.

Any combination of Mars and Neptune means that we are capable of acting (Mars) with secrecy (Neptune). In certain instances, such behaviour may be necessary in order to execute a job or transaction. However, the temptation to be dishonest or deceptive can lead to problems under difficult Neptune–Mars transits. We think we have covered our tracks as cleverly as possible, only to be caught out later by some unexpected circumstance or fluke. If possible, honesty is the best policy when transiting Neptune is aspecting our Mars.

During hard Neptune–Mars transits, our actions may periodically be taken over and governed by uncontrollable impulses stemming from our own unconscious. Neptune loosens the grip we have on ourselves, exposing aspects of our nature that we have previously managed to keep under control. As a result we may find ourselves acting in quite 'crazy' or compulsive ways, only to wonder later what in the world came over us. Betty is an almost classic example. When transiting Neptune in the twelfth came to square her second house Mars, she couldn't control her urge to buy things. She knew she was spending more than she had, and that sooner or later she wouldn't be able to cover the bills her credit cards allowed her to amass, and yet she couldn't stop herself. It was only through the help of a counsellor that she was able to discover and work through the deeper psychological reasons contributing to her need to spend – reasons directly related to a disappointing love affair in the previous year and the loss of her father early in her life. In general with Neptune–Mars transits, we will exhibit loose or uncontrollable behaviour most clearly in the area of life associated with the house our natal Mars is in, or the house(s) with Aries or Scorpio on the cusp. Although we might be shocked by the way we are behaving, these experiences do serve the purpose of revealing unconscious complexes, which for the sake of our psychological health and maturity need to be explored and confronted. Neptune has only brought to the surface what was there all along.

Sexuality is another area that can be affected by Neptune–Mars transits. With the harmonious transits, we could experience a softening or refining of our sexual expression; making love becomes more subtle or tender. The hard transits may bring more problems. Because Neptune loosens our control over unconscious drives and complexes, it is possible that sexual urges and fantasies could intensify during this period. Those of us who have as a rule tried to exercise restraint and propriety in this department will be most disturbed by these transits. Our first impulse may be to dismiss the kinds of fantasies and desires we are having at these times as mere aberrations which certainly have no real connection to anything going on inside us. This isn't the case; and while it is not necessary to act out our fantasies, we can still learn quite a lot about what makes us tick by taking time to analyse and explore their underlying psychological significance.

Some of us may not be able to contain our sexuality at this time, and might find ourselves driven by insatiable urges which no amount of actual sexual contact seems to quell. Again, the nature of these urges needs to be examined: it may be that we are trying to use sex to compensate for insecurities in ourselves which ultimately cannot be resolved in that way. Henry is a case in point. Transiting Neptune came to conjunct his first-house Mars at the age of 60, and he used sexual conquest to prove he was still young and potent. In doing so, he was avoiding the real issue – the fact that he hadn't yet come to terms with ageing. When transiting Neptune squared her Mars, Barbara also went through a period of sexual compulsiveness. Deeply convinced she was ugly and unattractive, she turned to sex to prove her worth and appeal. But no matter how many men she bedded, she was still left with inner feelings of inadequacy. Like Henry, she was using sex to try to resolve deeper issues which needed to be examined and dealt with more directly.

Neptune transits stirs a longing to reconnect to our lost wholeness. Some of the sexual compulsion associated with Neptune–Mars transits could stem from a desire to regain that lost unity through the sexual act. While it is possible to lose ourselves temporarily and merge with another through sexual union, the experience of wholeness with the rest of life can only be secured on any long-term basis by finding it from within ourselves.

Any Neptune transit can express itself in apparently opposite ways. While a Neptune–Mars transit increases sexual appetite in some people, other people may have the reverse experience, and go through a period in which their sexual drive is low or inactive. It may be that the libido or life-force is seeking to be redirected into other channels besides a sexual one – such as a creative endeavour or a particular mission or task which is engulfing us. The desire to transcend the sexual drive as a way of spiritual growth also could be activated at this time.

Mars is an animus principle, which means that during Neptune–Mars transits we could encounter Neptune through male figures in our life. Fathers, sons, bosses, boyfriends, husbands, or any men we know or meet now may be going through a Neptunian phase: they might be experiencing disturbing psychological or physical ailments, or a period of intense creative or spiritual inspiration. We should also watch for a tendency to attract dishonest or deceptive men.

Neptune–Mars transits can affect our physical health, depleting drive and energy. Some of us feel like sleeping all day, and it may be appropriate to limit activity in order to spend more time resting and being reflective. However, under these transits physical lethargy could be due to the fact that we are avoiding facing some problem or issue in our lives with which we should be dealing. Not attending to what needs to be done can give rise to depression, illness or fatigue. Examining what it is we need to take care of, and finding the courage to do it, will free our trapped energy.

Neptune–Jupiter

Jupiter is associated with the urge to give meaning to existence through a chosen philosophy or belief system. It is also linked to any experiences which broaden our awareness, such as travel or the pursuit of knowledge or higher education. Neptune inspires, but it also can confuse. When it transits in aspect to Jupiter, we will experience either or both of these effects – in some cases Neptune stimulates Jupiter's natural expansiveness and idealism; in other cases, Neptune clouds or distorts Jupiter's judgement and vision. Transiting Neptune sextile or trine Jupiter is generally a positive experience. The outcome of transiting Neptune conjunct Jupiter depends on how Jupiter is aspected in the natal chart. If natal Jupiter is not too adversely aspected, the transiting conjunction will have all the benefits of the transiting trine or sextile. If Jupiter is not comfortably placed in the chart, the transiting conjunction will expose and exacerbate the problems inherent in the birth map.

The harmonious transits stimulate that part of us which wants to believe in something: we see faith and belief as the path to redemption and fulfilment, and therefore we are open to being inspired or uplifted by some sort of religion, philosophy, political theory or belief system. Metaphysical or spiritual philosophies could appeal to us at this time – anything that enhances our sense of brotherhood or sisterhood with the rest of life, or gives us the feeling that we are participating in some grand plan or larger scheme of things. Our general outlook will be an optimistic one, and even if we are experiencing difficulties in our lives, we will still have faith in our future, a feeling that destiny is ultimately on our side. Opportunities come along which arouse our enthusiasm and energy, and we feel an increased desire to participate in life, meet people and have new experiences.

The harmonious transits of Neptune to Jupiter also indicate a good time to broaden ourselves through travel. We will attract experiences while travelling which arouse our compassion for humanity and enhance our understanding of life. It is a good time for an extended visit to another country, where we have a chance to settle in and absorb another culture more fully. These transits also favour any study which deepens or broadens the mind, and equips us with skills which can be used to help others and advance the quality of life on earth.

In general, transiting Neptune conjunct, square or opposing Jupiter stimulates similar issues as the trine or sextile, but in a more troublesome or problematic way – especially if natal Jupiter is not well aspected. For instance, we could be attracted to a religion or philosophy during this transit, but somehow get carried away by our own enthusiasm and become fanatic or extreme. Believing that what we have found is the answer to everything for everyone, we could try to push our beliefs too strongly on to other people. These are the kinds of transits under which people disappear off to an ashram in India or the States. While many good experiences can come through such associations, we could easily be disappointed or disillusioned if we pin too much hope on a religion or philosophy solving all our problems. Neptune can cloud or distort Jupiter's vision, and we need to be careful to whom we entrust our faith during this period: we might be easy prey for odd cults or misguided gurus.

Neptune also asks that we make sacrifices in relation to whatever principle it is transiting. Therefore, when it links up with Jupiter, the sacrifices may be in the area of religion or philosophy. This could mean we become involved with a cult or guru who insists we give up our ego, our name, or all our worldly possessions in order to find God. Or we may have to give up our belief-system itself. Jeremy is a good example of this. For years, he had been an active member of a meditation group, avidly following his mentor's philosophy and teaching. However, when transiting Neptune came to conjunct his natal Jupiter in Sagittarius, he became disillusioned with the organization. His faith dissolved and he felt he no longer had any clear direction in life. As in the case of all outer planet transits, something had died so something new could be born. His old philosophy collapsed, leaving him temporarily bereft, but it was only then that he was able to discover and formulate new beliefs by which to guide his life.

Travel is another area affected by difficult Neptune–Jupiter transits. The urge to travel could be linked with escapist fantasies at this time: we dream of faraway places that will take us away from our problems, or from a life which is too restricted, dull or mundane. We're sure the grass is greener somewhere else, but under a Neptune transit, such hopes are likely to prove illusory. During this period we should be wary of being deceived by people we meet when travelling. It would be wise to check and recheck all travel arrangements – these are the kinds of transits where you find yourself booked into a hotel which hasn't been built yet!

There is something quite manic about transiting Neptune square or opposing Jupiter, since both Neptune and Jupiter are both expansive energies. When they combine adversely, they produce a tendency to overdo things. Neptune also can confuse Jupiter – our perspective on life and our vision of what is possible may be nebulous or unrealistic. Put all this together and we have a formula for trouble. First of all, we might have an inflated sense of our own power or capabilities. Believing that we can do anything, we fly too high, taking on too much and over-extending ourselves. Secondly, these transits also give a naïve faith in life: we are convinced that no matter what we do, it will work out all right in the end. So we gamble with unwise risks, over-indulge in drugs and alcohol, and spend more money than we have, as if we are immune to the dangers involved. With transiting Neptune trine or sextile Jupiter, we genuinely might get lucky. But with difficult transiting conjunctions, squares or oppositions, we are more likely to be in the right place at the right time for the *wrong* thing to happen.

Most astrological textbooks warn us of impracticality, excessive idealism or clouded vision when transiting Neptune is adversely aspecting Jupiter. In general, I would agree with this counsel: this period is not the best time to undertake risky financial ventures. Even apparently sound investments could be thwarted by circumstances we were unable to see or predict.

Neptune–Saturn

By sign, house and aspect, Saturn indicates (among other things) where we feel weak, incomplete or insecure. We usually try to hide these uncomfortable feelings from both ourselves and others. However, when transiting Neptune aspects Saturn (and this applies to the harmonious as well as the hard transits), defences in that area fail, and we are forced to confront our innermost doubts and weaknesses. Consider, for example, the case of a man with Saturn in the third house, who fears he is not intelligent enough and feels inept at communication. Because he thinks he is inadequate in that area, he will do what he can to defend or protect himself against having to face those feelings. He will try to avoid situations in which he will appear stupid; he might accuse intellectual people of talking a lot of nonsense; or he might compensate for his insecurity in this area by working very hard to develop his mind and his ability to communicate – reading, taking courses, and collecting as many degrees as he can. Belittling the importance of third-house matters or the converse approach of trying to become a master of that sphere are attempts to protect himself against his basic feelings of weakness. Transiting Neptune aspecting his third-house Saturn will find a way to dissolve or erode these defences and expose his underlying insecurities and fears.

In addition to indicating areas of our life where we feel weak and inept, Saturn also shows where we feel pain. It is natural that we should want to hide from or avoid pain, so we find ways to protect ourselves. When transiting Neptune aspects Saturn, however, it undermines these protective barriers and reveals the hurt underneath. Paul, born with Saturn in Capricorn in the eleventh house of friends and groups, is a good example. His father was a British diplomat who married an Indian woman. When Paul was six, he was sent to a boarding school in England. Partially because of his half-caste background, he felt different from the other boys there, and was never fully accepted by them. His way of dealing with the situation was to decide that he would become so powerful and successful in life that people had to respect him. Which is precisely what he did. By the age of 35, he had built up a prosperous business; he was a rich and influential man. However, when transiting Neptune came to conjunct his eleventh-house Saturn at the age of 54, Paul sold his business and became involved with the human potential movement and other forms of psychological self-exploration. Through the catalyst of a therapy group, he reconnected to the vulnerability and insecurity he felt around other people; he came to see that the decision he had made at age six to be successful was nothing but a defence against feelings of hurt and inadequacy. Paul had structured his entire life as a way of avoiding that pain, and it was only in his fifties, when transiting Neptune conjuncted his Saturn, that he realized this. He was stripped bare, left with the original anger and pain he felt at six, but which he had managed to hide and compensate for all these years. The transit allowed him to see through his defences, and contact the feelings which were underneath. By acknowledging and attending to the hurt six-year-old in him, he was eventually able to free himself from the principle on which he had structured his life: he no longer needed to be successful in order to prove he was an acceptable human being.

Saturn, the boundary-builder, serves to bar from our awareness those parts of ourselves that we don't like and make us feel uncomfortable. Neptune, the boundary-dissolver, undermines the defences of Saturn, and exposes what we have kept hidden. Transiting Neptune in trine or sextile to Saturn may do this more gently or gradually than the transiting conjunction, square or opposition, but it is still not an easy experience for our egos to bear. We may even feel as if we are going crazy. And yet by letting go of our existing image of ourselves and reconnecting to what we have excluded from our identity, we can change and grow. We also should remember that it's not only 'negative' parts of ourselves which we repress or deny. Saturn tries to protect us against our pain and insecurity or any other 'nasty' feelings we don't wish to acknowledge, but we also might be repressing some of our positive potential as well – untapped resources or creative capabilities which have been stifled in the course of our development. Neptune–Saturn transits remove barriers that stand in the way of our developing these hidden gifts and talents.

Saturn also signifies restrictions imposed from the outside in the form of the rules laid on us by authority figures and social conventions. Transiting Neptune will undermine these boundaries as well. Under Neptune–Saturn transits we may be compelled to act in ways that are directly at odds with how our parents or society believe we should behave. For instance, a 'well-brought-up' white English woman with transiting Neptune in the seventh squaring her natal Saturn in the tenth fell in love and married a black man at this time – much to the disapproval of her family and many of her associates. Through this experience, she had to confront and step beyond the kind of conditioning and rules that had been imposed on her from the outside, and that up to this point she had never questioned. Under Neptune–Saturn transits our whole world view could change: new ideas and beliefs come to replace our old way of looking at life. With the transiting trine or sextile this could happen more gently – we have revelations or new insights which alter our perception of reality, and yet we don't experience any major difficulty integrating these into the already existing structures in our life. With the transiting square or opposition we will generally encounter greater inner or outer resistance in the process of assimilating our new ideas or visions. How easily these changes are accomplished under the transiting conjunction depends largely on the natal aspects to Saturn in the birthchart.

Neptune leans towards the mystical and spiritual and is easily carried away by flights of the imagination; Saturn has its feet planted firmly on the ground in the domain of practicality and common sense. Neptune dissolves our separateness and makes us aware of that part of us which is universal and unbounded; Saturn defines our individuality – where we end and others begin. Obviously these two energies are not the best of friends. None the less, transiting Neptune in trine or sextile to Saturn (and in some cases of the transiting conjunction) suggests a period in our lives in which we can successfully marry intuitive or spiritual vision with practicality and everyday reality. We have compassion and empathy for those around us, but we still know when to draw the line if others should ask too much or in some way invade our boundaries. However, in the case of the transiting square and opposition and a difficult transiting conjunction, we will experience greater tension when trying to integrate or blend the contrasting energies of Neptune and Saturn. Neptunian revelations about the interconnectedness of all life can threaten that part of us which has worked so hard to build and maintain an individual identity (Saturn). We fear that acknowledging our universality means forfeiting our individuality. To some degree this is true – in order to experience our essential oneness with the rest of life, we do have to relinquish the sense of ourselves as totally separate and distinct. And yet universality (which by definition means the inclusion of everything) does not exclude individuality: while not fully losing our individuality, it still is possible to recognize and experience that part of us which is universal and unbounded.

The harmonious transits of Neptune to Saturn also indicate times when, with patience and discipline, we can translate creative inspiration into some form of concrete expression. The transiting square and opposition will give more problems in this respect. We may have a vision (Neptune) of something we would like to achieve or express, but encounter numerous internal or external blocks and resistances (Saturn) in the process of giving form to what is in our imagination. Patience and persistence may help, but we also need to stop and examine more closely why we are running into difficulties – what the blocks mean and what they are trying to 'tell' us. For instance, the problem could be that we are lacking in some skill or knowledge (Saturn) which we will have to acquire before we can successfully implement our vision. Or it might be that what we would like to achieve is too grand or extreme and therefore impractical and unrealistic? If so, we may need to adjust the scale of an endeavour to align it with what is humanly possible or to make it more acceptable to others. (Whether we like it or not, when Neptune runs up against Saturn, we may have to work within the limits of what the more conventional elements of the establishment are able to condone.) And in some instances, failing to realize our dreams or visions has nothing to do with external forces blocking us, but with something inside ourselves which insists on sabotaging our efforts. If this is the case, then we need to ask ourselves why we fear success? Is there some part of us which is guilty about achieving our ambitions, or which unconsciously fears that others will envy and dislike us if we should succeed?

Saturn is associated with boundaries – and this includes the physical body which contains us. The more difficult Neptune–Saturn transits sometimes coincide with illnesses or ailments that drain our vitality. Tiredness and confusion are likely to be psychological in origin at this time; but it is always wise to consult a doctor if physical symptoms persist, of if we are suspicious of anything now which might be surreptitiously undermining our health.

Neptune transits to Saturn could make us feel that we are losing a grip on ourselves. In the past we may have been practical and disciplined, and now we are vague, lost, dreamy or just plain lazy. We thought we knew ourselves – that we were in control of our lives, but now we aren't sure what is real and what isn't. These transits sometimes deprive us of elements of our lives (property, people, possessions or belief-systems) with which we have been closely identified. As frightening as it may be, we might have to let ourselves fall apart before we can put ourselves together again in a new way. An experienced, supportive counsellor, therapist or analyst could help us through the process.

Neptune–Uranus

Since Uranus spends seven years in a sign, Neptune transits to it will affect large groups of people at the same time, indicating new ideas and trends which sweep through the collective. How Neptune–Uranus transits manifest in our individual lives is shown by the house placements involved – the house Neptune is transiting through, the house natal Uranus is in, and the house or houses where Aquarius is found.

Whenever Neptune contacts a planet by transit, it can make us more receptive to the planet it is touching. In the case of Uranus, we may be open to the idea of change or freedom. In 1988, the transiting conjunction of Neptune to Uranus was happening to people in their eighties. As the century progresses, this transit will occur later and later in people's lives. This late-occurring Neptune–Uranus transit indicates that while one part of us may fear death and the prospect of non-being, another part senses the time has come to disengage from ordinary life and leave behind what is known. In some cases, death under this transit could signify a freeing of the self from the restrictions of the physical body. However, the transiting Neptune–Uranus conjunction might force changes on us against our will. In other words, Neptune may be asking that we accept and go through some kind of Uranian disruption, even if this is not what we want. This could correlate with hospitalization, or being taken away from our own homes to be cared for in an institution for the elderly. These later-life Neptune–Uranus conjunctions might also correlate to the kind of mental confusion which older people sometimes experience. Neither Neptune nor Uranus are down-to-earth planets, and their meeting by transit could mark a time when we are not seeing concrete reality in a clear way. Our minds might be off somewhere far away, and our behaviour could become quite odd. More positively, for some older people this transit naturally draws the mind into reflecting on abstract or metaphysical concepts concerning existence and its meaning. Having lived so long, we have a better overview of life.

When transiting Neptune sextiles or trines Uranus, we are more receptive to new ideas, trends or currents in the atmosphere. If we have felt stuck or at a dead end in our lives, these transits could bring insights and revelations which enable us to progress. Rather than adapting ourselves to please others, we want to be free now to express who we are and what we believe. Our interest in life widens, and we could be drawn to philosophical or metaphysical studies as a way of deepening our understanding of how the universe works. We discover new ideals and principles we want to support, and look for ways we can improve and enrich life, not just for ourselves but for others as well. Political theories and social movements catch our attention, and we might become involved with societal reform – especially any cause which will aid those who are underprivileged or who we feel are being treated unfairly under the existing system.

With the harmonious transits of Neptune to Uranus we are so inspired by a new vision of life that we usually don't have too difficult a time adjusting to or accommodating these new insights. We feel ready for them. However, under the transiting square or opposition of Neptune to Uranus, changing our lives is fraught with tension and conflict. In the case of the difficult transits, Neptune sometimes works first to *undermine* our existing beliefs: the principles by which we have guided our life are called into question. What we once thought was the truth is no longer so convincing. We could experience a longish period of confusion, a phase when the old isn't working but nothing new has come to replace it. Or, caught in a no man's land, we vacillate between our old theories of life and the new ideas and ideals to which we are drawn. Either way we go, we feel insecure and uncertain. We are guilty or frightened of letting go of our old world view, but something inside urges us on. And yet we can't quite give ourselves to the new values and beliefs.

There is no escape from this tension, except to prevent ourselves to be confused, and allow the time we need to integrate new ways of being into our lives. William is a good example. Born with Uranus rising in the first house in early Cancer opposing Venus in Capricorn in the seventh, he had very strong ideas about what he wanted or didn't want in life. The product of an unhappy marriage and disruptive early home environment, he had decided he never wanted to marry or even live with a partner – he preferred to live alone and to keep his relationships open and at a distance. However, at the age of 37, when Neptune crossed over his descendant, conjuncted his Venus and came to oppose natal Uranus in the first, he met and fell deeply in love with a woman who knew for certain that she wanted marriage and a family. Caught between his feelings for her and his desire for space and independence, he would call an end to the relationship, then change his mind a few weeks later and beg to get back together again. He had never felt so torn and confused in his life – transiting Neptune in the seventh longed to be with her, but it opposed his natal Uranus in the first, that part of him that wanted to back off. After a year of painful indecision and soul-searching, Uranus conceded to Neptune, and William set up home with his girlfriend. Time and introspection enabled him to resolve his dilemma.

Neptune–Uranus transits are most significant when they activate natal aspects Uranus makes to other planets in the chart – especially to any of the personal planets. We've observed this in the case of William mentioned above, where transiting Neptune conjuncted his Venus and triggered off his natal Venus–Uranus opposition. Phoebe also had to adjust her world view when transiting Neptune opposed her Uranus. She was born with a close square between the Sun in early Libra and Uranus in early Cancer. When Neptune moved into Capricorn, it opposed her Uranus and simultaneously squared her Sun; and her mother confessed that the man Phoebe had been raised to believe was her father wasn't actually her real father. The Sun is a significator of the father, and its natal square to Uranus suggests something unusual or unconventional about Phoebe's relationship to him. Transiting Neptune, by opposing the Uranus and squaring the Sun at the same time, activated the natal Sun–Uranus square, and brought a revelation (Uranus) which dissolved (Neptune) her existing sense of identity (the Sun).

When transiting Neptune squares or opposes Uranus, we could be attracted to cults, groups or movements led by charismatic 'guru-type' figures who inspire us with new vision. As with any hard transit of Neptune, if possible, we should be careful whom we let influence us at this time. However, even if we are 'taken in' and later disillusioned, the experience could have some benefits, and it might make us more cautious next time someone comes along promising salvation.

All Neptune–Uranus transits open us to experiences of a mystical or psychic nature. With the transiting square or opposition, some of these may be upsetting or disturbing, especially if we are the kind of person who prided ourselves on our rationality and lack of gullibility in these matters. If this is the case, we should seek the help of people familiar with metaphysical or spiritual dimensions of being. Exploring the occult or supernatural during this period should only be done under the guidance of a mature, trustworthy and experienced guide.

Neptune–Neptune

When an outer planet transits in aspect to its natal position, the nature of that planet is brought sharply into focus in our lives. The various Neptune–Neptune transits coincide with issues specific to different ages or stages of life, so we shall consider each of these transits individually by aspect.

Transiting Neptune conjunct natal Neptune

Neptune's cycle is approximately 160 years; therefore it doesn't complete a full circle and return to its natal place in the span of a lifetime. However, the transiting conjunction can occur if Neptune crosses over itself shortly after birth. For instance, if a person is born with Neptune retrograde, it will eventually turn direct and transit back over its natal position. Or if someone is born with Neptune direct, it could transit over itself twice in the first year of the life – once moving backward and then again as it proceeds forward. These transiting conjunctions after birth coincide with an early experience of sacrifice or loss. To some extent, this is true for all of us – coming out into the world means relinquishing the uroboric oneness with life we felt in the womb. Another early Neptunian loss or sacrifice could occur if our mother, for whatever reason, is unable to look after us adequately. If this is the case, we are forced at a very early age to sacrifice something which is our birthright – the right to be nurtured and loved. As a result, in later life a part of us will still be seeking from others the kind of care and nurturing we failed to receive from her.

Transiting Neptune sextile natal Neptune

Transiting Neptune sextiles its natal position in our middle to late twenties, roughly the same time as Saturn approaches its first return and transiting Uranus trines its natal placement (discussed on p. 71). Together these three transits describe a stage in personality development which takes place just prior to turning 30, when almost everyone wants to make some changes in his or her life. Neptune gives us the ability to envision and imagine what we ideally could be. When transiting Neptune sextiles its own place, it activates that part of us which wants to become something more than we already are. Even if we have achieved much, Neptune still yearns for more. As this transit approaches, we grow increasingly restless. Women who have devoted their twenties to bearing and raising children will probably feel the need for other forms of self-expression. Men who have devoted themselves solely to work and carving a niche in the world start wondering what other aspects of life they are missing. Single women with careers may find themselves thinking seriously about marrying and having children. Men who have never stayed in one place long enough to amount to anything begin to feel the need to commit themselves and lay down roots. Neptune urges us to explore potentialities in ourselves which we have up to now ignored or put aside.

The concurrent Saturn return could prove an ally to Neptune at this time. First of all, Saturn's prominence now will help to keep our Neptunian vision of what is possible within realistic proportions. Should we overstep our mark and aim for something which is beyond our true capabilities, Saturn is not far behind to remind us of our limits and keep our perspective in place. Secondly, Saturn – the concretizer – will support us in the process of implementing Neptune's dream. Imagining what we could be is one thing, but taking the practical steps necessary to fulfil that vision is another, and no planet can do that job as well as Saturn.

Transiting Neptune square natal Neptune

This transit, which occurs around the age of 42, roughly coincides with transiting Uranus opposing natal Uranus (discussed on p. 73), and with transiting Saturn opposing natal Saturn. Taken together, these three transits describe the kinds of crises and changes associated with the passage into mid-life.

When transiting Neptune squares its own place, we will again have to confront the discrepancy between what we would have liked to achieve so far in our lives and what we have actually accomplished. We are not getting any younger, and this transit makes us painfully aware of our unsatisfied longings, our unrealized dreams and ideals. It's not unusual to experience a desperate urgency at this time: life is passing us by and we had better hurry if we are to have our share of the cake. To some degree, the dissatisfaction and dismay we feel now is a good thing – it is the spur which prompts us to do more with our lives. We are motivated to make changes for the sake of greater happiness and fulfilment.

This is fair enough. If we are in a job which isn't fulfilling, it makes sense to consider other lines of work which might be more satisfying. If we are not getting what we need or want in a relationship, the answer could be finding a different one which might work better. However, because this transit is a Neptune square, we need to be careful we aren't chasing after something unreal or illusory. We could overthrow all that we have built in our lives only to discover that the new 'perfect job' or the new 'Mr or Ms Wonderful' doesn't deliver all that was hoped for.

As usual with Neptune, the issues are not straightforward. Some of the greater happiness we seek might be found through implementing external changes, and it may be absolutely fitting to do so; but it's also possible that the crisis is an inner one, which cannot be resolved by simply making outer adjustments in our lives. For instance, ageing is something we all have to face at this time. No amount of jogging, working out, dieting, sexual conquest and outside validation will reverse the unavoidable truth that we are getting older. Neptune squaring Neptune ultimately asks that we let go of our youth. Rather than trying to hold on to it, the time has come to mourn its loss.

Neptune is the planet of dreams, but it is also associated with making sacrifices. When Neptune squares itself, we may have to sacrifice (Neptune) some of our dreams (Neptune). In other words, we might have to relinquish fantasies from earlier life, which we now realize are probably unattainable. By the age of 42 we have a fairly good idea whether or not we will ever be Prime Minister, President, or the richest person in the world. The time has come to let go of unreal dreams and focus on more feasible goals.

Even if we have achieved the degree of success we hoped for when we were younger, transiting Neptune square Neptune will still make us aware of where we are incomplete or unfulfilled. The wholeness and fulfilment we believed could be gained through work, relationships or material well-being just isn't enough. We may be rich, happily married, with beautiful children, living in a fine home, and yet something is still missing. What we are experiencing is a 'spiritual' crisis, or a crisis of meaning. The way through this crisis can be found only by looking inward in search of new goals and ideals which will give our life greater purpose and significance.

Transiting Neptune trine natal Neptune

This transit occurs around the age of 55, and may coincide fairly closely with transiting Uranus trining its own natal position (discussed on p. 72). It's easy to bemoan the loss of youth and dwell on the negative effects of ageing, but the harmonious triggering of both Uranus and Neptune at this time imply there are still plenty of new opportunities for growth and expansion. We might be tempted just to coast along, but if we are willing to make the effort, we will discover that life is far from over.

Although physical vitality and the mind's ability to absorb unfamiliar information do slack off with age, the combined effect of these transits suggest we are ready for new realizations and insights. By this time in life, we probably know ourselves better than ever before, and have a realistic idea of what we are capable of doing and what is truly out of the question. Transiting Uranus trine Uranus indicates that the late fifties is a period to give ourselves permission to be who we are – to do what we would like to do, rather than what we believe or think we *ought* to do. We might even have the courage to try a few things which up to now we haven't had the nerve to attempt – what Gail Sheehy in her book *Pathfinders* calls 'the last chance leap'.[2] And transiting Neptune trining natal Neptune adds yet another dimension to the kind of growth which is possible at this time – growth of an inner and spiritual nature.

Any important Neptune transit signifies the possibility of an increased empathy and concern for others. In particular, Neptune trining Neptune describes a time when we can appreciate and derive greater enjoyment from relationships and social contacts. Seasoned by life, we have a better understanding of ourselves and our own foibles and contradictions, and therefore more potential for tolerance of others. Roles are relaxed – men are freer to explore the feeling side of their nature, and women find it easier to assert themselves and to get what they want. As the demands of work and family subside, there will be more opportunity for companionship with a mate, and a chance to get to know our grown-up children as individuals in their own right.

The boundaries of Neptune extend beyond the concerns of our own personal self. Neptune trining its own place could coincide with an influx of transpersonal or superconscious awareness into everyday life. Freed from the busy strivings of earlier years, there is more time to stop and reflect on life's meaning, and to see beauty in things we hurriedly passed by before. Even if we are not mystically inclined, we may experience an increase in idealism at this time and a desire to engage in activities which promote our vision of a better world. The enhanced empathy we feel could find expression in community or charity work, where we serve and help people other than ourselves.

Any important Neptune transit entails making sacrifices of some sort. As in the case of Neptune square Neptune, we will have to let go of life-dreams or goals which we now recognize as improbable or unrealistic. However, the trine angle suggests that we encounter less trauma or pain in doing so – we are more ready to accept ourselves as we are even if we have not achieved as much as we hoped for, and to give our blessing to our own life.

Transiting Neptune opposition natal Neptune

This transit occurs when we are in our mid-eighties, and roughly coincides with the return of transiting Uranus to its natal placement (discussed on p. 78).

The negative manifestations of the Neptune opposition are all too obvious and common during this period. In line with Neptune's dissolving and weakening effect, our bodily processes run down and we become less resistant to illness. Energy diminishes as our physical organs wear out, making us slower and less flexible. We might be facing financial limitations and restrictions at this time. Mental confusion may set in, and we could suffer hallucinations and delusions which put us out of touch with the reality around us. We might end up institutionalized, bedridden, aimless and totally dependent on others.

While some of the effects of ageing are undeniably grim, it is still possible for many of us to use and understand this transit constructively. In fact, senility is not the rule in old age – the vast majority of people in their eighties remain unaffected by it. Many people in this age group report that even though their bodies look old, they don't feel that way inside. The Neptunian influence at this time indicates that we have no choice but to disengage from many of our past activities: we are unlikely to be pursuing a career or raising a family at this phase of our lives. However, withdrawing our energy from these activities also means that we now have the opportunity to find other dimensions of experience in which to engage. Old age is not just a period of decline: it offers – as does every stage of life – its own unique opportunities for development.

Even though short-term memory may be impaired, our longer-term memory is enhanced. Freed from social responsibilities, not only do we have more time to reflect on our life as a whole, but we are also better equipped to do so. By this I mean not just a nostalgic recollection of episodes, but the much more fruitful task of re-evaluating and reappraising past events within the framework of the overall context of our lives. It's time to weigh things up and to look back over our lives with the added insight that age allows. In doing so, we create the opportunity to come to terms and make peace with past experiences – the chance to discover how even the most distressing events also served some purpose or taught us a necessary lesson. We might even glimpse a quality of inevitability to all that has happened, what Erikson referred to as *ego integrity*, 'the acceptance of one's one and only life cycle as something that had to be and that, by necessity, permitted of no substitutions'.[3] Neptune opposing its own place does not have to leave us confused, bitter and full of regrets. Through the kind of introspection and soul-searching transiting Neptune invokes at this time, we are capable of achieving not only a healthier level of self-esteem, but also a greater respect for that higher ordering principle, both mysterious and wise, which guides and oversees all our lives.

While contemplation and philosophical speculation are ideal Neptunian pursuits, we should be wary at this time of disappearing into the oblivion of self-absorption. Old people are more capable than any other age group of enjoying long periods on their own, and yet satisfaction can still be gained from interaction with others. Associates weaker and less able than us may need our help, and we will feel better about ourselves if we can lend a hand where possible. Both younger and older people alike could benefit from the long vision our experience of life has given us. And even if we are severely handicapped or incapacitated, we are performing a Neptunian act of service when we give others the chance to be of help to us. Allowing ourselves to be cared for is yet another way of relinquishing our ego and separateness – something we all have to do when death comes.

This transit is a time to reflect not only on life, but also on death. What lies beyond? Will our spirit continue to live in some other form? And, as mentioned in the section dealing with the Uranus return, death requires more than just thought and speculation – it also requires preparation. If we can sort out the unfinished business and loose ends of our life, we are more likely to leave it behind in peace.

Neptune–Pluto

Because Pluto moves so slowly, large numbers of people will experience Neptune–Pluto transits around the same time. These transits describe stirrings in the collective which influence our individual charts according to the house placements involved (the house Neptune is transiting, the house of natal Pluto, and the house with Scorpio on the cusp or contained within it). How we are affected personally by Neptune–Pluto transits also depends on the aspects to natal Pluto in our chart. Any natal Pluto aspect will be activated when Neptune contacts Pluto by transit. For instance, take the case of a person born with Venus in 25 degrees Aries opposing Pluto in

23 degrees Libra. When transiting Neptune in Capricorn comes to square Pluto in Libra, it also will square Venus in Aries around the same period. Therefore, the Neptune transit will bring out the Venus-Pluto opposition at that time.

It is highly unlikely that anyone born in this century or in the first half of the twenty-first century will live long enough to have transiting Neptune come to conjunct his or her natal Pluto. However, transiting Neptune sextile, square, trine or opposing Pluto are all possible. Any contact between transiting Neptune and Pluto will arouse certain basic issues – although we will generally find the trine and sextile somewhat easier to handle than the square and opposition.

When Neptune transits in aspect to Pluto, we become more open and receptive to any of the things which Pluto represents. Primarily this means that whether we like it or not some part of us is seeking change and renewal at this time. Pluto – the planet which symbolizes death and rebirth – is nudged into action by Neptune via the spheres of life signified by the houses involved. For example, take the case of Gavin, who was born with Pluto in Leo in the seventh house. Gavin was 28 when transiting Neptune in Sagittarius in the eleventh house first came to trine his Pluto. At this time, he joined a psychotherapy training group (eleventh house) which had a profound effect on his consciousness. He also met and became involved with a woman in the group. After much soul-searching, he ended a long-term relationship in order to be with this new woman. So we can see the link between transiting Neptune in the eleventh (the house of groups) and the disruption of his present partnership (Pluto in the seventh). Even though the transit was a trine, it still created upheaval. His natal Pluto ruled his Scorpio midheaven, and he and his new partner decided to work together as co-therapists for other couples. In this way, the transit of Neptune trine Pluto not only altered his seventh-house situation, but also affected his tenth house, which Pluto in the seventh ruled.

As with any transit to Pluto, if we are not aware of that part of us which requires change, there is more likelihood that we will attract or provoke disruption into our lives. We will unconsciously set up our lives to fall apart in some respect. Or a collective phenomenon, such as war or an economic recession, could intercede and bring upheaval into our lives during this period.

When Neptune transits in aspect to Pluto, we are inclined to look more deeply into ourselves or life in general. This could stimulate an interest in depth psychology, metaphysics or the occult, and draw us to groups concerned with these matters. In Gavin's case, his desire to study as a psychotherapist reflected a growing collective interest in psychology, which was partly symbolized by transiting Neptune in Sagittarius trining a whole generation's Pluto in Leo. One mani-festation of this widespread transiting trine was that many people became fascinated (Neptune) by the idea of exploring the hidden dimensions of the psyche and themselves (Pluto in Leo), probably in the belief that some kind of personal or social salvation (Neptune) could be found through penetrating Pluto's realm. Gavin's individual participation in the trend created the circumstances which changed his life, particularly in the sphere of Pluto's natal house and the house with Scorpio in it.

As a general rule, Neptune–Pluto contacts draw us into Pluto's realm, often because we feel some kind of salvation lies there. Some of the generation born with Pluto in Virgo are already experiencing the effects of transiting Neptune in Capricorn trining their natal Pluto. The Yuppie movement reflects the earthy nature of this particular Neptune–Pluto contact, where nirvana is being sought through jobs (Virgo) which promise material success and well-being (Capricorn). In line with the respect for tradition evinced by earth signs, conventionality is becoming the fashion and is seen by many as the only road to happiness. This earthy transiting trine also symbolizes the increasing awareness people have of their bodies and what they are taking into their systems (Pluto in Virgo). Exercise and proper diet are the new gods, demanding obedience in the name of having a fulfilling life.

Of course, Neptune also elicits disappointment and disillusionment through any planet it is aspecting by transit. Therefore, when transit-ing Neptune aspects Pluto, we could be let down or experience losses in relation to the signs and houses involved. Some people with transiting Neptune in Capricorn trining natal Pluto in Virgo could find that their goal of material success constantly eludes them; or even if they achieve their desired financial status, they may discover that it hasn't brought the kind of bliss they hoped it would.

Neptune–Pluto transits draw out (Neptune) what is buried in us (Pluto). During these periods, we are more susceptible to unconscious complexes and compulsions taking us over. This can happen under any Neptune–Pluto transit, but the transiting square or opposition is likely to produce the most dramatic effects. Emotional complexes left over from early childhood, dislodged by transiting Neptune, float up to the surface level of consciousness, where they colour and influence how we see life and what we attract to us. This is particularly evident when transiting Neptune activates natal aspects from the personal planets to Pluto. Christina is a clear example. She was born with Mercury in Aquarius opposing Pluto in Leo. When she was 14, transiting Neptune in Scorpio came to square both ends of her Mercury–Pluto opposition, and her younger brother (Mercury rules relatives) was diagnosed as having leukaemia. The entire household was disrupted, and her parents focused their attention primarily on tending their sick son. Christina understood the necessity for this, but she also felt her own needs were being neglected as a result. Unable to voice this to her parents, she used getting into trouble at school as a way of indirectly diverting their attention towards her. Christina's behaviour worsened, and the school suggested a family therapist be brought in. In the course of the therapy, Christina's present needs were made clear, but it also came to light that Christina had been intensely envious of her brother all her life. Before his birth, she had been the only child, very much doted on by her parents. Her father desperately wanted a son, and after her brother's arrival Christina felt pushed aside and rejected. The transit of Neptune in square to her natal Mercury–Pluto opposition triggered an emotional time-bomb which she had been carrying inside for a very long time.

While any Neptune–Pluto transit could stir issues to do with sexuality, the transiting square and opposition are likely to be the most difficult in this respect. The sexual awakening attending adolescence is never easy, but this phase of life could be further complicated if Neptune adversely aspects Pluto during this period. This was the case for Robert, who was 16 when transiting Neptune in Scorpio in the eighth house moved into square with his natal Pluto in Leo in the fifth. Although he was interested in the girls in his class, he felt even more strongly attracted to other boys, and one older male friend in particular. Confused and embarrassed by his sexual urges, he didn't know how to cope with his feelings, and knew no one he could turn to for guidance. Robert's situation illustrates one manifestation of Neptune–Pluto transits – the arousal of drives we find overwhelming and uncomfortable. In his case, these were sexual urges, but other drives of a destructive or aggressive nature could also surface at this time. Young people with this transit can be helped if they are allowed to bring into the open and discuss their innermost feelings – especially those they are most ashamed of – with an understanding older person or trained counsellor.

Most people living now will experience the transit of Neptune in opposition to natal Pluto in their fifties and sixties. Any of the manifestations of Neptune–Pluto transits discussed so far apply to this transit as well. In particular, unresolved psychological complexes and various kinds of compulsions and obsessions could be brought out through people or situations we meet at this time. Some facet of our psyche we have buried or kept secret may have to be confronted, and issues we failed to come to terms with when transiting Neptune squared Pluto might re-emerge for us to examine more closely. Neptune draws out what Pluto has kept hidden, so physical weaknesses and ailments could be exposed under this transit. More specifically, with the transiting opposition we may be asked to accept (Neptune) something dying (Pluto) in our lives. For some people this transit could coincide with the loss of a parent, close friend or mate, or with other major life-changes, such as retirement, divorce, or the menopause. Again we see the influence of Neptune: one stage of life has to be let go in order to make room for something new. An attitude of willingness, acceptance and faith will aid the passage, and yet we still need to give space to the anger, resentment, guilt and pain engendered whenever anyone we are close to dies, or any phase of life passes.

Transiting Neptune Through the Houses

First House

When any outer planet transits over the ascendant and through the first house, our next major stage of growth involves a confrontation with the qualities of the transiting planet. The dissolution of our existing sense of self and our orientation towards life are the primary effects of Neptune moving through this area of the chart. Because an old self is dying, we might feel lost and confused at this time: we used to know who we were and what we wanted in life, but now we are not so sure. Neptune, the planet of leaky margins and fuzzy boundaries, diffuses our sense of identity and blurs our vision, and our immediate reaction is probably that of worry and fear: the ground has been taken away from beneath our feet, and we feel as if we're falling into a void. Every time we are about to establish a more solid footing, events seemingly conspire to undermine us. Even if we see a direction we would like to follow, something comes along to block our way or frustrate our plans. When Neptune is around the ascendant, we may have no choice but to accept our confusion and be with it. Essentially this means giving ourselves permission to tread water until the time comes when we are able to recover a grip on ourselves. This isn't easy. It entails trusting life enough to let go and see what happens next. Unfortunately, not everyone possesses that kind of faith.

According to the psychologist Erik Erikson, we are more likely to have acquired a basic trust in life if as a small child our survival needs were met and satisfactorily fulfilled.[4] But if our mother/caretaker consistently failed to respond adequately to our requirements, then we grew up with a lack of faith not only in life, but in ourselves as well. We form the opinion that we are bad, unworthy and unlovable – why else wouldn't mother have provided us with what we need? Without a basic trust in life or ourselves, the transit of Neptune over the ascendant can be especially difficult. How can we let go and trust that everything will ultimately fall back into place, when deep inside we believe that the world doesn't care about us?

With or without faith, the transit of Neptune over the ascendant may be one of the most frightening or lonely periods in our lives. This transit exposes any feelings of abandonment and neglect we felt as a child. It may help to realize that the emotions we are experiencing now are 'old' ones which are resurfacing. Taking the time to grieve for the ideal mother or father we didn't have is one way we can begin to use this transit constructively, and exploring these feelings with a therapist or counsellor will aid the process. We are vulnerable and exposed at this time, and the counsellor could provide the kind of support and containment we lacked as a child. Or we might transfer the rage we feel about not getting our basic requirements met as a child on to the therapist or therapy situation and work it through in that way. Bringing these feelings out into the open is the first step in coming to terms with them.

When transiting Neptune crosses over the ascendant and through the first house, we are often drawn into victim/saviour relationships. It's fairly easy to see how we could identify with being a victim at this time: this transit not only often produces confusion and a loss of direction, but it also can reactivate the feelings of helplessness we experienced in early life, when we needed someone bigger and more powerful than ourselves in order to survive. If under this transit we feel weak, 'little' or lost, we would naturally be in the market for a rescuer. Looking for another person to save us might be beneficial in the short term, but as a long-term proposition it is doomed to fail. The other person won't be able to sustain the role of saviour forever. Sooner or later he or she will let us down. Besides, finding someone else to take over our lives reinforces a sense of ourselves as small and weak, and perpetuates any tendency we might have to manipulate others by playing on their sympathy. However, if we have always appeared as the big, strong and capable one, this transit could be the time when we are meant – for the sake of wholeness and further psychological growth – to allow out that part of us which is more weak and vulnerable and to let other people see that side of our nature.

Playing the saviour is also tempting now, and sometimes appropriate. Neptune dissolves separateness and can confer a greater degree of empathy and compassion for other people. Our own boundaries are down, and we are more sensitive to what others are going through. To some degree, putting our own needs aside and attending to the plight of those less fortunate than ourselves is a positive and natural way to use this transit. However, in the name of psychological honesty, we should examine what personal benefits we are deriving by taking on the role of martyr or saviour. Helping others is one way of enhancing our own self-esteem. It also gives us power over other people. With Neptune around the ascendant and first house, some of our motives for serving people may be pure, but other factors can creep in as well. This transit is a good opportunity to examine more fully our reasons for wanting to rescue others.

Neptune enhances a desire to transcend our separateness and merge with something greater than ourselves, so urges and experiences of a mystical or religious nature could occur with Neptune passing through the first house. Devotional feelings run high, and we should exercise some discrimination in our choice of what to worship or surrender ourselves to at this time. Neptune's legendary gullibility makes for a funny story now and then; but there are charlatans around who could lead us far worse places than just up the garden path.

Because Neptune enables us to encompass realms beyond our ordinary ego-borders, this transit enhances our ability to serve as a medium through which archetypal images and feelings can flow. Creative people often feel more inspired at this time, and could do some of their best work. Regardless of our artistic capabilities, giving some form of creative expression to what we are experiencing now is an excellent way to use this transit.

Whether we know it or not, when Neptune transits the ascendant and first house, we want to 'lose' ourselves. Unwittingly we set up circumstances through which the structures we have built so far in our lives topple and collapse, so that we have to put ourselves back together in a new way. Drawn to pie-in-the-sky schemes or unrealistic proposals which are destined to fail, we are left emotionally or financially bankrupt, with little choice but to pick up the pieces, put ourselves together in a new way and start again. If we fall in love under this transit (which many people do), it's not just with anyone, but with the woman or man of our dreams. The problem is that sooner or later we wake up to discover that our beloved is not everything we imagined him or her to be. We may have been looking to another person to be the ideal parent we lost or never had. Under this transit, however, we will have to face the fact that we need to find our own ideal parent within ourselves, rather than importing someone else to play that role for us. Romantics will be in their element now: transported to the heights of ecstasy one day, and plunged into the depths of despair and disillusionment the next. If we have always lived a rigid, cautious but boring existence, it may be that the loosening and dissolving effect of Neptune is precisely what we need for our next stage of growth.

Anything that promises to deliver us from our shackles will be very tempting now. With Neptune transiting the ascendant and first house, we might be drawn to drugs and alcohol as a way of expanding our boundaries, or as a means of escaping from difficulties we don't want to face. People prone to addictions will have to exercise some restraint and discrimination during this period, and find healthier ways to deal with their problems and pain. We also could feel more tired and lethargic than usual – especially when Neptune is crossing the ascendant. We're sleepy during the day, then lie awake all night when we should be sleeping. We may suffer from periods of 'divine homesickness' – the yearning to return to the state of oneness with all of life we felt prior to birth – and there is a strong temptation to withdraw from the everyday world and to inhabit one of fantasy and dreams. To some extent, we may need to indulge these urges before we emerge ready to face mundane reality again.

Second House

While this transit brings change in the sphere of money, material possessions and our value-system in general, the exact way in which this occurs can vary significantly from person to person. In some instances, transiting Neptune in the second may increase the longing for money and possessions. We might find ourselves fantasizing more than ever about all the things we could do if we only had the financial resources. Wherever Neptune is transiting is where we are looking for the experience of something numinous and divine. In the case of the second house, we might see material success as the be-all and end-all of existence, as if wealth was heaven itself. The god Neptune had great riches under the sea and yet he still longed for the earthly possessions of his brother Jupiter. Neptune transiting the second could intensify a dissatisfaction with our existing material status: if we are poor, we want what rich people have; if we are rich, we want even more. Whether we do anything concrete about realizing these dreams is another story. Neptune is not the most practical of planets.

However, even if we achieve all the material success we hope for under this transit, we will find that something is still lacking. In the end it is only the infinite that will satisfy Neptune. Seeking material riches and wealth as a way of becoming complete just doesn't work. The kind of wholeness and fulfilment Neptune is looking for can't be found in anything external; it can be found only on an inner plane, within one's own self. By the end of Neptune's transit through the second, some of us will have learned the truth.

Neptune blurs distinctions, and can bring confusion, chaos and deception in money matters when it transits this house. In our fog, we make unwise investments and costly errors of judgement. Even something which appears to be a safe bet could be undermined by unexpected flukes and unforeseen circumstances. Neptune lives in a fairy-tale world, and any get-rich-quick scheme may be hard to resist for someone with this transit. Other people might deceive us with offers of work or money-making schemes which subsequently do not deliver what they promised. Thieves come in the night and deprive us of some of our possessions. Or we might be tempted to undertake illegal or dishonest ways of making money. A word of advice: underhanded dealings usually don't succeed when Neptune is moving through this house.

With Neptune transiting the second, we could have a great deal of trouble holding on to money, and our efforts to accumulate wealth may come to nothing. Money slips through our hands like water – we might wake up one day to discover we have turned into a 'credit card junkie', compulsively spending more than we actually have or can afford. Or we receive a big fat cheque in the first post, and then a bill for the same amount in the second. Neptune dissolves separateness and increases our sense of unity or oneness with others. When this happens in the second house, it can give rise to the feeling or belief that 'what's mine is yours'. As a result, we may find it difficult to resist a hard luck story: we can't help giving a little something to the homeless bum on the corner, or reaching for our cheque book to support another charity or disaster fund. (Thieves also glimpse the Neptunian vision of the oneness of life, but they see it the other way around – 'what's yours is mine', or at least it should be.)

There are deeper implications behind all the various workings of Neptune in the second discussed so far. Neptune dissolves boundaries which are too rigid or narrowly defined. Our deepest Self is unbounded and infinite, and Neptune doesn't like us to forget that fact. It we become too attached to anything, Neptune may take it away to remind us that our true identity does not depend on that specific thing being in our life. If we are deriving our sense of identity from our bank balance or possessions, transiting Neptune in the second will do what it can to upset the status quo. Our real worth cannot be measured in material terms, and ultimately this is what Neptune transiting the second wants to show us.

None the less, most of us adore our comforts and crave the security and power money brings. Ownership makes us feel safe, and we define ourselves by our tastes – those things we choose to possess. Most of us wouldn't consciously decide to give our money or possessions away for the sake of demonstrating that our true identity is unbounded. Therefore transiting Neptune has no choice but to work surreptitiously to teach us its lessons and to change our values and attitudes in this domain. Under this transit, unconsciously motivated by Neptune, we will unwittingly set up circumstances which result in our forfeiting or losing some of what we have attached to ourselves – in particular, our money or property. We forget to close the bathroom window or lock the back door, and we let ourselves be talked into unwise schemes and investments. Something in us seeks redemption through letting go of our attachments and discovering the Self that is there when everything else we thought we were is taken away.

As Neptune transits the second house, what we value will change. And when our values change, the choices we make in life also change. Carole is a good example. During this transit, she chose to leave a highly paid secretarial job and take a sizeable cut in salary in order to work for another firm whose product she believed in more. Money had always been important for her, but at this time her values shifted: working for something she considered worthwhile took precedence. When Neptune moved into Michael's second house, he gave up his secure job as a computer programmer to train as an actor – something he had always dreamed of doing. In keeping with the nature of Neptune, both Michael and Carole made financial sacrifices to pursue a path which promised greater fulfilment.

In certain cases, this transit manifests itself quite concretely – that is, we earn our money through a type of work which is 'Neptunian': acting, modelling, painting, poetry, dance, fashion, photography, healing, the selling of alcohol or drugs, etc. Professions as varied as that of a clergyman, chemist or merchant marine could also be connected to a transiting second-house Neptune.

Third House

Transiting Neptune through this house alters how the mind functions. In particular, Neptune's natural receptivity means we become more sensitive to undercurrents and nuances of feeling in the environment. Our intuition and perception increases – we notice things happening around us that we never registered before. However, Neptune's dissolving effect on the mind also indicates there will be phases when we experience mental confusion and scattered thinking. Those of us who have prided ourselves on a clear, rational approach to life will have the hardest time coping with this transit. Nothing is ever simply black or white in the house where Neptune is transiting. When Neptune moves through the third, we can view any situation from so many different angles or levels, we may find it more difficult to take a definite stand on issues about which we were once absolutely certain.

Neptune has a wide variety of effects on this house, some positive, and some potentially quite negative. An open mind is a mixed blessing. We are so receptive to others, we could easily be taken in by what they have to say. More gullible than usual, we are more capable of being deceived or misled by any powerful or charismatic personality who comes along. For this reason, many astrologers will warn us to be cautious about who we let influence us while we are under this transit. Also, Neptune can create confusion in dealing with others. We think they are saying or promising one thing, only to find we have understood them incorrectly. Or other people could misinterpret us. Many of these problems can be avoided if we take extra time to clarify the details of any transactions or exchanges we are involved with during this period. If not, perhaps we will learn from our mistakes, and be more careful in the future. Sometimes it's almost impossible to resist falling into the kind of traps any Neptune transit sets, and as a result we have to learn our lessons the hard way.

Neptune is paradoxical in this house. On the one hand, we are prone to misreading and misunderstanding others, and yet, on the other hand, we can be almost psychic in our ability to pick up on what people are thinking. We know what others are about to say before they say it. Or we might have thoughts which we believe are our own, when in actual fact we have absorbed the thoughts of those around us. We may even find ourselves voicing things which other people are thinking but not saying. Neptune acts like a sieve in whatever area of life it is transiting. When it transits the third our attunement to the mental plane of existence is so strong that we literally pick up on thoughts and ideas circulating in the atmosphere. This could work well for writers or public speakers, who are able to act as channels or mediums through which ideas and information can flow. Because we are more attuned to what people around us are experiencing and feeling, what we write or say is more liable to touch and inspire others. However, if transiting Neptune in the third is making difficult aspects to the rest of the chart, there is also the possibility that our perception may be distorted (usually by our own unconscious complexes), and we are giving expression to erroneous or ill-conceived opinions and points of view. Later on, we may have to admit our errors of judgement – a humbling experience, and a typically Neptunian lesson.

Even if we are not consciously trying to deceive people, this transit could make it difficult for us to express honestly or clearly what we feel. We feel things which are impossible to put into words. Or we attempt to speak what we believe, but as soon as we have spoken the words, we become aware of other factors which contradict what we have said.

In contrast to the increased gullibility and misunderstandings that often come with this transit, Neptune also makes us more aware of the hidden meanings and messages contained in what people say or do. A man tells his wife how much he loves her, and yet she senses other emotions in him. A father tells his daughter that everything is fine between himself and her mother, but the daughter 'feels' the hostility in the atmosphere at home. In other words, we are aware of what is not being said or expressed, even when people insist they are telling us the truth. This transit creates a great deal of confusion in our minds. Do we believe what we are being told, or what we feel? Are our deeper assumptions correct, or are we imagining something which isn't there? As one might expect with Neptune, there are no clear-cut answers. What we are sensing is probably right, but it's also true that our own inner insecurities and doubts could be obscuring our interpretation of the environment. The best we can do is to look inside ourselves and attempt to sort out the degree to which our anxieties are based on the reality of the situation, or whether they stem primarily from deep fears and complexes we carry around with us. In doing so, we also might come to recognize that our inner complexes actually influence the kinds of experiences we attract into our lives. For example, if we believe we are unlovable, we could act in ways which make it difficult for others to love us; or we might unconsciously choose partners who have problems with expressing or feeling their love. Exploring the connection between what is happening in the environment and what is going on inside ourselves is a fruitful use of Neptune transiting the third.

Education could be affected by transiting Neptune here. Young people with this transit sometimes experience learning problems, or have trouble adjusting socially with peers and classmates. Usually these difficulties can be helped by the caring intervention of an older, understanding person. The kinds of subjects which capture our interest or attention at this time may reflect any of the levels or meanings of Neptune. For instance, we may be drawn to a study of metaphysics, religion, psychic phenomena or the occult. Or there could be a desire to increase our knowledge of art, music, dance, poetry, film, the theatre or photography. This transit enhances a sensitivity to other people around us, and we may be motivated to become involved in work or projects which aid those who are less fortunate than ourselves. For this reason, the helping professions, healing arts, and ways of reforming or improving the educational system itself are other areas which could attract our interest when Neptune moves through the third.

The third house is also associated with relatives (siblings, uncles, aunts, cousins) and neighbours. Deceptions could occur in this sphere, or we may be asked to make adjustments and compromises on behalf of a relative or neighbour during this period. They may be going through a challenging phase of life, and we will probably be quite sensitive to their needs and difficulties. As with any Neptune transit, we need to be careful to set boundaries and limits; becoming too involved with the troubles of a brother, sister or neighbour could drain our own physical, psychological or material resources. Rather than 'taking on' all their grievances ourselves, it often is wiser to advise them to seek professional counselling or to direct them to relevant agencies which are experienced in dealing with their particular problems.

When transiting Neptune in the third triggers difficult aspects in the natal chart, latent mental and emotional problems or neurological disorders might be brought to the surface. In extreme cases, this could result in mental breakdowns or physical illness related to the malfunction of the brain and nervous system. In some cases, mobility, vision or hearing could be impaired. The effects may be severe, but it is only when these conditions are exposed that suitable treatment can be sought.

Fourth House

Neptune transiting the fourth touches us on a deep, personal level, and its effects will be manifested both outwardly and inwardly in our lives. Obviously, these two dimensions are connected: external contingencies will prompt inner changes, and any inner change will express itself externally in some way. We'll examine the inner, psychological consequences first, and then move on to the more mundane ramifications of this transit.

At any time during the period when Neptune crosses the IC and journeys through the fourth house, we may experience phases of inner confusion. We aren't sure exactly who we are or what we are here for. The fourth house is associated with our base of operations – on an external level it is our home, but psychologically it represents 'where we are coming from'. Neptune here can describe feelings of being lost; we don't know where we are, and we don't have a solid enough sense of ourselves on which to base an approach to life. Especially when transiting Neptune is hovering around the IC or cusp of the fourth, we may need to take time just to be with ourselves, time to look inward and make contact with what we are feeling deep inside. Through turning our awareness inward and withdrawing into the self, we will be better able to attune ourselves to our innermost needs and urges. When Neptune crosses the IC, it is appropriate to pause and take stock of our lives. Asking certain questions will help this process. What has motivated us in life up to now? Are these motivations still important to us, or is it time to allow new urges and goals to replace the old ones? Have our motivations been our own, or have our choices been influenced heavily by parents or society? Regardless of what others may want for us, what do *we* really want? What does our own psyche want to make happen for us?

With Neptune transiting the IC, the answers to these questions probably are unlikely to come quickly or dramatically. When Uranus transits this area, we might wake up one day jolted into a sense of who we are and filled with certainty about what we want in life. Neptune, however, doesn't operate that way. With Neptune, we just have to be with ourselves and wait until we can sense or feel more clearly the true urges stemming from our core Self. Neptune doesn't push and shove; it nudges. And when it transits the fourth, it asks that we find meaning and strength from inside ourselves – that we are true to our own psyche – rather than looking for something 'out there' to tell us what to be or do.

A re-evaluation of our deepest urges, needs and motivations at this time could be prompted by the feeling that our life is incomplete. Neptune transiting the IC can stir a deep malaise – we are not happy with existing circumstances surrounding us, and we don't feel fulfilled by the kinds of structures we have created or built for ourselves in our lives. In other words, we are frustrated with the whole way our life is set up. The fourth house has a rebounding effect on the tenth, and some of this frustration could be related directly to feelings of dissatisfaction with the work we are doing in the world. In fact, we may need to take some time away from work or other external commitments, in order to create more space for our own selves. By reducing our outer activity, we are better able to respect the inner process of unfoldment our psyche has in mind for us. By quieting down, we are better able to 'hear' our deepest needs and urges. In this sense, Neptune transiting the IC or fourth is asking that we give up or sacrifice some of our involvement with the external world for the sake of communing more closely with our inner selves.

Memories from the past could also be aroused at this time. Unconscious complexes and patterns related to childhood experiences and conditioning are dislodged from the depths of the psyche and float to the surface of consciousness. We may find ourselves in current situations which parallel earlier events in our lives, and trigger feelings which have been buried in us from previous stages of development. For instance, when Anne had transiting Neptune conjunct her fourth-house Sun, her husband was diagnosed as having cancer. This situation reactivated a long-forgotten experience – when she was four years old her father had to go into hospital for a major heart operation. The news of her husband's illness brought out the earlier fear, guilt and insecurity that had gripped her at the time of her father's hospitalization. In facing her present circumstances, she also had to confront unresolved emotions from her childhood. In the process, Anne's psychological understanding of herself deepened, and she was able to examine and apprehend more clearly a part of herself which somehow felt responsible if people around her were sick or unhappy. The transit of Neptune over her fourth-house Sun was a difficult period, and yet it provided the opportunity for her to discover and begin to work through a complex she had carried around inside her for many years.

Looking inside ourselves is the most subtle effect of this transit, but it can also be manifested quite concretely in issues to do with the home and personal life. Very often transiting Neptune in the fourth coincides with a phase of making major adjustments or sacrifices within the sphere of the home. We may have people living with us who require extra care or support. Sick relatives come to stay, or a spouse, lover, child or flatmate with whom we share our home may be experiencing a difficult time. What is going on within the home could drain us or demand so much of our attention that other areas of our life have to take second place. Any of these contingencies reflect Neptune's tendency to dissolve separateness by asking that we put our own needs aside for the sake of others. To do so may be right and appropriate under this transit; but we also need to acknowledge and deal with that part of us which might resent the sacrifices we have to make. Otherwise, the undercurrents within the home will be permeated with the poison of unrecognized resentment.

In some cases (usually when transiting Neptune in the fourth opposes natal or transiting planets in the tenth), we are caught in a conflict between our personal life (the fourth) and our professional life (the tenth). In this situation, the majority of people may feel the need to sacrifice the amount of time they would be using to pursue career activities in order to tend to pressing personal or domestic issues. However, sometimes this happens in reverse: we give up some of the time we would be putting into our personal life in order to engage in tenth-house activities. In the first instance, the career is given up for the sake of the home; in the latter, the home/personal sphere is compromised for the sake of career. In either case, we meet Neptune – the planet which teaches us about sacrifice and letting go.

Neptune transiting the fourth could indicate deception within the home – someone we live with is deceiving us. Or the dissolving effect of Neptune might be manifested concretely in collapsing foundations or rising damp. These situations, though real enough, often symbolize deeper issues which we need to examine. For instance, if the house is literally falling down around us, what does this say about our inner psychological state of being? Rationally minded individuals may laugh at trying to make such connections, but if we look deeply enough we will often discover a surprising reciprocity between the inner and outer dimensions of life. In a few cases, this transit coincides with our having to give up a home entirely. We may be forced to leave a house we treasure. Divorce, the death of a partner, the ending of a relationship, or the splitting up of a family could mean the structure of our home life as we have known it dissolves. Such occurrences may be the outer manifestation of a Neptunian process: the need to let go of old ways of being in order to rebuild life on a new foundation. Consciously we may not be choosing this to happen, and yet Neptune leaves us with no alternative: our inner growth demands these kinds of changes at this time.

We seek greater wholeness and fulfilment in the area of the chart where Neptune is transiting. A number of people I have encountered with Neptune moving through their fourth were working very hard to establish a more ideal home. Some were involved in revamping their home in order to make it more beautiful, comfortable or complete – which can be a positive, concrete use of this transit. I have also come across many people who purchased a home when Neptune crossed the I C and moved through the fourth. Since Neptune is the planet of deception, many astrological textbooks warn us of such transactions at this time. We may be unaware of something wrong with the house we are buying, so precautions should be taken to investigate such possibilities thoroughly. Or we set our sights on a property we love, but unforeseen circumstances mean that in the end we can't buy it. In any of these ways, Neptune can let us down. However, to say that we should *never* buy a house or flat under this transit is too extreme. Neptune doesn't only indicate disillusionment or disappointment. For some people, buying a home of their own at this time could be the realization of a life-long dream – another manifestation of Neptune. And, in most cases, acquiring a property is Neptunian: we are under the illusion that we own it, when in actual fact it belongs to whomever we borrowed the money from for the mortgage.

The fourth house can be associated with one of our parents, quite often the father (although the mother may fit better here in some cases).* Neptune transiting this sphere could describe something he is going through. He may be ill, depressed, or facing a major life-change, such as retirement or the loss of people close to him. He might find religion or take up writing poetry. The fact that these changes are happening for him when Neptune transits our fourth means that in some way we will be touched by what he is experiencing. He may need us to look after him, or we may have to be especially sensitive and understanding of his situation. In some cases, this transit could coincide with death of the father – we literally have to give him up.† However, what he is experiencing at this time could also have the effect of bringing us closer to him. Barriers that might have existed between our father and ourselves dissolve, and we can relate in a fashion not possible before. In this way, Neptune could help us heal earlier wounds in relation to the father, especially if we felt misunderstood, unloved or unap-preciated by him. On another level, this transit also suggests our capacity to find 'the father within' – the discovery of something within our own selves which can provide us with the strength and loving support we previously looked for in an external father-figure. Father also can be taken to be a symbol of spirit or God, and Neptune in the fourth could prompt an inner search to dis-cover and reconnect to the spiritual source of life. Which brings us back to the idea that, in its deepest expression, transiting Nep-tune in this house is asking that we turn our attention inward, where our soul lives.

Fifth House

Underlying the fifth house is the urge to distinguish ourselves as someone special and unique, the desire to express and radiate our individuality by putting our stamp on whatever we do. When Nep-tune – the planet that knows no boundaries and limits – transits the fifth, we could succumb to a tendency to self-aggrandizement or to

---

*See chapter 5, note 5.

†See p. 261 for a discussion of the issues raised by a parent's death.

assert inappropriately the demands of our ego. It is a law of life that depression follows inflation: if we become too carried away with ourselves under this transit, we inevitably invite a fall. With Neptune moving through the fifth, it is not uncommon to overdramatize and exaggerate whatever we are experiencing. Everything is bigger than life: we don't just feel happy, we are ecstatic; we don't just feel sad, we plunge to the depths of tragedy and despair. And somewhere in between these mood swings, we are capable of discovering a truer sense of our identity, worth and abilities.

Neptune enlivens the imagination, and for artistically inclined people this transit could be a fruitful period, bringing new vision and ideas. Those of us who have never really tapped our creative potential may be better able to do so at this time. However, unless we are prepared to put in the effort and discipline (Saturn) needed to take our inspired artistic vision and give it concrete manifestation, it will remain only on the level of fantasy. As usual, Neptune may ask that we make sacrifices in this area. Some of us may have to give up a reliable job or fixed income in order to pursue our artistic ambitions. Or the reverse could be the case. We may be forced to abandon or curtail creative aspirations in order to undertake work which offers greater stability and security.

The search for pleasure can be both rewarding and elusive when Neptune is moving through the fifth. Because there is usually a fascination for the affairs of the house where Neptune is transiting, in general I would recommend people under this transit to follow any urges they have to explore hobbies or spare-time pursuits which might interest them. This could be anything from an evening class in painting or calligraphy to regular nights out at the theatre or ballet. We might take up a sport or discover a penchant for rock-collecting or train-spotting. In fact, the difficulty with diffuse Neptune here could be deciding which of our many interests to choose to focus on. Once we finally settle on one, it could absorb us totally at this time, and contribute to feelings of greater well-being and completeness. On the other hand, we also run the risk of becoming obsessed or taken over by a spare-time activity. This in itself may not be problematic, unless we are using that form of recreation as an escape from other areas in our life we need to face. Should our spare-time pursuit entail some form of gambling, we are likely to find ourselves on the losing end. (With foggy Neptune transiting the fifth, speculative ventures may not turn out as hoped.) But whether we win or lose, the deeper psychological motives giving rise to compulsive gambling will need to be explored.

The fifth house is also associated with love and romance, and Neptune here raises a variety of issues, most commonly the problem of idealizing a relationship or a loved one. We might ascribe 'divine' qualities to partners, but fail to see their faults and shortcomings, and then become disenchanted when they don't live up to our expectations. Romance is not likely to be straightforward with Neptune around. We worship someone at a distance, or fall for a person who is already attached or who cannot love us back in the way we need.

Victim/saviour relationships are common with Neptune transiting the fifth, and we will be drawn to people wounded in some way or in obvious trouble or pain. Once again, our motives for embarking on these kinds of relationships need to be examined. Is playing the rescuer a means of bolstering our own sense of self-worth and power? Do we believe that serving others is the only way we can coerce people into loving us? Conversely, we may play the victim and look for someone to rescue us. While it's possible that sharing love can be healing for both parties, there are many pitfalls to such unequal relationships.*

Neptune will also be encountered through children, another fifth-house concern. A child born under this transit may have Neptune or Pisces prominent in his or her chart, or might be a dreamy or artistic type, or have difficulty relating to the world. We may have to make sacrifices for our offspring at this time. A child could be ill or disabled in some way and need special care and understanding. The more subtle issues around this transit may be our tendency to over-idealize a child, or an attempt to turn the child into someone who will redeem us. Why is it so important to us that our child be exceptional? What are we wanting the child to live out for us? We may have to

---

*See the section on Neptune–Venus transits (p. 141) for a further discussion of these issues.

stand by and watch our older children going through an emotional crisis which we are unable to prevent. Relinquishment is a key Neptune issue. If our children are coming of age, this transit could indicate the need on our part to let go of them; if they are suffering in some way, we may have to recognize the limits of our power to protect them, or our role as omnipotent parent. An older woman might have to face the menopause, and the passing of her childbearing abilities. In this case, she will need to mourn the loss of this capacity, and consider alternative avenues into which she could deploy her urges to mother and nurture others.

Unplanned pregnancies could occur under this transit. However, many psychologists would argue that there is no such thing as an accidental pregnancy, and if we end up in this situation we will learn a great deal about ourselves by examining any possible hidden motivations for getting pregnant at this time. Is the pregnancy a way of manipulating a partner or holding a relationship together? Or is pregnancy a means of avoiding other issues in the life, such as the establishment of a career? Honestly facing our ulterior motives may be difficult, but it is crucial, not only for our own sake, but for the sake of the father and the child as well. Abortions, miscarriages and the loss of children may also occur when Neptune is transiting the fifth, although these will be contingent upon other aspects of the natal chart. The accompanying grief, anger, guilt and resentment all need to be understood, and some form of counselling is highly recommended at these times.* Neptune uses suffering to change us – in whatever house it is transiting, we sometimes experience losses which hurt us very deeply. Pain hurts, but it may help to remember that suffering is one of the paths which lead to greater consciousness.

Sixth House

This transit affects two areas of life in particular – work and health. Because Neptune dissolves boundaries, when it transits the sixth

*See Suggested Reading (p. 386) for a list of books dealing with death and the grieving process.

house the boundary between what is inside us and what is outside us becomes more permeable. If we observe the body closely at this time, we will see the way in which it registers what we are feeling and 'picking up' from the environment: we walk into one room and we feel physically light, buoyant, and expansive, and we go into another situation and our stomach tightens and neck tenses. A great deal could be learned about ourselves and others now by taking time to examine the body's reaction to different people and environments.

Also, since our physical defences are weakened, we are more prone to invasion by germs, illnesses or stress in the atmosphere, and for this reason we should do what we can to strengthen our nervous system. Exercise, proper rest and diet can help to counter-balance some of the possible detrimental effects of Neptune in this house. We are more sensitive to what we take into our systems; therefore, over-indulging in alcohol or drugs could be very danger-ous. We might discover certain foods to which our body has a negative reaction. Making dietary adjustments is one form of sacrifice Neptune may call for when moving through the sixth. However, Neptune can cause us to be carried away in whatever house it is transiting, and we run the risk of becoming obsessive about health and diet. In our quest for ideal health, we could put all our faith into one specific dietary programme. Approached sensibly, some of these regimes – grape fasts, raw food or low mucous diets, for instance – can have a cleansing and beneficial effect on the system. But we should exercise discernment and common sense in this area, and seek the guidance of a qualified practitioner before embarking on diets of an extreme nature, especially since health problems may be hard to diagnose: there are cases of people with Neptune transiting the sixth who have been treated for the wrong illness, or who have been prescribed medication which produced unfortunate side-effects. Under this transit, we might benefit from alternative or comple-mentary medicines such as homeopathy, naturopathy or acupunc-ture, which seek out the subtle causes of illness, and generally treat the body more gently. With Neptune around, illnesses may be emotional or psychological in origin, and could be serving some ulterior motive or purpose. For instance, when Neptune transited

Kate's sixth house, she developed a stomach ailment which a number of specialists were unable to diagnose or cure. Eventually Kate sought the help of a holistic medical practitioner, who not only examined her body but also enquired into the overall situation of her life. Through their talks, Kate came to see that her illness did have a psychological basis. At the time she became sick, she was employed by the social services in an extremely demanding job looking after emotionally disturbed adolescents. Rather than admit the work was beginning to get the better of her, she used sickness as a way of taking time off. She desperately needed someone to look after her for a change, and illness offered a legitimate excuse to ask for this. When Neptune transits the sixth, health problems may be the catalyst through which we re-evaluate our lives, and arrive at a degree of psychological or spiritual understanding we previously didn't have.

Faith and attitude play a large part in the course of recovery from any illness, and this is especially crucial with Neptune transiting the sixth. If we want to live and believe we can be helped, our chances of returning to health are increased. If we are fed up with life, and have been told that there is no possible cure, we are more likely to give up and die. In *Love, Medicine and Miracles*, American surgeon Bernie Siegel reports on his experiences with patients who have participated in influencing the course of their illness and miraculously recovered from serious life-threatening diseases.[5] People with Neptune transiting the sixth, whether they are ill or not, would benefit from his insights.

Work is another area that Neptune affects when moving through this house. In some form, adjustment or sacrifice may be called for in this sphere. We might yearn for employment which offers greater fulfilment than what we are doing already, and yet our attempts to find such a job keep failing. Or we may be forced, probably for practical or financial reasons, to stay in a job we don't find totally satisfying. With Neptune moving through the sixth, we might have to accept a work situation we can't significantly alter, at least for the time being. But in doing so, Neptune could be teaching us one of its lessons: sometimes it is only when we give up trying to change things that a solution to our problem appears.

The element of sacrifice can make itself felt in relation to work in a number of other ways. Wherever Neptune transits, we may have to give more than we receive. We might be working very hard at a job which doesn't offer a fair remuneration. Or our work may involve having to live somewhere we wouldn't choose ourselves; or the job could be draining, so that our health and personal life suffers. This transit also means that we are more sensitive to the atmosphere and conditions at work. The job itself may not be secure, or we might be working under conditions of confusion and uncertainty. Co-workers could burden us with their problems, or look to us for help and support, and we might become very entangled in their lives unless we know where to draw our boundaries. Misunderstandings with employers, employees, or fellow workers could arise. We might be the victim of an employer's or co-worker's deceit, or scapegoated by people we work with. One woman with this transit was deeply hurt when another woman in her office wrongly accused her of stealing.

At certain times during this transit, we may find ourselves unable to cope with the ordinary and mundane practicalities of everyday life. Our daily routines seem incredibly boring or pointless; we want a more glamorous life, not the drudgery of cooking, dusting, and worrying about paying bills. Or we might find that even simple tasks become more complicated and difficult than usual. We take our car to the garage to be serviced, and it comes back in a worse condition than when we took it in. An *au pair* could let us down, and the milkman may charge us twice for the same delivery. And yet the transit of Neptune in the sixth also increases our capacity to perceive beauty in little, everyday things we might have overlooked before, a chance to discover the truth of the saying 'In every speck of dust, there are a million Buddhas.'

In spite of all the potential difficulties this transit can bring, it is possible for Neptune in the sixth to describe a period when we are absorbed in a job we find very fulfilling. In particular, this can be a good time for creative or artistic work, or for employment which involves caring for or helping others. In *Planets in Transit*, Robert Hand makes an interesting and valid point when he says that this transit is best used working in a field of social service looking after people in need, or employed in a hospital, prison or similar institution. Neptune has what he calls an 'ego-denying' effect: if, under this transit, you are in a job just for your own benefit – solely to bolster your ego or bank balance, for instance – you probably won't be happy or very successful. But if you are working with a spirit of service to others, then you are complying with Neptune's tendency to dissolve separateness, and you are acknowledging your connectedness with the rest of creation – which is the main thing Neptune wants to teach us.[6]

Seventh House

When Neptune transits the seventh, we will be changed through situations we encounter in the sphere of close partnerships. Some of these experiences will not be easy, but they offer the possibility of gaining greater self-awareness and increasing our insight into the realm of relationships in general. Even if we are already in a relationship, we could fall for someone new we meet at this time. But there are likely to be complications. We might not be perceiving this new person clearly. With transiting Neptune in the seventh, we may be looking for a god or a goddess – a knight in shining armour or the fair damsel of our dreams. We project an image of our ideal partner on to other people, and fail to see what they are really like. In the end, we will be disappointed when they turn out to be human, flawed or less than perfect. This doesn't have to mean the end of the relationship, but rather the end of our illusions about the other person. We can then begin the task of building the relationship on a more solid footing.

We will be attracted to 'Neptunian' types at this time, possibly falling for people who are deceptive and treacherous. They may not be this way intentionally, and yet they somehow involve us in a web of confusion and deceit. We could be drawn to someone with Neptune, Pisces, or the twelfth house strong in his or her natal chart, or a person who is experiencing an important Neptune transit. Planets transiting the seventh often mirror attributes and traits we are now ready to discover in ourselves or build into our own nature. In the case of Neptune, we may fall for an artist whose creativity we admire, and this is an indication we are ready to explore our own creative side. If a mystically inclined or religious person powerfully appeals to us, this means the time is appropriate to connect with the mystic in ourselves. If it is a deceitful person, then the time has come for us to examine more closely our own capacity to deceive and betray.

Victim/saviour relationships are common with this transit. We could become involved with people who need rescuing – alcoholics, drug addicts, or other confused and lost souls. A partner might be experiencing fairly severe emotional difficulties, or problems with health, money or work; whatever the case, they need our support, care and understanding. Sometimes this transit coincides with our falling in love with people who aren't free to commit themselves to us, or who are unable to love us back. We might have to make major sacrifices and adjustments for the sake of a relationship. While it may be appropriate to give a great deal to others at this time, we should be careful not to be foolishly altruistic and turned into a doormat – someone who too easily is walked over and abused. If we have been too selfish, intolerant and ungiving in the past, this transit asks that we become more flexible and less demanding. However, if we have repeatedly allowed others to take advantage of us, this transit will bring hard lessons which serve to teach us the necessity to draw firmer boundaries and to have more respect for our own rights and needs.

Transiting Neptune in the seventh is also a phase in which we might look to another person to save and redeem us – someone who will take our pain away and fulfil our deepest longings. Unconsciously, we are seeking the lost ideal mother or father, who will understand us perfectly, and always be there in every way we need. Unfortunately, no partner is capable of such a feat, and inevitably a time will come when we are let down and disillusioned. However, it is only when this happens that we can initiate the process of grieving for the lost ideal 'other', and begin to look inside our own selves for the kind of loving acceptance and understanding we have been seeking from a partner.

With Neptune transiting the seventh, we may be in a relationship which is far from ideal, and yet refuse to admit this is the case. We pretend everything is fine and try to present to the world the façade of a perfect partnership. But Neptune has an uncanny way of catching us out: unexpressed feelings bottle up, and eventually explode to cause a mess, or they turn inward and attack us in the form of ill health or depression. Neptune, like Pluto, is an underworld deity. As in the case of Pluto transiting the seventh, this is a period when we need to bring the frustrations we are feeling in a relationship to the surface so they can be faced and, we hope, resolved. This takes courage, and the willingness to admit that something is wrong in the first place. In the long run, it doesn't pay to deceive ourselves in the area of life being transited by Neptune.

If we over-idealize or over-romanticize relationships or another person at this time, Neptune sets traps to catch us out. However, it is possible to meet someone now with whom we have an uncanny psychic rapport and closeness. And yet, no matter how divinely ordained the union might seem, we will still have to make adjustments and compromises. Even true soul-mates might find themselves arguing over who's turn it is to do the washing up, or the proper way the toothpaste tube should be squeezed. With Neptune around, as much as we might hope otherwise, relationships do not arrive pre-packaged as perfect. I have come across people under this transit who have been so hurt and let down in a relationship that they have decided to give up the idea of marriage or close partnership altogether. Or for religious or spiritual reasons, some people decide to be celibate and focus primarily on their relationship with God. With Neptune transiting the seventh, we might believe, consciously or unconsciously, that giving up a relationship or making sacrifices in this area is a way of being spiritually cleansed or purified. It's worth recalling the story of the god Neptune who, dissatisfied with the rulership of his own watery domain, coveted the city of Attica belonging to Athene, goddess of wisdom, and threatened it with destruction by flooding. Such contradictory feelings of possessiveness and an urge to destroy what we cannot have may threaten our relationships unless we use Athenian judgement.

Sometimes this transit signifies the loss of a partner – through death, divorce, or some other form of separation, and if this occurs, Neptune is working through fate to teach us a lesson in non-attachment and letting go. We have been robbed of the happiness and fulfilment we once hoped the relationship would provide; we have been robbed of intimacy and can no longer 'lose' ourselves in someone else. Before we can forgive or come to terms with our loss, we must come to terms with feelings of abandonment; we have to mourn the person and dreams we have lost and we have to grieve for our old self which is dying – and we need to do this without permanently over-identifying with an image of ourselves as 'tragic' victims of fate, for ultimately grief must be left behind if we are to have a new life.

The seventh house describes more than just close personal relationships. Many astrologers associate this area of the chart (along with the eighth house) with business partnerships, and we should be careful of confusion, deception and misunderstandings in this sphere as well. The seventh is also linked to law courts: legal battles could be messy, complicated and drawn-out if undertaken at this time. More broadly, the seventh house describes something about our interaction with society in general – what we have to offer other people, and what they see in us. With Neptune transiting here, we are capable of expressing greater sensitivity and compassion with others. Artists, musicians, healers, counsellors, fashion designers, photographers, models or those involved in any other 'Neptunian' profession might find the public quite receptive to them at this time. However, because Neptune is also the planet of the victim and the scapegoat, this could be a period in which we become the focus of a public scandal, or find ourselves punished and admonished for qualities we exhibit which other people have difficulty accepting in themselves.

Eighth House

Neptune dissolves boundaries and separateness, and what better place to do this than the eighth house of sex, death, intimacy and sharing. Neptune can create confusion, deception or disappointment in any of these areas, and yet it also brings experiences of an inspiring, even ecstatic nature in relationships when transiting this house.

Exchanges between people – whether the currency is monetary, emotional or sexual – will be affected by any of the possible influences of Neptune. On a mundane level, this transit indicates a propensity towards misunderstandings in our transactions with other people. Any contractual arrangements we enter need to be made as clear as possible, otherwise we might discover that how we understand an agreement is quite different from the way another person understands it. At this time it is necessary to secure promises in writing and to read the fine print; this applies particularly to financial dealings, which could become confused. Neptune creates vagueness or gullibility – we don't see other people or situations clearly for what they are, and the wool could easily be pulled over our eyes now. We might be offered gifts or money from people whose motives appear honourable, but who are really trying to manipulate or control us in this way. Therefore, if possible, we should be quite careful in our choice of people with whom we do business. Wherever Neptune is transiting, we often unconsciously set ourselves up for a fall: unless we keep our eyes wide open and seek advice on our dealings from practically minded people we trust, we might walk right into a trap. Conversely, we might be tempted to try to fool others at this time. The eighth house is commonly called the house of other people's money, and is associated specifically with the finances and resources we share with another person (usually a marriage or business partner, or someone with whom we have a fairly close tie), and under this transit it pays to be scrupulous in the way we handle other people's money or resources. In issues to do with business, taxation, property or investment, honesty is indeed the best policy.

Alternatively, it could be that our partner might be experiencing financial problems, or a relationship we hoped would bring us material gain fails in that way. Difficulties and confusion over inheritances and legacies are not uncommon when Neptune is moving through this area of the chart. But concrete resources such as money or possessions are not the only kind of values described by the eighth: this house denotes a partner's value-system, what he or she believes in or holds dear. Neptune moving through the eighth renders us more open to what other people value or espouse. We may be so moved or won over by what others believe that we alter our own views or biases as a result. Or we could find ourselves in a situation which requires us to make concessions on behalf of others: our partner's values conflict with our own, and we are the one who ends up making the adjustments and compromises. In either case, Neptune in the eighth asks that we 'give up' something – our money, possessions, some of our beliefs or values – in the course of blending or merging with others. Because we are more susceptible to another person's influence at this time, we should try to be cautious about whom we put our faith in.

The eighth house describes how we die as an 'I' to be reborn as 'We': the kinds of issues we encounter when we attempt to be intimate or to fuse with another human being. In many ways, Neptune, which by nature is concerned with the dissolving of separateness and ego-boundaries, is at home in this area of the chart; and this transit not only can enhance our receptivity to others, but it also can make it easier for us to 'let ourselves go' in the process of merging or relating more closely with a partner. The sexual act is a profound exchange of energy between two people; it also is a way of fusing and merging with another. For these reasons, sex is associated with this house. Neptune transiting the eighth will influence our sexuality in various respects, all of which are in accord with the different levels or meanings of Neptune. Under this transit, sex can be the symbolic means by which we transcend the isolated self, either by losing ourselves in another person or by absorbing somebody else. Love and sex can be an escape, a way of abandoning or forgetting the self – we let go and give ourselves to another. Or sex is the area through which we abnegate personal responsibility and control: a partner captivates us, and we are carried away by a force more powerful than we can resist. With transiting Neptune in the eighth, sex also can be an expression of worship and reverence, a way of offering ourselves to somebody else. In certain cases under this transit, giving of the self sexually can be experienced as a form of service, or an attempt to please or heal others. The reverse is also true – loving sexual contacts could heal some of our emotional wounds at this time.

However, there are other levels of Neptune which affect sexuality during this transit. Some people experience confusion as to their true sexual identity or proclivities. Neptune's diffuse and fluid nature can make it hard for us to know exactly what it is we want or desire. By nature, Neptune yearns for greater fulfilment and ecstasy. During this period of our lives, sexual fantasies could increase both in amount and intensity, as if we are looking for something more satisfying and exciting than we already know or have. And yet, even if we succeed in finding and acting out our fantasies, we might be let down or disappointed; we still feel unfulfilled and left with an obsessive hunger that no amount of sexual activity is able to quell. If this is the case, we will need to examine what inner needs we are symbolically trying to fulfil through the act of sex, and look for other ways to satisfy or come to terms with those needs in us.

Under this transit, we may choose or feel compelled to make sacrifices in the area of sexuality. A relationship we are in might not satisfy us sexually in the way we would like and yet we choose to maintain it. Or, for any number of reasons, we could find ourselves forgoing or turning down a sexual relationship with someone to whom we are strongly attracted. Some people might decide to transcend libidinal desires altogether, for the sake of channelling these energies in other directions. In other words, giving up sex is seen as the path to God, a way of purifying or spiritually redeeming ourselves.

The transit can also bring experiences to do with death, another eighth-house concern. Again, Neptune's influence will vary: some of us with Neptune transiting here may try to escape from facing the reality of death, our own or someone else's. However, this transit offers the chance to deepen our understanding of death and the process of dying. Dr Elisabeth Kübler-Ross had Neptune transiting her eighth house throughout the decade of the 1960s, years in which she worked closely with terminally ill patients. Her book *On Death and Dying* was written and published during this period, and records her pioneering efforts to bring death out into the open and to ensure that dying people are treated with compassion and sensitivity.[7] Under this transit, we can give care and comfort to the dying, but they have just as much to give to us – insight into an experience we all sooner or later must go through. With Neptune transiting the eighth, we could learn to accept death, and in doing so, tremendously enrich our capacity for life and living.

More negatively, a death-wish or suicidal longing could be activated at some point during Neptune's transit of the eighth. We long for the peace of non-being and see death as a release, a respite from pain and the harsh realities of life within boundaries. Suicide is a complicated issue, made even more so with a transit of Neptune, the least clear-cut of all the planets, through this house. Faced with the kinds of horrors that accompany some terminal illnesses, suicide may be an act of courage, a rational choice to abandon and give up the physical body. However, in the majority of cases the desire to kill oneself when Neptune is moving through the eighth is not a desire to end one's life forever, but a desire to die *and* be reborn into a new or happier existence. Suicidal people with this transit need help to see that they are confused about what they really want: their goal isn't a physical death, but a psychological one. And with the right form of counselling or support, this can be achieved.*

Our sensitivity to undercurrents in the atmosphere increases under this transit. We more readily feel or register what is passing between people, even things not spoken or overtly expressed. For some, this can inspire an interest in psychology, or a desire to explore the mysterious and hidden dimensions of life through such subjects as the occult, esoteric philosophy or metaphysics. Our receptivity to intangible and non-material forces can operate constructively or destructively depending on the kinds of aspects transiting Neptune in the eighth is making to other planets in the chart. Most positively, we might receive – as if out of nowhere – helpful guidance and inspiration, which not only helps us in our own life, but can be of use to other people in times of crises. However, psychic openness can manifest in less pleasant ways: there may be times we feel gripped by forces or compulsions over which we have little conscious or rational control. We might interpret this as possession, the belief that we have been invaded by some psychic entity or that we have been taken over by another human being. Such cases as these may exist, but it is more likely that the overwhelming forces we feel now originate from our own unconscious minds. When Neptune transits

*The concept of psychological death is more fully discussed in chapter 8, p. 221.

the eighth, parts of our psychological make-up we would rather keep hidden or at bay seep through the barrier we have erected to keep them out. We haven't necessarily been taken over by disembodied spirits, poltergeists or other external agents, but by dispossessed parts of our own psyches. If we can find the right kind of psychological help at this time, we will be able to integrate more properly into our conscious awareness aspects of ourselves we have never been able to face before.

Ninth House

This transit activates the area of the chart associated with philosophy, travel and higher education. With Neptune moving through this house, we may be drawn to a religion, philosophy or belief system in the hope that it will be the means of our salvation: we put our faith in faith – if only we can find something to believe in, we feel we will be saved. While many people can have positive experiences along these lines, there are also certain problems and pitfalls which frequently accompany this transit.

Neptune could confuse us in our search for higher truths and principles by which to guide our lives: we yearn to merge with something greater than the self, often through a devotional adherence to a philosophy, religion, cult or guru. But, as usual when Neptune is around, we might not be discriminating enough about whom is to be trusted. Irresistibly attracted to anyone or anything that promises enlightenment and redemption, we could find ourselves involved with rather strange groups or sects. The main danger is giving too much power to those people leading these groups. If they tell us to believe or do something, then we do it, in the belief that they know best what we need. I have seen many cases of people with Neptune transiting the ninth who allowed themselves to be misled in this way, and have been psychologically damaged as a result. Even if friends we normally trust warn us against such involvements, Neptune's capacity to engender passionate feelings (perhaps even a Dionysian desire for dismemberment) makes it difficult for us not to be carried away or taken in by charismatic figures when it is transiting this house. Putting our faith in a guru or cult and then being disappointed or disillusioned may be an unavoidable or even necessary lesson under this transit.

Of course, not everyone will become entangled with charlatans or frauds. There are many gurus and teachers with a great deal of integrity, who have much to offer people exploring a spiritual path. The problem may not be the guru or group itself, but our own mishandling and distortion of the teaching. With Neptune in the ninth we could become fanatic or obsessive about a religion or belief-system. We might believe that the truth we have found is the answer to everything for everyone, or we could fall prey to the 'buddha disease', and emulate our guru or teacher to such a degree that we only eat, think, say and do those things that he or she does. We mistakenly believe that imitating an enlightened being is the way to become one. However, there is a flaw in this way of thinking. Acting in the way we believe a realized being would act doesn't make us enlightened. Consciousness is not the by-product of behaviour. When our consciousness changes, then our behaviour will naturally change. It doesn't work the other way around.

A philosophy we embrace when Neptune is transiting our ninth could entail some form of sacrifice or relinquishment. In order to find God, we feel we have to give up something – our ego or separateness, our possessions, or anything to which we are overly attached. Our image of the deity will probably be coloured by Neptune: God is seen as caring and compassionate, and someone who can be found through devotion, love and prayer, not through intellectual arguments or discourses.

At some point during this transit confusion could set in over what we believe. The dissolving effect of Neptune may mean that a philosophy or world view we once counted on and respected could let us down, or no longer seem valid. As a result, we are left adrift, unsure of what to believe in or how to guide our lives. We might experiment with different philosophies, hoping that one of them will be able to replace what we have lost, but repeatedly find ourselves disappointed. We need to take time to grieve for our lost beliefs, and to mourn illusions about ourselves and life in general which need to be let go of now. Ultimately, under this transit, we may have no choice but to exist temporarily in a state of uncertainty and not-knowing, until the time comes when we formulate or discover a new way to give meaning to existence. But even this 'un-knowing' may ultimately be felt as something akin to a state of grace: with no illusions, no need to verify one's faith or to have it demonstrated by logic or experience, we may approach life unburdened by pre-conceived philosophical notions and expectations.

Neptune also will influence travel at this time. Under this transit, some people embark on a pilgrimage to places which hold special importance for them. If transiting Neptune is not making too many difficult aspects, we are likely to discover places abroad that we find enchanting or captivating. This is usually a good time to absorb another culture, and we might be drawn to living in a foreign country. However, a stressful transit of Neptune in the ninth inclines to deception and disappointment in travel: a holiday might let us down, and work out completely different from how we hoped or expected. Unless we learn to keep our eyes wide open, we could be the victim of treachery or deceit while travelling.

Generally, transiting Neptune in this house opens the mind and inspires the imagination. We become concerned with what Maslow called 'the farther reaches of human nature'. We yearn to realize and expand our potential, and enrol on courses or training which promise greater fulfilment and self-actualization. This can be a good transit during which to pursue an in-depth study of healing, medita-tion, philosophy, religion, metaphysics, painting, music, dance, the theatre, film, photography, chemistry, or other related 'Neptunian' topics. However, difficultly aspected Neptune transits in the ninth can create confusion about what direction to take in life, and an uneasy uncertainty about our future. These feelings could manifest in the sphere of higher education: students applying to colleges when Neptune is making a hard ninth-house transit may experience the disappointment of not being accepted by the school of their choice. We might be confused about what course of study to follow, or find ourselves disillusioned about or unfulfilled by an educational institution or system. One way or another we meet Neptune in the halls of academia: we fall in love with a married professor or run into problems with drugs or alcohol. The entire duration of this transit could be a period when our view of life and our future swings from extremes of ecstatic optimism to utter despair. And somewhere in between these swings, we might discover a truer sense of our potential, and a deeper understanding of the nature of reality.

On a more mundane level, the ninth house is associated with in-laws. Neptune here may ask that we make compromises, sacrifices or adjustments on their behalf, especially if they are experiencing difficult passages in their lives. However, as always with Neptune, it is wise to know where and when to set our boundaries.

Tenth House

While Neptune is in the tenth house (especially when it first crosses from the ninth into the tenth), we may go through a period during which we are confused about what we are doing with our lives. We're no longer sure who we are and what we really want. Should we stay on our old path, or follow a new one? What new one should we choose? What is our true vocation or calling? Taking time now to engage in some serious reflection about ourselves, our ambitions, and what it is we want from life, is a constructive way to use this transit. It may help to seek the guidance of a careers advisor, someone who is trained to assist people examine these kinds of issues.

Neptune transiting the tenth often expresses itself in dissatisfaction with our existing work. We crave something more exciting and fulfilling; we want to go after our dreams rather than settle for what we already have. The time may be right to give up one form of work for the sake of another, but we need to examine carefully the new direction we want to take in order to be sure of its plausibility. With Neptune in the tenth, there could be the danger that we are fantasizing about career possibilities that are truly impractical, unrealistic or beyond our reach. However, if our aims and goals are within reason, then it is appropriate now to let go of our old work, and begin the process of concretely realizing our new ambitions.

Neptune doesn't only signify delusion and uncertainty: it also brings idealism and passion. Some of us could feel a calling at this time – a vision of what we are here on this planet to do. We are drawn towards a particular line of work which excites and arouses us emotionally. For some people, this could be an artistic or theatrical career, or work in film, photography, fashion and even politics. Or we are inspired to pursue a profession which involves helping and caring for others: social work, nursing, and other forms of healing or counselling. We may be pulled towards a religious vocation or a career as a meditation or yoga teacher. We need a career we believe in, work that satisfies deep yearnings within us. However, under this transit, we need to examine our motives. In whatever house Neptune is moving through, we could be driven by a desire for glamour and recognition. Is a career in the arts enticing us mainly because of the glamour associated with these professions? Is the idea of being a therapist, counsellor or healer appealing because of the power and image it bestows on us? Are we choosing a career because we think it's impressive and we like how it will sound when we tell others what we do?

In this house, Neptune can stir delusions of grandeur. If we are seeking a career primarily for the sake of aggrandizing our worth in our own or other people's eyes, we are likely to encounter difficulties under this transit. Ultimately, Neptune's task is to dissolve, not inflate, the rigid boundaries of the ego. In some form, when Neptune transits the tenth, our work ideally can be a means of transcending our sense of isolation and separateness. In the end, the kind of job we are doing is less important than the spirit with which we do it. Undoubtedly, some desire for personal recognition and success will be present in most work we undertake, but it is the degree to which this motivates us that is the crucial deciding factor when Neptune is transiting the tenth. If aspiring artists are primarily seeking fame and fortune, Neptune – the ego-dissolver – is more likely to frustrate their overtly egotistical ambitions. However, if artists are more concerned with acting as mediums through which ideas and images can flow and find concrete expression, the presence of Neptune in the tenth will aid them in this process.

Probably no action is completely altruistic. When we help or take care of others, we may do it for reasons of compassion, but there are likely to be other more personal reasons as well – the need to be needed, for instance, or the apparent control over pain (ours or someone else's). If, when Neptune transits our tenth, we are drawn to the helping professions, it is advisable to examine all the different levels of motivation that exist inside us. If our ego is too wrapped up in our work, we will encounter many problems in our job at this time.[8]

Setbacks and sacrifices in the area of career often accompany this transit of Neptune. Our ego might be denied the affirmation it seeks or deserves, which could occur when we work hard at something for which we receive inadequate recognition or remuneration. Initially, at least, we may have to give more than we get back in return. We could experience ego-deflating disappointments at work, such as a colleague being chosen for a promotion rather than us. A boss or employer may be going through a difficult or chaotic time which makes demands on our patience and understanding, or the job itself might be in some kind of jeopardy. For some people, this transit may coincide with the loss of work, perhaps through redundancy. This can be devastating, not only for financial reasons, but also because losing a job means forfeiting the identity and sense of worth the work has given us. Being made redundant can evoke anger and outrage. We may not be able to understand why this had to happen to us. Again we meet the dissolving effect of Neptune, which asks that we relinquish an existing sense of self so that something new can be born. It is frightening when our life falls apart in this way, and yet falling apart can be the first phase in a process of building ourselves anew.

Older people may have to face retirement under this transit. Like redundancy, retirement can entail a great sense of loss: it strips us of an identity; it deprives us of a workplace where we had a chance to meet and interact with others; it robs us not only of a salary, but also of a source of self-worth and a way of proving our competence. Even if we use our newly gained free time to explore various hobbies or to take trips around the world, we still can be left feeling useless and unnecessary. And yet, if approached in the right way, old age and retirement can be a productive and fulfilling time of life.*

The tenth house also describes our public standing, and how we

---

*Issues around retirement are also discussed on p. 73.

are seen by others. For some of us, this transit could mark a period in which we are idealized and worshipped by segments of the populace. Something about us captures the collective's imagination and interest, or we become the living embodiment of a movement or force sweeping through parts of society. Musicians, artists, fashion designers, actors and actresses, politicians, social prophets and reformers could find themselves in the limelight when Neptune is transiting their tenth. Even if we enjoy the fame and attention, handling this situation may not be easy. Our personal lives become food for public consumption, and we could feel robbed of our privacy and peace. Or the adulation we are receiving might distort our ego out of all proportion; and when this happens, Neptune will not be far away, construing some means of toppling us off our pedestal. In a few cases, this transit also could coincide with a period in which we are the focus of a scandal, or we end up assuming the role of a public scapegoat or outcast. It's not a good time to engage in anything illegal or dishonest – Neptune has a way of catching us out, no matter how clever we think we're being.

Aside from career issues, the tenth house is associated with our mother or father, describing the parent who has exerted the biggest influence on our socialization – that is, the one who has done the most to prepare us to meet and fit into society. (Usually this is the mother, but the tenth may apply in some cases to the father.)* If we take the tenth to mean the mother, this transit indicates that we will encounter Neptune in some way through her. She may be facing physical, psychological, or material difficulties in her life, or experiencing a phase of increased religious or creative inspiration. She might legitimately need our help or support, but she also could be making impossible demands which drain or anger us. As usual with Neptune, we have to reconsider what boundaries are appropriate; with a demanding mother, for example, it may be appropriate to be there for her in the way she needs, but it's also wise to recognize the limits of our duty or patience, rather than totally sacrifice our personal lives on her behalf. Conversely, this transit could indicate a time

*See chapter 5, note 5.

when we look to her to save or redeem us in some way. In certain instances, transiting Neptune in the tenth might coincide with her death. A time, in other words, when we have to let her go.*

Eleventh House

When Neptune is transiting the eleventh house, we experience phases of uncertainty and confusion about our life-goals and objectives. This is because our ideals are changing – the vision of what we hope to gain or achieve in our lives is in flux. Existing ideals seem too narrow, too circumscribed, and thus lose their validity or power. Until a new set of ideals can be formulated, we are adrift, not knowing what to believe in or hope for. Given time, the uncertainty will pass and we will emerge from it with a renewed sense of vision or purpose, not only for ourselves, but possibly for the whole planet as well.

Most of us have a skin-encapsulated identity – we define ourselves by the boundary of our skin. What is inside the skin is us; what is outside is not us. But we also define ourselves by what we own, by our job, by a relationship or marriage we might be in, by children we produce, by our religious beliefs, etc. In other words, our individual identity is expanded to include things beyond the borders of our physical body. With Neptune transiting the eleventh, it's possible to take this even further so that we transcend our ego and separateness through identifying ourselves with a group of people or with all of humanity itself. We might even glimpse what the mystics describe as our oneness with the rest of life, a deep interconnection with others which extends beyond traditional ties of church, state or family.

Einstein spoke of 'widening our circle of compassion to embrace all living creatures'.[9] Will Durant, a historian and philosopher, expressed something similar when he wrote: 'the meaning of life lies in the chance it gives us to produce, or contribute to something

---

*See p. 261 for a discussion of the issues raised by a parent's death. See also Suggested Reading (p. 386) for a list of books on death and the grieving process.

greater than ourselves'.[10] Rather than being concerned solely with our personal needs and requirements, we can support and promote the needs of humanity, especially those segments of the population we feel are ill-treated or misunderstood. Transiting Neptune in the eleventh, in one of its broadest manifestations, promotes this kind of altruism and concern for others: it inspires a utopian vision so that we are motivated to join groups promoting humanitarian, social or spiritual causes. We want to join with others to bring our idea of truth, justice or beauty to the world, and it could be a period when we give of our time and of ourselves to promulgate ideals which we believe will benefit the planet.

Such causes and ideals may be noble and can achieve many positive effects. However, when Neptune is involved, we could be carried away with our beliefs and visions. We also might put our faith in something which later lets us down or doesn't deliver what it first promised. To make matters worse, Neptune brings with it a tendency to proselytize, an emotional certainty that what we see as the truth is what others also need. We lose ourselves in a cause; we fly too high. Neptune is paradoxical: it inclines us to such flights of emotion and feeling, but if we go too far, it will at some point stick a trident in our bubble and bring us back down to earth. What goes up must come down. Many astrologers will warn us of the dangers of this kind of Neptunian inflation, and advise that we avoid going over the top in any eleventh-house concern at this time. This is sound counsel, and yet there is still much we can learn from making the 'mistake' of getting carried away. Yes, we are in danger of going too high and then landing flat on our face, but the whole experience may enable us to mature and 'grow up' in a way which wouldn't have been possible otherwise.

However noble or ill-conceived our notions might be, not all of us will use the transit to embark on the path of redeeming humanity. There are many other ways Neptune can be experienced via the eleventh-house issue of groups. We could be drawn to secret sects and societies, to artistic groups, or to spiritualist and psychic circles. Or we look to a group for our own redemption and salvation, as if through the experience of participating in it we will be cleansed and purified. We could be let down by a group, or make sacrifices on its behalf – we give our money and time away to causes, or abandon other activities in order to attend meetings or follow a particular group's code of conduct. Group involvement may be a way of escaping from problems in other areas of our life which need attention. There is a temptation to lose oneself in a group, or to become caught up in a social whirl, seeking 'glamorous' friends who bolster our image and sense of self-worth, thus deriving our sense of identity from the group rather than from within.

This transit will be experienced through issues around friends and friendship. Manifesting itself most positively, Neptune here could indicate friends who are supportive, caring and there when we really need them, or friends who broaden our horizons and open us to new visions and goals. Likewise, our capacity to help and nurture associates will be enhanced. However, if we are repeatedly looking to friends to save and rescue us, we will not only tax their patience, but also fail to develop within ourselves the qualities we need to deal with our own problems. Conversely, under this transit, friends may want us to be their rescuer, or we may make it our mission to 'save' them in some way. As usual with Neptune, we need to examine any hidden personal motives which are contributing to our taking on this role. Is saving others the only way we feel worthy of friendship? What kind of power does this position give us? What is it we want to 'cure' in them or rescue them from, and why does it bother us so much?

At times during this transit, we may have some difficulty finding a group we feel comfortable in or friends with whom we fit. In general, new friends we attract now will reflect the qualities of Neptune – they may have Pisces, Neptune, or the twelfth house strong in their natal chart. They may be artists, healers, dreamers, or involved in any of the professions and interests associated with Neptune. During this period, old or new friends could be undergoing significant Neptune transits – they might be experiencing physical, psychological or material difficulties, or opening to artistic or mystical inspiration. This transit also makes us more susceptible to the influence of friends and groups in general. Their influence may be constructive, introducing us to useful new activities or ways of behaving, but under this transit it is just as easy to abnegate personal responsibility for our actions and be swept along by the crowd into forms of behaviour that are negative and destructive. In whatever house or sphere of life Neptune takes over, discernment and clear-sightedness are not the rules of the day. If at all conceivable, we should be discriminating in our choice of friends or groups at this time. If not, Neptune may have some hard lessons to teach us.

When Neptune moves through the eleventh, we might have the experience of being betrayed, let down or abandoned by friends. In other words, our ideals of comradeship are not met. Sometimes a friend may act in a way that is unforgivable, and we will feel we have no other choice but to call off the relationship. However, if we repeatedly find ourselves blaming friends for not living up to our expectations, perhaps it is our expectations themselves that need to be examined, let go of or modified. If we believe a friend should share all our tastes, goals and passions, we are asking too much of friendship. If we insist that a friend should feel only absolute love and trust for us, we are expecting too much from that person (or any human being, for that matter). On one level, friends will rejoice in our achievements and successes; but at the same time, they secretly or unconsciously might feel envious of our good fortune. They want to hear of our triumphs, but another part of them could feel competitive and resent our being happier or more successful than they are. With Neptune transiting the eleventh, friends whom we hoped would 'fit' us perfectly could let us down; or they might admit to or display the 'darker', negative emotions they have for us – feelings we may not believe should accompany friendship. Rather than always ending the relationship in these cases, Neptune could be asking that we let go of the unrealistic expectations we put on friendship, and learn instead greater forgiveness and acceptance of others.

In some cases under this transit, we will lose friends, perhaps through death. As with any death, we will need time to acknowledge and accept the loss, and to be with the grief, anger or guilt associated with it. If we have the opportunity to be close to a dying friend, Neptune's influence in this house indicates that we may be able to ease or help our friend with this transition. What we gain from this kind of experience not only will teach us a great deal about death and dying, about surrender and faith, but also about life and living as well.

No matter how hard we try to pursue them, some of our aims in life could continually elude us during this transit, and we may be forced to recognize that certain of our goals and expectations are unrealistic or improbable. Childhood dreams of wealth, fame, and fairy-tale romances that last forever may have to give way to more realistic ideals that are within our capacity to achieve. Even if we do actualize many of these wishes, we will still feel vaguely dissatisfied. With Neptune transiting this house, we put our faith in our dreams: 'If I could have this or that, then I would be complete.' Rarely, however, can the kind of fulfilment Neptune seeks be completely satisfied, certainly not by anything external – be it material wealth, a loved one, or noble principles and causes. That lost feeling of wholeness we all seek to regain does exist, but it can't be found by searching for it outside ourselves. It can only be found within.

Twelfth House

The twelfth is Neptune's natural house, and this transit can be very powerful, describing a period when we are more than usually sensitive not only to forces operating in our unconscious, but also to feelings and undercurrents in the atmosphere around us.

In whatever house Neptune is transiting, we are drawn into the spectrum of life represented by that domain, and we feel (sometimes not consciously) that our redemption, renewal or wholeness will come through the affairs of that house. In the case of the twelfth, this can mean we become fascinated by or are drawn into the workings of our unconscious mind and what is going on inside us. We feel a pull to look inward, both to understand ourselves better and to find greater fulfilment in our lives. The motivation to reflect more deeply on ourselves and life in general could be prompted by a growing sense of dissatisfaction with our present existence. We might have achieved a great deal materially in the world, but a nagging sense of incompleteness tells us that there is more to life. Even those of us who have been engaged in a fair amount of self-analysis or self-examination may feel under this transit that we are ready to explore the psyche more thoroughly than ever before.

Transiting Neptune in the twelfth stirs deep feelings: the emotions it brings out exert such a strong force that we will have difficulty resisting or denying them. One of Neptune's objectives in this house is to overwhelm the ego and our existing sense of self – to break down the control we have over what we allow into conscious awareness. Obviously, many of us will find this threatening, because we have little choice but to accept and go with emotions and feelings which we were previously able to manage or keep at bay. In this sense, we become a victim to our own unconscious: hitherto buried or curtailed drives and urges gather power and engulf us in such a way that they can no longer be denied or excluded. To many people, this will feel as if they are being swept away by uncontrollable inner forces and compulsions – an especially frightening state of affairs for those who have always kept themselves tightly held together. Some people might believe they have been taken over and possessed by evil spirits.* But there will be others who experience Neptune transiting the twelfth as the breakthrough they have been waiting for, a welcomed chance to gain deeper insights into their own nature.

However we feel about it, the floodgates are open. What do we do? We can try to resist Neptune and re-exert even tighter controls over ourselves, but such efforts are not likely to prove successful. Night time dreams and daytime fantasies will persist all the same, reminding us of those parts of ourselves we are trying to forget. So much energy can go into denying what we are feeling that there is little left with which to live our lives. It is wiser and more productive to co-operate and work constructively with this transit through some form of counselling, therapy, spiritual guidance or self-exploration which will facilitate and give meaning to what the psyche is trying to make happen. Whether we like it or not, Neptune is heading towards our ascendant and we are on the edge of major psychological change and renewal. New growth demands that an old self is shed.

Transiting Neptune in the twelfth reveals what is hidden in us so that we can attend to aspects of our psyche we have previously ignored. Neptune, the planet which knows no boundaries, asks that

*This topic is discussed more fully on p. 202 in the section on transiting Neptune through the eighth house.

we treat *all* of ourselves with compassion and non-judgmental love, even those parts of our nature we have banished because we believed them evil or wrong. In the name of psychological growth and honesty, all of what is inside us needs to be accepted. Negative and destructive urges may now float to the surface of our awareness, and these can be distressing to acknowledge and experience. While such feelings don't have to be acted upon or expressed openly, they do need to be examined and faced for what they are: they are part of us, just as much as our arms and legs are a part of us. We cannot transform or resolve anything we condemn or deny in ourselves.

At this time, we need to have faith in the wisdom of our unconscious. This does not necessarily entail exhibiting every urge or whim bubbling up from inside, but it does mean listening to and acknowledging what we are feeling. Under this transit, we might have certain intuitions and impulses which, if followed, affect us in ways we might not have imagined. The urge to pursue a particular course of study, to contact somebody we haven't seen in a while, or to visit certain places, may be messages from the unconscious directing us towards experiences which unexpectedly benefit ourselves or others. The unconscious is smarter than we may believe. Even supposed mishaps or slip-ups could turn out to be the intervention via the unconscious of a 'higher intelligence' which has our well-being in mind. We leave the house, realize we have left something behind, and go back to find the telephone ringing with some urgent or timely news that we would have missed if we hadn't returned just at that moment.

Hidden in all of us is the urge to reconnect to a lost unity and oneness with the rest of life which we unconsciously remember as having experienced somewhere in the past. Mystics call it 'divine homesickness' – the longing to find God or return to our source. Psychologists might label it the desire to restore the blissful symbiosis we once felt with mother, when we were one with her and she was the whole world to us. However it is understood, this transit stirs a longing for wholeness and harmony with something greater than ourselves, something beyond the lonely boundaries of our isolated ego.

As Judith Viorst explains in her book *Necessary Losses*, restoring this connection may be an act of sickness or one of health.[11] We might seek that boundless place through alcohol, drugs, various forms of escapist behaviour, or ultimately through suicide (literally the destruction of the separate-self). Or we look for it in 'healthier' ways, through meditation, prayer, religion, art, or through communion with nature. We hope to regain our lost paradise in love and in the sexual act, where we lose ourselves and merge with another. And yet, that same quest for cosmic union is not dissimilar to some forms of schizophrenia and madness – a childish blurring of reality, or the failure to establish clear boundaries between ourselves and the rest of the world. When Neptune transits the twelfth, any of these ways to heal the primal wound of lost unity may be sought. Some are more positive than others, and it helps to be conscious of our true goal. If we are aware that transcending our separate and fragmented existence is the goal we are seeking, we can embark consciously on a constructive path to arrive there, rather than inadvertently taking the more haphazard routes, by which we risk destroying our health, our sanity or ourselves in the process.

Transcending separateness also means a greater sensitivity to what those around us are feeling or experiencing – especially people in need or suffering pain. Their plight will touch us and in some way resonate with our own wounds and vulnerability. This kind of receptivity might entice us into work, paid or otherwise, which involves caring and helping others. Or we could become identified with and swept into collective struggles for social reform – such things as campaigning for nuclear disarmament, working for an AIDS charity, or fighting for animal rights. Even though we probably are motivated primarily by genuine social concern, altruism or compassion, we should examine other more personal reasons why service of this sort appeals at this time. There can be a glamour attached to being the kind of person who rescues or fights for others, or it may be the only way we can feel we have any worth or power. Serving others also could be a means of assuaging some deep-seated guilt left over from childhood and early life, which needs to be examined and better understood for what it is. The discovery of personal motivations needn't deter us from such undertakings; on the contrary, an awareness of all the charged psychological reasons why we are drawn to causes and crusades can help us achieve our larger aims more cleanly and effectively. Under this transit, however, we should bear in mind that we are more easily invaded or drained by people and environments with whom we come into contact. Accordingly, we may need more time on our own in order to cleanse ourselves of the 'psychic smog' which we have absorbed and accumulated from our interaction with the world.

The twelfth house is associated with institutions (hospitals, day-care centres, orphanages, prisons, libraries, museums, charitable organizations, etc.). When Neptune transits this house, we will meet any of the levels of Neptune through this sphere of life. How this happens can vary. On the negative side, we might encounter mal-treatment in our dealings with such places: we feel inadequately cared for in a hospital, or end up a victim of bureaucratic confusion and red tape. And yet, with Neptune here, an involvement with an institution (either as an inmate or as a worker) could yield positive experiences of an inspirational or healing nature. Generally, the kinds of aspects transiting Neptune is making to the rest of the chart will be some indication of how we fare in this respect.

When Neptune transits the twelfth, unresolved issues from earlier in our life (or from past lives) could come back to haunt us. Old resentments and hurts reappear, sometimes disguised in the form of new conflicts and crises, sometimes through recurring dreams or memories. In some cases, the actual people associated with an earlier trauma or period of pain in our lives turn up on our doorstep or cross our path again. The good news is that Neptune in the twelfth can ultimately have a cleansing effect on the psyche, enabling us to feel the kind of love, understanding and forgiveness needed to make peace with people and events from our past, or with parts of ourselves. We can surrender to these feelings of reconciliation as a prelude to our new life which will occur when Neptune crosses the ascendant.

PART FOUR

Pluto Transits

8

Plutonian Crises

So long as you do not die and rise again,
You are a stranger to the dark earth.

GOETHE

People tend to be afraid of Pluto transits, and they have a right to be, for we are dealing here with the god of death, whose domain is the dark and shadowy underworld. Transiting Pluto often brings us painfully into contact with death. In some cases this can mean a literal death – our own or that of someone close to us – but more usually these transits correspond to psychological deaths or 'ego-deaths': the death of a part of us, the death of ourselves as we know ourselves.

Most of us establish and bolster our identity through attaching ourselves to things that give us a sense of who we are. The people with whom we associate, the person we marry, the work we do, the money in our bank account, the children we produce, the religion or philosophy to which we adhere – all these are used to help shape and support identity.

In the course of development, we also come to form opinions or beliefs about ourselves and about life 'out there', and these 'scripts' or 'life-statements', as they are sometimes called, also contribute to our sense of identity. One person's script may be 'I am able to achieve what I want'; another person's statement about life may be 'I always lose.' One life-statement could be: 'The world is a safe place I can trust', while another could be 'The world is dangerous and out to destroy me.' We derive our psychological identity not only through relationships or a job, a vocation or a talent, but also through these kinds of statements and beliefs about life and about ourselves. They are part of our personal mythology, and, more to the point, may be unconscious and therefore unchallenged. Under a Pluto transit, any of the 'props' from which we derive our identity could collapse or irretrievably break down, for with Pluto there is no going back, no return to innocence. Psychological deaths of this sort are not infrequent: we have all experienced the end of 'chapters' in our lives, the end of a phase or career or important friendship – the death of ourselves as we have known ourselves. With Pluto, however, such pain may also bring to the surface much darker emotions – rage, a dreadful sense of humiliation – forcing us to look at the ferocity with which we cling to things. Even giving up negative attachments – a bad relationship, an unsatisfying job, or a 'loser' script – demands that we acknowledge how great is our sense of loss, and requires major readjustments in our life. We may be perfectly aware that letting go of an unfulfilling or destructive partnership is the best thing we could do – we may spend years in psychotherapy attempting to transform negative patterns brought over from childhood – and yet we still feel a sense of loss and a reluctance to free ourselves of these attachments. Intellectually we may know that we will be reborn and that the changes are positive, but we still experience the death of our attachments as frightening and painful.

Blessed are those who mourn, and especially those who learn that mourning involves not only grief and sadness, but also anger or guilt we might feel about our loss. We might be angry because something we relied on is deserting us, or we are angry at ourselves for not having let go of an outworn part of our lives sooner. We might feel guilty or responsible for having caused the death of someone or something which has passed away, or guilty because the changes we go through hurt or disrupt others around us. In order to ease our death and rebirth process, we need humility and patience and to give time to all the feelings engendered by loss, for only then can we be fully open to the new unknown 'I' that is wanting to be born. There is no way to avoid grief, and no easy way to mourn: especially under Pluto transits do we learn that any attempted 'heroic' struggle or wilful assertion against it only deepens our anguish. The ego – our sense of a 'me-in-here' – tries to preserve those internal or external attachments which give it a sense of stability and solidity. The ego is not interested in its own destruction. Pluto, however, the god of the underworld, represents a force that operates from beneath the surface level of consciousness – a force inimical to the ego's efforts at self-preservation. Pluto symbolizes a part of our own psyche that unconsciously 'sets up' or attracts situations through which we fall apart, not simply because it is 'malefic'. Pluto does tear us down, but it does so for a purpose: in order that we can be rebuilt in a new way. Transiting Pluto may well create pain, crisis or difficulty, but it does so in the name of growth and needed change.

Our true and deepest nature, although unrecognized in most of us, is unbounded and infinite.* If we derive our identity mainly through 'props' – whether things or people – or if we overly identify with a particular belief-system or one overriding self-image, transiting Pluto may disrupt these attachments and identifications. And it does this in order to help us re-identify ourselves in a broader and more inclusive way. The house or planet transiting Pluto is affecting shows the areas of life in which attachments are being torn down and restructured. For example, if transiting Pluto is making an aspect to natal Jupiter or moving through the ninth house, it will challenge an existing world view or philosophy to which we have been overly attached or may severely disrupt the direction of our education. In this way Pluto reminds us that our true identity is not contingent on any particular perspective on life.

Images of Scorpio

Scorpio, co-ruled by Pluto, is a complex sign, for unlike the majority of the other signs which generally have one symbol – Aries the Ram, Taurus the Bull, Gemini the Twins, etc., – Scorpio has a number of different representations: the scorpion, the snake, the eagle and the phoenix. Scorpio, moreover, is much more than just one sign of the zodiac, where your Sun, Venus, Mars or ascendant might be, but also represents a principle or facet of life which we are all subject to: the cyclic process of change, decay, death and renewal. The different

*See section entitled 'Oneness and Separateness', chapter 6, pp 114–17.

images associated with this sign illustrate the kinds of deaths and transformations which are part of a universal evolutionary process; they also illuminate the ways in which Pluto acts as an attachment-breaker.

The lowest level of Scorpio is symbolized by the snake – a reptile which regularly sheds an old skin for a new one – and by the scorpion, the animal with the deadly sting in its tail. People dominated by this feeling-level of Scorpio act almost exclusively from their own emotions and desires: they are totally at the mercy of their moods, and express themselves in a way which is vehement, instinctive and primitive. When they're feeling good, they couldn't be nicer to people. When they're feeling miserable or nasty, no one is safe – not even their closest friend. This level or phase of Scorpio (which some people never outgrow) is described in an old story about the meeting of a scorpion and a frog.

The story begins at the side of a lake the scorpion wants to cross. He asks the frog if he wouldn't mind giving him a ride on his back to the other shore, and the frog – hesitant – says: 'I'll give you a ride across the lake, but you must promise not to sting me.' To which the slightly offended scorpion replies: 'Of course not; why would I do a thing like that?' The scorpion mounts the frog's back, and they start their journey. Halfway across the lake, however, the scorpion stings the frog. As they both sink to their deaths, the frog asks 'Why did you do that? – you promised me you wouldn't.' With its last breath the scorpion answers: 'Because I felt like it.' There are people who act like this scorpion and sting because they feel like it. That is, they are compulsively dominated by their moods and instinctive responses to life, and can suddenly turn against people to whom they have been close, or destroy structures in their lives that have been supporting and bolstering their identity. They may attack for any number of reasons – revenge, anger, a need for change and new growth, or sometimes purely for the sake of excitement if life has become dull. Sometimes in the process they destroy themselves as well – and sometimes they even *know* this risk and seem to court destruction in a perverse exercise of will.

However, the death of the scorpion in the water is also symbolic of a potential transformation and renewal. Lower-level Scorpions can die and be reborn on to another level – that of the eagle. People on this second level of Scorpio are not identified solely with their emotions or whatever they happen to be feeling at a particular time, but instead derive their identities and their sense of meaning and purpose in life from something outside themselves: a relationship, a cause or project in which they are involved, or a philosophy or vision that excites them. They will serve their loved one or their cause with admirable single-mindedness, dedication and vitality. Like the eagle who flies higher and sees farther than any other bird, and is a deadly hunter, people who have attained this eagle-level of Scorpio usually possess lofty principles and ideals but still retain their deadly sting. Should anything threaten what they value or believe in, the eagle-level Scorpion will swoop down and attack, perhaps even viciously destroy, its opponent. Clearly, the main problem with people at this stage of Scorpio is their intensity. They may be serving noble sentiments such as truth, justice or love, or worthwhile ideals which promote the welfare of humanity, but they pursue their aims with such passion and in such a focused manner that they lose sight of everything else. They become so absorbed in the object of their devotion that they forget their true nature is unbounded and infinite, or they burn themselves out from righteous indignation or from the superhuman physical demands they impose upon themselves. A further stage of growth – another ego-death – is needed, and this is when the phoenix may be born.

The phoenix was a mythical Egyptian bird. It was consumed by fire, but then rose out of the ashes to live again: it thus became a symbol of immortality. People who resonate with the eagle-level of Scorpio may find that the passion of a significant relationship 'burns itself out'; or a cause in which they have so fervently believed exhausts them or proves false. When this happens, it feels to them as if they themselves have been annihilated. Like the phoenix, they are reduced to ashes and may remain in that state for some time before rising renewed out of the cinders. When we attach ourselves to something – no matter how noble or transcendent – we limit our identity and forget that our true nature is unbounded and infinite. In the process of growing towards greater wholeness, we have to let go of our attachments in order to learn that who we really are is that part of us which remains when everything else we thought we were is taken away. By transit, Pluto represents a force which tears down our ego-identities until we discover our essence, the transpersonal Self, the eternal and universal core of our being. This is a difficult lesson, which transiting Pluto will bring to us again and again by bringing us to our knees. We can still have and enjoy relationships, beliefs, causes or ideals; but we must remember that our true and most basic identity is not dependent on any of these things.

Images of Descent

Pluto's domain was the underworld and, in psychological terms, the underworld is synonymous with the unconscious. The ego is the centre of consciousness, the centre of what we are aware of or identified with in ourselves. However, beyond the ego level of aware-ness lies the unconscious – all those attributes and elements of our being which we have not yet contacted or integrated. The nature of life is to move towards wholeness, and Pluto serves this drive by breaking down the boundaries and attachments of the ego and forcing us to recognize those parts of ourselves that the ego has excluded from consciousness. We have discussed how Pluto acts to put us in touch with our universality and unboundedness – some-thing to which most of us are not consciously attuned. In a similar manner, and also in the name of wholeness, Pluto will force us to confront anything that is buried in us – be it our untapped potential or our repressed demons and complexes.

Pluto transits evoke images of descent – a voyage into the under-world of the unconscious, a voyage to discover what is hidden in us. It must be emphasized again that the unconscious is not only the storehouse of disavowed negative or destructive emotions, complexes and feelings, although we will find no shortage of 'demons' of this kind lurking in the depths of our psyche. The unconscious is also the repository of undeveloped potential and positive traits which have yet to be recognized and integrated. In a later section, we shall examine the buried treasure hidden in our unconscious. But first we must confront the beast . . .

Facing the Beast

Pluto transits entail meeting the primitive, instinctive and unregenerate side of our nature. Feelings of anger, hurt and pain from childhood; greed, envy, jealousy, and infantile desires for omnipotence and power; unbridled sexual yearnings and ferocious destructive urges – all these and more lie festering in the deeper recesses of our unconscious mind. Pluto is the servant of wholeness, and to live our wholeness we must face these primal drives and emotions. Reconnecting to what is hidden in us means reclaiming lost and repudiated parts of our own psyche. In doing so, we also create the possibility of freeing the energy trapped in infantile complexes, and reintegrating it more constructively back into the personality. But before we can transform anything in ourselves, we first have to accept that it is there.

Much of what is buried in us stems from our infancy and childhood. Our inner world as a small child revolves around three major states or feelings: need, love and hate. We are born helpless; we need the love and care of someone else to survive. We feel tremendous love when our mother or caretaker gives us the nurturing we require for our survival. However, we also feel tremendous anger and pain when she isn't there. If we're hungry and she doesn't come, or if we need to be held and she doesn't respond, we fear she has abandoned us . . . we fear we are going to die. And naturally this gives rise to fury, frustration and rage.

In the womb and for the first six to nine months after birth, we have not yet fully distinguished ourselves as separate from the environment and therefore our feelings are not localized. If we feel anger, the whole world is angry. If we feel hungry and cold, the whole world is hungry and cold. According to Melanie Klein, when we are angry, we fantasize tearing and destroying mother's breast; but since in our infant mind we are the same as the breast, we actually are fantasizing attacking ourselves as well.[1] Obviously, such a state does not feel pleasant. In fact, it is so unbearable that the only way we can deal with these emotions is by cutting off from them. Accordingly, our early destructive rage is suppressed, and remains unfinished and unresolved, festering in temporary abeyance in some neglected corner of the psyche. The rage hasn't disappeared; it is just on hold. Later in life, under a powerful Pluto transit, our global undifferentiated infantile hate and anger can resurface, triggered by an external catalyst of some kind.

Rage isn't the only emotion buried in us. We might also harbour a deep and early sense of ourselves as bad or loathsome. These feelings of shame and self-hate stem from a mechanism known as *introjection* – the tendency as an infant to identify with the mother. If mother can't provide us with what we need – in other words, if she is a 'bad mother' – we introject or take in that 'badness', and we believe that we are bad. Since we think we are the whole world, if we are bad, then the whole world is bad. Again, it is too painful to stay with such feelings, so we cut off from these as well. However, like our early destructive rage, they too lurk and fester in the hidden recesses of our psyche until a Pluto transit comes along to reactivate them.

In addition to rage and self-hate, there is a whole range of other early buried emotions and drives which important Pluto transits can disinter. Envy and jealousy have their roots in infantile complexes, but they are as alive as ever in the adult psyche, and are susceptible to a passing Pluto transit. Although they are not the same thing, envy is commonly confused with jealousy. The main difference is that envy involves two people, while jealousy involves three. In terms of psychological development, envy pre-dates jealousy. Again, according to Kleinians, we first feel envy towards the breast (or bottle) that feeds us. We love the good things it gives us, but we hate the breast when it fails to provide what we need – or when it is forced on us after we have had enough. We not only love or hate the breast, but we also are envious of the power it has over us – whether we are happy or sad, full or empty, content or miserable, all depend on it. Because we resent our dependence on the breast, a part of us of us wants to destroy or spoil it, and we fantasize defecating on the breast and tearing it to pieces. These same feelings are transferred on to the mother: we both love and hate her, and we also envy the power she has over our life and well-being.

We grow older and fall in love, and the same ambivalent mixture of need, admiration, envy and destructive rage will again be acti-vated. Closeness, dependency and anger are intimately related. The closer we are to someone, the more our happiness depends on that person, and one part of us resents being in that position. We envy the power the other person has over us, and as a result, there may be times we want to destroy our partner or the relationship itself. Some of us may be so frightened of our own envy, resentment and rage that we avoid closeness altogether, rather than risk having these emotions aroused and exposed in the course of a relationship. Pluto transits often revive our early feelings of envy and the anger associated with them, only this time it will not necessarily be directed at the mother, but towards someone else with whom we have a close bond, or towards any person who makes us feel 'small' and inadequate.

Jealousy is also a primal emotion. As infants, our survival depends on the love of the mother/caretaker. If we are special to her, she will want to fulfil our needs and keep us alive. Winning her love and attention reassures us that she will be there whenever we need her. However, if we do not feel that special tie with the mother – if there is another person around whom she loves and pays attention to more than us – then we become anxious and threatened. What if she gives all her care and nourishment to that person, and there is nothing left for us? What if a hairy predator comes to eat us just at the moment mother is busy with somebody else? Envy is a two-person situation, an issue between us and mother. Jealousy, however, involves three people: ourselves, mother and the rival for her attention. Later in life, if our partner should pay too much attention to another person (or a job or hobby), the frightened infant in us will be aroused again. As adults, we are probably not totally dependent on our partner for our survival; we can find ways to look after ourselves, and yet the infant in us, when confronted with a rival, will be thrown into a state of panic, a feeling of 'Help! I'm not the most special, I'll die!' Because part of us still believes that our survival depends on being our loved one's primary focus of attention, jealousy triggers intense emotions of hate, fear, rage and anxiety. These are the kinds of reactions a transiting Pluto aspect can stir when it reawakens the jealous child in us.

Because envy and jealousy are almost universally seen to be 'bad', we are taught not to have such feelings. Accordingly, many of us deny and suppress these emotions, along with a whole array of other 'sins', such as lust and greed, and we may refuse to recognize their unconscious hold over us. But Pluto demands that we face our shadow and confront these darker feelings. If we are to grow and become whole, we have to expand our sense of identity to include our primal emotions, our 'uncivilized' instincts and conflicting desires. We need to accept that they are part of life, and not to condemn ourselves for having them. However, contacting such early complexes as rage, jealousy or envy doesn't mean we have the right to act out these feelings or indiscriminately unleash them on others. Prisons are filled with people who have attempted just this. Our primal emotions need to be recognized and accepted, but they also need to be *contained*. By admitting they are there and by accepting them as part of our human inheritance, we can begin the process of redirecting the energy trapped in such complexes into more productive modes of expression. Again, we can turn to myth to provide us with some clues as to how this is done.

Hercules and the Hydra

In his journey of individuation, Hercules has 12 tasks or labours to perform. The eighth labour, that of slaying the Hydra, illuminates the kinds of lessons and issues we encounter through the sign of Scorpio and the planet Pluto. Pluto transits, in particular, often designate a phase in our lives when we have to do battle with the Hydra, the beast in us.

Hercules' eighth labour begins with his teacher assigning to him the task of slaying the Hydra, a nine-headed monster which has been plaguing the land of Lerna. But before setting out to find the Hydra, Hercules is given a piece of advice by his mentor: *We rise by kneeling; we conquer by surrendering; we gain by giving up.* Equipped with his club and this aphorism, Hercules begins his search for the beast. She is hard to find – like the buried emotions which hide in the muck and slime of our unconscious, the Hydra hides in a 'cavern of perpetual night'[2] alongside a stagnant swamp; that is, in a part of ourselves most resistant to 'illumination' or rational explanation.

When he locates the cave, Hercules shoots his arrows inside, hoping to lure the Hydra out, but she doesn't stir. Finally, he dips his arrows in pitch, lights them, and sends them flaming into the monster's lair. Outraged, she emerges from her dwelling, murderous and vengeful. By shooting his burning arrows into the cave, Hercules has succeeded in bringing the Hydra out of hiding. Likewise, under Pluto transits, we consciously or unconsciously set up situations which force us to confront the beast in us, or in those around us. Now the Hydra is in the swamp with Hercules standing over her. Using his trusted club, he stands to confront the Hydra and tries to lop off her heads, but each time one falls off, three more appear in its place. His attempt to slay the Hydra this way mirrors how we try to destroy our beastly emotions by severing them from consciousness. And yet they keep reappearing, angrier and more intense each time. Finally Hercules remembers his teacher's advice – *We rise by kneeling, we conquer by surrendering, we gain by giving up.* Instead of beating her while standing, he kneels down in the swamp, immersing himself in its fetid slime, and lifts the monster by one of her heads into the light of day where she begins to wilt. It is only when she is in the swamp that she has any strength; when she is brought up into the light, she loses her destructive power. Hercules can then cut off each of her heads and none regrow, but after he severs all nine, a tenth one appears; Hercules recognizes this as a jewel and buries it under a rock.

What does all this mean? If left to fester in the stagnant waters of the unconscious, our blindly instinctual drives and our infantile complexes (our early destructive rage, self-hate, envy, jealousy, greed, lust, etc.) have enormous power and control over us. But if they are brought into the light of day, into the light of consciousness and held there, they begin to lose their strength. What we are unconscious of has a way of sneaking up behind our backs and hitting us unexpectedly. However, if we are conscious of something in us, we have a better chance of resolving it. If we do not admit to our hidden jealousy, for instance, that jealousy will find disguised ways to express itself. Our partners act in a manner which arouses our jealousy, but we insist we are not feeling that way – even though we spend the next few days acting cold and remote, or sulking about how superficially they behave at parties. But when we lift our jealousy out of the swamp and bring it into the light of day, we create the possibility of analysing that part of us and learning a great deal about ourselves. Upon examination, we may discover an Oedipal rivalry we didn't know we had, or a hitherto unacknowledged resentment towards our parents for paying more attention to a sibling than to us. In other words, we may discover the origins of those feelings we have about our current partner. In doing so, we are better able to distinguish just how much of what we are feeling is appropriate to the present situation, and how much really belongs to unresolved emotions from the past. If we insist on denying or cutting off from our jealousy, this kind of exploration is not possible. The Hydra remains in the swamp and retains her destructive power over us.

The key to conquering the Hydra is not just lifting her out of the swamp. Many people unleash the Hydra from its unconscious bondage and are locked up in prisons or asylums for doing so. The key is lifting her out of the swamp and *holding* her there in the light of consciousness. Holding is a psychological term, closely related to the idea of containment. Holding means recognizing and accepting the whole range of our feelings, and allowing these 'space' without acting them out indiscriminately. We can write about our emotions, paint or draw them, or give expression to them in some form of psychotherapy or counselling. In the course of therapy, for example, a client may unearth some deep anger towards mother or father which then might be transferred on to the therapist. In this way, the therapy sessions become the vessel in which these angry feelings can be held and contained until the client can resolve them and move on to other issues. Without being denied, judged or condemned, the feelings are examined and given space. (Even outside the context of therapy, the best relationships are those which are able to contain both the love *and* the hate we inevitably will feel towards the other person. It's impossible to be close to someone and not have our early infantile emotions aroused. A healthy relationship can withstand and contain the good as well as the bad feelings.)

When Hercules lifts the Hydra out of the swamp and holds her by one of her necks in the air, she loses her power. It isn't easy and it may take some time, but the same can be done with our jealousy, rage, envy, lust, and any other basic instinctive drive buried in us. We can lift these out of the unconscious, accept them as part of us (even though society has told us we shouldn't have such feelings) and examine them in the light of day. By forming a relationship with hitherto denied feelings, we create the possibility of transmuting these aspects of our nature.

After Hercules has raised the Hydra and cut off all nine of her heads, a tenth one appears, which is a jewel. The monster yields something precious in the end. The poet Rilke touched on a similar theme:

> Perhaps all the dragons of our lives
> are princesses who are only waiting to see us
> once beautiful and brave.
> Perhaps everything terrible is in its deepest
> being something helpless that wants help from us.[3]

Though accepting, containing and working on our infantile complexes, we are reconnecting to parts of ourselves we have banished and repressed. Even though these complexes reappear at first in a negative form, the energy contained within them, once denied but now reclaimed, will eventually become available to integrate back into our psyche in more constructive ways. We will free not only the energy imprisoned within the complexes, but we will also regain for new use all the energy we have been employing to hold back our complexes. None of this is possible until we have confronted and admitted the beast back into consciousness. In the end, the battle with our Hydra leaves us more fully alive and present, no longer out of touch with the rich, instinctive side of our nature – no longer living life just from the neck up.

Rilke also wrote: 'If my devils are to leave me, I am afraid my angels will take flight as well.'[4] It is only by accepting our hate that we can choose to love. It is only after we have accepted our rage that we can choose to be understanding. Otherwise we are just pretending to be nice.

The Rape of Persephone: Pluto in Love

In mythology, Pluto wore a helmet which rendered him invisible when he left the underworld. He thus represents a force that operates from beneath the surface level of consciousness – a facet of our psyche that unconsciously attracts situations through which we will fall apart in order to put ourselves back together again in a new way. Pluto came to the upper world only twice, once to seek healing for a wound, and the other time to abduct Persephone. Pluto transits are often experienced most clearly through issues to do with health and relationships. We meet Pluto in illness, when accumulated toxins and poisons are drawn to the surface and eliminated from the body in order for the system to function healthily again. We also encounter the god of the underworld in relationships when emotional complexes are brought to the surface and exposed. Pluto transits may bring new relationships or create tensions in existing ones – tensions designed to arouse and reawaken what is buried in us. Again we can turn to myth to amplify and to elaborate on the effects of Pluto on this area of life.

In spring we find the maiden Kore playing in a field with other virgin goddesses, happy and content in the protective embrace of her mother, the earth goddess Demeter. Kore is young and inexperienced, at peace living in the upper world on the surface level of life, but Aphrodite, the patroness of sensual love, looks down on Kore from Olympus and finds her too naïve and innocent to be true. In her capacity as the redresser of imbalance, Aphrodite decides to teach Kore a lesson, and she instructs Eros to pluck Pluto (who happens to be in the vicinity) with an arrow of love.

Unaware that it is a flower associated with the underworld, Kore picks a narcissus. The earth opens up and Pluto appears in his black chariot drawn by four fire-breathing horses. He abducts Kore and takes her to the underworld where he rapes her. In one fell swoop, she is taken from the spring meadow in the upper world into a place that is dark and unknown – a place of passion, sex, and intense emotion. After this, Kore's name is changed to Persephone, which means 'the one who loves the darkness'. Initiated into womanhood by Pluto, she is no longer a maiden. Symbolically at least, she has freed herself from her mother's domination and is now a woman in her own right.

Demeter, distraught over the loss of her only daughter, sinks into a deep depression, and forbids the crops to grow or the trees to bear fruit. For seven years the whole word is cold and barren, while humanity starves. Finally, the gods, worried that no people will be left to worship them, intercede and arrange for Persephone to be reunited with her mother. Because Persephone has eaten of the pomegranate fruit in the underworld (a symbolic way of saying that blood has been spilled and she has lost her maidenhood), she is allowed to return to the upper world only for six months each year. The remaining six months must be spent with her husband Pluto, in her role as queen of the underworld.

To the Greeks, this myth provided an explanation of how the seasons came into being. Before the rape of Kore, it was perpetual spring and summer; but now whenever Persephone has to leave her mother and return to the underworld, Demeter mourns – the trees lose their leaves, the crops die, and winter descends. The story also describes a passage, a rite of initiation: the adolescent must break away from the womb of the family or ancestors in order to become a person in his or her own right. But no matter what age we are, the myth portrays what happens when we become involved in a close, passionate relationship. Like Kore, we are plunged through love into the underworld where we meet our hidden emotional complexes. Intimacy and closeness expose the secret inner world of the infant still alive and kicking in our unconscious minds – a world of passion, rage, envy, jealousy, lust and greed. Our partner may be unable to provide us precisely with what we need or want at a particular time, and up comes our raging infant again. Our partner flirts with someone else, and up comes the jealous infant inside us, fearful of abandonment and death. There are times we feel like killing our loved ones; and there are times we want to destroy or spoil the relationship, because we resent the power a partner has to determine whether we are happy or sad, fulfilled or unfulfilled. Intimacy stirs all these emotions in us. And we were told that love was meant to be a joyful state.

In the end, Persephone becomes the mistress of two worlds. She is at home in the upper world, living on the surface level of life. She can be light, easy, gay, innocent and good at small talk. But she also is familiar with the underworld; she has contacted the darker emotions that live beneath the threshold of consciousness. Under an important Pluto transit, we too may have a Persephone experience: the experience of having to confront the underworld of our own destructive emotions via the catalyst of a close relationship. Like Persephone, our existing sense of self is violated by Pluto, and we discover more about who we are and what lurks deep within us. And like Persephone, we can be born again, a new and more whole person.

Pluto: the Balancer

In the Persephone myth, Aphrodite used Pluto to achieve her ends – to take the innocent and naïve maiden Kore and initiate her into another side of life. In this sense, Pluto acts as a balancer; wherever this planet is transiting in the chart is where we are shown another dimension of ourselves, a side we have ignored or denied. If we are too identified with the 'masculine' or 'animus' principle (power, assertion and outer achievement), a Pluto transit may strip us of our power and drive in the name of putting us more in touch with the 'feminine' side of life, the 'anima' – the realm of soul, feelings and relationship. If we are overly identified with the anima and are mainly deriving our identity through what another person needs or wants us to be, then Pluto may rob us of that relationship, so that we are forced to find out who we are in our own right. If we have grown inflated in any way – believing we are a god or a superhuman being – Pluto transits will cut us down to size. If we have swallowed whole the values of our culture and society, Pluto will confront us with choices and temptations that lead us away from the norm, and show us (to our shock and surprise) other sides to our nature and other ways of conducting life which are radically different from those that parents or society have tried to instil in us.

Pluto is also the avenger of natural law. Every living thing has its place and its limits: if we step too far beyond these limits, a major Pluto transit will bring the Furies upon us. Pluto may do this through illness, where pain and disease are the messengers informing us that something has gone awry, that we are out of balance in some way. If we have not heeded any of its earlier warnings, Pluto will use the body to make us listen. Illness may be the only avenue open to Pluto to break us down and change us. Sickness draws the toxins and poisons hidden in us to the surface, so they can be eliminated and our body cleansed. In some cases, a cleansing illness of this sort can accompany or facilitate the psychological regeneration of long-standing emotional complexes and disorders.

The Dark Goddess

Persephone is just one of many mythic figures who have been transformed through a journey into the underworld. Reputedly the oldest known recorded myth (written on clay tables in the third millennium BC), the Sumerian legend of the descent of Inanna[5] also illustrates the kinds of changes associated with Pluto as it transits important points in the chart. Inanna, an earlier form of Ishtar, is a goddess of the heavens: she is radiant, alive, sensual and joyful, and her life flows relatively smoothly. But she has a wicked sister, Ereshkigal, who lives in the underworld, and whose name literally means 'the lady of the great place below'. Greek mythology is comparatively late, and before the Greeks, the underworld was ruled by a goddess, not a god. In this sense, Ereshkigal is an earlier form of Pluto.

As the story begins, Ereshkigal's husband has just died, and a funeral is to take place in the underworld. Inanna feels impelled to attend the funeral, to make a journey into Ereshkigal's domain. She has to go down into a place which she doesn't really like, a region with which she is unfamiliar, a place that is not her realm. When Inanna arrives at the first gate into the underworld, Ereshkigal greets her with a dark and poisonous stare: 'How dare you come into my realm? Even though you are my sister, I will subject you to the same treatment that all souls receive when they enter the underworld.' Ereshkigal is in a foul mood, and when she feels that way, everyone is made to suffer. She doesn't stop to consider that Inanna has come to be by her side at her husband's funeral. Ereshkigal is not concerned with being reasonable or fair. She represents the early, global rage of the infant: when she is angry or unhappy, everything is bad and nothing is good.

Seven gates or portals lead into the depths of the underworld. Ereshkigal orders Inanna to pass through these gates, and at each portal the queen of the heaven must strip something off – her garments, her robes, her jewels – until she arrives in the deepest underworld utterly naked. Then she is instructed to bow before Ereshkigal, to honour the force that has stripped her.

Pluto transits can be similar to a meeting with Ereshkigal. We may have to let go of those things through which we have been deriving our sense of identity. Relationships, jobs, belief-systems, possessions or other forms of attachment can be stripped and taken away, or they lose their validity and appeal. And yet in the myth Inanna is forced to bow before Ereshkigal – to honour as one would a deity the force which has stripped her. Ereshkigal is a goddess, a dark goddess, but a goddess none the less. She is a divinity through which a higher law operates, and in the end she must be honoured as part of life. Being stripped of our identity and attachments is not pleasant: it feels more like a curse than the workings of a divinity. As difficult as it may be to comprehend, Ereshkigal (like Pluto) serves a higher purpose. However, the nature of that purpose is not always immediately clear.

In fact, in Inanna's case the situation gets worse before it gets better. As if stripping Inanna naked and making her bow low isn't enough punishment, Ereshkigal then kills Inanna and hangs her on a meat hook to rot. The once happy, beautiful and thriving goddess of heaven is left to hang on a peg in the underworld like a dead piece of meat, stewing in her own decay. This is what Ereshkigal does to her; and this is what a difficult Pluto transit can feel like. Pluto may banish us to a place where we feel rotten and miserable, an ugly, nasty, depressed, alone and abandoned place. These feelings have always been there in us, hidden away in the darker recesses of our psyche, left over from childhood traumas or past life experiences. We may have defended ourselves successfully against such emotional states, but Pluto/Ereshkigal finds a way of confronting us with them.

Meanwhile, Ereshkigal – who has just lost her husband and killed her sister, and is torn by grief and rage, is also pregnant and having a difficult labour. Nor is she happy with her role as goddess of the underworld. She was raped as a child and banished to the underworld as a punishment, and she is still enraged at this injustice. Ereshkigal not only represents death and decay, but also symbolizes the outraged instincts of the angry, hurt and frustrated child which many of us continue to carry inside, no matter how much we try to hide these feelings from public view. With Inanna dead and the vindictive Ereshkigal in the throes of painful labour, we reach the low point of the story. And yet, though something has died, something new is being born. A death requires a birth; and a birth requires a death.

Inanna, before embarking on her journey into the underworld, had wisely instructed her servant Ninshubar to rescue her if she hadn't returned from her sister's dark realm after three days. Inanna knew she had to go into the underworld, but also knew that she mustn't get stuck down there. She is willing to go down into a dark place, but she takes precautions to ensure she will come back up again. Three days pass, and Inanna is not back yet, so Ninshubar desperately appeals for help. She approaches Inanna's father and paternal grandfather to plead with them to do what they can to rescue Inanna. Both reply they can do nothing to alter what Ereshkigal decrees. Here we have two strong masculine figures who have no power over Ereshkigal, meaning that the 'masculine' prerogative of force and subjugation (which by nature would try to overpower, suppress or fight an opponent) is not what is needed to deal with Ereshkigal. Taking a heroic stance against Ereshkigal does not work. If we try to battle with her, she will only retaliate more angrily and ferociously than before.

Finally Ninshubar approaches a god called Enki, Inanna's maternal grandfather, who is known as the god of water and wisdom. He is fluid and compassionate and understands the laws of the underworld. In some versions of the myth he is portrayed as bisexual, both male and female: he can be tough, but he is also flexible and yielding. Enki agrees to do what he can to rescue Inanna. Using dirt he scrapes from beneath his fingernails, he fashions two small figures called 'the Mourners' – tiny, androgynous, unobtrusive little creatures. Whispering some words of advice to them, he sends the Mourners down into the underworld to rescue Inanna. It seems unbelievable that these tiny and insignificant figures will be able to

deal with the mighty Ereshkigal, but it is because they are so small
that they manage to slip into the underworld unseen. They are not
apprehended by Ereshkigal's henchman along the way, nor do they
have to endure the stripping ordeal Inanna had to go through.

Quietly, the two little Mourners creep up to Ereshkigal and Inanna.
Their task is to save Inanna, but they approach this in a very
unusual way. Even though they are there to retrieve her, they
totally ignore Inanna, and concentrate first on Ereshkigal. Rather
than berating Ereshkigal for killing Inanna, they actually choose to
commiserate with Ereshkigal, to empathize with the dark goddess.
Ereshkigal, in the pain of labour, laments her fate: 'Woe is me, woe
my inside!' The Mourners take pity on her: 'Yes, you who sigh are
our queen. Woe your inside!' Then, because she hates being the
goddess of the underworld, she cries, 'Woe is me, woe my outside!'
and they reply 'Yes, you who sigh are our queen. Woe your outside!'
In line with the principles of current-day Rogerian therapy, the
Mourners mirror back to Ereshkigal what she is experiencing. In
doing so, they make her complaining and moaning sound more like
prayer or litany. The Mourners have been taught by Enki to affirm
the life-force even if it reveals itself through pain and suffering. Even
in darkness and negativity, there is still something to honour, something to be redeemed.

Ereshkigal is amazed. No one has ever honoured her in this way
before. Most people spend their lives trying to avoid pain, darkness
and everything Ereshkigal represents. But the Mourners have
accepted her; they have graciously allowed her the right to moan
and complain. Effectively they are saying to Ereshkigal, 'You have a
right to be. You can complain and carry on as much as you want,
we still accept you.' Ereshkigal, grateful for this kind of recognition,
wants to reward the Mourners and offers them any gift they would
like. They ask for Inanna back. Ereshkigal agrees, sprinkling Inanna
with new life, and the queen of the heavens is revived, free to return
to the upper world again.

Pluto transits often symbolize an encounter with Ereshkigal, a
time when we have to go down 'into the pit' and face that which is
painful, loathsome or ugly in ourselves. Pluto transits can bring a

deep despair: everything is terrible and life has no hope. People we thought cared about us may let us down; ideals seem hollow and dead; what previously has given our life meaning and substance now amounts to nothing. But the myth teaches us how to deal with these states. Enki's Mourners are the key, the way of responding which will help us out of the dark underworld when we are stuck down there. In the same way that Enki's Mourners accept Ereshkigal, we also can learn to accept depression, darkness, death and decay as part of life, as part of the great round of nature. We need to be willing to go into our depression and pain, to explore it, feel it, and wait it out. We need permission to grieve, mourn, and feel angry – not only for people or things which we have lost, but also for lost phases of our life and lost ideals which no longer serve us. Acceptance allows the healing magic to work. It is only when Ereshkigal is honoured and revered as a deity in her own right that we, like Inanna, can return to the upper world again. This is Enki's lesson to us; this is Enki's way of helping us through difficult Pluto transits and bringing us back from the underworld into new life and hope.

The story ends with an interesting twist. There is a rule that if you are freed from the underworld, you have to find someone else to take your place. When Inanna returns to the upper world, she seeks out her consort Tammuz, who didn't help her when she was down there, and says: 'Now it's your turn, you must take my place in Ereshkigal's realm.' If one component of a system changes, then the whole system will have to be altered in order for it to function properly. If one person in a relationship experiences a major psychological change, unless the other person changes as well, the partnership is in danger of breaking down entirely.

Inanna was stripped of everything which had given her an identity and was left for dead, yet she rose again renewed. The only way we find out we have the capacity to survive our own ego-death is to go through our own ego-death. When everything we thought we were is taken away, we discover a part of us that is still there – that aspect of our being which is eternal and indestructible. When what we thought supported us is taken away, we find out what really supports us. This is the gift of Pluto/Ereshkigal.

Head, Heart, and Belly

Every situation we encounter in life can be experienced through the head, the heart or the belly. For instance, let's say you have arranged to meet a boyfriend at the theatre. You have the tickets and he is supposed to meet you half an hour before the show begins. You are there on time, but he doesn't appear. Ten minutes go by, 15 minutes go by, 20 minutes go by, and he still doesn't come. How do you react to this?

If you are dealing with this situation through the head, you will try to figure out what has gone wrong and look for a reason why he hasn't appeared. You may check your diary to see if you have the right place and time. You may buy a newspaper to see if there was a train strike. The head will try to find meaning in what is happening, so you might think: 'Maybe the cosmos intends for me to do something else tonight; that's why he didn't come' or 'I must have stood someone else up in a previous lifetime, and now I have that coming back to me.' In other words, we use our minds to stand back and view the situation from a detached or objective point of view. But there are other dimensions of our being that will be stirred by this event.

The experience of being stood up will also activate feelings in the heart. The heart may worry about the other person: 'I hope he is all right. Wouldn't it be terrible if he had an accident while coming to meet me?' The heart may try to be compassionate: 'Maybe he had a hard childhood, that is why he is the kind of person who can't keep appointments on time.' Above all, the heart will feel sad: 'Isn't it the story of my life? I was so looking forward to this and now I am let down.' You go home, have a cry and write a poem about what has happened. You put on sad music, pour a glass of wine, and feel sorry for yourself or for the condition of humanity in general.

But what about the reactions happening in your belly? What do you feel in your gut when someone you have been waiting for and wanting to see doesn't turn up? Most likely, the area around your belly will become agitated and tense, which is the physical body's spontaneous response to the experience of being let down. Your gut will churn, and you will feel angry and perhaps vindictive: 'Wait till

I see him again; I'll show him that he can't do this to me!' You may be fuming: 'I knew there was something devious and untrustworthy about him all along. Why didn't I listen to myself?' You might even fantasize killing him. These instinctive and primitive responses originate from the belly region, and are our natural reactions to betrayal. The belly isn't objective, it doesn't stop to analyse a situation or try to find logical and sensible reasons for what has happened. Nor does it respond in the same compassionate manner as the heart. The belly may fear that something dreadful has happened to the other person which has prevented him from getting there, but this feeling will be accompanied by a greater degree of terror and stark horror than if it stemmed from the heart centre.

Transiting Pluto stirs the belly in the sphere of the chart it is transiting or in relation to whatever planetary principle it is aspecting by transit. And in every case, when the belly is aroused, it not only agitates over the immediate event which has triggered its responses; the present situation will also activate feelings and emotions from earlier times in our lives when we have been let down or betrayed. A boyfriend stands us up at the theatre, and we feel angry and hurt, but the rage and pain we are feeling are not just from that situation. Our reactions also could stem from when we were six months old and we urgently needed mother to come and hold us, but she didn't come. The present disappointment will resonate with that earlier time and expose the emotions from that experience as well. When we are disappointed or frustrated as infants, our reactions are very intense because our survival depends upon a caretaker being there for us. Our life does not depend on somebody arriving at the theatre on time, but when they don't appear as promised, it reactivates a rage that originates from a period when another person being there on time was a life or death situation. For this reason, the infant in you feels as if your life has been threatened by someone not coming as promised.

Generally, as in the example of being stood up at the theatre, we will probably have reactions on all three levels at once. The head will attempt to ascertain what has gone wrong and try to find meaning in the experience; the heart will feel sad and may worry about the other person's well-being; and the belly will be experiencing terror, anger and rage. Our head, heart, and belly fight with one another – the head compelling us to be reasonable and mature about the situation, the heart urging us to be compassionate and forgiving, and all the while our belly is fantasizing ways to defend ourselves and to take out our revenge and hurt on the other person.

Under a Pluto transit, we often try to be reasonable and understanding too quickly, at the expense of the belly. We are afraid of our gut reactions, and use the head or heart to keep the belly at bay. However, if this is done over too long a period of time, the pent-up instinctive responses fester and become toxic. Unexpressed anger turns in on itself and attacks the body. The end result could be any number of psychological and physical disturbances – a nervous breakdown, a cancerous growth, stomach disorders, heart problems, skin diseases or sexual dysfunctions. This does not mean that we should indiscriminately unleash our belly feelings on whomever is unfortunate enough to trigger them. To do so is not really fair to the other person, because the intensity of our anger and hurt are actually related more to unresolved emotional issues from childhood than to the present situation. The person who stands us up at the theatre is just the catalyst that brings what is buried in us to the surface.

Even if we choose not to unleash our gut reactions on to another person, we shouldn't deny the emotions which have been stirred. We arrive again at the idea of acknowledging and accepting the instinctive and primitive side of our natures, without necessarily acting out this part of ourselves directly onto others. Once more, the key is acceptance, holding and containment. We need to find ways to give space and time to our primitive, instinctive emotions – ways that don't require rushing out and buying a gun to shoot whoever has triggered the beast in us. Giving our belly reactions some form of creative expression is one means of working with them. We can take time to write down what we are feeling – to let out on paper whatever thoughts and emotions we are having. In doing so, we are not only giving these feelings the space to be, but in the process we also might discern a connection between our present reactions and earlier events in our emotional history. Or we can paint, draw, dance or sculpt our feelings. Any of these outlets are advisable under a Pluto transit, because they give our belly-emotions room to express themselves. Feelings which are denied at the time of a Pluto transit will only bottle up and come back later with greater force. But if we accept our feelings and give them a safe form of expression, they naturally will begin to shift, change and transform themselves in some way.

After taking time to be with our belly responses, we will discover that other reactions to the present situation start to emerge. Our energy can shift in a natural way from the belly to the heart: we begin to experience glimmerings of compassion towards those who have upset us, and to see their point of view or their perspective more clearly. Or we gradually find ourselves looking at the situation from a more objective stance, and we are able to perceive some meaning in it or some greater purpose for it having happened. Pluto transits activate the root *chakra*, the energy centre at the base of the spine. Once this energy is tapped, it is possible for it to flow up into the higher *chakras*.

Buried Treasure

Earlier I mentioned that the unconscious is not just the storehouse of negative emotional complexes and our denied primitive drives, but the unconscious is also the repository of undeveloped potentialities and positive traits that have yet to be recognized, worked on and integrated. Pluto was the god of buried treasure, and a journey into what is buried in us will unearth hidden riches, some of which we might not have known were there.

Before analysing Pluto transits in this respect in greater detail, we need to examine more closely the dynamics of ego-development and the mechanism of repression in general. We are born into this world totally helpless; without the love of a mother/caretaker we would not survive. In order to win this much-needed support, we soon learn to hide, suppress or deny altogether those parts of ourselves which the environment does not condone, usually – and especially – our aggressive and sexual urges. This process can be mapped in this way:

Drive→Anxiety→Defence Mechanism[6]

We all have certain drives which we feel are not acceptable to the environment. Because we fear losing love, we become anxious about these urges and defend ourselves against them. Repression is one kind of defence mechanism that can be employed, but there are a host of others. In this way, the ego, or sense of 'I', is generally formed to include those urges and qualities that the environment supports, and to exclude those that the environment disapproves.

However, it is not only our sexual or aggressive urges that are frowned upon. It also is possible that those people on whom we were dependent for survival were ambivalent or disapproving of our more positive traits, such as our innate energy, curiosity or spontaneity. If we sensed as a child that the environment was not approving of these qualities, we would feel anxious and try to deny these traits as well. In short, we banish them from our ego-identity and become what is known in Transactional Analysis as the 'adapted child'. We develop a false self which is safe to show the world. And after a while, we forget what was originally there and come to believe that this false self is who we really are. In doing so we are left feeling incomplete – alienated from parts of our own being and out of touch with our wholeness. Pluto transits break down existing ego-boundaries and allow what is hidden in us to be included in our identity, and therefore they give us the opportunity to integrate positive potentialities which we previously have denied.

The humanistic psychologist Abraham Maslow was very aware of how we repress our positive potentiality. He coined the term 'the Jonah Complex' to describe the fear of our own greatness:

> We fear our highest possibilities (as well as our lowest ones). We are generally afraid to become that which we can glimpse in our most perfect moments, under the most perfect conditions, under conditions of greatest courage. We enjoy and even thrill to the god-like possibilities we see in ourselves in such peak moments. And yet we simultaneously shiver with weakness, awe, and fear before these same possibilities.[7]

Why should we fear our own greatness? One reason is a fear of

responsibility. If we fully acknowledged our potential talents, resources and skills, we would have to shoulder the burden of doing
something to develop them further. We would rather avoid knowing
than face the task of taking responsibility for what is there. Another
reason for denying our full potentiality might be the fear of the
power it would give us. We wouldn't be able to be 'little' any more.
Would we use our power wisely, or would we mishandle it? Or
maybe we are afraid that if we were truly in touch with the living
our greatness, other people would be envious and resentful of our
achievements. Transiting Pluto, in making us more aware of what is
buried in us, may ask that we confront these fears in order to grow
into the self that we truly are.

Facing Ultimate Concerns

We have discussed how some of our infantile drives give rise to
anxiety and to the employment of defence mechanisms to quell that
anxiety. Existentialist thinkers, however, believe that it is not just
unacceptable drives that make us uncomfortable. They speak of
certain 'ultimate concerns' – basic facts of life we have to face by
virtue of existing – which also create anxiety, and therefore energize
defence mechanisms into action. Pluto transits may strip away these
defences as well, and ask that we confront directly life's ultimate concerns.

What are these ultimate concerns, these inescapable 'givens' of
existence? Irvin Yalom, in his book *Existential Psychotherapy*, lists
these in four main categories: *death, freedom, isolation,* and *meaninglessness.*[8] We will consider them one by one.

Anything which is born will one day die. We are alive now, but
one day we will cease to exist, and although there is no escape from
death, we construct all kinds of defences against facing this fact.
Christianity suggests an after-life; esoteric philosophers believe in
reincarnation and in our soul's essential immortality. These concepts
may be true, but many existentialists would claim that such beliefs
are ways to avoid acknowledging the finality of death. One part of us
is aware of the inevitability of death, and yet another part of us is
terrified of the prospect of non-being, and wishes to continue to be.

We assuage our death-anxiety by finding ways to make ourselves 'immortal'. The idea of becoming famous and living forever in people's memory helps to alleviate the anxieties our ego has about its own finite existence. Writing books, creating works of art which will live on after we have passed away, is also satisfying to that part of us which craves immortality. Having children is another symbolic way of ensuring our continued existence: we may die, but a part of us will live on after we have gone. However, under a Pluto transit, we may be forced to face death, through being confronted with the inevitability of our own, or with the death of someone close to us.

According to existentialist theory, another ultimate concern is freedom. We alone are responsible for what we do, and the state of our lives is a result of choices we make, whether consciously or unconsciously. We alone are responsible for these choices. If our lives are not the way we would like them to be, we cannot blame anyone but ourselves. We could have made other choices; we could have handled things differently. No one is to blame but us. The fact that we are responsible for our own lives is frightening, for what if we make the wrong choices? In his book, *Escape from Freedom*,[9] Erich Fromm postulates that some people would rather live in a totalitarian state where all their decisions are made for them, rather than having to undergo the anxiety of making choices in their lives. We try to coerce others into making decisions for us. We attribute the ultimate responsibility of our lives to fate, to the gods, to our unconscious – anything but ourselves. Under Pluto transits, we may have to face the fact that no one but ourselves can be held responsible for the choices we make in life.*

Another basic given of existence which we find frightening is the fact that no matter how close we are to other people, certain unbridgeable gaps still remain. No one can ever fully know us, nor can we fully know another person. We are born alone and we die alone. We attempt to defend ourselves against feeling our existential isolation by seeking love and relationship, especially symbiotic

---

*Olivia's case study (pp. 360–8) is a clear example of how Pluto transits can work in this way.

unions where we merge or blend with another person. We exist alone, and yet yearn to be part of something greater. Under Pluto transits, we may lose relationships or people we thought would never let us down and as a result have to face our basic alone-ness in life.

Finally, there is the issue of meaninglessness. Most existentialists believe there are no ultimate truths – that the universe has no meaning, except that which we attribute to it. 'The only true absolute is that there are no absolutes.'[10] If this is the case, why are we here and how should we live? Even though there may not be any pre-existing truths, as human beings we need meaning in order to give purpose and direction to our lives. We need something to live for, guidelines by which we can steer a course through life. Under Pluto transits, we may find that the way we have given meaning to our life doesn't work any more: a belief-system, religion, philosophy or set of ideals could crumble into insignificance. We may have to face the possibility that the universe has no pre-ordained meaning, or we are forced to re-evaluate and redefine the way in which we give our existence purpose and relevance.

Pluto and Power Struggles

Wherever Pluto is transiting in the chart, our existing ego-identity is in danger of being destroyed through the affairs of that house or through the principle symbolized by the planet Pluto is aspecting by transit. The ego, whose main desire is to maintain itself, attempts to resist destruction by trying to exert power and control in that area of life. For instance, if Pluto is transiting the seventh house, we may be frightened that something our partner might do will be too much for us to cope with and will somehow endanger the relationship. Therefore, in an attempt to keep trouble at bay, we try to control our partner or the relationship itself. We hope that by dominating or manipulating the other person (often through guilt) we can avert disaster. Ultimately this doesn't work. Whether we wish to or not, Pluto will find a way to force us to confront changes in that area of life. These changes needn't signify the end of the relationship, but probably do require some alteration to the nature of the partnership, or a need on our part to face some of our worst fears in that area of life.

As a general rule, power-struggles are common in whatever house Pluto is transiting, or in connection with whatever planet Pluto is aspecting by transit. These conflicts may be motivated not only by the ego's desire to preserve itself (as explained above), but also from a need on our part to strengthen, affirm and to define further our identity by battling with another person or group who is taking a different stance from us. Therefore, if Pluto is transiting the third or making an aspect by transit to Mercury, we may fight with siblings or neighbours. If Pluto is transiting the tenth or making an aspect to Saturn by transit, power-struggles could ensue with authority figures such as the government, bosses or parents.

Pluto and Past Lives

Reincarnationists believe that the human soul is on a journey towards perfection which takes many lifetimes to achieve. With each new incarnation, we carry our *karma* – the harvest of experience from previous lives – with us. The actions we have performed in prior existences affect what we will meet in the present one.

It is not my purpose in this book to debate the truth of the philosophy of karma and reincarnation. However, those people who do believe in the theory may be interested in exploring Pluto transits in terms of the karma we are bringing over from past lives. I have discussed at length the fact that Pluto activates deep-seated drives and complexes rooted in childhood, but reincarnationists would assert that the kinds of emotions and feelings stirred by Pluto stem not only from childhood, but from experiences in previous lives as well. For instance, when transiting Pluto aspects our Venus, if we meet someone to whom we are powerfully attracted, it may signify that this is a person we knew in a previous incarnation. This person has come back into our lives because we still have something to resolve with him or her from the past. Or under this transit, a present partner could be the agent through whom karma returns to us: he or she walks out on us or cheats on us, because in a past life we were the one who abandoned or deceived others. Transiting

Pluto aspecting the Sun could bring karma back to us through our father or through men in general. If our father is cruel to us under this transit, reincarnationists may interpret this as our own cruelty as a father in the past coming back to us. Transiting Pluto aspecting the Moon could symbolize our meeting a woman with whom we have karmic ties, or attracting experiences via the mother which are related to occurrences in past lives.

The house Pluto is moving through will also indicate the area of life through which we are meeting past karma. If it is transiting the eleventh, for example, a group involvement or a situation with a friend could stir painful issues from previous lives. Transiting Pluto through the fifth could bring past karmic difficulties back to us through children. One woman with this transit was terrified of becoming pregnant: she was beset by an irrational fear that she would die if she tried to have a baby at this time. She sought the advice of a psychic, who told her that in a previous life she had in fact died while giving birth to a child. The psychic reassured her that the apprehension was there because it had happened in the past, and since it had already happened, it was not likely to repeat itself. Once the woman in question was able to pinpoint her fear and attribute it to something specific she had gone through before, her present concerns about getting pregnant were eased.

Not all karma is bad karma. Abilities, strengths, talents and resources we have developed in previous lives can also be carried over into our present existence. A Pluto transit could bring these to the fore in connection to whatever planet or house it is affecting by transit. For instance, when transiting Pluto moves through the sixth house, we may rediscover a skill or talent which we have developed in a past life. Or when transiting Pluto aspects Mercury, we could gain access to knowledge or wisdom we have accrued in other incarnations.

Seen in terms of karma and reincarnation, both the positive events and the catastrophes we meet in life are not random or accidental, but reflect the working of divine justice, and serve the soul in its journey of evolution and return to its divine source. For many people, understanding present difficulties in the light of this philosophy helps them give meaning to what they are having to endure. Because they can discern some reason or purpose why they have to meet these tests and challenges, they are better able to find the strength and resolve to deal with them constructively. Whether the theory is true or not, if it is understood wisely and approached with common sense, it can be of great value to people in times of crises.

Externalizing Pluto

Our discussion so far has emphasized the kinds of inner, psychological adjustments associated with Pluto transits – the death of an existing ego-identity and the reclaiming of lost parts of the self. It also is possible to externalize transiting Pluto's urge to tear down and rebuild through finding things in the outer world which need to be changed or transformed. Joining a cause or group which attempts to regenerate society by promoting needed social reform is one way of expressing Pluto's energy externally. Battling famine and disease in a Third World country could be another 'outer' manifestation of a Pluto transit. And Pluto's impetus to face darkness and expose what is hidden could express itself outwardly in medical and scientific research or any form of investigation into the mysterious and unknown.

Pluto asks that we confront what is raw, primitive or instinctive in us. This too can be approached externally by pitting ourselves against nature and the elements. Living alone in a jungle for a month, for instance, would teach you a great deal about the more primitive or instinctive side of life. Pluto is a boundary-breaker, and this too can be expressed outwardly in any attempts to stretch ourselves beyond our usual limits in some way. We could look for the highest mountain to climb in difficult weather conditions. We could try to beat a personal athletic record, or effect a major change in ourselves physically through a strict diet or body-building or other forms of strenuous exercise.

However, if we do express a Pluto transit by battling darkness or negativity in the world, we should be careful that in the process we are not disowning and then projecting what we don't like in ourselves on to others. It is a fact of life that what we despise most in others is what we are most intolerant about in ourselves. If we are unwilling to acknowledge and deal with our own capacity for jealousy, envy, deceit, treachery, violence, lust or greed, then we will dislike anyone or anything displaying these qualities. In our intolerance, we may embark on causes and crusades to eliminate such negativity from the world; but to do this before we have looked at our own dark side or unconscious compulsions is both fake and hypocritical – like shouting for peace while brandishing a sword.

If, under a Pluto transit, we find ourselves involved with others who deceive or betray us, or with people who are jealous, possessive or envious of us, we had better ask ourselves 'Why?' Why do we keep running into the Hydra around every corner? Why do we act as a magnet for these kinds of people? Are we unconsciously setting up these situations? Are we unconsciously provoking other people into these states? The nature of life is wholeness. Whatever we are not conscious of in ourselves, we will draw to us from the outside, as if by fate. If we are repeatedly meeting treachery, anger or envy in others, then we need to look inside and explore our own denied or repressed capacity to behave in any of these ways. Also, if at the time of a Pluto transit, we attract disruption and change via external calamities or through other people's behaviour, then we need to look inside for that part of us which doesn't want to remain in an existing mould or structure. Again, this doesn't mean we have to act on our destructive drives, but it does ask that we become more aware and understanding of aspects of ourselves which we are suppressing. If we totally deny Ereshkigal in us, she grows very angry and retaliates by sending her minions our way.

Attracting Plutonic people or situations into our lives often brings out what is Plutonic in us. A Mexican woman who had emigrated to England came to me for a reading, and her natal chart revealed Sun, Mercury and Venus all rising in Aquarius, opposite Pluto in Leo on the cusp of the seventh. She identified primarily with her Aquarian qualities, and saw herself as fair, just and principled, but was not in touch with the Pluto in Leo opposing her Aquarian planets, and adamantly denied any capacity to act treacherously or in a cold, underhanded way. Other people might be that way, but not her! I saw her again a few years later when transiting Pluto in early Scorpio was squaring her Sun, Mercury and Venus in Aquarius, and coming up to square her natal Pluto as well. At the time of this transit, her father died and she discovered that her brothers and sisters (who still lived in Mexico) had devised a plot to take advantage of her absence to cheat her out of her share of what the father had left to the family. When she told me this story, her face turned cold and bitter. She was determined to do whatever she could to punish them for their injustice to her. The Pluto transit, working through the treachery of her siblings (transiting Pluto was squaring the natal Mercury-Pluto opposition), had managed to expose a revengeful side to her own nature which she had never known was there.

Pluto Transiting the Planets: an Overview*

The first part of Chapter 9 on Pluto transits to the planets is designed to give the reader guidelines on what to expect under each transit, and some suggestions as to the best ways to use the transit constructively. A number of other books also contain excellent material on Pluto transits. Robert Hand's *Planets in Transit*, Betty Lundsted's *Transits: The Time of Your Life*, Stephen Arroyo's *Astrology, Karma and Transformation*, Liz Greene's *The Astrology of Fate*, and Tracy Marks's *The Astrology of Self-Discovery*, (see Suggested Reading at the end of this book), all include sections on Pluto well worth reading. Donna Cunningham's book *Healing Pluto Problems* deserves special mention: entirely dedicated to issues to do with Pluto, her warmly written book provides a deep insight into the nature of this planet and the kinds of difficulties, traumas and rewards Pluto transits offer. She also recommends specific healing techniques – Bach Flower Remedies, California Essences, meditations and chants – which can be employed for the various issues raised by different Pluto transits.

Even when transiting Pluto trines or sextiles a natal planet, we may not have an easy time. These transits can bring as much upheaval as the transiting conjunction, square, opposition or quincunx. Generally speaking, however, with the transiting trine or sextile we may be more in touch with that part of us which is

---

*See also p. 259 for a brief summary of how transiting Pluto affects natal planets.

demanding a change or rebirth, and therefore we offer less resistance to what wants to happen.

Because of Pluto's slow movement and its periodic retrogradation, any transit of Pluto to a natal planet or angle will last between two to three years, sometimes longer. Sensitive people may feel the reverberations of Pluto even when it is as far away as 4 or 5 degrees from the exact transiting aspect. As Pluto approaches an exact aspect by transit, the stage is being set for needed changes or breakthroughs. After aspecting exactly, it will then change direction and go retrograde, during which time the process initiated with the advent of Pluto may slow down, and we feel stuck or held back in some way. Finally, when Pluto turns direct and completes the aspect for the third time, the process moves forward to some sort of resolution. For example, as Pluto approaches and makes the first square to your Moon, it could become obvious to you that you need to alter your living situation. But when Pluto goes retrograde and makes the square again, you may find that all your efforts to move are thwarted or blocked. When it moves direct again and squares the Moon for the third time, you are more likely to succeed in making the necessary change.

However, we shouldn't expect everything to fall back into place as soon as Pluto has finished transiting the third time. There is usually a period of 'fallout', a phase of adjusting to the effects of the transit, which can last until Pluto is 2 or 3 degrees beyond the exact aspect to the planet in question. We might not realize just how much the transit has changed us until a year or so after it has passed and we can look back over the whole period more clearly. As a general rule, Pluto transits often exhibit two separate stages: the first half of the transit involves breaking us down in some way, and the second half is the rebuilding phase. Or we could say that the first half of the transit involves journeying down into Ereshkigal's realm, and the second half entails returning from that place, we hope renewed and wiser as a result of what we have experienced.

Transits of Pluto to the Planets and Through the Houses

Pluto–Sun

Pluto–Sun transits radically alter our basic sense of identity. Our old self and old ways of being will no longer be viable at this time. In particular, false or outdated aspects of our personality need to be let go of and changed.

These transits put us more closely in touch with the qualities represented by our Sun sign. If for any reason we haven't been living our Sun sign characteristics, we will be compelled to develop these traits. Take the case of Christopher, for example, born with the Sun in Taurus in the eleventh house, but with a strong water component in his chart (a Jupiter–Venus conjunction in Pisces on the MC, and the Moon rising in Cancer square to Neptune). For the first 34 years of his life, he was much more identified with and ruled by his watery and Neptunian side. Moody and changeable, he drifted from one job to another, and after leaving the family home at 22, never lived in one place for more than a few months. Transiting Pluto entered Scorpio and came to oppose his Sun in the early degrees of Taurus. Through a new relationship which started at this time, he became interested in psychology and embarked on a three-year training course in psychotherapy – a course which involved a great deal of self-examination both individually and within groups (note that transiting Pluto is moving through the fifth house of romance opposing and activating his natal Sun in the eleventh, the house of groups). One result of the training has been to make him aware of his deep desire to put down roots, build more lasting structures in his life and earn a decent living. In this way, transiting Pluto awakened his Sun in Taurus, enabling him to discover more fully a central aspect of his identity.

However, if we are already fairly in touch with our Sun sign, transiting Pluto aspecting the Sun may ask that we explore dimensions of that sign we have not yet expressed. For instance, a woman with the Sun in Sagittarius who had already travelled extensively turned her attention to another level of Sagittarius and began to study philosophy and religion when transiting Pluto squared her Sun. A man with the Sun in Pisces who had spent years living out the victim side of Pisces as an alcohol- and substance-abuser, found that transiting Pluto in Scorpio trining his Sun provided him with the strength needed to free himself from these addictions. He now works counselling others with drug problems: the Pluto transit shifted him from the victim to the healer level of Pisces.

In other cases, a transit of Pluto to the Sun actually could exaggerate the expressions of one's Sun sign qualities. Pluto deals in extremes and brings out the very best or the very worst of whatever planet it touches by transit. Some people with transiting Pluto conjunct their Scorpio Suns could find themselves overwhelmed by previously latent sexual compulsions, or obsessed by intense feelings of rage or hate they never suspected they had. Transiting Pluto square the Sun in Aquarius could arouse a person's ideals and convictions to such a degree that any means would be advocated to achieve a political or social aim. Transiting Pluto square a natal Leo Sun could expose a lust for power or an overwhelming need to be famous or special. Although such states of mind are extreme, dangerous or unpleasant, Pluto is working to reveal qualities in us which need to be better understood, worked on and healed. Extremism under Pluto transits almost certainly will invite a fall, and yet as a result it is possible to learn from the experience: we can pick ourselves up again, perhaps a little wiser and more balanced.

The Sun represents the *animus* principle of power, assertion and self-expression. Any Pluto–Sun transit in a woman's chart is a chance for her to become more aware of her need to have an identity in her own right, rather than solely defining herself through those to whom she is close. If over a long period of time she has allowed herself to be dominated and defined by others, a transit of Pluto to her Sun could increase her unhappiness and frustration to such a degree that she may have no choice but to let go of this pattern, often in a dramatic and decisive fashion. This is the kind of transit that prompts a woman to leave her husband and sometimes her children behind, in the name of discovering who she is in her own right. However, it isn't true to assume that Pluto–Sun transits in a woman's chart only indicate the need for her to contact her own power and self-assertion. More generally, Pluto operates to change the way we have defined who we are. Pluto transits to the Sun revolutionize the self: if she has always maintained that she would never marry, have children or settle down, she may find herself doing just those things under these transits.

For some women, transiting Pluto aspecting the Sun (and this applies to the transiting trine and sextile as well) could describe changes or difficulties men in her life are going through. I have seen many instances of women with these transits whose husbands are experiencing crises in the form of business or financial upheavals, health problems or major life-transitions such as redundancy, retirement or the death of a parent. In these cases, the woman meets Pluto indirectly through the man, and one way or another she will be changed as a result of what he is experiencing.

Encountering a Plutonic or Scorpionic type man (or sometimes a female of this nature) who transforms her life is another possible manifestation of a Pluto–Sun transit for a woman. Someone she meets could exert a powerful, almost spellbinding influence over her, and there may be little she or anyone else can do to stop this attraction. The new person will mirror or help her contact qualities in herself which are ready to become conscious during this period.

A man with transiting Pluto aspecting his Sun will have to confront issues to do with power, identity and assertion. If he has not yet developed or expressed his will or authority, these transits can help him do so. In charts I have seen where this is the case, the Pluto–Sun transit brought opportunities to exercise greater power and assertiveness in a work situation, as if the outer world is encouraging him to discover this side of his nature at this time. He may at first mishandle his newly found authority, and yet it is only by having power that he can begin to learn to use it wisely. However, if a man has been accustomed to positions of power and control, and has chiefly determined his identity through his office in life, a transit of Pluto to the Sun could have a very different effect. In other words, if he has already risen to the top and demonstrated his authority both to himself and the world, it may be time for him to change directions. He may wish to employ his energies in an entirely new arena, switching from one line of work to another. Or he might divert altogether from positions of power and responsibility in order to tend to other sides of his nature, and turn his attention towards his personal life or to the development of latent artistic or creative urges.

From these two contrasting examples – the man who is catapulted into learning about power, and the man who already has power and feels the need to alter his course – we can detect an underlying *modus operandi* of any Pluto transit. Whenever transiting Pluto aspects a planet, it can work on the sphere of life represented by that planetary principle in three different ways:

1   If we have been out of touch with the sphere of life symbolized by the planet Pluto is aspecting by transit, we have a chance to reconnect to and develop that side of ourselves. In the case of the Sun, this means further developing our power and authority.
2   If we are already involved to some degree with the sphere of life designated by the planet transiting Pluto is aspecting, then the transit suggests that this is a time when we need to refine, deepen or improve how we are expressing or relating to that principle. In the case of the Sun, this means learning how to use power more wisely and skilfully.
3   If we have over-identified with the side of life associated with the planet Pluto is transiting, Pluto will ask that we develop ourselves in some other way, rather than adhering to the direction we have followed so far. Pluto will bring about changes by choice (we decide to change), or by coercion (the outside decides it for us). In either situation, it is time to explore other levels or dimensions of the principle represented by the planet Pluto is

contacting. In the case of the Sun, instead of exercising our authority in an already existing career, we may need to find another outlet through which to define and express ourselves.

For either sex, the relationship with the father could come into focus. A child or young person with this transit might experience problems with the father – power-struggles with him, violence, incestuous undercurrents, the father moving out of the family home, and in some cases the father's death. Any of these issues will profoundly affect the child's character and identity later in life. Unattended wounds from this period will leave deep scars on the psyche, and a young person needs extra care, help and understanding at the time of a difficult Pluto–Sun transit.

Regardless of age, if we have been overly identified with, attached to or controlled by the father, this transit indicates the need to break that tie and to free ourselves from his dominance in order to discover ourselves in our own right. Battles with the father could occur at this time. He may want us to take one direction, but we feel the need to go in another. He believes in one thing, but we assert our belief in something else. These power-struggles may be necessary as a way to draw clearer boundaries between the self and the father, and to establish greater autonomy and independence. In some cases, this transit denotes a fairly radical severing of ties with him, a feeling that we need to burn our bridges behind us. After the transit passes, we may change our mind and seek a reconciliation.

A total break with the father is one way a Pluto–Sun transit might manifest itself. However, the opposite situation is also possible under these transits. Pluto changes our relationship to whatever principle it touches. If there have been long-standing difficulties with the father, a transit of Pluto to the Sun could alter these circumstances. We have a chance to bring to the surface and work through old problems with the father and improve our relationship to him. Pluto sometimes agitates problems, but it also gives us the opportunity to transform existing patterns, even ones that have been with us for a very long time.

In some cases, Pluto–Sun transits may indicate the father himself experiencing a difficult or disruptive period – illness, retirement, or various other emotional and psychological crises. Sometimes these transits correlate to the death of the father – an event that inevitably will have a profound effect on us. When a parent dies, all the old issues and conflicts surrounding that parent come to the surface. We will need time not only to mourn the loss of the father, but also to grieve for the passing away of the chance to resolve some of our problems with him while he was alive, or the loss of the opportunity to demonstrate our unexpressed love or gratitude to him. Feelings of anger, resentment or guilt to do with the father may re-emerge, and it is essential to give ourselves the time and the space to be with these feelings. In her book *Healing Pluto Problems*, Donna Cunningham suggests that it is still possible to confront and deal with unresolved emotional problems with our parents even after their death.[1] This could be facilitated through some form of bereavement counselling, and, in certain cases, with the help of a competent medium or psychic. The death of the father, properly mourned, also can free us to express ourselves in ways which were not possible when he was still living.*

Although there is no substitute for the grieving process, a belief in the immortality of the soul can be of great consolation in situations such as these. Spiritualists talk of 'the other side', the plane of existence on which our soul resides in the after-life. It is believed that the deceased, once comfortably settled on the other side, are able to view events on the earth plane, and even may try to contact or pass messages on to us. These messages can come through dreams or through the vehicle of a medium. A father who has passed on and who is released from the encumbrance and rigidity of the physical body, may be able to offer us love, support and understanding in ways which he couldn't have done when he was alive.

Pluto destroys forms, but it also can create new ones as well. Under Pluto transits, births occur as frequently as deaths. When Pluto transits in aspect to the Sun in a man's chart, he could become a parent, perhaps for the first time: he dies as the son to be reborn the father.

---

*See Suggested Reading (p. 386) for a list of books dealing with death and the grieving process.

Pluto–Moon

Whereas Pluto–Sun transits concentrate on issues to do with assertion, power and authority (*animus* issues), Pluto–Moon transits more
directly affect the realm of emotions and feelings (the *anima*). Pluto
transits to the Moon activate deeply ingrained images and patterns
left over from childhood. As children, we form 'opinions', based on
our interaction with mother and the environment, about what kind
of place the world is and what kind of person we are. For instance, if
mother is attentive to our needs, we will form the opinion that the
world is a safe place to be in. We develop a basic trust in life, the
feeling that life will provide us with what we need, that it is on our
side. What's more, we introject or identify with the good mother,
and this will contribute to a positive self-image: 'Mother loves me
enough to look after me; therefore I must be a good person.' However,
if mother or the early environment are not receptive to our needs,
we will form an opinion, life-statement or script which views the
world as unsafe. In this case, we will introject the bad mother, and
deduce that we must be lacking or inadequate because mother does
not care about us.

Our childhood experiences leave a deep impression – even though
we don't consciously remember these formative experiences, their
effects reverberate on an unconscious level. They are part of our
personal mythology, a set of beliefs and expectations about ourselves
and life in general. We carry them around inside us, and we continue
to interpret later events through the lens of these early images and
assumptions. An experiment illustrates this principle. One group of
young pups were subjected to an escapable electric shock, while
another group was given electric shocks they couldn't avoid. Later,
both sets of dogs were given escapable shocks. The dogs who had the
earlier experience of being able to avoid a shock were easily able to do
so again; however, the dogs who originally experienced an inescapable
shock were not able to find ways to avoid the escapable ones. Their
previous experience taught them that shocks were unavoidable –
although this was not the case in the latter experiment, they were still
governed by their old expectation or pattern. Their earlier framework
obscured their ability to find new possibilities in the situation.[2]

Likewise, as humans our childhood experiences set up certain expectations, and a predisposition to perceive later events in life in ways which confirm our earlier beliefs. If we have a positive expectation or belief about ourselves, we selectively perceive or filter out from experience those things which fit what we expect to see. If our self-image is negative or we hold the belief that the world is dark and threatening, this is precisely what our observations will mirror back to us. Life has a way of obliging our expectations.

How we experienced mother, the environment and ourselves as children is shown in part by the sign placement and natal aspects of the Moon in our charts. If the Moon is trine to Venus or Jupiter, let's say, then the image of mother and the early environment will probably include some positive feelings and associations. However, if the Moon is in difficult aspect to Saturn, Uranus, Neptune or Pluto, the likelihood of early bonding problems is increased, because the stressful aspects of these planets describe difficulties in the relationship with the mother and with problems in successfully satisfying our early needs. Later in life, when transiting Pluto aspects the Moon, it will reactivate any of these early patterns, often through problems – sometimes quite threatening – in a present relationship. For this reason, Pluto transits to the Moon – especially when the Moon has hard natal aspects – are not always pleasant. And yet these transits do offer us the opportunity to discover and learn more about our deep-seated complexes. Used wisely, Pluto–Moon transits can initiate a process that enables us to understand and perhaps resolve detrimental emotional patterns which have dogged us since childhood. How can we best facilitate this possibility?

We can't go anywhere until we accept where we are. We first need to allow into awareness whatever emotions are surfacing at this time. After we accept our feelings, we can begin to analyse them more closely. We can ask ourselves what early experiences would have contributed to our developing these kinds of patterns and beliefs in the first place. Pluto–Moon transits not only activate early complexes, but in accord with the investigative and penetrating nature of Pluto, these transits also allow us to examine our emotions in greater depth. Insight doesn't automatically bring change, but it heralds a step in that direction.

For example, take the case of a man born with the Moon square Saturn. This suggests an inner image of difficulty (Saturn) around the mother (the Moon), as well as problems (Saturn) having one's most basic emotional and physical needs (the Moon) met. He came from a poor family and his mother had to work to supplement his father's income. As a child, this man would cry out for her, but she often wasn't there for him at those times he most wanted her. Accordingly, he formed an inner image or belief that he wasn't worthy of love and that the world was not conducive to fulfilling his needs. The feelings associated with not having his needs met were so painful that he soon learned to protect himself in the only way he could as a child: he simply denied his need. Eventually, after repeated failure, he stopped reaching out for her.

When transiting Pluto came to conjunct his Moon, it triggered off the natal Moon–Saturn square. The images and issues associated with this natal square were revived again. At this time, he tentatively formed a relationship with a woman, but he was terrified to open up to her and show his feelings. Experiencing him as cold and withdrawn, she broke off the involvement. Our deep-seated complexes have a way of proving themselves true: his personal myth told him that he was someone who doesn't get what he needs and therefore it is better not to admit to feelings; but his reluctance to display his emotions was what, in the end, drove the woman away. The disappointment he encountered when transiting Pluto brought out his Moon–Saturn square awakened the same kinds of emotions he experienced with his mother. In this case, he was so devastated by the failure of his latest attempt at a relationship that he sought the help of a psychotherapist. Here we see transiting Pluto's ability not only to expose complexes, but to enable us to begin to change them as well. By admitting he needed help (admitting to a need), he was making his first step towards altering his pattern.

For both sexes, Pluto–Moon transits can reawaken a whole range of feelings from the past: the love and hate we felt for mother, our envy of her power, our early rage, frustration, sadness and depression. No matter how much psychological work we have done on ourselves previously, we can still do more under these transits. We might have tried for years to shift some of our emotional baggage, but it won't move until we have the right transit to help it along. There isn't a better time for emotional house-cleaning than under a Pluto–Moon transit.

For men, a Pluto–Moon transit can be very important because it is an opportunity for them to delve more deeply into their feeling nature. A man is likely to feel unusually touchy, over-reactive and over-sensitive at this time. He might be surprised at the kinds of emotions he discovers in himself. Previously, he confidently stepped out to meet life, but then this transit hits, and he feels anxious, moody, irritable, distracted and no longer so sure of himself. In short, his feelings overwhelm him at the expense of his rationality, intellect and common sense. Like the Hydra's heads, the feelings activated by a Pluto–Moon transit cannot be dealt with by trying to clobber them to death. However, most men are not accustomed to spending time with their feelings: they will try to rationalize emotions out of existence or seek ways to rise above feelings and put them in their 'proper' place. When Pluto is aspecting the Moon, this may not be possible. Ereshkigal is demanding to be acknowledged and given attention, and she doesn't take kindly to being shut up or denied. Men with these transits need time to be with and explore their feelings – even if this isn't considered the 'manly' thing to do and their normal efficiency is undermined in the process. If a man runs away from his emotional problems now, they will reappear later with more force than ever, often taking the form of physical illness.

A man also can experience this transit through a woman in his life: his mother, wife, girlfriend or daughter could be undergoing a difficult time. Or a man may meet a woman now whose nature is coloured strongly by Pluto or Scorpio, and she will have the effect of transforming him in some way. For either sex, it may signify the death of the mother.* Women with this transit also may find that at this time they attract or are around women who are of a Scorpionic or Plutonic nature, or who are going through a 'Plutonic' phase of some sort. A mother, daughter, sister, female friend or co-worker could be the agent through which Pluto in any of its forms is met.

---

*See p. 261 for a discussion on coping with the death of a parent.

The Moon is one of the astrological significators for the physical body, and when Pluto transits the Moon, the body itself can go through many changes. This is especially true for women. In some cases, Pluto–Moon transits may indicate problems with the feminine organs, the womb or breasts. Anything to do with feminine functions – menstruation, pregnancy, etc. – is prone to complications when Pluto transits the Moon. Hidden problems which have previously escaped detection could be seen and diagnosed now. This transit can manifest in other ways beside physical disorders, and my intention is not to frighten women about it. However, if you will be under a Pluto–Moon transit within the next five years or so, it makes sense to maintain a programme of regular yearly examinations in order to detect any possible trouble in its early stages. Most of the potential health threats of this transit, if spotted soon enough, can be treated successfully.

A woman's relationship to her own femininity can change when Pluto transits her Moon. She may become pregnant and bear a child for the first time; no longer just a daughter, she is now a mother. Pluto–Moon transits sometimes correlate with abortion, so care should be taken to avoid unwanted pregnancies at this time.[3] Pregnant women with this transit are best advised not to overdo things: plenty of time is needed to rest and adjust to the changes the body is going through. For older women, Pluto–Moon transits sometimes correlate with the need to transform how they have been expressing their Moon function. As children grow up and begin to lead their own lives, mothers may have to find other ways besides just caring for their own offspring to satisfy their nurturing desires. When Demeter lost Persephone to Pluto, she went into a deep mourning, but later she adjusted to her changed status by establishing a school to teach her mysteries. Mothers whose children have grown and left home can follow Demeter's example. Time is needed to grieve for the phase of life which has passed, but then they can search out new outlets that will fulfil them emotionally. Some women may find work which involves caring and looking after others, and in this way express their Moon function on a more impersonal scale. Others may turn to study, and enrol in courses which provide food for the mind and soul. In some cases, Pluto transits to the Moon manifest physically in the menopause and the need for a hysterectomy. If this is the case, it will be necessary to mourn for the passing of a phase of life and the loss of part of the self until a new sense of one's own worth and identity as a woman can be found.

Children with a difficult Pluto–Moon transit will normally experience it through the mother. She may be going through a major change or disruption, and as a result the child's sense of security is threatened. Children or young people having these transits may need extra care, understanding and reassurance. For adolescents, Pluto–Moon transits correlate with the radical transformation of the body at puberty. For either sex at any age, a transit of Pluto to the Moon can signify an important move or change of home, the pulling up of roots and the need to re-establish the self in a new environment. Some people will express this transit on a very practical level and undertake redecorating the home. It is likely that these outer alterations reflect inner, psychological changes.

Pluto can bring out the best or the worst in whatever planet it touches by transit. I have emphasized some of the more problematic emotional complexes and patterns which both the harmonious and hard transits can stir, and the potential for transformation and psychological growth these present. Pluto–Moon transits also can activate some very powerful positive feelings. I have seen many cases of individuals under these transits who tap depths of feeling they never knew existed in themselves. Fuelled by renewed emotional strength and conviction, their capacity to appreciate life and to love and empathize with others is experienced more strongly than ever. On some very deep level, they have never felt so alive.

Pluto–Mercury

Pluto's realm is the underworld far beneath the surface level of life, and this is where transiting Pluto beckons Mercury. One of the most obvious effects of a Pluto–Mercury transit is the urge to delve more deeply into the nature of reality, both inner and outer. A superficial understanding of life isn't what satisfies Pluto – more than any other planet, Pluto represents the urge to get to the bottom of things. When it transits Mercury, it asks that we use our mind and intellect to probe and explore as thoroughly as possible into whatever issues concern us.

For this reason, a Pluto–Mercury transit would obviously lend itself to study and research work. Hours, days, weeks and years can be spent investigating a specific field or topic. Pluto is a planet associated with intensity and passion, and the mind needs something to be stimulated or excited about when it transits Mercury. In general, it is an excellent time to pursue knowledge or embark on a course of study – anything that will engage or captivate the mind. Any Pluto–Mercury transit is easier to handle if Mercury has something constructive to focus its attention on.

Pluto beckons Mercury to explore and learn more about what is hidden and less obvious in life – to ferret out secrets and probe into mysteries. This could mean anything from investigative journalism or scientific research to a study of the occult. To some degree, knowledge confers power, and understanding how something works is the first step in gaining mastery over it. Under a Pluto–Mercury transit, the underlying motivation to master a field of study could be linked to this desire to have power and control in that sphere of life. In many instances, this is an admirable and healthy endeavour. Medical researchers need to understand what causes a disease before they can find a cure or prevention for it. In other cases, however, seeking knowledge for the sake of power can easily be corrupted. Under a Pluto–Mercury transit, the temptation to use knowledge in a negative way – as a means to manipulate or blackmail others – may be a path some people can't resist following. Black magic is more than just the theme for countless movies of a certain genre: it actually exists, and is practised far more widely than many people assume. With Pluto–Mercury transits, the whole issue of the uses to which we put knowledge comes into question.

As we have seen, Pluto lends power to whatever planet it touches by transit. Mercury is not only associated with the mind, but also with speech, writing and other forms of communication. When Pluto transits Mercury, it isn't only mental power which is increased: the ability to influence and sway other people through speech and writing is also enhanced. Conversely, our own opinions and ideas are open to change when Pluto transits Mercury. Pluto tears down and rebuilds whatever it touches, and when it contacts Mercury, someone we meet or something we read or study could revolutionize our beliefs and our usual ways of thinking and looking at life. The significance of a change in belief or attitude is not to be underestimated. Albert Schweitzer once wrote: 'the greatest discovery of any generation is that human beings can alter their lives by altering their attitudes of mind'.[4] Werner Heisenberg, a researcher into the field of atomic physics, also demonstrated that 'the act of observation itself affects that which is being observed'.[5] Over two thousand years ago, the Greek philosopher Epictetus observed: 'We are not troubled by things, but by the opinions which we have of things.'[6] Our mind thus plays a crucial role in determining what the world is like for us. Under a Pluto–Mercury transit, the way we perceive life changes, and therefore our whole world changes.

In the geography of the psyche, one boundary-line stands out above the rest: the division between what is conscious and what is unconscious. Pluto is associated with what is hidden or buried in the unconscious recesses of the psyche. When it transits Mercury, Pluto compels us to turn our attention towards that region, to probe what is down there in us. Pluto dispatches Mercury to act as a messenger between the unconscious and conscious minds. These transits ask that we delve into our unconscious in order to bring what we find there back up into conscious awareness. For this reason, any Pluto transit to Mercury is an ideal time to explore what makes us tick. Pluto enables Mercury to go deeper than usual, and this is a period during which psychotherapy, meditation, introspection or dreamwork could serve to open up the mind in ways not previously possible. Under Pluto–Mercury transits, Pluto is capable of leading our minds into places inside ourselves which we really haven't examined up to now, and some of what we discover in the depths of our psyche may not be all that pleasant to face.

Impressions and memories from early life, consciously remembered or not, distort and obscure how we see life in the present. The experience of being unloved or repeatedly pushed away as a child predisposes us to expect rejection later in life. As an adult, we will interpret other people's behaviour and attitudes towards us in light of the expectation or belief that they won't like us. They may not be rejecting us; but because this is what we expect, this is precisely how we will view their actions in relation to ourselves. In this way our earlier beliefs are reinforced. It's a vicious and painful cycle, and one that is hard to break. However, when Pluto transits Mercury, our minds can probe more deeply than usual, allowing us the opportunity to catch a glimpse of some of our deeply rooted unconscious beliefs and life-statements. In doing so, we become more aware of the scripts and patterns that govern the way we perceive, digest and interpret experience. Becoming aware of these unconscious scripts is the first step in doing something towards changing them.

Sometimes a Pluto transit to Mercury (especially the conjunction, square or opposition) manifests in the form of depression. For much of the time during these transits, our mind may be heavier or more serious than usual. Thoughts or feelings we were once able to shrug off easily will cling to us, even obsess us. It is not uncommon to be obsessed with the thought of death during this period. (Pluto, the god of death, is touching Mercury, the mind). Dreams or fantasies about accidents or illness and other frightening thoughts and premonitions may intrude into consciousness, awake or asleep. The mind may periodically be taken over by images of an instinctive or primitive nature – overwhelming sexual images, powerful aggressive urges, angry and destructive thoughts and impulses. Pluto grips the mind, and draws forth images and thoughts that we have usually managed to keep hidden or have previously denied were there.

Many of us may be shocked by what we are thinking and imagining now, and this can be a disturbing time, especially if we haven't thought of ourselves as the kind of person who entertains such compulsions. It may be difficult for us to see anything constructive in what is happening, but it would help if we realized that Pluto is at work to bring to the surface parts of ourselves we need to confront in order to be more whole. Again, as we have discussed earlier, Pluto is not asking that we act out these thoughts and urges. But in order to deal effectively with our subterranean impulses and images, they first need to make themselves known – and that is what Pluto transiting Mercury does. After they are recognized, we can then work with the energy contained in these compulsions and complexes. Working with them – perhaps therapeutically with a counsellor or analyst or on our own in some way – means accepting and coming to a better understanding of the motivations behind these urges. Taking time to write down our thoughts or to give them some sort of creative expression though drawing, dancing, etc., could help us deal with them more productively. Bach remedies or various kinds of body therapies – shiatsu, homeopathy or acupuncture, for instance – could also enable the body to cope more efficiently with the changes Pluto–Mercury transits are trying to effect. These transits sometimes coincide with a temporary mental or creative block, which we have to face and endure before new energy makes itself felt.

The unconscious is not only a storehouse of early scripts and patterns: it is also the reservoir of untapped potential and abilities awaiting to be developed. A journey into the unconscious means the possibility of contacting talents and facilities which are yet to be more completely realized. In particular, Pluto transits to Mercury could serve to reveal latent mental or verbal skills that are not being utilized to their fullest. We could discover a flair for languages, an intellectual capacity, or an ability to write and communicate.

Mercury is associated with routine and day-to-day interactions with the immediate environment. Popping out to the local shop for more milk, a letter or phone call to or from a friend or relative, a conversation or chat with the neighbours, a week-end jaunt to the country – these all come under the domain of Mercury. During a Pluto–Mercury transit, it's possible that something fairly routine or ordinary might end up embroiling us in more complications than expected, or even could develop into an event of major significance.

In particular, negative undercurrents and unresolved problems with siblings or other relatives often come to the surface when Pluto is transiting Mercury. A present concern or situation might be the agency through which childhood resentments and jealousies re-emerge. Pluto brings them out into the open, where they have more chance of being resolved. Unfortunately, this is not always the end-result, especially in the case of the hard Pluto–Mercury transits. Some people are unable to transmute the hate, pain or hurt they feel towards a sibling, or they can't deal with the feelings a sibling has towards them. If this is the case, they may break off relations with the relative in question at this time. But, besides describing a direct conflict between ourselves and a sibling, Pluto transiting Mercury in one's own chart could signify siblings or relatives who are facing a difficult period or phase of life. A relative may suffer emotional or financial setbacks or could fall ill. In some cases, these transits, particularly if linked to the fourth or eighth houses, indicate the death of a relative. As with any death, a time to grieve is necessary. Grieving may involve not only working through sadness, but also confronting feelings of guilt ('Why didn't I do more?'), or anger and resentment ('Why did you die now before we could sort out our problems or do the things we wanted to do together?'). Generally speaking, Pluto–Mercury transits are a time when exploring issues to do with death can lead us to a deeper understanding of it.

Pluto–Venus

The planet Venus is linked to three basic spheres of life: relationships, creativity and values. When transiting Pluto makes an aspect to natal Venus, it is within these three areas that change, disruption or transformation are most likely to occur. We'll examine each separately.

In terms of relationship issues, Pluto–Venus transits manifest in a number of different ways. If we are already married or involved in an important relationship, transiting Pluto will test the strength or truth of the union, forcing us to look at what is wrong in the relationship. Things we have been unhappy about in the partnership, but have never acted on or paid much attention to, make themselves felt with such an intensity that they have to be acknowledged and confronted. For instance, a woman came to see me when transiting Pluto was squaring her natal Venus. For years she had been sexually frustrated in her marriage, but she kept pushing aside her dissatisfaction. The relationship worked well in so many other ways that she tried to ignore the sexual problems. However, with transiting Pluto square her Venus, she could no longer contain her frustration, although she was afraid to tell her husband and risk stirring trouble between them. In the end, she found the courage to share her feelings with him, and they were able to work through their sexual problems. As a general rule, if we can face and successfully resolve the kinds of concerns that Pluto raises when it aspects Venus by transit, there is a good possibility the relationship will deepen and grow stronger as a result. What is potentially undermining and threatening is brought to the surface and cleared. In this way, Pluto cleanses Venus and purifies the relationship. The relationship dies as it has been, and is reborn on to a whole new level or way of being.

In some cases, however, a Pluto transit to Venus (even the transiting trine or sextile) could stir up difficulties or issues which prove insurmountable. Pluto may reveal such deep-seated differences that, even with the best intentions, the union cannot survive. One or the other of the partners may be unwilling to admit to the problems in the relationship, or may simply be unable to change his or her habitual patterns of relating. If Pluto is making a conjunction or square by transit to our Venus, we are often the one who initiates the break-up. If transiting Pluto is opposing our Venus, then the other person may end the relationship. However, in practice, even with a transiting conjunction or square, it may be the partner who walks out or finishes things. As with any of the transits of the outer planets to Venus, we will meet change or disruption by choice or by coercion. If we are unwilling to face the truth in a relationship or are reluctant to deal with problems that need to be brought to the surface, then our partner may act in a way which forces us to confront what we have been avoiding or denying.

A Pluto transit to Venus also could indicate a partner or loved one experiencing a very difficult and challenging phase of life. He or she may fall ill, or there could be serious psychological troubles, or problems with work. In these cases, we are put through tests and changes as a result of what the partner is facing. In our efforts to support the other person, we may find resources in ourselves we didn't even know we had. Finally, in some instances, a Pluto transit to Venus coincides with the actual death of a partner.* If it is the relationship itself which 'dies' under this transit, it will need to be

*See Suggested Reading (p. 386) for a list of books dealing with death and the grieving process.

mourned in the same way we would grieve for a person who has died.

When Pluto transits Venus, present relationship problems act as a catalyst to awaken deep-seated emotional complexes left over from childhood. For example, if we discover that our partner is having an affair, we will not only feel the hurt and betrayal associated with the immediate situation, but we also will reconnect to emotions still lurking inside us from infancy when we were threatened by our caretaker paying more attention to another person. As a child, our life depends on having someone there to take care of us; not being the central focus of our caretaker's attention is very frightening, and gives rise to fears of being neglected, abandoned, or left to die. These early-life insecurities and traumas can be triggered again by our present partner's infidelity. This is not to say that the immediate situation of a partner's indiscretions isn't upsetting in itself: we have been tricked, deceived and let down, and this alone will provoke strong reactions. But these natural responses increase in complexity and intensity when they become entangled with childhood fears of abandonment and death. Most likely as an adult, our actual physical survival doesn't depend on our partner's fidelity, and yet the frightened child who lives inside us will react to our mate's unfaithfulness as if our lives were really at stake.

If this is the case, it's understandable that our reactions to the situation are going to be more fraught and extreme; we even may feel like murdering our partner or the other person involved. The young child who fantasizes destroying a bad parent isn't capable of carrying through the act, but the adult whose inner child is stirred in this way is physically mature enough to turn destructive fantasies into reality. Transiting Pluto to Venus in itself probably wouldn't evoke a reaction ferocious enough to lead to murder or violence, but if this transit (or another significant one happening at the same time) also activates natal Mars, it might provide the necessary impetus to lead to such extremes. Actually taking it this far – although it happens – is fortunately not the norm. But it still leaves us with the question of what can we learn from these situations – what value is there in having our unresolved infantile complexes brought to the surface? It is only through reconnecting to complexes buried in our unconscious that they can be reclaimed and eventually transformed. The present difficulties with a partner that occur under a Pluto transit to Venus serve to bring these complexes to the fore. Once they are brought to the surface level of awareness, they can be more fully explored, which is the first step towards working productively with them. Once freed, the energy trapped within a complex can be reintegrated into the psyche in more constructive ways. Counselling, therapy, meditation or certain forms of healing – such as homeopathy, Bach Flower Remedies, acupuncture, etc. – will aid the process.

We have been discussing Pluto–Venus transits in terms of a partner arousing our jealousy and anger. However, in many instances I have seen, these transits (especially when transiting Pluto opposes Venus) manifest in our being on the receiving end of somebody's rage and jealousy. We may be the one who is threatening the existing relationship, and in doing so, act as the catalyst to activate our partner's jealousy, envy or rage. (Even if we are completely innocent, our partner might be imagining that we are engaged in some kind of deceit, and read his or her worst suspicions into what is innocuous behaviour on our part.) When Pluto transits Venus, it asks that we encounter intense emotions and feelings through love and relationship; if it is not our own feelings that are stirred, we will then find ourselves the target for someone else's. Again, we must ask ourselves why have we attracted such a situation. Is there any truth to our partner's accusations; if so, what needs to be looked at and discussed in the relationship? Or are we somehow provoking a partner to express and act out feelings inside ourselves which we have disowned and projected?

Whether or not we are already involved in a relationship, Pluto–Venus transits could bring a new person into our lives for whom we feel a strong, irresistible attraction. Something deep is touched and there may be little choice but to go with our feelings, even if it means endangering an existing partnership. With Uranus–Venus transits, a new relationship could serve as a catalyst to change our lives in some way and then end as suddenly as it began. With Neptune–Venus transits, a new relationship could let us down and disintegrate within a number of years. But if a new relationship develops under a Pluto–Venus transit, there is more likelihood it will last and replace an already existing one. The kind of person we fall for under these transits often is someone whose natal chart shows the planet Pluto or the sign of Scorpio prominently configurated. Given the strong feeling nature of such a person, it's not surprising that these relationships are very intense and call for more commitment and involvement than a partnership that develops when Uranus or Neptune are transiting in aspect to Venus.

Pluto transits to Venus are times of discovery – we are meant to learn about parts of ourselves we haven't been fully in touch with before. For a young person who is new to the whole sphere of relationships, this transit could mean a fiery, passionate, all-consuming involvement, and an initiation into the arena of sex and intimacy. For someone who has had previous experience of relationships, there is still something new, exciting and more complete about a partnership which is begun when Pluto is affecting Venus. In either case, the relationship is likely to stir parts of us that other relationships haven't touched, and to arouse our deepest feelings, emotions and complexes. Those of us who have prided ourselves on our calm, rational and controlled nature may be in for a surprise.

If we are involved in artistic or creative outlets, these also will be affected by Pluto transits to Venus. In some instances, the medium in which we are accustomed to work changes: actors turn to directing, non-fiction writers take up fiction, and dancers become choreographers. The medium may remain the same, but the message could alter significantly, reflecting a major shift in philosophy or belief-system taking place at this time. In a few cases, a Pluto–Venus transit has coincided with a person abandoning his or her career in a creative field in order to pursue some other kind of profession; but it is more likely that creative people will experience an increase in artistic inspiration under Pluto–Venus transits. An idea, image, or theme totally absorbs them, and they are obsessed with giving it some form of expression. Anything creative which is worked on at this time will stir powerful emotions, and force artists to face deep complexes or hitherto buried and unresolved feelings.

However, before new creative inspiration is tapped, it may be necessary to go through a period in which our creativity is apparently blocked or stifled. This is because the energy normally used to drive the creative process has been temporarily appropriated by the psyche for other reasons – probably to effect and support important psychological changes that need to take place at this time. In other words, our libidinal energy turns inward, and we have less at our disposal to continue creating in our usual fashion. It's best just to go with this process – once the inner changes have been effected, a new influx of creative energy will be available and the whole period can be looked back upon as a necessary pre-creative depression. Unfortunately, many people, frightened and disturbed by a block of this kind, may try to force themselves to carry on working during this period, only to find that the end-results are far from satisfactory. Others may turn to alcohol or drugs as a way of soothing their frustrations, or in the hope that these substances will somehow renew their inspiration. While it's quite natural (and even part of the process) to fight a creative block in this manner, we will serve our work best by flowing with a temporary lull in creativity. A non-productive phase may be necessary in order to give the psyche the time and space needed to effect the changes dictated by the deeper levels of the unconscious at this time.

The planet Venus is also associated with the whole issue of *values*: what it is we value, find beautiful or hold dear in life. The value of something is very often determined by its financial worth – therefore Venus is traditionally linked with money and wealth. Accordingly, a Pluto transit to Venus could change our financial status; depending on the nature of the transiting aspect (trine, square or opposition, etc.) and other factors in the natal chart, extreme reversals of fortune either way might occur at these times. More broadly, a Pluto transit to Venus often indicates a shift or change in our value-system in general: what we previously valued, treasured or hoped to gain no longer seem so worthwhile or attractive. When Pluto transits Venus, our old values slowly fall away and die, and for a while we may be left confused and uncertain, no longer sure what it is we really want or desire. An uncomfortable period could ensue during which we know what we don't want, but don't know what it is that we do want. By the end of the transit, however, new values and desires will emerge to replace the old ones.

Our value-system dictates the kinds of choices we make in life. If we value money, we make choices for money; if we value freedom, we make choices which would lead to greater freedom; if we value security, we opt for whatever would give us more security. A change of values has a far-reaching effect. We may have achieved admirably in terms of our old value-system, but if these things are no longer what we find fulfilling, then major adjustments have to be made. In this way, a Pluto transit to Venus can dramatically undermine the foundations on which much of our life has been built.

Probably the most important and dramatic change we could experience under a Pluto-Venus transit is that of learning to love and value ourselves more. This is easier said than done, and usually involves having to explore our early life, and those situations, people and events that contributed to our forming a negative self-image in the first place. If we don't value ourselves, we are likely to make choices in life that don't make us very happy. If we come to love and respect ourselves for who we are, we will naturally make choices that reflect and support a healthy self-esteem. The kinds of crises associated with Pluto–Venus transits are far from easy; but if in the end these enable us to find a greater sense of our own value, our struggles would certainly not have been in vain.

Pluto–Mars

When transiting Pluto aspects Mars, it is a time for us to learn more about our aggressive drives, power urges, desire-nature and sexuality. In many cases, the effects of these transits can be quite dramatic, especially when transiting Pluto conjuncts, squares or opposes Mars. Transiting Pluto trine and sextile Mars generally are easier to handle.

Pluto burrows beneath our usual boundaries and defences: it will thus bring out of hiding and force us to confront any planetary energy it aspects by transit. If we have not been in touch with our aggression, a Pluto transit to Mars will force us to come to terms with this part of our nature. Just as the sexual drive is an essential part of our human instinctive behaviour, so too is aggression; the natural or root aggression we are born with makes it possible for us to grow and to master life, and is a force that provides the impetus to move forward, learn new skills, and evolve into all that we could become. If we have been lazy and have allowed other people to tell us what to do and where to go, a Pluto transit to Mars can have the effect of waking us up. Something happens and we discover a drive for power or urge for self-expression we didn't know was there. Under these transits, we may find, perhaps for the first time, what it is we really want in life and connect with the will and energy needed to implement and realize these desires. Suddenly there are goals we are determined to achieve, places we are determined to go, things we definitely want to learn and do, and people we no longer will allow to stand in our way.

However, if we already have a grip on our Mars and for years have been forging ahead in a definite direction, a Pluto–Mars transit could actually stop us dead in our tracks. External circumstances may come and block us, and it is impossible or just not feasible to carry on in the direction we have been heading. Or we lose interest in our present endeavours – what we have been seeking no longer seems relevant: something inside says 'Hold on, it's time to take stock and reconsider your drives and desires.' During this period, it may feel as if we have no goals or desires at all, but this is an in-between stage, when the old isn't working but the new hasn't yet made itself felt. We may just have to sit and wait until new drives and fresh desires take hold.

Like the Sun, Mars is an *animus* principle and represents that part of us which seeks to express our individuality through action, asser-tion and power. In a woman's chart, a Pluto transit to Mars could serve to put her in touch with animus energy inside her. If she has been too passive and submissive, Pluto–Mars transits most likely will make her more aware of a need to assert herself in her own right. Dreams about male figures – especially ones who are violent, or who chase and try to attack her – are indications that the animus is awakening. However, if she has been too dominated by her animus side, Pluto–Mars transits could have the effect of blocking or stifling (temporarily) her aggression and assertion in an attempt to help her discover ways to relate to the world other than through her Mars.

Pluto–Mars transits also activate animus issues for men, and if a man has not been living out his assertive side, he will probably discover it under these transits. However, if he is too animus-driven, then Pluto–Mars transits could be the time when he needs to learn how to alter or temper his overpowering drive or ambition.

So far, we have discussed two different ways in which Pluto transits act on Mars. In the first instance, these transits awaken a previously latent or hidden assertive nature, whereas in the second case, our assertive side is already active, but Pluto changes the focus of our aims and drives, or modifies the manner in which we vent our aggression. As a general rule, transiting Pluto will (1) intensify whatever planetary energy it aspects by transit, or (2) will challenge and transform the usual way we express the principles represented by that planet. For example, consider the effects of Pluto–Mars transits on the expression of anger or aggression. If up to now we really have not been in touch with our anger, a Pluto–Mars transit could reveal a bottled-up rage which we hadn't even suspected was there. Some degree of anger in life is healthy – we need it to fight injustice or to deal with people and things that are blocking us getting on with what it is we feel we have to do. But a Pluto–Mars transit (in particular transiting Pluto conjunct, square or opposing Mars) will often reveal a different kind of anger – a much earlier, more primitive infantile rage that has been buried deep inside us for a long time. And this kind of rage is anything but civil*

However, for those of us who always have exhibited a tendency towards anger and rash behaviour, Pluto–Mars transits will serve a different purpose. We don't need to discover our deep rage – we already know it's there and are frequently taken over by it. Instead, our lesson is to transmute or redirect that destructive anger into more useful or constructive channels. In these instances, Pluto–Mars transits have an uncanny way of stirring anger at the same time as creating circumstances which make it impossible or impractical to express our venom. Rather than unleashing our rage and attacking other people, we have to find alternative ways to give expression to our anger, or to find the root cause of our anger and frustration in order to eradicate it.

---

*For a fuller discussion on the nature of infantile rage and how to work with it, see ch. 8, pp. 226–33 and pp. 242–5.

For example, a woman came for a reading who had transiting Pluto in Scorpio conjuncting her natal Mars. She was not someone who needed to discover her belligerent side, since all her life her immediate response to people who frustrated or hurt her had been to hurl rage and abuse at them. In the course of 35 years, she had managed to accrue two broken marriages, a whole string of friend-ships that had ended badly, numerous jobs she had stormed out of, and three lawsuits lodged against people she felt had maligned her. At the time of our reading, she was very angry at her father over a remark he had made about her. However, he was so ill and in such a confused state that she didn't feel right about expressing that anger directly to him. She found herself in an awkward situation: her normal pattern would be to act out her rage, but in this case she felt that the circumstances prohibited her from doing so. The Pluto–Mars transit was asking that she deal with her anger differently than she would have done in the past. Pluto wanted her to transform the use of her Mars energy, to contain it and sit with it rather than unleash it. Over the following few months, she joined a dance and movement class which allowed her some physical expression of these emotions. She took time each day to write about her feelings and explore the kinds of frustration and hurt she carried in her from childhood. In doing so, she not only physically discharged her anger, but she was also able to use her rage as a way of looking more deeply into her psyche and early complexes.

When transiting Pluto conjuncts, squares or opposes natal Mars, we may be feeling violent, although many of us will do what we can to deny it. However, if we try to suppress these feelings, we increase our chances of provoking others to be violent towards us (this is true of any hard transit of Pluto to Mars, but especially in the case of transiting Pluto opposing Mars). What we deny in ourselves, we tend to attract from others. Denying our violent feelings also can result in these emotions turning inward against the self, manifesting in the form of self-destructive urges and behaviour (more likely in the case of transiting Pluto conjunct or square Mars) or even illness. If we can find the courage to face our anger and rage, we lessen the risk of attracting it from the outside and stem the dangers inherent in allowing it to fester inwardly. Again, owning our violence does not mean having to live it out; once it is acknowledged, we have the opportunity to find other ways to work with or direct that energy.*

Under Pluto–Mars transits, we can sublimate, redirect or learn more about our Mars energy through various kinds of external outlet. For instance, the aggressive urge and need to exert power and influence could be satisfied by joining causes and organizations in which we fight for changes we feel need to be made in society. Some people may become involved with projects designed to battle poverty or disease. Or we could test our assertiveness and power through body-building, competitive sports or by pitting ourselves against the elements – camping, climbing or sailing.

It's not only assertiveness and aggression that Pluto transits to Mars stir and alter. These transits can also affect our sexual nature and drive. There are a few general rules we can apply here: (1) people who have been out of touch with their sexuality could wake up to its existence; and (2) people who are already venting their sexual drives quite openly or freely may find that a Pluto–Mars transit inhibits or blocks their usual mode of expression and ultimately changes the way they relate sexually to others. Obviously, how these transits manifest depends a great deal on age. If we are 15 years old and transiting Pluto aspects Mars, it is likely to manifest in issues related to the awakening of sexuality. Teenagers under these transits could become obsessed with sex or frightened by the strong feelings and compulsions it arouses in them. In certain cases, they may be the victims of sexual abuse.[7]

In adults, Pluto–Mars transits can also indicate the need to confront and to understand better their sexuality. These transits may force people to acknowledge sexual frustration and difficulties. One woman who came for a reading had been married for 20 years and had never felt sexually satisfied with her husband. She had put up with the problem for all that time, but when transiting Pluto squared her Mars she could no longer tolerate the situation. Unable to resolve the sexual problems with her husband, she left him and soon after became involved with a man with whom she found a fulfilling

*See ch. 8, pp. 242–5.

physical relationship. In another case, a man had been celibate for most of his life, but when transiting Pluto conjuncted his Mars he finally acknowledged his homosexuality and joined a group through which he could meet other men. These examples illustrate how Pluto compels us into the sphere represented by the planet it is aspecting by transit.

However, Pluto also can have the effect of blocking, inhibiting or altering sexual expression – especially if our tendency has been to misuse or overdo that energy. Previously celibate people may discover sex under these transits, but the converse is also true: if we have a pattern of promiscuity or have been dominated by our sexual drives and appetites, a Pluto transit to Mars could bring experiences which result in our changing these trends. One stage of the process of change may involve temporarily losing our sexual drive. We might fear that it is gone forever, later to discover that it returns, but with a different quality.

Pluto–Mars transits can affect our sexual expression, aggressive urges, the animus side of our nature, or the way we pursue our goals. Transiting Mars conjunct, square or opposing natal Mars in particular can be very difficult and not everyone will succeed in handling these times in a positive way. But if we can face and successfully deal with such transits, they offer a tremendous opportunity for psychological growth, personality development and for the wise and judicious use of our strengths.

Pluto–Jupiter

Faced with a world which often seems indifferent or chaotic, we search for ways to give meaning to our existence. We feel more secure if we can make sense of what happens to us in life by fitting our experiences into some larger pattern or all-encompassing explanatory framework. The planet Jupiter is associated with the symbol-making capacity of the psyche – the inclination to attribute meaning to events and random incoming stimuli which we encounter in the course of daily living.

Because Pluto tears downs and rebuilds whatever it touches, when it aspects Jupiter by transit, we may find ourselves disillusioned or let down by what we have previously believed in. The way in which we have been finding meaning in life or making sense of the world may no longer work, and anomalies in our belief-systems become apparent, or we question our image of God. Is there a God at all? If God exists, how could He allow the kind of suffering and pain we see all around us? The death of a philosophy or religious conviction can leave us shattered, bereft and confused: the ground is taken from under our feet and we don't know what to believe in any more. The loss of a dearly held belief-system needs to be mourned in much the same way as any death. We will not only feel sad and aimless, but we also could feel angry and betrayed by our faith, or guilty and punishable for no longer believing in it. Eventually, after an empty period during which our old beliefs aren't working but no new ones have yet been found, we can emerge renewed and with a restored vision of life and its meaning.

However, Pluto can also arouse and bring to life the principle represented by the planet it is aspecting by transit. If up to now we have not been very concerned with the overall meaning of existence, a Pluto–Jupiter transit could change all this. A book we read, a lecture we attend, a 'chance' meeting with someone who opens us to new ideas could plunge us into the whole realm of metaphysics, philosophy and religion. Under these transits, our lives could change radically as a result of a new faith or belief-system that grips us intensely. The effect is similar to a conversion – we sometimes become totally absorbed with our newly found beliefs or with the entire sphere of philosophy and religion in general. Neither Jupiter nor Pluto does things by halves, and when these two planets are linked by transit we go to extremes – we can't read enough, we can't study enough, we can't devote ourselves enough. Suddenly there is an urgency, a pressing need to probe the 'whys and wherefores' of existence, to find the truth and to live it. Friends and family may look on in amazement, wondering what has come over us.

A change of philosophy that occurs under a Pluto transit to Jupiter is likely to take hold and last for a long time. Transiting Pluto conjunct or square natal Jupiter are the clearest indications of major changes in our belief-system or the discovery of a new philosophy that obsesses us. When transiting Pluto opposes Jupiter, difficulties could also come through external agencies: other people challenge and oppose our views or we are victimized for our religious convictions, whereas transiting Pluto trine or sextile Jupiter will not usually affect us as dramatically: changes will come but normally they will be easier to accommodate.

Jupiter is also associated with travel and long journeys. When transiting Pluto aspects Jupiter, it means that we will meet Pluto through this area. Since Pluto is the deity associated with death, in a small number of cases, it's possible that travelling under difficult Pluto–Jupiter transits could entail facing danger, intrigue, risk, or even a life or death situation. However, rather than an actual physical death, these transits are more likely to manifest in our going through a major psychological death and rebirth: our whole lives and way of seeing the world could be drastically changed as a result of a journey we make. This could happen in a number of different ways, but one thing is certain – while travelling or visiting abroad, we will attract experiences that profoundly affect us. Under these transits, we might fall deeply in love with someone we meet while travelling, or come across people who open up our lives in a new way. We may have a life-changing inner experience on a journey, moved by the site of an ancient ruin or a visit to a holy land or temple. The culture and philosophy of the country we are touring could stimulate whole new ways of thinking and looking at ourselves and the world. If we travel when transiting Pluto is aspecting Jupiter, we are not likely to return home the same person as when we left – if we return at all. Under a Pluto–Jupiter transit, we might leave our homeland and emigrate to another country. This could happen by choice or because political, social or economic circumstances force us to do so.

With a difficult natal aspect between Jupiter and another planet in our birthchart, we sometimes express the principle represented by the planet Jupiter is aspecting in a rather extreme fashion. For instance, if we have a hard natal Jupiter–Sun aspect, our ego or sense of self will be over-inflated at times. If Jupiter is squaring the Moon at birth, we are prone to excessive displays of emotion: we go overboard with our feelings or experience dramatic mood swings, one day very high, the next day very low. Stressful natal Jupiter aspects to Mercury indicate a proclivity to live too much in the head – to overdo cerebral activity – or the tendency to talk too much, and to embellish or exaggerate what we communicate. When transiting Pluto makes an aspect to natal Jupiter, it will also trigger any planet which Jupiter aspects in the birthchart – therefore the transit will also bring out our tendency to go to extremes in the sphere of life represented by that planet. As a result, we are given an opportunity to learn about that part of our nature, and possibly to do something to alter or transmute our pattern of overdoing in this area.

An example will help illustrate how this works. A young man of 22 was born with a natal square between Venus and Jupiter. When transiting Pluto conjuncted his Jupiter it also squared natal Venus at the same time. In effect, the Pluto transit brought out the Venus–Jupiter square, which in him manifested in his getting carried away in romantic situations. As might be expected, he fell in love under this Pluto transit, but this was no ordinary romance – it was the love to end all loves. Nor, to him, was she an ordinary woman, but a goddess whom he idealized and worshipped. He totally centred his life around her, giving up a promising career and abandoning his friends and social circle in order to move to the city where she lived. By the end of the first year of their relationship, she was finding it increasingly difficult to cope with his passionate and intense nature, and she began to feel unbearably cramped and suffocated. As she grew more irritated and distant, he reacted by holding on even tighter. Finally, after 18 months of living together, she asked him to move out. Devastated by the break-up, he sank into a deep depression and finally sought the help of a psychotherapist, with whom he was able to examine and better understand his behaviour, and what in his nature and background contributed to his tendency to over-idealize women and glamorize his relationships with them. Transiting Pluto brought to the surface the Venus–Jupiter square in such a way that he was broken down, changed and transformed through the experience.

Sometimes the kind of obsessiveness indicated by Pluto–Jupiter transits can be highly productive. A woman came to see me while transiting Pluto was conjuncting her Jupiter. Her natal Jupiter squared Mercury, so the Pluto transit was also activating this square, and the overall effect was to stimulate her mind in a way it had never been aroused before. She would wake up in the middle of the night, her mind afire with revelations and insights into different situations in her life, both past and present. Under this transit, her perception was heightened and she was able to understand concepts that previously had eluded her. She started to keep a journal at this time and in doing so discovered she had a talent for writing.

Jupiter represents a principle which encourages us to look towards the future – to our aims and direction in life. For instance, during a Jupiter return (when transiting Jupiter comes back to its natal placement), we often become excited about new prospects or possibilities we see for ourselves in the near future. However, when transiting Pluto forms a hard aspect to Jupiter, we are likely to go through a period during which our already existing aims are questioned or challenged. What formerly enticed us or pulled us forward may no longer seem so desirable, or we could meet insurmountable blocks that force us to rethink the direction in which we have been heading. We may experience a phase of not knowing what our goals are – a depressing feeling of being lost: we used to know where we were going, but now it seems we have no future and nowhere that beckons us. Or we see a future, but it looks doomed, dark, frightening and bleak, as if something threatening and ominous awaits us around the next corner, maybe even death itself. Our immediate reaction may be thoughts of suicide and ending it all. But the best advice is to wait it out, while our psyche reorganizes itself. As with any death or loss, we need time to mourn for our lost future, for those possibilities we hoped to realize but which have now betrayed us. We may have little choice but to stay stuck in this dark place for a while, since Pluto might temporarily force Jupiter and our sense of future 'underground'; but, given time, new directions and aims will emerge and we will act from greater conviction and a deepened sense of purpose.

Pluto–Saturn

In order to understand the effects transiting Pluto has on Saturn, we have to remind ourselves about the nature of Saturn in the chart. In general, Saturn shows our weak spots, those spheres of life in which we are insecure, vulnerable and easily wounded. We all worry about something – whether we are lovable enough, pretty enough, masculine enough, smart enough, etc. Saturn reveals where we are afraid to be seen as stupid, ugly, inadequate or inept. For instance, if Saturn is in Gemini (or in difficult aspect to Mercury or in the third house), we are concerned about our intellectual abilities as well as our capacity to communicate and to be articulate. If Saturn is in Libra (or in difficult aspect to Venus or in the seventh house), we feel uneasy in close relationships; we fear others won't like us or that we are incapable of forming satisfying partnerships. Sometimes we compensate for our Saturnian insecurities by trying to improve ourselves in the area in which we feel weak. Saturn in the third, for instance, could make a great deal of effort to develop the mind. Saturn in the seventh may work hard to improve the quality of relationships. In the end, through hard work and perseverance, we become increasingly adept in the area of our chart Saturn influences.

Gaining mastery and security in Saturn's domain takes time, and until we do achieve this (if ever), many of us will attempt to hide or deny where we feel weak and vulnerable. As a way of protecting ourselves against hurt, we erect defences in those areas. We don't enjoy having our weaknesses and inadequacies exposed, so we carefully try to avoid any situations which could trigger them. We put on a good show, doing our best to appear fulfilled, happy, attractive, intelligent or whatever. Such endeavours to conceal our pain and insecurities could succeed for a while; but when transiting Pluto aspects Saturn our defences will be challenged and we may be forced to face what we are most afraid of looking at in ourselves. Saturn builds barriers; Pluto, however, tears them down.

Transiting Pluto trine or sextile Saturn tends to do this more gently and with less upheaval, but the conjunction, square or opposition often hit very hard. They strip away our masks and expose that part of us which is most vulnerable and raw. In some cases, this is akin to a breakdown – the devastated ego is laid bare, and we may find it difficult to function as usual in everyday life. We might look for ways to fight or escape from the pain we are feeling, but the real healing can come only after the pain is accepted and faced. A brief case history will help to clarify how this works.

Jim was 31 when transiting Pluto first conjuncted his natal tenth-house Saturn in the early degrees of Scorpio. He had worked hard to establish himself in a business career, and had hopes of advancement within the company that employed him. However, when the post he had his eye on became vacant, another person was given the job. Jim was shocked and hurt. He had never readily expressed many of his feelings, but this situation triggered an overwhelming reaction, and he couldn't hide the anger, outrage and jealousy he felt. Transiting Pluto over his Saturn broke down his 'nice guy' façade, and revealed an array of intense 'Scorpionic' emotions beneath the surface. He sank into a deep depression, at which point he sought astrological counselling.

Through the chart reading, Jim became aware of a sense of inadequacy and fear of failure he had carried inside all his life. As long as he did well at his job, he was able to defend himself against these feelings of worthlessness. But as soon as he didn't receive the kind of recognition he needed to bolster his identity, his defences collapsed and he was forced to face his underlying negative self-image. His immediate response was to leave the company and find another job through which he could prove himself. It didn't take him long to realize that in doing so, he was only seeking another way to compensate for the inner belief that he was a useless and incapable person. Up to that point, his whole life was one attempt after another to deny and prove wrong what he inwardly felt about himself – that he was no good.

Instead of looking for a different job, Jim decided it would be more beneficial to stay with his feelings, unpleasant as they were, and use them as a pivot point from which he could explore his inner world. Where had his personal myth of inadequacy come from? Why did he feel that way? With the help of astrological counselling, he came to understand how his early childhood environment had contributed to his feelings of insecurity. His father was intelligent and hard-working, but didn't have the kind of personality or flair which inspired confidence in others. He stayed in the same firm for his whole working life, but never achieved much recognition and never advanced within it. Jim's mother, who was born with Sun conjunct Saturn in her tenth house, was disappointed by her husband's lack of success, and didn't hide the fact. Father is the first role-model for maleness, and in Jim's case, the model he inherited was one of failure and defeat. To combat these feelings, Jim was determined to rise to the top. In effect, his basic motivation in life was to win his mother's love. If he were successful, he would prove to his mother that, unlike the father, he was worth loving.

Failing to achieve his promotion opened the way for Jim to discover the deeper, hidden motives underlying his ambition and need to succeed. Underneath he was convinced he (like his father) was no good, and as a result, he was determined to prove his worth. But how could he really succeed if deep inside he felt he was inept and ineffective? How can we find love if underneath we believe we are unlovable? Ultimately, life reflects back to us our deepest beliefs about ourselves. In the end, despite all his efforts to achieve positive recognition, Jim felt a failure. The only way he could free himself from this vicious cycle was to become aware that he was in it. Transiting Pluto conjunct his Saturn toppled the framework upon which he was building his life, and created a situation which compelled him to look inside himself. Now that he had gained some awareness of his early wounds and conditioning, he could begin the process of healing them and finding his sense of worth from within himself, rather than having his self-esteem remain dependent on pleasing his mother. He could now begin to make more adult decisions about what it was he really wanted in life.

Saturn is the planet associated with boundaries. When transiting Pluto aspects Saturn, a force is set into operation which challenges the boundaries, limitations, and inhibitions we have imposed on ourselves. We might feel these destructuring urges so strongly that we are compelled to break free of restricting self-definitions with which we have circumscribed our lives. A married woman previously committed to her husband and family could find herself no longer able to function happily solely within that structure: she may want to break out, and experience other parts of herself and other aspects of life. A man who always has been quiet, responsible and contained may, under these transits, experience a powerful urge to free himself of this persona. The boundaries between conscious and unconscious, between what is allowed and what is not allowed, between what is and what could be, are among the first restrictions that Pluto will try to tear down and change when it transits Saturn. If Pluto succeeds in undermining any of these boundaries, much of what we have suppressed or kept buried will erupt into consciousness, demanding its due. Obviously, such transits play havoc with our lives. And yet they offer the possibility of growth and change in a way that few other transits can. An astrological reading at this time won't stop what is happening or remove the conflicts, but it enables us to perceive more clearly what is going on and gives some indication of the kinds of changes that need to be made and the areas of life most affected. The chart can give us a perspective through which to view what we are experiencing, and in this way make the whole process more meaningful, smooth and effective.

However, in many instances when transiting Pluto aspects Saturn (especially in the case of transiting Pluto opposition or square natal Saturn), we don't feel as if something inside us wants to break down boundaries and make changes; rather we feel as if something *external* is forcing us to change, over which we have little control. Call it fate or the deeper Self working through outside circumstances, but the result is the same: we have to face some kind of change or crisis in our life. How we have been deriving our sense of security or our sense of who we are will be disrupted, and even though it doesn't seem to be of our own conscious choice or making, it has none the less found its way to our doorstep for us to deal with. At this point, some of us may try to dig our heels in and resist change more strongly than ever. We can rant, rave and moan about our fate – we can blame it on others or on God – and yet, in the end, what we are confronting is our problem and our challenge. If we can find meaning or relevance in what we have to go through, we will be able to make constructive use of this period.

Saturn is associated with anything that limits or defines us – and the most obvious thing that does this is our physical body. Most of us define where we end and another person begins by the boundary line of our bodies. When transiting Pluto aspects Saturn, it may in certain cases break down the body through illness. Sometimes physical illness is the last resort – the only way the psyche can speak to us or get through to us that certain changes need to be made in our lives. Olivia's case history on page 360 is an example, among other things, of a Pluto transit to Saturn working in this way.

Pluto transits to Saturn sometimes indicate a period in our lives when we run into trouble with authority figures or with the law itself. Again, in these situations, we can detect the attempts of Pluto to tear down and de-structure anything that represents a boundary, rule, or ring-pass-not (especially those that are unfair or stand in the way of progress and needed change). None the less, issues with authority figures can be quite a complex psychological matter – usually relating to problems with parents during childhood and the growing-up years. We may have a genuine grievance against our boss, the law, the state or the Prime Minister; but if the way in which we express our dissatisfaction is accompanied and mixed up with unresolved anger or resentment towards mother or father, it will manifest with an uncontrollable intensity and produce extreme behaviour that in the end will hinder our achieving the kinds of changes we wish to implement. The task here is to disentangle our infantile anger towards mother or father from the legitimate and positive reforms we are promoting. No easy job, but a worthwhile one, not only for the sake of promoting a cause, but also in the name of gaining greater psychological self-knowledge and maturity.

Obviously, the effects of these transit (as with any transit) depend to a large degree on our age. Children with transiting Pluto aspecting Saturn are more likely to experience this as a time when their security is threatened in some way, usually through disruptions happening to the family that upset existing routines or structures in their lives. Teenagers and young adults could experience the more rebellious side of these transits, or go through a phase in which they feel exceptionally vulnerable and tested by the kinds of difficulties naturally associated with adolescence and the task of breaking away from the womb of the family and establishing an independent existence. Adults generally relate to these transits in terms of changes in self-definition and periods in which their defences break down and they have to face their innermost fears or insecurities. For elderly people, retirement issues and the loss of loved ones could arise under Pluto–Saturn transits. Illness could occur under Pluto–Saturn transits at any age.

No transit exists in isolation. Not only are there other transits and possibly important progressions occurring, but a single transiting planet will quite often aspect more than one planet. For instance, if there is a natal Venus–Saturn square, then transiting Pluto aspecting Saturn also will make a transiting aspect to Venus around the same time. This means that transiting Pluto will rout out and stir deeply ingrained issues not only to do with natal Saturn but with the natal Venus–Saturn square as well – such as problems with one's sense of self-worth and esteem, long-standing difficulties in relating to others, or conflicts and blocks within the sphere of creativity. And when transiting Pluto aspects Saturn, it will also be influencing the house or houses in the chart that Saturn rules, i.e. the houses with Capricorn and Aquarius on the cusp or contained within them.

Pluto–Uranus

Both Pluto and Uranus symbolize forces that tear down what is existing in order to make room for the new. When they are brought together by transit, their combined effects can be both explosive and revitalizing.

Uranus spends seven years in one sign, and people born within that period will share its sign placement. Therefore, when transiting Pluto aspects Uranus, many individuals will be experiencing the same transit. These periods often mark times when new ideas, movements, fashion or trends sweep through the collective and captivate the interest and attention of large groups of people around the world. We might observe that a number of our friends or associates seem to be experiencing changes in their lives and in their way of thinking similar to those we are going through. Such changes usually reflect evolving social trends and ideas that are circulating collectively, and how these shifts in collective consciousness affect us personally will be shown by the house placements involved (the house placement of natal Uranus, transiting Pluto, and the house with Aquarius on the cusp or contained within it).

Basically, a transit of Pluto to Uranus intensifies Uranus's natural predilection for change, expansion and growth. Even though we are probably being influenced by larger social trends, most of us will experience these Uranian urges as stemming from inside ourselves – especially in the case of transiting Pluto conjunct, sextile, square or trine natal Uranus. Transiting Pluto opposing Uranus, however, could carry with it a greater sense of external factors forcing disruption or upheaval onto us. With the opposition, we are also more likely to find that our vision of how things should be is in conflict with society or with others around us. In general, transiting Pluto sextile or trine Uranus indicates a fairly smooth and gradual transition into a new phase of life, while the harder transits such as the conjunction, square or opposition may be accompanied by more obvious turmoil, drama and strain.

Mythologically, Ouranus was essentially a sky-god who viewed life from on high. In astrology, this planet is associated with abstract systems of thought and with the search for visions and ideals which help order and give meaning to existence. It is also linked with the revolutionary and the inventor, both of whom are concerned with finding new and better ways to do things. When transiting Pluto aspects Uranus, a part of us is activated that wants to break free of habitual patterns of behaviour that are no longer serving our growth. The psyche does a flip: if we have crystallized into rigid and predictable routines and set beliefs, these transits disturb the status quo. We might find ourselves excited by some new ideas or visions, which come to us through something we read or hear. Our political or social awareness could also blossom and draw us into causes or groups with which we become intensely involved. In her book *The Aquarian Conspiracy*, Marilyn Ferguson discusses what she calls 'the entry-point' experience – inner or outer events that disturb our old way of viewing the world, alter our priorities, and open us to the possibility of a brighter, more expansive and meaningful dimension of life.[8] Pluto–Uranus transits often coincide with such entry-points: they mark times when we are so stimulated and aroused, we can no longer stay the same as we have been.

Extremism can be a problem with Pluto–Uranus transits, especially with the transiting conjunction or square. We could easily be carried away by a need to completely change our lives, and in one fell swoop throw away everything we have worked hard to establish or anything which represents the past. Or we could be taken over by a compulsion to change the world, fanatically advocating any means to achieve our ends. Or we think we have found the one answer to everything for everyone, and feel it is our mission to convert others to this truth. In the case of transiting Pluto conjunct Uranus, the house in which this is taking place will indicate an area of life we actively want to revolutionize and transform, or in which change and disruption is somehow forced on us. One way or another, we won't be able to carry on with the affairs of that house in our usual fashion. Both the conjunction and the square evoke stubborn behaviour, and a tendency to stick adamantly to our views. With Pluto transiting Uranus, whatever we feel we feel strongly: we are absolutely sure we are right, and are not likely to listen to anyone who tries to tell us differently.

We have been discussing Pluto–Uranus transits in terms of throwing off the shackles of tradition and conservatism. However, if we have always opted for independence and freedom and never settled down or adhered to conventionality, it is possible that a Pluto–Uranus transit could turn us round the other way. Seemingly overnight our motivation shifts and all we want is to put down roots, and find security. In some cases (especially with the opposition), these kinds of change may appear to be forced on us by circumstances in which we find ourselves caught. And yet, some part of our psyche has probably unconsciously created the situation, because, whether we like it or not, the time has come to move in other directions from those we have already travelled.

Most positively, Pluto–Uranus transits give us the opportunity to contact and make better use of our latent talents and abilities. We discover new things about ourselves and about the world we live in. Previously we may have felt limited by certain blocks or apprehensions, but now barriers break down, and our creative expression, our unique attributes, are able to flow more freely. We are especially capable of inventive and original achievements at this time. These transits also can indicate a period when we become so enthused or excited about a new field of interest that we are motivated to study and learn as much about it as possible – computer technology, astrology, metaphysics and other 'new-age' philosophies are commonly associated with Uranus, and an interest in these could be stimulated now. However, there is an erratic or haphazard component to the hard Pluto–Uranus transits: we venture off enthusiastically in one direction only to decide later it doesn't suit us, and then run off excitedly towards something else.

In general this is a time to be flexible, to experiment with new ways of being, and look to the future rather than the past. The danger is in going overboard and too far, too fast. If we can channel the intensity associated with Pluto–Uranus transits into constructive changes and outlets, we may find ourselves looking back on these periods as some of the most eventful and exciting times in our lives. And even if we do fly too high and crash down to earth with a thud, we have probably learned valuable lessons in the process.

Pluto–Neptune

Pluto can stimulate and arouse whatever planet it touches by transit, but it can also break down and transform that planetary principle as well. Neptune is associated with dreams, fantasies, ideals, illusions, transcendence and creative inspiration. When transiting Pluto contacts Neptune, facets of our desire-nature are powerfully awakened – we might become obsessed or 'taken over' by strong yearnings or ideals. However, these transits also could denote a period when dearly held dreams and ideals are shattered or destroyed. Because of the slow movement of both these planets, people alive today will only experience the conjunction, sextile, or square of transiting Pluto to Neptune. In general, transiting Pluto conjunct or square natal Neptune is more potent than the transiting sextile and more difficult to handle.

When transiting Pluto aspects Neptune (especially in the case of the conjunction and square), significant inner changes take place. Pluto wakes up and activates the Neptunian principle in us, that part of us that seeks to dissolve our rigid ego-boundaries and merge with something greater than ourselves. For some people, this entails the awakening of spiritual yearnings – the desire to transcend the confines of material existence or go beyond the usual 'me-in-here versus you-out-there' way of seeing life and others. We might be drawn to religion, mysticism, depth psychology, meditation groups, or any cult which promises access to the divine and numinous. Often this is a positive experience, an opening to another dimension of life which can give greater meaning and fulfilment. However, whenever Neptune is activated some degree of discrimination is needed. Otherwise, we could lose ourselves and be swept away into cults or groups which later on we realize are misguided or extreme.

Pluto–Neptune transits don't only arouse spiritual aspirations. Humanitarian, social or political visions of a better and more ideal world also are stimulated under these transits. Conversely, Pluto–Neptune transits sometimes shatter our dreams and challenge the beliefs or goals upon which we have based our lives. For instance, many of the people born with Neptune in Virgo who believed material wealth and success were the most important things in life experienced a change in their dreams and ideals when transiting Pluto passed through Virgo in the 1960s. In certain cases, they gave up secure jobs in the 'rat race' in order to participate in the pursuit of the spiritual aims and objectives embodied by the hippie movement, humanistic psychology, and the influx of ideas into the West from Eastern religion. Similarly, the generation with Neptune in Libra who held a vision of love and peace for the planet found their ideals slipping away and transforming as Pluto moved through Libra in the seventies. Discovering that what we have believed in is not the answer to everything can be very disorientating, as if the ground has been taken away from beneath our feet. Yet we will not be going through these changes alone. Neptune spends approximately 14 years in a sign, so whole groups of people will experience a Pluto transit to Neptune around the same time. Again, as in the case of any outer planet contact to another outer planet, many of our contemporaries will be facing crises or changes similar to those we are experiencing.

The kinds of longing stimulated by Pluto–Neptune transits also vary according to the house position of Neptune in the birthchart (as well as the house with Pisces on the cusp or contained within it). For instance, if Neptune is in the eighth and Pluto comes along to conjunct or square it, sexual compulsions could be activated. People with this placement may find themselves driven or taken over by intense sexual urges and fantasies, perhaps in the form of an obsession about a particular person who may or may not be attainable. The effect of transiting Pluto aspecting a third-house Neptune might be a thirst for knowledge and learning. If transiting Pluto makes a contact to natal Neptune in the tenth house, the urges and longings of Neptune are likely to manifest in the sphere of work and career ambitions. But we must remember that Neptune is also the planet associated with making sacrifices and giving up attachments. Therefore, a transit of Pluto to Neptune in a particular house could also ask that we sacrifice or let go of some of our dreams and longings in that area. Transiting Pluto aspecting Neptune in the eighth might not only arouse our sexual fantasies, but it can also mean that these may have to be given up, transcended or redirected in some way. Even if we successfully realize our fantasies in this domain, we may discover that they haven't fulfilled us in the way we hoped they would. Similarly, transiting Pluto aspecting Neptune in the third can entail having to make sacrifices in relation to a third-house concern – one young woman with this transit left school in order to look after her mother who fell ill during this period. Transiting Pluto aspecting a tenth-house Neptune could mean that certain of our career goals will have to be abandoned – perhaps we realize that our existing goals are unattainable and need to be relinquished or levelled down in scale.

In general, Pluto transits to Neptune (especially the conjunction and the square) will activate the unconscious mind and the feeling side of life. Creative inspiration can be aroused, along with greater empathy, compassion and openness to others. Intuitive and psychic faculties come to the fore, and we may experience an increased capacity to love and to perceive beauty around us. However, for some people Pluto–Neptune transits are not so easy, especially if natal Neptune is in difficult angle to the personal planets. In these cases, the transit of Pluto to Neptune will bring out the troublesome natal aspect, intensifying the difficulties. For example, a man came for a reading who had the Moon in 4 degrees of Leo squared to Neptune in 3 degrees of Scorpio. When transiting Pluto came over his Neptune, it squared the Moon in Leo as well, triggering the natal Moon–Pluto square. He fell madly in love with a woman whom he believed was the true love of his life, only to be painfully disillusioned within six months. This same man had lost his mother when he was very young, and the transit reactivated all the feelings connected to that early loss. A Pluto transit to Neptune which activates difficult natal aspects to Neptune can be very hard going – we are prone to deception and disillusionment or we may find ourselves at the mercy of unconscious compulsions or complexes. However, we must remember that such times, although painful, can be productive: they highlight psychological patterns existing in us which are in need of attention.

Pluto transits to Neptune can also affect and alter creative expression. A number of artists with these transits have experienced a period when their creativity temporarily was blocked, although in most cases they eventually came out of this phase with renewed inspiration and energy. Some turn to a new medium through which to express themselves. Actors take up directing, painters change to sculpting, or vice versa, or perhaps change their focus: for example, a professional photographer who had mainly worked within the fashion industry became disillusioned with that sphere and turned instead to photographing nature and wildlife.

We often meet trouble through whatever planet Pluto is transiting, and in the case of Neptune this could involve the misuse of drugs and alcohol. The desire to escape or transcend the confines and difficulties of everyday life may in part contribute to substance abuse at this time. Both Pluto and Neptune are planets associated with underworld deities, and when their influences are combined, they exhibit a pull which can drag people down to the depths. Even though we may be unconscious of such urges, self-destructive forces could be operating during this time. The urge to fall apart and put ourselves back together again in a new way is not necessarily negative, since it is only when the old collapses that new beginnings occur. However, some people under these transits do become dependent on drugs and alcohol and then have to face the difficult task of freeing themselves from these addictions.

Sometimes, with transiting Pluto conjunct or square to Neptune, we may feel as if we are losing control of our lives. Things we have taken for granted or always thought we could count on let us down, leaving us unsettled and adrift. Whenever Neptune is activated, it is a time of letting go, and this is never easy, especially if we have grown attached to or reliant on certain structures in our lives. Yet there may be very little we can do to stop changes from happening during these transits, and we may have no choice but to flow with the tide and trust that new things will come along to replace what is being taken away. We only make it harder on ourselves if we resist too long.

Pluto–Pluto

Pluto stirs and activates whatever planet it is aspecting by transit. When it transits in aspect to itself, it signifies a time when forces inside us push for a major change and renewal of the personality. Whether we like it or not, under these transits we will attract circumstances into our lives that compel us to come to terms with elements of our nature that are not easy to face. Because Pluto has a 248-year cycle, the Pluto return or transiting conjunction does not occur, except in some cases within the first six months or so after birth. Transiting Pluto conjuncting its own place at this time (either by moving retrograde or direct over it) might indicate an early traumatic experience that leaves a deep psychological impression, the ramifications of which could be explored through analytical psychology, hypnotherapy or some form of regression therapy. Transiting Pluto will not oppose its natal place in the span of a normal lifetime. However, most people will experience the sextile and square of transiting Pluto to its own place, and many of us will also have transiting Pluto trine to natal Pluto at some point in later life.

Transiting Pluto sextile and trine natal Pluto are less difficult to handle than Pluto square Pluto. With the sextile and trine, we are often in accord with the changes that need to be made – they 'feel' right and necessary. During these transits, parts of us which are touchy and sensitive can be brought out, and yet we are usually willing to co-operate and learn from life at these times. In other words, the trine and sextile indicate periods when we are more able to flow with the kind of radical psychological growth and development required of us. Provided that we don't doggedly dig our heels in and resist moving on to new phases of life, these transits, even when there are difficult lessons to be learned or challenges to be met, can be handled with relative dignity and grace. In fact, they could indicate a fairly exciting phase of life.

However, transiting Pluto squaring its own place – from my observation of this transit in the charts of clients – is among one of the most testing transits we will experience in the span of our lives. This is especially true if natal Pluto is difficultly aspected in the birthchart, because the square of Pluto to its own place will activate these natal configurations as well. For instance, if you were born with Pluto conjunct Saturn, then transiting Pluto will also be squaring natal Saturn at the same time. If you were born with the Sun opposing Pluto, then transiting Pluto squaring natal Pluto also will square the Sun around the same period. If you were born with Venus square Pluto, then transiting Pluto will either be conjuncting the Venus or opposing it at the time it squares its own place.

Transiting Pluto aspecting natal Pluto brings out what is grumbling in us, revealing where we are frustrated, discontented and unhappy with the status quo. On the whole, this is a good thing, because it is only when we acknowledge what is bothering us that we can begin to do something about it. When transiting Pluto squares natal Pluto, we can no longer get away with burying our heads in the sand, and it's a most opportune time to look at and do what we can to change what is not right in our lives. As stated earlier, transiting Pluto trine or sextile Pluto are easier to handle – we are more willing and able to make adjustments and accept what has to be changed. Transiting Pluto square Pluto however, is more likely to activate what is *most* raw, intractable, reprehensible and vulnerable in us – to force us to confront parts of our nature that are particularly difficult to face. The kinds of personality changes required with the transiting square are so threatening to our existing sense of self that we offer more resistance to them.

How old we are when transiting Pluto squares its own place depends on our year of birth. People born between 1900 and the late 1920s will experience this transit when they are in their fifties and sixties. People born from 1930 to the late 1980s will have Pluto squaring Pluto slightly younger, in their late thirties and in their forties. People born in the 1990s will have this transit in their forties and fifties. Obviously, its exact effects will depend to some degree on age, but certain general remarks still apply.

Clients with this transit who come for astrological counselling often bring concerns about sexual issues. Many of them complain of sexual frustration. They may have been married for some time, but they admit that the sexual side of the relationship is unfulfilling. They have put up with this situation for many years, but now, with transiting Pluto square Pluto, they can no longer ignore it. These sexual problems are often symptomatic of a deeper issue – the relationship they are in has no 'life' left in it. Communication between partners is virtually non-existent or other problems that have been there for a long time are no longer bearable. When Pluto squares Pluto, we need something to be passionate about, something that grips and engages us. If that is not being satisfied through a marriage or ongoing relationship, we become restless and irritable. A number of people with this transit have turned to extra-marital affairs through which they rediscover passion and sexuality. In some cases, an inner battle ensues between the desire to preserve the marriage or relationship they are in, and the urge to destroy it, and the indecision can be crippling. In general, with Pluto square Pluto, we feel there are important decisions or changes to be made in our lives, but for one reason or another these are frightening or extremely difficult to carry through.

Conversely, some people with these transits report that they are 'going off' sex, or find themselves in situations that require them to change their sexual habits and patterns. When Pluto squares Pluto, we have to alter those areas of our life associated with Pluto – and sex, regardless of what houses in the chart are involved, is one of Pluto's main concerns. Pluto is also associated with feelings and emotions which are buried deep in us – primal wounds from early life which have left us with anger, rage, jealousy, envy and pain. When Pluto squares Pluto, these 'darker' emotions have a way of surfacing through present circumstances related to the house position of natal and transiting Pluto and the house with Scorpio on the cusp or contained within it. At this time, we may be quite shocked or overwhelmed by the nature and intensity of what we are feeling. We might have believed we were a kind, sweet person, only to discover that underneath there is a rage and vindictiveness which knows no bounds. Or, through the areas of life associated with the houses involved, we meet circumstances that hurt or threaten us deeply – situations that trigger our worst fears and force us to confront our deepest anxieties, insecurities and complexes. We may have succeeded fairly well in protecting ourselves from our deepest neuroses and problems, but transiting Pluto square Pluto clearly reveals where we are most damaged and wounded. We can rigidly try to defend ourselves and do what we can to prevent difficult situations from arising, but we will most likely be thwarted in these attempts. Even if we manage to protect and defend ourselves against what is painful, by doing so we are cheating ourselves of growth, change and transformation.

An example will help make the workings of this transit clearer. John and his wife Louise were both actors, but of the two he was by far the better known. When transiting Pluto in the tenth came to square his seventh-house Pluto, the situation reversed. Louise landed the leading role in a television series, which brought her a great deal of public attention. Meanwhile, his career seemed to have stopped dead. For the first time, he was forced to acknowledge his feelings of competition, jealousy and envy – emotions he had always managed to keep under control, mainly through ensuring that the people with whom he associated closely were less successful than himself. At first he expressed his bitterness and resentment in devious and indirect ways. He went out and had an affair, and found any excuse to criticize and hurt his wife. Eventually, she confronted him, and he admitted to his jealousy of her success. He sought the help of a therapist in order to explore his feelings more deeply. At first, he found this jealous side of his nature difficult to accept – he had never thought of himself as petty or envious. In the course of therapy, he realized that these emotions had always been there. When he was a child, his mother continually compared his development and achievements with those of his twin sister. Although he and his sister were friendly and close, John came to see that there was a great deal of unacknowledged rivalry and resentment between them. As children, our security depends on the love of our caretaker, usually our mother; if we feel special in her eyes, we are reassured she will protect and look after us. However, if someone else is more special to her, we worry about being rejected or left to die. In John's unconscious mind, his survival depended on outshining his sister. As a result, he worked very hard to surpass her achievements and later to outdo his peers. These same feelings were transferred on to Louise. Everything was all right as long as he was on top and doing better than she was. But when she became more successful, the little boy in him feared losing the kind of love he needed in order to survive. Transiting Pluto square Pluto brought this complex to the surface. It was a very trying time for John, and yet through it he was able to recognize and work on aspects of his nature he had never seen or admitted to before.

The square of transiting Pluto to natal Pluto frequently coincides with important transitions life requires us to make. For instance, I have seen this transit in the charts of women who have dedicated themselves to raising a family. Now, with their children grown, they have to find other ways in which they can define themselves and be useful. For men, these transits often mark critical points in their careers. Some men have to face the fact that they have not succeeded as they hoped they would. Others are trying to decide whether to stay where they are or branch out in other ways, perhaps establishing their own business rather than continuing to work under others. If this transit occurs in our late thirties or forties, we may find ourselves taking on work that stretches us to our fullest capacity. But if transiting square Pluto (or transiting trine Pluto) takes place in our fifties or sixties, it could manifest in retirement issues and the major changes in lifestyle that this entails.

When Pluto makes a transit to its own place, we may have to confront death in some form. On a symbolic level, this could mean the passing of old or outworn phases of life. However, the transit of Pluto square or trine natal Pluto is likely to occur at a time when death could evince itself more literally – the loss of a parent, or the death of friends and colleagues. Such losses prompt us to examine our own lives more closely. We realize, more clearly than ever, that we are getting older and are not going to be around indefinitely. What have we done with our lives so far? What more can we do? What isn't right that could be changed? What have we missed out on? These Pluto–Pluto transits challenge us to make changes in our lives in order to make better use of the time we have left.

Transits of Pluto to Pluto (particularly the square, but in some cases the sextile and trine as well) also may mark periods of illness. Pluto brings what is buried in us to the surface, and this includes hidden impurities and debilities which may have been lingering in the body for years. Hopefully it is not too late to change or alter the negative habits that have contributed to any illness appearing under these transits. While attending to the purely physiological aspects of the malady, it also is useful to examine the possibility that our physical symptoms are symbolic of deeper psychological issues. For instance, skin problems which appear under Pluto–Pluto transits could indicate long-term irritations and resentments now manifesting physically. Stomach complaints often are emotional in origin – what is it that we can't stomach, or which is hard to take in and digest? When any Pluto transit expresses itself in illness, there is likely to be a psychological factor involved.

It is helpful to give some kind of creative expression to what we are experiencing when transiting Pluto aspects natal Pluto – through writing down, drawing, dancing or painting our feelings. The problems and tests we meet under these transits are deep and poignant ones, and if we avoid looking at them, we deprive ourselves of the kind of wisdom and maturity that facing them has to offer. Pluto–Pluto transits may wake up our 'demons', but they can also activate a desire in us to explore more deeply into philosophical, psychological, or metaphysical concerns. Our ability to fathom the kinds of laws or truths governing existence is increased, and any Pluto–Pluto transit is an excellent time to study not only the workings of one's own psyche but the cosmos as well.

Transiting Pluto Through the Houses

First House

When transiting Pluto passes over the ascendant and moves through the first house, our whole way of looking at life alters, and our sense of self is radically transformed. This transit sometimes correlates with striking changes in physical appearance, such as a new style of dressing, wearing the hair or presenting ourselves to the world. Overweight people slim down; previously thin or scrawny people put on weight. These external physical transformations are the outward expression of an internal shift in awareness and consciousness.

Obviously, the exact way any outer planet transit affects us depends on our age and other factors occurring in the chart at the time. None the less, some general conclusions can still be drawn. With Pluto crossing the ascendant and moving through the first house (the most easterly point in the chart and the house of the self), the core Self is asking that we explore new ways of expressing ourselves and experiencing life. If we are not in touch with our need to change, the environment will force us into it. For instance, children with Pluto transiting the first may face disruption because of difficulties their parents are going through. Adults under this transit who are unaware of, or unwilling to acknowledge, the inner need to alter their lives during this period could unconsciously coerce another person to force change upon them – they could provoke a partner to leave or an employer to fire them. In other words, disruptive outer circumstances occurring when Pluto is moving through the first reflect the core Self's desire that we change at this time.

This transit can reverse our life direction in ways we didn't think possible: people who thought they would never get married change their minds; people who thought they would always stay married get divorced; conservatives turn liberal; and liberals turn conservative. What we thought we were is no longer what we are. During this transit, our personal style and way of approaching life is meant to reflect and embody any of the principles which Pluto symbolizes. Some people will 'live out' Pluto at this time by acting as agents of disruption for others or for society in general, and the changes we make in our lives will force those around us to change. Or we can employ Pluto's regenerative energy by aligning ourselves with causes or groups which promote social transformation or by confronting the darker undercurrents buried within both the individual and group psyche. Hidden facets of our personality come to light under this transit, and we have to face aspects of our nature we have not fully acknowledged before. Unconscious contents break through into conscious awareness: previously unrecognized anger, sexuality or power drives erupt and challenge our existing self-image. We might never have thought of ourselves as someone who was manipulative and controlling, but now we see that side of our nature. We might have been unaware of our capacity for anger, jealousy, envy and destructive behaviour, but now there they are, unleashed and out of control. Like a harrow dragged across ploughed land to level or break up the soil, Pluto transiting the ascendant and first house brings to light our hidden depths, what has been 'underground' in us, and breaks up previous complexes or rigid patterns of behaviour. This is a time of discovery, cleansing and renewal, a fertile period for any form of self-exploration or self-development.

The unconscious is not only a storehouse for repressed infantile complexes. When Pluto dredges subterranean contents of the psyche up into consciousness, we also have the opportunity to discover and reclaim latent or untapped strengths, aptitudes and talents previously not at our disposal but now ready to be developed. If we have predominantly identified ourselves as weak and inept, this transit could unearth hidden strength and hitherto denied wellsprings of power, and reward us with a whole new sense of what we are capable of achieving. Many people under this transit discover, sometimes for the first time, an ability to take charge of their lives, a feeling that they are a creative force able to shape their destiny.

Pluto transiting the ascendant and first house thus signifies a time of rebirth, but because there is no birth without pain, this transit of Pluto is not without difficulties. The ascendant and first house are areas of the chart directly related to the physical body, and Pluto transits here can correspond with illnesses that profoundly affect our lives. The gifted astrological thinker John Addey – founder of the Astrological Association of Great Britain and the Urania Trust – is a case in point. In 1942, when Pluto was transiting over his Leo ascendant, he was struck down by an acute form of rheumatism that left him crippled. However, John himself was later to remark that had he not been 'forced to stay still for a moment and reflect on life . . . he would have probably been all too happy to spend his days between golf and the horses!'[9] John's illness was a crucial factor in turning his attention to astrology and philosophy – two subjects that had always fascinated him, but which he hadn't up to that point fully pursued. Dramatically changing the direction and focus of his life, the transit of Pluto over his ascendant heralded the death of one phase of his existence and his rebirth into a whole new way of being.

Second House

As Pluto transits the second house, we experience changes in the area of life associated with money, material possessions and values. On the most obvious level, this can mean a radical change in income. Pluto moving through this house could coincide with the loss of a job, and we may have to face the stark terror of worrying about whether there will be enough food to eat or enough money to pay the bills. This situation will bring childhood fears to the surface – in particular, those times we were terrified that mother couldn't provide us with what we needed to survive. Although harrowing to live through, losing the identity we derive from our work forces us to redefine ourselves: we have an opportunity to find an internal sense of worth not dependent upon how much we are accomplishing in the world, how much power we wield, or how much money we bring home each week. People who find this internal sense of worth gain an inner strength and equanimity not contingent upon the external world, but based upon a better estimation of who they really are and what they really need. In some cases when Pluto transits the second, the loss of one job paves the way for the discovery of another and of work which may be more in line with what we really want to be doing. However, a drop in income is not the only way Pluto operates in the second: in some cases I have seen, people have increased their income and wealth under this transit and as a result their sense of identity, potency and self-worth is enhanced.

On a deeper level, the second house is concerned with our sense of values. As Pluto transits the second, our values may change. If money and security have always been important to us above all things, we might discover values of a different nature at this time. In some cases, people with Pluto transiting this house have chosen to switch to an occupation which pays less, but offers greater satisfaction and fulfilment in other ways. The reverse, however, also is true: individuals who have never valued money or security could find themselves obsessively concerned about these things for the first time in their lives. And I have seen instances in which people with this transit take a business that is not worth much and transform it into something of great value.

Pluto makes us look more deeply into any house it is transiting, and in the second it asks us to examine what money and possessions really mean to us. If we passionately seek money, then why? Is money seen as a way of controlling others? Is it tied up with our sense of sexual attractiveness? Are we accruing money and possessions to compensate for a lack of love or security in childhood and to prove our worth to the world? If we continually fail at attempts to make money and find security in life, we need to explore why this is. Is there a part of us which doesn't feel we are worthy or good enough to achieve what we want? If so, we need to explore how we came to form such a low self-opinion. Or are we afraid of invoking anger and envy from others if we become successful? Asking these kinds of question with Pluto transiting the second will help us gain a deeper understanding of the issues we have around money.

When Pluto transits this house, a desire for wealth could bring out 'the beast' in us. We might go to any lengths to obtain money, resorting to ruthless and underhanded behaviour if necessary. We could find ourselves intensely jealous and envious towards those who have more than us. Pluto also stirs fears in whatever house it is transiting, and as it moves through the second, we may become obsessed by a fear that something will come along and take away our job, money or possessions. In certain cases people do lose everything under this transit, and it may be that Pluto is asking them to discover a new sense of self or the true ground of their being which is not reliant on their material status. In fact, under this transit we might unconsciously provoke or attract such a catastrophe so that an inner and more permanent sense of worth and security can be found.

Third House

Transiting Pluto in the third house can deepen our mind and this is a good time to take up a demanding study. In fact, we may be gripped by an urge to go beyond our superficial understanding and to probe more deeply the essence of a subject. Pluto transiting the third believes that knowledge is power: knowing how something works gives us greater mastery and influence over it. Moreover, what we learn under this transit we will probably never forget. Because the third house also describes our relationship with the immediate environment, Pluto here often activates a desire to understand more deeply what is going on around us. Like a detective, Pluto seeks to fathom the hidden motives behind the actions and behaviour of people we come in contact with in daily life. Pluto could also make us more suspicious than usual of other people. What do they really want from us? What do they actually mean when they say or do something?

In extreme cases, Pluto transiting the third correlates to a literal breakdown of the mind, or a long period of mental stress, paranoia or depression. Pluto takes us into the underworld via whatever house it transits, and previously hidden or repressed thoughts and feelings erupt to the surface under this transit. The mind, overwhelmed by deep primal emotions and fears, will not be able to function as normal. We might project dark images from early childhood – 'the suffocating mother', 'the punishing father' etc. – on to everyone in the immediate environment. The world around us becomes a living nightmare, peopled by the unconscious phantasies of the frightened inner child of our past. Prescribed drugs may be necessary to keep the mind under control, but this form of treatment will be most useful if given in conjunction with some form of psychological counselling or therapy. Understood most positively, the eruption of unconscious complexes into conscious awareness is an opportunity to begin to work constructively with hidden thoughts and feelings which up to now have been denied or kept at bay. We may not be able to cleanse ourselves totally of these psychic 'demons', but by fully acknowledging their presence and source, we have taken the first step towards facing and coming to terms with them.

The third house is also associated with siblings, relatives and neighbours, and Pluto transiting here can stir difficulties in this sphere. A conflict with a brother, sister, cousin, uncle or aunt, or a disagreement with a neighbour could awaken 'the beast' in us at this time. Again, through such conflict buried feelings from the past are brought to the surface. We hope that through becoming aware of these deep and unresolved tensions, we can begin to work with them more positively.*

Transiting Pluto through the third affects communication, writing, teaching, lecturing and the media, so that developing any latent writing ability or finding ways to improve our capacity to communicate and relate to others around us is a good use of this transit. We may be more impatient than usual with 'small talk', and will urgently want to get to the heart of a matter and talk deeply with others about what really concerns us. Under this transit, we can achieve a greater degree of honesty with people in our immediate environment. Conversely, some of us may experience this transit as temporarily inhibiting or interfering with our ability to communicate easily and openly with others. There are various reasons for this: what we are thinking or feeling may be so subtle or intimate that it is hard to put into words, or it may be that we are afraid to reveal our innermost thoughts – we are embarrassed by their intensity or frightened what other people would do if they really knew what we were thinking. We may fear that exposing too much of ourselves will give other people power over us, and therefore we carefully guard our thoughts. If this is the case, it is still useful under this transit to keep a diary or journal which allows us to express in a safe way what we are feeling. Or we can find a counsellor or psychotherapist with whom we are able to express ourselves freely. Without such outlets at this time, thoughts and feelings will fester, and the psychic pressure become so intolerable that our minds could break down under the strain.

The third house is also linked with early education. Younger people with this transit could encounter problems at school – difficulties with learning or trouble relating to their peers. Children

*For a discussion on dealing with deep-seated complexes, see ch. 8, pp. 226–45.

sent to boarding school during this period sometimes interpret being sent away as a punishment for something they have done wrong, since, in a child's mind, the thought of an action easily can be confused with the deed. A young boy, for instance, in a fit of anger might wish his little sister dead, and if she hurts herself or falls ill the next day, he will believe that his thought caused the mishap and feel shamefully guilty and responsible as a result. If children or adolescents have Pluto transiting the third when a sibling or relative dies or goes through a difficult phase, they may also feel somehow responsible for the event. In such cases, they will need help from an understanding parent, adult or trained counsellor to work through these feelings. If this is not available and their guilt remains unresolved, these children could be left deeply scarred by the experience.

Fourth House

The IC and the fourth house mark the very bottom of the chart: when Pluto transits here, it is a time to look into the depths of the self. At any point during this transit (but especially when it first crosses the IC and enters this house) we may feel more strongly introverted than usual. There is nothing wrong or pathological about this – being alone with ourselves at this time may be necessary in order to facilitate the kind of psychological metamorphosis this transit heralds. Pluto crossing the IC is an opportunity to make a new start, a new beginning in life, and even if we are not conscious of an inner need to change and progress, events will conspire in ways which make us do so.

The fourth is traditionally labelled the house of 'the home, the soul and the roots of the being'. It depicts the home and what kinds of activities go on there, and, on a deeper level, it also describes much about our childhood conditioning, the effects of the parental home on us, and how we might have been influenced by our ancestors. The fourth house also signifies father or mother, depending on which parent the astrologer feels fits most accurately with this house.* The influence of transiting Pluto through the fourth can be felt in any of these spheres.

What happens early in life forms a deep impression on us: we may not be consciously aware of it, but we carry these impressions from childhood around with us and they continue to influence how we perceive and experience life far into adulthood. In other words, how we see and evaluate the present is very much conditioned by our conscious or unconscious recollection of what has happened to us in the past. When Pluto transits the IC and fourth house, the effects of early conditioning are brought out into the open. Childhood issues are relived, either through the present relationship with our parents or through interaction with those we have close contact with during this period. Deeply ingrained beliefs and statements we hold about life and ourselves come to the fore, revealing what is operating in the inner recesses of our being. If we remember that the situations we attract into our lives now are replays of earlier traumas and difficulties, we not only learn more about what is buried in us, but we also gain added perspective and insight into our immediate concerns.

The case of a 25-year-old woman who came for a reading when transiting Pluto was conjuncting her fourth-house Libran Sun illustrates this point. Her father, who had hoped she would be a boy, had been exceptionally critical of her. Nothing she did was right, and she grew up feeling inadequate and worthless. Under this Pluto transit she became involved with a man who occasionally teased and made fun of her. Other people might have laughed this off, but his teasing stirred the early shame and hurt she had experienced with her critical father. The chart reading helped her to see the connection between her reactions to her boyfriend's behaviour and her feelings as a child. She joined a women's group in which she explored the early relationship with her father, and, in doing so, gradually freed herself from the negative conditioning stemming from his attitude towards her. Subsequently she found she was more relaxed with her boyfriend – she could see his jesting for what it was, and it no longer triggered her earlier wounds in the way it had previously done.

Getting to the bottom of long-standing problems and issues from childhood makes it possible to break out of old patterns and implement some profound and fundamental changes in our lives. Some of us may

*See ch. 5, note 5.

even confront our parents directly at some point during this transit. Transiting Pluto in the fourth could indicate the need to stand up to them, to say 'This is who I am, and if you don't like it, that is too bad.' In other words, this is a time when we can separate more completely from our parents – to define who we are as people in our own right, rather than continuing to be what they expect or want us to be. However, the converse situation can occur as well. If we have continuously rejected anything to do with our family and rebelled against them in extreme ways, this transit could indicate a change in that pattern – we may realize that some of their values or beliefs actually do fit with who we are. In general, Pluto in the fourth is a period when we are called upon to distinguish between those family traits that accurately describe us, and those that have been imposed on us and need to be rejected in the name of individuation. If the fourth house is associated with the father, this transit may focus specifically on issues to do with him. We might have to confront the father by standing up to and separating from him; or conversely, we come to realize just how much of our father's nature we have inherited. Transiting Pluto here heralds breakthroughs which enable us to relate more deeply or honestly with him than previously possible. Passages he is going through in his life at this time (a psychological crisis, an illness, retirement, etc.) will profoundly affect us as well.*

The fourth house describes the ancestral inheritance – our genetic and psychological link to the antecedents in the family line. Unresolved issues and conflicts in the ancestral line are passed down to us: we not only inherit our progenitors' physical traits, but we also inherit their psychological complexes or unfinished emotional problems. Transiting Pluto in the fourth could stir conflicts and crises in our own lives that in some way are related to unresolved issues in the family heritage. Being aware of this possibility and exploring as best we can our psychological family tree will help us better understand the kinds of concerns we are confronting during this transit.

In addition to childhood and ancestral patterns which are exposed through present crises at this time, transiting Pluto in the fourth

---

*See p. 261 for a discussion of the issues raised by the death of a parent.

coincides with changes and upheavals on the home front. If we move house when Pluto is passing through this sphere of the chart, it is likely that the move will significantly affect the whole of our lives. Under this transit we might purchase a home of our own for the first time, or embark on extensive repairs and redecoration in the place where we live. These external alterations reflect inner changes of a psychological nature. Transiting Pluto through the fourth can also indicate important changes in the lives of those with whom we live. Exactly how this manifests depends on the natal placements in the fourth, the rest of the chart, and the other transits and progressions occurring at this time. In some cases transiting Pluto through the fourth coincides with separations and divorces. In other instances, this transit indicates new arrivals to the home – the birth of a child, or a family member returning after a long absence (fathers coming home from war, etc.), or someone new entering the household. Transiting Pluto in the fourth could also signify departures from the home – a child who grows old enough to leave the nest, any family member leaving, or even the death of a household member. 'The beast' in us is awakened in whatever house Pluto is transiting, so during this time the home sphere will be the main arena where vicious quarrels, intrigues and power-struggles might take place. Traditionally the fourth house is associated with our country of origin. When Pluto is moving through this house, some of us might uproot and change countries, or return to our homeland if we have been away from it for any significant length of time.

Fifth House

The fifth house is broadly associated with self-expression, creativity, hobbies and recreational pursuits, children and romance. Transiting Pluto through the fifth will affect any of these areas. That part of us that yearns to give concrete external expression to our individual thoughts, feelings and imagination gains impetus at this time. We might discover a new interest, hobby or recreational activity in which we become intensely involved, sometimes to the point of obsession. If we are already engaged in a creative outlet, we may change from one medium to another; on the other hand, if up to now creativity has not interested us, it could turn into a major concern. Under this transit, however, any form of creative undertaking is not likely to be achieved without a great deal of effort, and we will have to confront psychological blocks and complexes that stand in the way of our freely expressing ourselves. Such creative blocks and difficulties can often be tracked back to the kinds of messages we received about the worth and value of what we created or gave expression to as children. The psychologist Erik Erikson pointed out that the crucial developmental issue between the ages of two and four was 'Autonomy versus Shame and Doubt'.[10] During this phase of life (what the Freudians refer to as 'the anal phase'), we develop either a positive sense of our own power, autonomy and effectiveness, or we come to believe we are shameful, bad and dirty – the feeling that what we have to offer the world is inadequate or unacceptable. Toilet-training occurs at this time and is directly related to later issues around creativity. As children, we don't inherently feel that our faeces is shameful or dirty; on the contrary, we take pride in what our bodies are creating. Eventually we are conditioned into believing there is something dirty or wrong about faeces – our first creations – and this can establish a pattern of feeling inadequate or shameful about anything we attempt to create later in life. When Pluto transits the fifth, early traumas and unresolved issues from this stage of development resurface in the process of self-expression. Whether we consciously realize it or not, we feel as if the dark face of the mother (or controlling parent) is watching over what we are trying to accomplish during this period. In order to free our creativity, we have to do battle with that figure.

Even if we have managed to pass through the anal stage and toilet-training without too much damage to our self-worth and self-esteem, transiting Pluto in the fifth can still activate psychological difficulties when we are trying to express our individuality and creativity. We could be so worried about how our creations will be received by others that our free flow of expression is inhibited. When Pluto is transiting the fifth, power issues also complicate creative endeavours, especially if we are engaged in projects that involve other people. If our sense of worth and identity is closely linked with what we are working on, we will insist that it is done our way, and we won't find it easy to make adjustments to how other people feel things ought to take shape. This was the case of a film director who came for a chart reading when transiting Pluto was conjuncting his fifth-house Mars. He so adamantly clung to his particular understanding of the film he was directing that he became embroiled in fierce arguments with the producer, who did not agree with his interpretation. Unwilling to relent or alter his view, he eventually broke his contract rather than compromise his opinions. Later, he came to understand that the intensity of his convictions stemmed from 'the little boy in him' who was still contesting the authority to which his overbearing father had subjected him as a child. Problems with creative self-expression that occur when Pluto transits the fifth serve to expose unconscious patterns and unfinished issues from early life, and offer us the opportunity to resolve them.

Children – creative extensions of the self – also come under the heading of the fifth house, and transiting Pluto through the fifth can affect this sphere in many different ways. The birth of a child during this transit will take on special significance, indicating the death of one phase of our lives and the beginning of a new one. It may be the first child, ushering us into the world of parenthood. A child born when Pluto is transiting our fifth will often show Pluto, Scorpio or the eighth house strong in his or her chart; or the synastry between our chart and the child's will highlight these areas. Somehow, the child will exert a Plutonic influence on us, forcing major readjustments in our lives. A woman carrying a child when Pluto is transiting the fifth may need to take extra caution during the pregnancy. In some cases, Pluto moving through this house indicates abortions, miscarriages, or stillbirths, events which require a period of mourning similar to any death or loss. In a few instances I have come across, the transit of this planet through the fifth coincided with the death of an offspring. One woman with transiting Pluto conjuncting her fifth-house Sun lost her eight-month-old baby son from a cot death, and her subsequent anguish and guilt led her to seek counselling and provided the entry point into a very intense and thorough psychological re-evaluation of herself, her marriage and her life as a whole.*

*See Suggested Reading (p. 386) for a list of books on death and the grieving process.

When Pluto transits the fifth, our children could be troubled or in crisis, and their experiences may present us with major challenges and lessons. The type of problems they are facing depend to a large degree on their age during the period we have this transit. In a number of cases, transiting Pluto in the fifth of the parent's chart has occurred when a child was going through puberty and the awakening of sexuality, but I have also seen this transit synchronize with an offspring getting married or divorced or experiencing other kinds of life-changing passages. Children may be exceptionally difficult to handle during this period, and yet Pluto here suggests that we have something to learn from what they are undergoing. Intense power-struggles between parent and child are a common manifestation of this transit. Some children may need to break radically with a parent at this time in order to establish more clearly their own separate identity. If we try to over-control children at this point, problems could escalate. Usually we do this because we are frightened that, if left to their own devices, they will harm themselves or act in a way that threatens our own sense of what is safe, right or appropriate. However, we need to accept that, in the name of growth and development, they may have to go through certain experiences from which we cannot or should not shield them. Also, under this transit unresolved issues with our parents can resurface through problems we encounter with our children. For instance, if we battled with parents for greater freedom and autonomy, we may find our children battling with us over the same issue. Or if we didn't feel loved by one of our parents, we may find ourselves fearing that one of our children doesn't love us, or we might be concerned that we don't love that child enough. In whatever house Pluto is transiting, patterns and problems from earlier in our lives reappear in a thinly disguised form. It is as if Pluto is saying 'you didn't resolve this issue before; here it is again for you to work on.'

The fifth house also relates to sex and romance, and Pluto transiting here will colour this sphere of life. A person we become involved with may have Pluto, Scorpio, or the eighth house strong in his or her chart, or the inter-aspects between charts accentuate these placements. A relationship during this period will change us in important ways. Involvements are likely to be intense, passionate and complex – they may be kept secret or riddled with power-struggles, intrigue, betrayal and jealousy. Liaisons formed now often reactivate the hurt and angry child of our past who is still trying to get mother or father to love us in the way we needed then. We discover 'the raging infant' or 'the beast' in us, and in this way are presented with an opportunity to explore and work through unresolved infantile complexes.* Pluto transiting the fifth can also coincide with the first awakening of our sexual passion, or this transit might rearouse our sexual energy after a long period of quiescence. However, while Pluto here often awakens sexuality, it can also manifest in temporary sexual blocks or a change in the nature of our sexual expression. Some people chose to transmute their libidinal desires into creative outlets or physical activities such as sports at this time.†

Sixth House

Work, health, and the running of everyday life are the main concerns of the sixth house. This area of the chart not only describes how we relate to our own bodies, but also how we get along with co-workers and those people we are serving or who serve us. As transiting Pluto moves through the sixth, we are challenged and transformed through the different kinds of problems and experiences we attract in any of these spheres.

Transiting Pluto in the sixth can manifest itself as health trouble. Pluto, the god of the underworld, brings what is buried in us out into the open: chronic but not terribly significant symptoms may erupt to

*See ch. 8, pp. 226–33.
†For a more complete discussion of the effects of transiting Pluto on sexuality, see the sections on transiting Pluto aspecting Mars, and transiting Pluto through the eighth house.

the surface in the form of illness and disease, the result of a long-standing imbalance. But even if we suffer ill health during this transit, it is not fair to view Pluto's effect on our bodies as totally malevolent; one of Pluto's main tasks as it moves through the sixth is to expose accumulated toxins and poisons in order to help cleanse the body and facilitate the healing process. Pluto here also wants to remind us of the intimate relationship and undeniable reciprocity between the body and the mind. Body and mind form an integrated system: our mental and emotional states have a direct bearing on our health, just as our physical condition affects the way we think and feel. The sixth house, more than any other area of the chart, is concerned with this *body–mind* connection, with the close relationship between *pysche* and *soma*, and it is well known that psychological issues play a part in aggravating a disease. Noxious agents are always present in the body, but whether we develop an illness or not depends upon our ability to resist them. Psychological stress, and negative thoughts and feelings (conscious or unconscious) impair our immune system and weaken the body's natural defences, making us more susceptible to what we previously were able to ward off. If we fall ill with Pluto moving through the house, we should not take the illness at face value. Poor health at this time is Pluto's way of informing us that our lives are critically unbalanced.

The root causes of health problems, not just outward symptoms, need to be treated when Pluto transits the sixth. By examining our whole life, we move in the direction of better health. Linda is a case in point: she came for counselling when transiting Pluto in Libra was moving through her sixth house coming up to square her Sun in Capricorn in the ninth. A lump on her neck had been diagnosed as malignant, and she was desperate to know what the chart might reveal about the illness and her future. Transiting Jupiter was making some good contacts to her chart at the time, and I encouraged her to fight the disease in any way she could. She sought the help of an alternative therapy centre specializing in cancer, and through the counselling and treatment the centre offered, she explored the factors in her past and present life that were contributing to her illness. A number of years before the onset of the cancer, she had given up a promising career in the arts to attend full-time to the needs of her husband and family. She hadn't realized how much bitterness and resentment she felt about this. With the diagnosis of a life-threatening illness, however, she gained a new perspective on her life. The old rules she lived by needed to be questioned, and the illness gave her permission to act in ways she hadn't allowed herself before. She openly expressed the anger she felt at giving up her career, and arranged for some part-time help to take over some of the responsibilities running the home so she could begin to work again. She became aware that she had the power to change her life, and with that realization, she felt increasingly positive and optimistic about the possibility of getting well again. She pursued various alternative therapies and followed a special diet recommended to her by the cancer centre. Within two years, the tumour disappeared and she was declared fully recovered. Transiting Pluto in the sixth, expressing itself through the medium of her body, had alerted her to what was wrong in her life and the kinds of change needed to steer her on the right path again. Linda summed up the effects of the illness in these words:

> Through my efforts and attitude, I was able to influence the course of my disease, and this showed me just what I was capable of. The illness made me realize how passively I had been meeting life. I never believed I had the power to make things the way I wanted them. Now that I've been through this, I have a much more positive sense of self, and feel that I have more control over my life. I'm not such a victim anymore.

Not everyone with Pluto transiting the sixth house will fall ill. But it *is* a time to listen to the body and respect its needs and limits and to examine any areas in our life that need adjustment or attention. Pluto tears down in order to rebuild and can exert a very positive regenerative influence in whatever house it is transiting. During the years this transit is in effect, we have the chance to remake ourselves physically. People who are not happy with their weight or shape often find the will-power and stamina at some point in this transit to undertake and stick to a diet or exercise regime.

Work is another sphere transformed by Pluto moving through the sixth. Wherever it is transiting, Pluto brings out what is grumbling in us. If we are not happy with the type of work we are doing, this transit provides the impetus to seek something different, either within the general area we have been working in or in an entirely new field. Pluto marks a time when the old has to go so that new things can happen. Very often, it will be our choice to leave or change employment; we feel we have grown or progressed as far as we can in our present job, and it's time for something new or different. However, in some cases under this transit, fate will have its hand in pushing us in new directions. We might be fired from the work we are doing, or be made redundant. If this should happen while Pluto is moving through the sixth, I would still read it as an indication that the time is ripe for fresh growth in new areas. We may not be fully conscious of that part of us which wants change, and yet if disruption or humiliation comes under this transit, it is likely that the core Self or deeper levels of the psyche are calling for it – perhaps we have become too staid, complacent or stagnant in our present employment. Doing what we can to co-operate with that part of us which needs to branch out or expand into something new is a good use of this transit. And even though the loss of employment could have a serious effect on our psychological or physical well-being, examining the emotions and feelings which are brought to the surface by such contingencies will lead to greater self-knowledge and further personal growth.

Everything in the world has both an inside and an outside. The urge behind the sixth house is to make the outer forms of our life – our body, our work, how we dress or keep our home – a truer reflection of what we are inside. The sixth house asks that we continually make adjustments and refinements in our lives in order to be more true to the self that we really are. This urge to be true to the self provides another motivation for changing work when Pluto is transiting here. We keep searching until we find the employment which best suits and reflects who we are. If under this transit we find a task which really grips us, we will execute it with an intensity and dedication that borders on the obsessive. Some of us may do the best work of our lives when Pluto is moving through this area of the chart. It is also possible that at some point during this transit, we will be attracted to a line of employment that is Plutonic in nature –

undercover or detective work, secret projects, mining, psychology, medicine or anything that involves tearing something down in order to rebuild it.

Under this transit, Pluto could be reflected in working conditions – we may be working long hours or against great odds. Or Pluto may reveal itself through problems with co-workers: 'the beast' in us or in others could be loose in our office, factory or consulting room. We may be jealous of a colleague's success, or sexually obsessed with a workmate or client. We may feel that co-workers don't like us or that they are plotting something behind our back. Power-struggles could flare up between ourselves and those we work with or under. During this transit, our own deep psychological complexes, insecurities and fears will surface in the workplace, or a co-worker or client may be going through an exceptionally traumatic time which affects us. On the other hand, we could also experience trouble and pain in connection with people we hire or use to serve us in some capacity. For instance, a woman with this transit found out that her husband was having an affair with the *au pair*, who had just become pregnant with his child, while another woman discovered that her home help was stealing from her. A trusted butler or domestic servant could die or go through a difficult time. Or we might find ourselves entangled in a long and fierce legal battle with the garage mechanic, after our car is returned to us in a worse state than when we took it in. Pluto will use the affairs of whatever house it is transiting to bring powerful and complex emotions to the surface.

The sixth house is associated with those routines and rituals of an everyday nature which we have to perform in the course of mundane existence. At some point during Pluto's transit of this house, even the most simple daily tasks could take on great importance. Just deciding what clothes to put on in the morning, or just keeping the house clean and the bills paid can become fraught with great anxiety. If this is the case, we are probably displacing deeper psychological concerns and complexes on to these ordinary tasks, and the root source of our tension needs to be fathomed out and explored.

Finally, Pluto transiting this sphere of the chart sometimes indicates transformative experiences or problems that arise out of our relationships to domestic animals and pets, another sixth-house concern. For some people, the death or disappearance of a beloved pet is as painful as any kind of loss that can be encountered in life, and the ensuing grief could activate a host of psychological concerns that need to be examined and worked through – such as unfinished mourning for others we have lost who were once close to us, or fears about our inadequacy as a carer, or the feeling that whomever or whatever we love in life we somehow destroy. On the other hand, the transit of Pluto through the sixth can indicate positive experiences with pets. One elderly woman who had constantly complained of loneliness and physical debility inherited two small cats from a relative just as Pluto was moving into her sixth house. Caring for these animals and the kind of attachment they formed with her gave new meaning and happiness to her lonely life. Another woman overcame a lifetime of feeling she had nothing to give to people and discovered a new sense of her value and worth when she took in a stray dog who found its way to her back garden when Pluto was transiting her sixth house.

Seventh House

When Pluto transits the seventh, close relationships become the catalysts or agents for personal transformation, growth and change. If we are already involved with someone, transiting Pluto entering the seventh or making important aspects by transit from this house will test the truth or depth of that relationship. Pluto in the seventh will bring out where we feel dissatisfied, incomplete or unfulfilled in the area of partnership. If the difficulties that arise now can be met and resolved, the relationship will become stronger and more solid as a result. It doesn't help to run away from problems in this area when Pluto is transiting this house. The frustrations we are feeling will continue to simmer and seethe under a wilfully calm surface and eventually find some way to undermine the partnership. Besides, if we try to deny that anything is wrong in order to avoid a crisis or confrontation, we are cheating ourselves of the kind of growth and transformation that comes through honestly facing the reality of the situation.

Pluto stirs deep feelings in any house it is transiting, and in the seventh, our entry into the underworld will come through other people. At this time, relationships will activate deep-seated emotional complexes lurking in the recesses of the psyche. Through issues that arise in the course of relating, facets of our nature that have been repressed or kept under lock and key will erupt with full force into everyday life. We might be overtaken by feelings of jealousy, envy, rage or uncontrollable sexual passion. Even though these emotions are felt and directed towards a current partner, they stem from childhood, when we experienced similar feelings about mother, father or others in the early environment. Transiting Pluto in the seventh, through the context of a present close relationship, offers us the opportunity to discover and resolve such long-standing emotional patterns.*

Alternatively, in some cases with Pluto transiting the seventh, it may be our partner who unleashes his or her jealousy, envy or fury on to us. In other words, we don't directly experience these emotions ourselves, but they come at us through the agency of another person. Should this happen, we need to look into what we might have done to help create this situation. It is a psychological precept that what we disavow in ourselves, we attract in others. The nature of life is wholeness; we draw to us those parts of ourselves we have denied or suppressed. For example, if we deny our own capacity to be jealous, we are more likely (unconsciously) to keep choosing partners who openly display this part of their nature; even if our partners aren't usually inclined to jealousy, we will somehow act in a way that provokes these feelings in them. The same dynamic applies to anger. We may successfully curtail or circumvent the owning or expression of our fury and rage, and yet uncannily choose partners prone to such outbursts, or subtly coerce them into responding in that manner. As Pluto moves through the seventh, partners or people we become involved with will mirror our shadow or unconscious back to us. This is hard to accept and admit to – we

---

*For a more detailed discussion on dealing with emotional complexes, see chapter 8, pp. 226–45.

would much prefer to blame them and the way they are for the unpleasant course of events. It feels better to have the burden taken off our backs, and yet in the end, accusing the other person of being the source of all the trouble does nothing to further our own psychological maturity or growth.

Treachery, ruthlessness and betrayal are other hallmarks of transiting Pluto in the seventh. We might be obsessed by a fear that a partner will leave us, or that he or she is secretly involved in an affair with someone else. Again, we need to look at this in terms of projection. Are we restless or dissatisfied with the relationship and projecting these feelings on to the partner by imagining the other person living out what we are holding back in ourselves? If we discover such feelings in ourselves, we don't necessarily need to act on them by running off and having an affair, but we should be psychologically honest enough to explore that part of us that entertains fantasies or desires of this nature. Instead of labelling our partner the culprit, the responsibility is now on us to analyse why *we* are unhappy, bored or discontented with the relationship.

Of course, it is possible with Pluto transiting the seventh to discover that a partner is actually conducting an affair. Should this be the case, Pluto is working to expose issues within the relationship that need to be confronted and discussed. This situation also is likely to stir such powerful emotions in us that we may be shocked by our own reactions – we always thought we were so reasonable and in control, not the kind of person who could ever display feelings of such violence or intensity. Pluto is making us face parts of ourselves we would rather not know about. After some psychological self-investigation, we may come to realize that these overpowering emotional reactions can be traced back to feelings we had in early life, when our survival depended on mother and we were terrified we would die if she abandoned us. Our partner's infidelity reactivates these old fears, and gives us the chance to learn more about the kinds of complexes lurking in the depths of our being.

Then again, we might be the one to fall in love with someone else when Pluto is transiting our seventh. Pluto complicates the issues of any house it is moving through, and in the seventh its target is our relationships. If, under this transit, we find ourselves strongly attracted to another person outside our main relationship, we will be forced to re-examine and re-evaluate our existing partnership as well as our whole attitude towards relationships. What is the new relationship giving us which our present one isn't? Has our existing relationship run its course and is something new now right for us? Is there a part of us which is afraid of commitment and therefore looking for a way out of the existing partnership? Grappling with these kinds of questions leads to a deeper understanding of ourselves and the nature of relationships in general. This is precisely what Pluto wants to make happen when it transits the seventh.

Transiting Pluto moving through the seventh sometimes indicates that our partners themselves are experiencing a Plutonic phase. Their natal Pluto may be activated by an important transit or progression, or transiting Pluto may be hitting key points in their chart. They may be having various kinds of emotional difficulties, a hard time at work, or health troubles. However this manifests, the kinds of problems they are facing will directly affect us and our relationship to them. We will be changed by what they are going through. In some cases, transiting Pluto through the seventh could coincide with the death of a partner. All that we have discussed earlier about the necessary process of mourning obviously applies here.*

Pluto transiting the seventh reveals deep-seated tensions and problems in our close partnerships, some of which we may not be able to overcome or resolve. For this reason, this transit could mark the end of a relationship. When anything we have been attached to or identified with dies, it must be properly mourned. Otherwise our ability to form new, meaningful relationships will be severely impaired. While in some cases Pluto may require the complete breakdown and elimination of an existing union, it is not an absolute law that a relationship must end when Pluto is moving through the seventh. This transit could also indicate that the relationship will go through a series of mini-deaths and rebirths, and in the end be stronger as a result.

*See Suggested Reading (p. 386) for a list of books dealing with death and the grieving process.

If we are not involved in a close personal relationship, Pluto moving into or through the seventh often brings one to us. During this period, we might become involved with others who have Pluto strong in the natal chart, or who are going through a major Pluto transit at the time of our meeting. In other words, their nature is probably complex and intense, or they are in the middle of a major life-crisis when we meet them. Relationships that take place at this time may also involve intrigue or require some degree of secrecy. People have been known to fall in love with a boss's wife or a best friend's husband under this kind of transit. Whatever the case, we can be sure of one thing about relationships which begin or form when Pluto is moving through our seventh – they are meant to have a powerful and transformative effect on us. However long they last, we won't be the same person afterwards.

Power-struggles are another feature of a Pluto transit through the seventh. We might try to control or dominate partners, usually in order to prevent them from acting in ways that threaten or wound us. Or we could become involved with a person who wants to control us in this manner. When Pluto moves through this house, the issue of who has the power in the relationship comes to the fore, and we may realize that we don't feel safe unless we are the ones in charge. Conversely, we may be looking for someone to give our power to – someone who will swallow us up, make decisions for us, and tell us who to be or what to do. In either case, the balance of power is not being shared evenly, and lessons of true mutuality and co-operation still need to be learned. Sooner or later, transiting Pluto in the seventh will ask this of us, and it will work in two ways: people will act as agents of change and transformation for us, but we too will find ourselves in a position to help others through times of crisis and transition. The seventh house also describes our relationship to society in general. When Pluto passes through this sphere of the chart, we may be drawn into groups or activities concerned with changing or reforming aspects of society. This could be quite a productive use of this transit, provided we don't succumb to destructive extremes in our attempts to tear down old structures to make way for the new.

The seventh house isn't just about marriage and close partnerships, or our relationship to society at large; it also rules open enemies and the lower law courts. In *Planets in Transit*, Robert Hand gives the reader some good advice: he warns us to be cautious about power-struggles with enemies at this time.[11] If we engage in battles when Pluto is going through the seventh – legal ones or otherwise – they are likely to be long and drawn out, and could turn quite nasty. When Pluto is in our seventh, 'the beast' or 'raging infant' in us is on a collision course with the 'the beast' and 'raging infant' in other people. Others may not be willing to look at the deeper psychological implications of why they are feeling hostile towards us at this time, but that doesn't mean we shouldn't examine where our angry feelings are really coming from.

Eighth House

The eighth house, carrying on with the seventh-house theme of close relationships and marriage, probes deeply into what could be called 'the nitty-gritty of relationship': the kinds of issues that arise when two people (each with his or her own temperament, value-system, resources, needs and inner biological clock) come together to share with each other and merge as one, to die as an 'I' to be reborn as 'We'. Put very simply, the eighth is an indication of 'that which is shared' between people – in particular the kinds of exchange that take place on a monetary, emotional, physical or psychic level. When Pluto transits the eighth, it is through this sphere of life that we are broken down, changed and transformed. Let's examine this in more detail.

The eighth is often labelled the house of 'other people's values' and describes how we fare with money and resources that are shared in marriage, close relationships or business ventures. On the most concrete level, transiting Pluto in the eighth could indicate that we will be profoundly changed or affected as a result of someone else's money or material resources. For instance, a number of my clients have either married or become closely involved at the time of this transit with a wealthy partner, and in this way their material status altered significantly. This transit could mark a time when our partners experience a major swing (up or down) in their financial affairs. They might come into millions or go bust, but in either case this transit means that our lives will be profoundly affected by their changes of fortune. This transit might also bring conflicts and power-struggles with a partner revolving around issues to do with money or joint resources. Sometimes Pluto moving through the eighth coincides with divorce, and represents a complex or intense battle over who gets what. Or it could describe problems with a business associate – some kind of financial treachery, intrigue or deception taking place. As Pluto transits the eighth, we may end one business partnership in order to begin another.

The eighth is also concerned with issues of taxes and inheritance. If we have been wildly cheating on taxes, when Pluto comes to transit the eighth we could find ourselves in trouble with the government. Or we might be on the receiving end of an inheritance that considerably alters or improves our material security. However, should transiting Pluto through the eighth make difficult aspects to other planets in the chart, there could be some complications in matters of legacy, or conflicts with other people over the execution of a will or bequest. The eighth also indicates money we receive on loan, or through government grants or other forms of assistance. Again, if transiting Pluto in the eighth is making hard aspects to other planets in the chart, going too far into debt could lead us into deep water or give rise to much psychological discomfort. And yet, sorting through the emotional issues that such money problems bring up at this time could ultimately help us come to a deeper psychological understanding of ourselves. For example, if we go into debt we may need to learn to defer 'instant gratification' and to tolerate frustration of our needs and wants; beyond this, however, we may need to look at *why* we think we need specific material things. The problems concerning money, attachment and responsibility are all intimately connected.

Money isn't the only thing shared between people. The eighth house also denotes the emotional undercurrents that pass between two people involved in any kind of joint venture, and the feelings that are stirred when we relate closely with another person. Pluto, Mars and Scorpio are the natural rulers of the eighth reflecting the well-known fact that relationships arouse very powerful emotions in us, which we either express with ease, indulge or defend ourselves against. When transiting Pluto moves through its natural house, we can expect a fair amount of crisis and upheaval in our close contacts. This transit has the effect of drawing to the surface unresolved issues from previous relationships, especially early bonding problems with our mother. The fear, for instance, that our partner doesn't love us any more will reawaken primal emotions in us. Just the thought of being abandoned by a current partner can arouse a high degree of anxiety and outrage – the same kinds of feelings we experienced when we equated the loss of mother's love with abandonment and death. Much of the anger and destructive rage we sometimes feel or unleash on partners can also be traced back to infancy. Because of our extreme helplessness as children, we experience tremendous frustration when our needs are not being met; later in life, when a partner thwarts us in some way, the 'raging infant' in us could be awakened once again. Transiting Pluto through the eighth exposes the early fears and complexes lurking in the deeper recesses of the psyche. This may not be pleasant, but it is only through facing what is there that we can begin to come to terms with our early pains and wounds.*

If during this transit we find ourselves repeatedly on the receiving end of a partner's destructive rage or negative outbursts, we had better explore why we are attracting such hostile reactions at this time. Are we somehow projecting our own unexpressed feelings on to other people, and getting them to live these out for us? Or is it time we learned to stand up to others, and not allow ourselves to be the dumping ground for their unresolved infantile complexes?

The eighth house – the house of intimacy – also reveals something about the nature of our sexual expression. In sex, we expose and share intimate parts of ourselves which we normally keep hidden. And it is through sex that we might attain, even for a brief moment, a more complete physical, emotional and spiritual union with another. When Pluto transits the eighth, we can expect changes in the

*For a more detailed discussion on working with emotional complexes, see chapter 8, p. 226–45.

expression of our sexuality, or experiences in this sphere of life that have a profound or devastating effect on us. Pluto intensifies whatever part of the chart it transits. In some cases, this transit could mark the awakening of our sexuality in a way it has never been aroused before. Transiting Pluto in the eighth may help us to break through certain defences which have held us back from fully relaxing and letting ourselves go sexually. However, the reverse situation can also occur, at least temporarily. One of my clients, a man aged 50, who had always enjoyed an active sex life, began to have sexual difficulties when Pluto entered his eighth house. At first he thought the problem would just go away. It didn't, and eventually his impotency caused him such distress he sought the help of a psychotherapist. In the course of therapy, he explored his deeper attitudes towards women and sex, and discovered a misogynistic side he had never acknowledged was there. The therapy also gave him a chance to discuss other emotional and psychological problems he was going through at the time – primarily the feeling that he had failed to achieve in life what he had hoped he would. Through various sex therapy techniques, he overcame his impotency. Moreover, the psychological work he had done on himself helped him to feel more open, trusting and less critical of his partner; and as a result, he found it easier to express feelings of tenderness during sex. All this was the work of transiting Pluto through the eighth.

The eighth-house label of 'other people's values' can extend beyond monetary resources to include their sense of values in general – what others believe in, hold dear or find important in life. As Pluto transits our eighth, we could be dramatically transformed or changed through a close encounter with another person's beliefs and values By expanding or altering our understanding of life to embrace a philosophy and perspective on the world other than our own, we symbolically die as we have been and are born again. However, a transit of Pluto through the eighth could indicate battles and power-struggles with other people, in which we pit our sense of values and view of the world against theirs. This is more likely to occur if transiting Pluto in the eighth opposes natal planets in our second house (the house of 'my values'), or squares placements in our eleventh (the house of 'friends, hopes, wishes, goals and objectives').

The eighth also denotes our relationship to what esoteric philosophers call 'the astral plane', a level of existence where apparently intangible, but none the less powerful, emotions and feelings collect and circulate. As Pluto transits this house, we become more sensitive to undercurrents in the atmosphere and open to the hidden or unexpressed feelings of those around us. We may find it difficult at this time to take life or other people at face value; instead, we feel the need to probe beneath the surface or superficial level of our relationships and interactions with others in order to ascertain what is really happening on a deeper or more subtle level. Along similar lines, this transit could activate an interest in occult or psychic phenomena, metaphysics or any branch of psychology that explores the hidden or unchartered dimensions of life. However, if transiting Pluto is making hard aspects to other planets in the chart or triggering troublesome natal placements in the eighth, some caution is advised when exploring anything to do with the psychic or occult: we could tap forces or powers that are difficult to handle wisely. Should we venture into this realm when Pluto is transiting our eighth, it is wise to do so only under the guidance of someone we trust and who is experienced in such matters.

Pluto was the god of the dead, and the eighth house is one of the areas of the chart associated with death. Accordingly, transiting Pluto in the eighth could mean that we will have to grapple with death itself. Freud theorized that we all harbour a death-wish, a desire to return to a tension-free state we experienced some time before birth. Transiting Pluto through this house might activate a death-wish of this sort, and we may be tempted to flirt with death by putting ourselves in very risky or obviously dangerous situations, or by unconsciously playing out self-destructive urges at this time; these are best dealt with by bringing them into conscious awareness and examining their true source. I have encountered a number of people who have had close brushes with death while under this transit. As a result of their near-death experience, they have reassessed their priorities and made major changes in their lives.[12] During this transit, it's also possible that some of us may experience the death of someone close to us. One way or another, we may be asked to look death squarely in the face. Death is an inextricable part of life

– to deny it is to deny life. Confronting it, however, can plunge us into living more authentically and enhance our ability to appreciate life.

The transit of Pluto through its natural domain may not be an easy time, and at some point we may feel deeply depressed or find ourselves trapped in our own personal hell – an underworld of intensely disturbing emotions and feelings. But we shouldn't forget that Pluto has the power not only to destroy life, but to create it as well. Like Inanna, who is condemned to death in Ereshkigal's realm, this transit also carries with it the possibility that we may rise again, reborn and transformed.*

Ninth House

During the years that Pluto transits this house, our whole world view – how we perceive life and the cosmos in general – will undergo major adjustments. Up to the time of this transit, we may have held a belief system or religion that worked reasonably well, providing a framework through which to view and interpret life. However, as Pluto enters and moves through the ninth, our existing belief-systems and religious allegiances will be challenged in some way. What previously provided us with a sense of meaning or purpose may no longer seem suitable or appropriate. What we once worshipped and respected as the truth is called into question and may no longer appear to us as absolute. In short, transiting Pluto in the ninth often means the death of our existing philosophical value-system. The loss of a philosophy or religion can be a shattering experience. Belief-systems and religious precepts help guide us through life, enabling us to make choices about the most appropriate way to act or behave in different situations. When our existing philosophy is no longer seen as valid or, for whatever reason, doesn't work for us any longer, it feels as if the ground has been taken away from beneath our feet. We no longer have concrete guidelines or rules by which we can judge or determine the 'right' way to be.

In my years as a professional astrological consultant, I have

---

*See 'The Dark Goddess', chapter 8, pp. 237–41.

observed 'this effect of transiting Pluto through the ninth on many occasions. John is a good example. Up to the time that Pluto entered his ninth by transit, he avidly followed the teachings of an Indian guru. He regularly practised his meditation techniques, participated in courses and retreats, and tried to live according to the laws and truths which his guru taught. John was happy with this way of looking at life, and he derived much security and comfort through having definite beliefs to guide and give structure to his daily existence. When transiting Pluto crossed his ninth-house cusp, however, all this changed. He began to encounter new ideas which forced him to question his existing beliefs and much of his guru's philosophy and outlook. John had always believed implicitly in his guru's teachings, but now he was seriously re-evaluating its validity for him. For a number of years after Pluto entered his ninth, he was still confused about what to believe in and vacillated between his old beliefs and the newer ones that were gradually replacing them. Letting go of his connection to his guru was a frightening prospect: he had gained security from belonging to his particular meditation group, and without that identification he felt adrift in the world. He feared some kind of calamity or disaster would befall him because he was no longer meditating regularly or adhering so strictly to the guidelines that had previously dominated the way he had conducted his life. He felt as if he were betraying both his guru and the meditation society and he expected to be punished for straying from the path he had followed for so long.

John's sense of identity had been very much linked to his belief system. When that changed, he went through a desperate period when he didn't know who he was. People who change religions or turn their back on the church when Pluto transits the ninth may go through a crisis similar to the kind John endured. John still maintained a respect for his guru and the meditation practice he had done, and yet he knew that at this particular stage in his life something new was needed. However, in other cases I have seen of Pluto transiting the ninth, people have rejected or discarded their old philosophy or religion with much more resentment and bitterness than John felt.

Transiting Pluto in the ninth fuels the urge to explore deeply the meaning of life. If we have never felt this 'calling' before, if we have been content with received wisdom and an undemanding life, this transit will activate 'the seeker' in us. As Pluto moves through the ninth, we will keep searching for the philosophy or belief-system that will help us make sense of existence and give purpose to our lives; and we will keep rejecting different philosophies in the name of finding the one which works best, in the Plutonic mode of 'tearing them apart' to find the essence or hidden meaning. Any philosophy or belief-system we sincerely embrace during this transit will have a deeply transforming effect on us. But Pluto transiting the ninth can also mean that we become obsessed with our new religion or creed – be it born-again Christianity, *est*, or Jungian psychology. And we may fall into the trap of believing that what we have found is the answer to everything, and everyone should be converted to it. Pluto stirs intrigues, obsessive allegiances and strong feelings in whatever house it transits. Those of us with Pluto transiting the ninth could also find ourselves caught in the middle of fierce 'in-fighting' within the sect or group to which we belong. And, in some cases, people under this transit become involved with a cult or movement which is the target of persecution or prejudice – either from other groups or from mainstream society itself.

Pluto is the god of death and rebirth, and when it moves through the ninth, travel (another concern of this house) may be the catalyst for major changes in our lives. Under this transit, we meet Pluto when we are travelling. Usually, this doesn't mean our literal death, but travel could provoke psychological deaths and rebirths during this period. We will attract experiences while travelling which have a life-changing effect on us, or meet people who profoundly influence our lives. In many cases I have seen, people take up residence abroad during this transit and are dramatically transformed through immersion in a foreign culture. Because transiting Pluto arouses deep or buried emotions, we may find ourselves battling with inner 'demons' and complexes while travelling; or we may discover that what we thought was a universal moral concept is actually a 'cultural construct', something valid for our own world but not *the* world. Joseph Conrad's book *Heart of Darkness* is a profound exploration of this dilemma.

Higher education is another ninth-house issue, and transiting Pluto through this house could affect this area of life as well. If we are at college or university during the time of this transit, we will be significantly changed as a result of experiences we encounter there. With Pluto transiting the ninth, conflicts and passions are likely to be aroused in the pursuit of higher education: this could be anything from falling madly in love with a professor to becoming involved in political or ideological battles with the academic establishment. At some point during this transit, we may choose to make a dramatic shift in our major focus of study – a change from arts to science, or vice versa. Embarking on an in-depth course of study in a topic that engages us is a good way to use this transit at any age.

The ninth house also covers writing and publishing. If we write during this period, we will meet Pluto in some form. The writing itself may be experienced as a challenge or struggle, or what we write could have a profound effect on the field or discipline with which we are involved. Problems and entanglements with publishers is another possibility if transiting Pluto makes difficult aspects to the natal chart from this house.

Finally, the ninth house is traditionally associated with 'the higher courts', and during Pluto's transit through this domain, legal battles could be complex and drawn out. The ninth is also the house ruling our relationship with in-laws (it is the third house from the seventh, therefore connected with our partner's relatives). In a number of cases I have seen, transiting Pluto through the ninth brought conflicts and battles with in-laws: a mother-in-law at odds with a daughter-in-law; sisters-in-law or brothers-in-law at each other's throats, etc. Under Pluto's influence, an in-law may be the agent through which our simmering resentment and dilemmas about power in relationships are brought to the surface – we hope, to be integrated or transformed.

Tenth House

The transit of Pluto through the tenth is very powerful, not only affecting our career goals, but helping us arrive at a deeper understanding of who we are and why we are here. This can happen in a number of different ways. As Pluto approaches the tenth-house cusp, we may find ourselves feeling increasingly dissatisfied with the work we are doing. The nature of the career itself may be called into question. Is it the right one for us? Does it engage us enough? Wherever Pluto transits we tear down, alter or destroy existing circumstances in order to create new ones. Often we want to clear the decks ruthlessly and completely remove what is already there in order to build anew. Not all of us will have the experience of Pluto transiting the tenth house, but if we do, it often indicates we are more ready than ever to pursue the kind of career we feel is most true or right for us. Some people feel a 'calling', choosing a true vocation during this transit. Or they discover their ambition for the first time in their lives.

In some cases under this transit, changes in career may be forced on to us through involuntary redundancy or other such circumstances. If some part of us desperately wants or needs change and we are not acknowledging this, we could unconsciously provoke an employer to fire us or our business to collapse in order to be free to pursue new lines of work. In a number of charts I have seen, people with this transit leave a job on a matter of principle – they reach a point where they no longer can tolerate how things are being run. No matter how it happens, Pluto will find some way to effect change in this area of life. Rather than changing occupations altogether, we might stay within the same field, but become involved in an angle or aspect of it that we have never tried before.

Pluto often stirs issues around power, and its transit of the tenth house can manifest in various ways. I have seen people promoted to positions of greater power within their work sphere, where transiting Pluto brought increased authority over others, as if they were being given a chance to explore more fully how to handle power wisely. This was the case with Tony, promoted to a higher position when Pluto crossed his tenth-house cusp only to discover that wielding power intelligently wasn't an easy task. Shortly after taking up his new post, he implemented changes in work schedules that antagonized many of the people under him. Determined not to be overruled, he dug his heels in and maintained a hard line. It wasn't long before protests were organized, and Tony found himself with a major mess on his hands. Eventually the heads of the organization had to be called in to sort out the difficulties. They made it clear to Tony that unless he learned how to dispense his authority with a better understanding of the people who worked under him, he wouldn't be in his new position much longer. By being given more authority, and by his early mistakes, Tony learned the uses and abuses of power from this transit.

Pluto creates intrigues and power-struggles in whatever house it is transiting, and as it moves through the tenth we might find ourselves engaged in more battles than usual with colleagues, bosses or employees. These conflicts can awaken early infantile complexes – in other words, unresolved power issues between ourselves and our parents reappear in the guise of struggles with authority figures or co-workers, and we need to assess and re-evaluate any hidden, underlying motives that fuel our ambition and need for power or worldly success. Are we trying to succeed in order to please a parent? Are we seeking recognition to prove to people that we are a worthy and lovable person? Did we suffer so badly at the hands of others when we were young that we desperately need power now in order to feel secure?

One way or another under this transit, Pluto will find its way into the work situation. An employer might die, leave or be replaced by someone else. Secret talks and negotiations could be going on at the executive level that will have a profound effect on the way things are run. We may wake up one day to discover that the company we work for has been taken over by another organization that plans to make important changes in work procedures. A career we pursue at this time may be of a Plutonic nature: medicine, psychology, investigative science or journalism, politics, mining, or even atomic research. We might be working on something which has to be kept secret, or promoting a cause to reform outworn or out-dated societal institutions. This transit of Pluto can also mean that we become intensely involved or obsessed with a work we are engaged in during this period. In *Planets in Transit*, Robert Hand emphasizes that transiting Pluto in the tenth often stimulates a desire to take control and dominate situations or other people. He warns that if we act ruthlessly in the pursuit of our goals at this time, we are likely to suffer as a result.[13] With transiting Pluto in the tenth, should we behave in ways that are untoward or illegal, there is a good chance we will be caught out. If discrimination is not exercised, some people with this transit could invite public scandal and humiliation or a professional downfall. In *Transits: The Time of Your Life*, Betty Lundsted echoes Hand's warning when she advises people with transiting Pluto in the tenth not to engage in 'short cuts, graft or underhanded dealings'.[14] I would agree with both these authors: it may be appropriate to pursue goals avidly while under this transit, but it is safer to play fairly and by the rules.

The tenth house is also associated with mother or father, depending on which parent the astrologer feels 'fits' best with this house.* If we take the tenth to signify the mother, Pluto's transit here could indicate a period when she is going through transformative experiences in her life. These may be positive, but in some cases she might fall ill or face difficult emotional problems. In certain instances, this transit coincides with the death of a parent – especially at the time Pluto crosses the tenth-house cusp. When I see transiting Pluto approaching the tenth house of a client's chart and discover that the mother is elderly or ailing, I will advise the person to do whatever he or she can to resolve unfinished emotional issues with her, since she may die under this transit. The loss of a parent at any time in our lives will stir deep emotional pain and confusion that needs to be faced and gone through, but these reactions will be felt even more strongly with transiting Pluto in the tenth – especially if we have not prepared ourselves.†

Under this transit it is also possible that a parent's death will free us from long-standing restrictions and insecurities we have experienced in connection with that parent, and we may then feel reborn as a result. Even if a parent's death isn't apparent or imminent, Pluto entering and moving through the tenth is a time to take stock

---

*See chapter 5, note 5.
†See p. 261 for a discussion of issues raised by a parent's death. See also Suggested Reading (p. 386 for a list of books on death and the grieving process.

of where we stand in relation to one or both of our parents. The transforming influence of Pluto could help us clear difficult issues and blocks between the parent in question and ourselves. We may be unable to confront a parent face-to-face with what we are feeling or what we would like to say, but we still can work through unresolved issues with our 'inner' parent by seeking the help of a therapist or counsellor or finding some way to do this on our own. In some cases I have come across, this transit occurred many years after the death of a parent, and yet it stirred unresolved feelings about that parent. Even if mother or father is already dead, transiting Pluto in the tenth may ask that we work on finally transforming our relationship with that parent, extricating ourselves from guilt, anger and resentment in order to live our own lives more fully.

Eleventh House

The eleventh house is associated with friends, groups, and long-term goals and objectives. When transiting Pluto moves through the eleventh, we will experience challenges, disruption and change in these spheres of life.

Transiting Pluto in the eleventh often reveals itself through issues around friendship. On a positive note, this transit could indicate important and profound liaisons which endure over many years, even through periods of separation and change. However, Pluto moving through the eleventh also suggests complications in this area. While we could come to value friendship very deeply during this time, we are likely to encounter difficulties and dramas as well. Psychological complexes and problems we have been carrying around inside us from childhood and the past could be projected and re-experienced through circumstances involving friends. We might find ourselves very angry, hurt, resentful, jealous or competitive with close associates, or sexual undercurrents or rivalry could complicate a friendship.* At some point during this transit, we may feel let

*See chapter 8, pp. 226–45, for a discussion of infantile complexes and how to work with them.

down or betrayed by a friend or group of friends whom we trusted, or we may be the one to turn our back on old friends and desert them for new allegiances. Power-struggles between friends is another possibility with Pluto transiting here. We may want to control and dominate friends, fearing that unless we are in charge they may act in ways that harm or hurt us. Or we may feel that a friend is trying to suffocate, over-control or dominate us, and as a result we want to break free of the relationship.

With Pluto in this house, some of our friendships may have to end: they are outworn or negative, or the other person is no longer on the same wave-length as we are. A close friend may move away or die, stirring grief, anger, guilt and a host of other psychological issues that we need to confront. Conversely, this transit also signifies the formation of new friendships that can have a profound and transformative effect on our lives. Friends can be the catalysts who bring change to us: an old or new friend could introduce us to new ideas, new fashions or new groups that alter our whole outlook and approach to life. Pluto deepens whatever area it transits: in the eleventh, it asks that we examine more closely our reasons for forming friendships – are there secret or ulterior motives for wanting to be a particular person's friend? More positively, transiting Pluto in the eleventh can help enrich our appreciation of the value, meaning and importance of friendship. However, this is usually achieved only after the relationship has been tested or tried in some way.

Besides circles of friends, the eleventh house is also associated with groups or our experience in groups, and transiting Pluto can bring expansive and positive experiences in this sphere: we may join a social group that broadens our contacts with other people, or we might align ourselves with groups of a political or humanitarian nature, and find new meaning in life through contributing to causes and immersing ourselves in activities that help other people. We could be drawn to groups interested in the radical reform of society's existing structures and institutions, but should we act too ruthlessly or treacherously to achieve the group's aims under this transit, we are likely to come into direct conflict with the law; our cause may be just and we may feel extreme tactics are necessary, and yet it is still wise to look inside ourselves to understand better why our reactions are so violent or emotional. The fervour we feel for a cause could be entangled with unresolved infantile rage towards parents or authority figures, but by analysing the original source of our anger, we can view the immediate situation with more objectivity; this will help us to choose more clearly the most effective ways to realize our goals.

During this period, a group may serve to break down our existing ego-boundaries and open us in ways we haven't experienced before. Some people under this transit jump right in at the deep end and join therapy groups expressly for the purpose of psychological growth and exploration. However, the group experience can also be frightening or difficult for us when Pluto is moving through this house. Deep emotional complexes and unresolved issues from early childhood (or past lives) may be revealed in group situations. We may find ourselves exceptionally uneasy or disturbed within a group context, or we may fear that the group won't accept us. With Pluto moving through the eleventh, we could project the destructive force of Pluto on to a group – if so, we will feel as if one of its members or the group itself is trying to destroy us. Some of us with Pluto transiting here could end up playing the scapegoat for a group, or find ourselves in the role of 'group shadow', attracting hostility for expressing what other members are afraid to admit to in themselves. While such experiences are not pleasant, exploring why we attract these kinds of projections can help us come to a deeper psychological understanding of ourselves.

The transit of Pluto through the eleventh could make us confused about where we fit into society or the collective of which we are a part. We may go through a period of feeling isolated and lonely until we can arrive at a deeper understanding of our relationship to humanity and other people in general. Conversely, for some of us this transit may coincide with a breakthrough – what Marilyn Ferguson calls 'an entry point experience' – in which we realize our interconnectedness or unity with the rest of creation.[15] This could prompt us to join groups that serve the evolution of society and the planet in general, or promote the well-being of those whom we feel are being unfairly treated.

The eleventh house also describes our goals and objectives in life, and the ideals we wish to realize in the future. By the end of Pluto's transit of the eleventh, we will have significantly altered our sense of direction and purpose in life. Goals we once thought important or desirable may not seem so central to us any more. As our objectives and ideals change, so too will our choice of friends and groups. During a Pluto transit, the manner in which we set about realizing our desired aims also needs to be examined: if we are continually vague about our goals or sluggish in pursuing them, we need to fathom the reasons for this, and to transform such a pattern. However, as discussed earlier, when Pluto is affecting this house we should be careful about employing extreme measures, for if we fail to modify an overbearing or over-aggressive way of pursuing our aims, transiting Pluto in the eleventh may make life very difficult for us until we are willing to change.

Twelfth House

We tend to identify with and live out certain parts of our chart, while other facets of the birth map are relegated to the unconscious. The ego – or sense of 'I' – builds walls to keep out what threatens it. We are capable of denying or suppressing any factor in the chart: we might be out of touch with Mars, or we might suppress the Moon or our Neptunian side. Although we may be unconscious of any chart placement, the twelfth house is one of the clearest indications of those drives, motivations and elements in our nature that are likely to be operating below the surface level of awareness. The task of Pluto transiting the twelfth is to bring into consciousness those parts of ourselves which are hidden, weak or undeveloped, so that they can be faced and integrated into the ego-identity. In other words, when Pluto transits the twelfth, we have an opportunity to discover and form a relationship with those aspects of our being that we have hitherto denied or repressed.

Freud first perceived the unconscious as a repository of what is primitive, evil or anti-social in us. However, the unconscious is not just the storehouse of negative drives – it also contains positive potentialities that have yet to be recognized fully. As children, our survival depends on winning the love of a caretaker. Certain drives – our aggressive and sexual impulses in particular – are usually not acceptable to the environment and therefore we deny or repress them for the sake of winning love and securing our survival. But it is also possible that our caretakers may not wholly approve of other, more positive traits we might exhibit – our innate spontaneity, curiosity or creativity, for example. Should we as children sense that the environment does not validate such qualities in us, these too will be banished to the unconscious. Positive drives as well as so-called negative ones can be denied or repressed.

As it transits the twelfth, Pluto will conspire in any way it can to bring us face to face with those parts of ourselves from which we have run away. During this transit, we will attract circumstances and events that force us to look inside and discover more of what we are. Reclaiming missing parts is not always a comfortable task. Something in us still believes that acknowledging our hostile or sexual feelings entails losing the love of others and therefore endangering our survival. Accepting untapped positive potential is just as frightening. If we fully own our latent talents, resources and skills, we will have to shoulder the responsibility of doing something to develop these potentials. Refusing to know is a way of not having to take responsibility for what is there. And yet doing so means we remain half a person, incomplete and unfulfilled. Whether we like it or not, the aim of Pluto transiting the twelfth is to help us rediscover those parts of ourselves we have denied, so that when Pluto reaches the ascendant we can emerge reborn – more completely in touch with who we are than ever before, and ready to express more openly our newly discovered self.

Pluto moving through the twelfth not only stirs and awakens whatever planet it aspects by transit, but it also gives us the opportunity to transform or regenerate the way we have been expressing or using that planet. This was the case with Jean, a woman who came for a reading when transiting Pluto was conjuncting her twelfth-house Mars. She had always considered herself extremely withdrawn and shy. But under this transit, she was promoted in her work to a position of greater power and authority over others, and as a result she had to explore and utilize more of her Mars energy. Similarly, a man had transiting Pluto in the twelfth conjunct his natal Moon. During this period, he discovered and more fully expressed feelings he normally kept hidden – he found himself in situations that forced him to reveal his emotional needs and frustrations in ways he had never dared previously. The same dynamic applies to transiting Pluto in this house aspecting other planets in the chart, even if these are not natally in the twelfth. So if transiting Pluto through the twelfth squares natal Mars in the third or ninth, for instance, qualities of Mars will be brought into the open and made available for transformation

Pluto transiting the twelfth has an uncanny ability to reactivate issues from earlier in our lives that we have not yet fully resolved. This can happen quite concretely in the form of people from the past turning up with whom we have some sort of unfinished business. For example, when transiting Pluto in the twelfth aspected one woman's natal Venus, she ran into her first serious boyfriend (whom she hadn't seen in 20 years) at a party, and the meeting rekindled an old passion between them. However, it's not only people who come out of the woodwork – any kind of unresolved situation from the past can reappear in a slightly altered but thinly disguised form. For instance, a man who had experienced fierce power-struggles with his father met the same situation with an employer when transiting Pluto in the twelfth opposed his natal sixth-house Sun; in other words, his father complex resurfaced through problems with his boss at this time. Transiting Pluto through the twelfth acts like a clearing house – it forces us to face issues we might have run away from or left dangling in the past. We can also find ourselves intensely reliving old encounters or experiences through powerful dreams we have at this time, as if the dreams are serving to bring to our awareness problems we still need to come to terms with.

Fears, complexes and insecurities from early life come clearly into focus during this transit. Based on our childhood experience and perception of mother and the early environment, we form opinions about what kind of person we are and what life 'out there' is going to be like for us. We carry these early impressions and assumptions around inside us, and for the rest of our lives they continue to influence our self-image and what we expect from the world. They become part of our personal mythology – the framework and belief-systems we have about ourselves and life in general. As transiting

Pluto moves through the twelfth and makes aspects to other planets in the chart, our early life-statements and beliefs come to the surface through current situations we are encountering in our lives, or possibly through dreams which evoke our most deep-seated fears and complexes. For instance, if transiting Pluto in the twelfth makes an aspect to our natal Moon, the kinds of opinions and images we formed around mother and the kinds of expectations we have about getting our emotional needs met will be brought to the fore; or if transiting Pluto in the twelfth aspects the natal Sun, our unresolved issues with father and our feelings about our own power and worth will resurface. As mentioned earlier, transiting Pluto through the twelfth manages to arrange our meeting 'ghosts' from the past through the agency of current events. This transit creates the ideal breeding ground for what is known in analytical psychology as *repetition compulsion*: the tendency to keep re-creating early-life traumas and difficulties, perhaps in order to resolve and work through them as best we can. By facing and dealing with our deeply ingrained complexes, we will feel less fated to repeat these patterns over and over again in life. Transiting Pluto in the twelfth helps to cleanse and free the psyche from the unconscious repetition of the past. When Pluto finally reaches the ascendant, we can look at life from a whole new perspective.

If we consider the ascendant to relate to birth, then the twelfth house, which precedes the first, can be understood as what is in the back of the mind before birth. The developing embryo is receptive not just to physical substances that the mother ingests, but is also affected by her overall psychological state during the gestation period, and her attitudes and experiences are transmitted through the umbilical connection to the foetus in the womb. The nature of what is passed on to the child in this way is shown by the twelfth house (i.e. planets and signs there, as well as the placement by sign, house and aspect of the planet ruling the sign on the cusp of the twelfth). Therefore, as Pluto transits the twelfth, this area of life is reactivated and experiences we had in the womb will resurface in some way through present life circumstances. I did the chart for a woman with Saturn ruling the cusp of the twelfth. After her mother's death, she found a diary in which her mother had written that she had not wanted to have a child; throughout the pregnancy, the mother had wished she wasn't pregnant, because it conflicted with her work as an artist. I believe that these were the kinds of messages transmitted via the umbilical effect to my client, while she was still in the womb, for she grew into a woman who unconsciously harboured a deep belief that nobody really loved or wanted her. When transiting Pluto went through the twelfth house and squared her natal Saturn which ruled the twelfth, all these negative expectations came to the surface in a relationship she was having at the time. The relationship brought into the open fears and self-doubts which had formed during her gestation. With the help of the chart reading and subsequent psychotherapy, she was able to make a connection between her strong current feelings of rejection and what she had felt in the womb in relation to the mother. In the therapy, she was able to express the anger she felt towards her mother, and she came to see how she kept repeating her early hurt through falling in love with men who had difficulty loving her back. By becoming more aware of the complex and its origins, she began the process of freeing herself from blindly repeating its pattern. Transiting Pluto through the twelfth had exposed the deep early feelings and gave her the opportunity to come to terms with them.

The twelfth house shows influences from the past that are affecting us now, but these could stem from even farther back than the womb. Many astrologers refer to the twelfth house as the 'house of karma', the area of the chart which most directly shows the debits we are carrying over from previous incarnations. Understood in this way, transiting Pluto through the twelfth could reactivate problems or difficulties that have their origins in unresolved past-life issues. But we should also remember the *continuity principle* of karma, the concept that positive traits and potentials developed in one life will be carried over into the next. Therefore, the twelfth will show our ingrained assets – acquired abilities and qualities that may be latent in us until transiting Pluto through the twelfth brings them out into the open again.

The twelfth house is an indication of what is stored in the unconscious from early childhood, the womb, or from our past lives, but there is another branch of memory – what is called our 'ancestral inheritance'. Just as biophysical traits are carried in the genes, we inherit a mental and emotional legacy as well. Our psyche teems not only with our personal experience, but also with the parental, ancestral and racial memories that are handed down from one generation to the next. We are the beneficiaries of our ancestors' unresolved psychological difficulties, and also the recipients of their positive traits and drives. The natal placements involving the twelfth house describe the nature of our ancestral inheritance, and transiting Pluto through the twelfth brings this more fully into the open. As Pluto transits the twelfth, we can find ourselves unwittingly living out and trying to resolve the kinds of psychological dilemmas with which our ancestors also contended. Or the transit of Pluto here could activate latent abilities and potentials which we have inherited through the family line.

The twelfth can be associated with an even larger pool of memory than just the ancestral inheritance, the pool Jung referred to as the collective unconscious: the entire memory bank, not only of the individual, the family or the tribe, but of the whole human race. The collective unconscious represents the sum total of all the thought substance of humanity. Every cell in our body has coded within it everything that has ever happened before us. In some way, as shown by our twelfth house, we are linked to the past and to all of creation, carrying records of experience far beyond what we have personally known. People with a strong twelfth-house emphasis have a natural access to this collective memory bank. Therefore, transiting Pluto moving through the twelfth can enliven the ability to tap into this realm. What we write, say, create, do, dream or experience during this transit could in some way be an expression of our attunement to images and thoughts circulating on the level of the collective unconscious.

The twelfth house represents the greater whole of which we are a part. One way or another, transiting Pluto in the twelfth will make us more aware of our essential interconnectedness with the rest of creation. When Pluto transits here, we may have to contend with the less pleasant aspects of the collective shadow, experiencing a period during which we are more susceptible to dark or destructive undercurrents in the atmosphere around us. We could be exceptionally sensitive to anger or hostility in the air, and even 'taken over' by such feelings. In other words, some of the feelings we are having at this time may not be entirely our own – but those of people around us which we have absorbed as if we were a psychic sponge or vacuum cleaner. With Pluto transiting the twelfth it is also possible to be 'used' as an agent of change or transformation for society by embracing some cause or reform, thereby acting out Pluto's predilection to tear down what is outworn and to rebuild new, more authentic structures. As we become more aware of our unity with the rest of life, our motivation to serve and help others also increases.

The twelfth house is associated with institutions – hospitals, prisons, schools, libraries, museums, etc. When Pluto transits this house, we will meet Pluto through this area of life as well. Some of us with Pluto transiting the twelfth may work to transform outmoded institutions, removing the old or moribund to make room for something new or innovative. Or we could be transformed ourselves through significant encounters with institutions – a period in prison, confinement in hospital, or through work we are doing for a charity, library, museum or other such place. Unpleasant experiences within an institution of any sort could awaken 'the beast' in us, activating our early infantile rage, fears and complexes. One thing is certain: if we have close associations with any of society's institutions when Pluto is transiting the twelfth, we will emerge from these crucial, perhaps painful, encounters with a deepened sense of ourselves, with a renewed sense of what we may offer the collective, and with an increased possibility to contribute to its – as well as our own – transformation.

PART FIVE

The Light at the End of the Tunnel

Three Case Histories

A transit to any placement in the birthchart can be fully understood only in light of the whole chart. A transiting planet aspecting natal Mars, for instance, will not only affect Mars, but it also will activate any natal planet in aspect to Mars. Furthermore, during any crucial period of a person's life, there will usually be more than one important transit influencing the natal chart; for example, transiting Uranus might be conjuncting Mars and opposing Saturn at the same time that transiting Neptune is squaring the Sun and trining the Moon, while transiting Pluto is passing over the midheaven and conjuncting the Venus/Uranus midpoint. In assessing the effect of any transit, many astrologers will also examine the simultaneous secondary progressions, taking into account the transits to these progressions as well. A person's age, background, temperament, level of self-awareness and self-understanding all have a direct influence on how a transit or progression is experienced, so these too must be taken into consideration. Someone with a fiery chart and prominent natal Uranus, for example, is likely to have an easier time adjusting to Uranus transits than a person with six planets in earth, while a person with a stellium in Pisces and a strongly placed natal Neptune would probably cope better with a Neptune transit than someone with a preponderance of air in the chart. With so many factors to consider and to synthesize, interpreting outer planet transits is a complex task that challenges the skill of even the most experienced astrologer. The following case histories are included as a teaching aid to illustrate the workings of transiting Uranus, Neptune and Pluto within the framework of the whole chart, and to examine in greater detail how periods of pain and crisis can offer opportunities for profound psychological growth.

Betty

Betty met her future husband in 1971, and they lived together for four years before getting married in 1975. In 1977, two years after the marrriage, Betty left her job in public relations to pursue a life-long ambition to become an actress. Focusing primarily on establishing herself in her new profession, she was prepared to delay having children for a number of years, although her husband was more keen to start a family right away. From 1977 to 1979 she toured the world with various theatre companies, receiving praise and recognition for her work. However, in November 1979 her husband, who had begun an affair during one of the periods she was away, announced that he was leaving Betty for this other woman. He refused to investigate why the marriage had broken down or to consider any ways in which the difficulties could be resolved. On reflection, Betty feels she underestimated how much her huband wanted to have children and the degree to which he resented her not playing the role of a traditional 'mothering' type of wife. He finally left to live with his girlfriend in January 1980. Betty was devasted, literally beating the walls and screaming in unbearable pain and agony. And yet by March 1980 she could look back on the experience and begin to see value in it: 'It was extremely creative for me and something I'm glad I went through. I was very upset at the time and wanted Stan back, but eventually I realized it had to be. The break-up of my marriage marked a clear dividing line in my life, a personal BC/AD.'

The transits and progressions occurring during this period (see fig. 1) describe not only the outer events but also Betty's inner experience – what the dissolution of the marriage meant for her. Her natal Sun in Pisces had progressed to 23 degrees of Aries moving through the eleventh house. The movement of the progressed Sun is an augury of a shift in self-definition, and as it aspects natal planets, we are presented with new opportunities for change and growth. Betty's unfoldment at this time was symbolized by the progressed Sun in

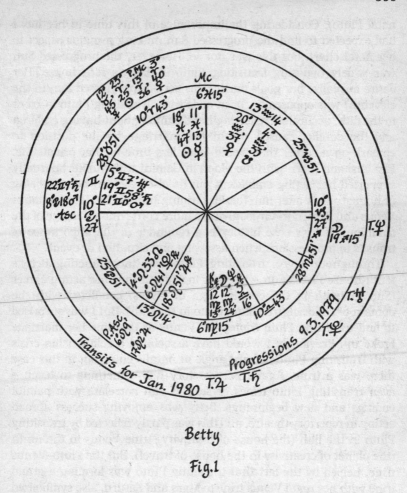

Betty

Fig.1

Aries in the eleventh house – the fervent pursuit (Aries) of the goal (eleventh house) to establish herself as an actress. (In 1977, the year she changed professions to go into acting, the progressed Sun exactly sextiled natal Mars in 21 Gemini in the twelfth, activating her desire to fulfil a hidden ambition. And in February 1979 career issues were further emphasized by a solar eclipse in 7 degrees of Pisces, which conjuncted her midheaven, squared natal Uranus and inconjuncted

natal Pluto). Considering the importance of this time in her life, I
had expected to find the progressed Sun making a major aspect to
her natal chart, but this was not so. However, the progressed Sun
was widely opposing transiting Pluto in Betty's fifth house. Her
desire to realize her goals during this period (progressed Sun in the
eleventh) was opposed by, or at odds with, transiting Pluto in Libra
in the fifth, accurately reflecting her dilemma about having children
and the conflict caused within her marriage by the decision to
embark on a career that would leave less time for her private life.
Her husband (born with the Moon in Gemini trine Jupiter) partially
supported her acting ambitions, but he also resented her not being
at home to look after him (besides trining Jupiter, his Moon squares
Venus and Saturn in Virgo, giving a more conventional image of the
feminine). Betty's case history is a reminder of the importance of
transits to progressions when assessing any situation or event.

Throughout 1979, transiting Pluto was inconjuncting Betty's
tenth-house Pisces Sun – another indication that her acting career
(Sun in tenth in the creative sign of Pisces) conflicted with the
domain of children (transiting Pluto in the fifth). But I was surprised
to find transiting Pluto *trining* her Venus at the time her marriage
broke up. Previously I would have associated a relationship crisis
with transiting Pluto in hard angle to natal Venus, but in this case
there was a trine. Again, Betty's story had something to teach –
even transiting Pluto trines or sextiles can correlate with painful
endings and new beginnings. Betty was enjoying success abroad
acting in repertory theatre, and this was partly reflected by transiting
Pluto in the fifth (the house of creativity) trine Venus in the ninth
(the planet of creativity in the house of travel). But the Pluto–Venus
trine, helped by the fact that transiting Pluto was forming a grand
trine with her natal Venus trine to Mars and Saturn, also symbolized
the way she reconciled herself fairly quickly to the end of the
marriage. She felt a great deal of pain, but within a few months after
the event she was able to find meaning and relevance in what she
was going through. Had Pluto been making a conjunction, square
or opposition to natal Venus, Betty might have fought much harder
and longer against this crisis; instead, she came to terms with the
inevitability of her marriage breaking down and could accept the

painful loss which none the less resolved her dilemma and further contributed to her creative growth.

When she was younger, Betty's family were happy for her to explore her creative talents as a hobby, but they discouraged her from taking up acting as a profession and she was persuaded to develop secretarial skills instead. However, between 1977 and 1979, when transiting Pluto in Libra came to trine her natal Saturn and Mars in the twelfth, Betty found the courage, determination and strength (Mars and Saturn) to be true to herself and follow her deepest inclinations. Progressed Mars moving out of the twelfth and over her ascendant likewise described the ability to express more openly her personal will and desires at this time. The transit of Pluto sextile to Jupiter in Leo in the third correlated with her success abroad and the sense of pride and self-worth this gave her. However, the progression of the ascendant over her natal north node conjunct Pluto in Leo in the second was also highly significant in this respect. The north node is a point of growth and evolution in the horoscope, and it is conjunct Pluto in Betty's chart – in other words, crisis (Pluto) is intimately connected with growth (north node). The progressed ascendant reaching this point in her birth map signalled that Betty's next step in development demanded she stand up for herself and follow her personal desires and value-system (Leo second house) even if it meant conflict and crisis; it was a time when she had to find her identity, power, value and self-worth from inside herself (north node in Leo in the second) rather than through a partnership or by adjusting to her husband's preferences (south node in the eighth). The progressed ascendant hitting Pluto in the second carried another meaning. Betty had been deriving a sense of security and safety (the second house) from her marriage, but when it collapsed she found she was capable of surviving even after what she thought she needed for survival was taken away. In other words, through the progressed ascendant activating Pluto, Betty discovered her own indestructability.

Neptune, by transit and progression, also played an important role in the changes Betty was experiencing during this period. In late 1979 and early 1980 Neptune was between 18 and 21 degrees of Sagittarius moving through her sixth house and filling the empty leg of her T-square (Sun–Mercury in Pisces opposing Moon in Virgo squared by Saturn–Mars in Gemini). Neptune in the sixth house (the house of work) indicated both the choice of a creative field of work and also the fact that sacrifices had to be made in relation to that sphere of life – a theme reiterated by transiting Neptune squaring her Sun in the tenth (the house of career). One way or another, a Neptunian sacrifice was called for. If she chose to have children, then her acting work would have been sacrificed. If she chose to pursue her career, she would have to give up the idea of mothering at this time. Transiting Neptune in the sixth opposed natal Saturn, the ruler of her seventh house, and through this we can see that the relationship was in danger of dissolving because of issues around work (the sixth). In addition to these Neptune transits, transiting Neptune was also sextiling her natal Venus as well. As in the case of transiting Pluto trine Venus, we once again find a soft aspect – a transiting sextile to Venus – coinciding with a crisis and the break-up of a marriage. Normally we might associate a transiting Neptune square or opposition to Venus with the letting go of a relationship, but in this case the aspect was a sextile. Her husband's clandestine affair is shown by transiting Neptune (deception) square the Sun (the male principle), and by her progressed Venus opposing natal Neptune during this period: any fantasies or ideals (Neptune) she might have had about her 'perfect' husband (Sun) or relationship (Venus) were undermined by his infidelity. The progression of Venus in Aries in the tenth opposing Neptune in Libra in the fourth also correlated to the domestic sacrifices (Neptune in the fourth) required of Betty for the sake of developing a creative career (progressed Venus in Aries in the tenth).

During this period transiting Uranus trined her Sun and squared her natal Venus–Jupiter opposition. The Uranus–Sun trine supports the idea that Betty was freeing and expanding her self-expression, personal will and spirit at this time by pursuing her career goals in spite of what others felt. The fact that her marriage was disrupted by her choice to delay having children and to focus instead on developing her creative talents was shown by transiting Uranus in the fifth (the house of children and creativity) square to Venus in the ninth (ruling Libra in the fifth) and Jupiter in Leo in the third ruling

Sagittarius in the sixth house (touring with repertory companies took her away from the relationship). In 1979, Uranus, Neptune and Pluto in the heaven were lined up in adjacent signs: Pluto moved back and forth between 16 and 21 degrees of Libra; Uranus moved between 19 and 23 degrees of Scorpio; and Neptune stayed within 18 to 20 degrees of Sagittarius. For this reason the natal planets between these degrees in Betty's chart (Sun, Venus, Jupiter, Saturn and Mars) were affected simultaneously by each of the transiting outer planets. In particular, transiting Pluto trined her Venus in Aquarius, transiting Neptune sextiled the Venus, and transiting Uranus squared it. With all three of the outer planets stimulating her Venus in Aquarius, Betty discovered that the kind of relationship she really wanted was one based on values of an Aquarian nature:

> The pain I went through was for the best. I realized that I had been playing the wife – playing out certain roles – and not really being myself. My relationship with Stan was immature . . . it was too symbiotic – we were too enmeshed and dependent on one another. One of the first books I read after we broke up was Erich Fromm's *The Art of Loving*, and I started to assess what love really means. Love has to do with freedom rather than hemming in.

Her progressed Venus in Aries was coming to sextile natal Uranus in the twelfth – again we can see the linking of Venus with Aquarian values, and an unconscious need for change, freedom and space (twelfth-house Uranus). Progressed Venus also was about to trine her north node and Pluto, suggesting that the disruption was painful and traumatic, but none the less dictated by a need to evolve.

In 1979, Saturn was moving through her fourth house, where it passed over the Moon–Chiron conjunction, opposed her tenth-house Mercury and Sun in Pisces, inconjuncted Venus and squared the Saturn–Mars conjunction in Gemini in the twelfth. The fourth and tenth are both parental houses and the twelfth is related to the unconscious and the past. Transiting Saturn's influence on these houses meant that at this time Betty was confronting issues from childhood inherited via the family. Betty had been brought up in an environment where communication was a problem – nobody in her family had found it easy to express themselves or come out and say what they really wanted (Mars conjunct Saturn in Gemini in the twelfth square Sun–Mercury in Pisces in the tenth and the Moon in Virgo in the fourth). With Saturn affecting the fourth, tenth and twelfth, and with all three outer planet transits hitting Venus (ruling Libra on her fifth-house cusp and Taurus on the cusp of the twelfth), Betty had the opportunity to confront and break through parental patterns and childhood conditioning by asserting an inner need to delay mothering so that her creative and professional ambitions could be fulfilled. However, the dissolution of the marriage was the price she had to pay for her honesty: her husband left her in January 1980, but by March, when transiting Jupiter conjuncted her IC, she was already aware of a new sense of self emerging from within:

> As soon as I got through the initial crisis and March came, I saw the garden starting to grow again – and I started to feel that I was growing again. When I began to put the pieces of my life back together, I put them back in a slightly different way and realized the importance of what had happened in terms of my own development. After years of being what other people wanted me to be, I felt like I was finally becoming my own person.

Olivia

In late 1979 Olivia, aged 55, discovered she had cancer. She agreed to immediate surgery, assured that the removal of the tumour would stop the disease from spreading. A year later, however, in December 1980, secondary cancer was diagnosed. Olivia was told that unless she consented to another operation, she had only between six weeks and six months to live. She refused to be operated on again, but now – over seven years later – she is more alive than ever, not just healthy but enjoying great well-being and energy. She faced despair, disease and death, and emerged from the experience transformed.

If we include Chiron – the image of the wounded healer – in her chart (see fig. 2), Olivia has three T-squares. One T-square is in cardinal signs (Saturn in Libra opposing Chiron in Aries, squared by Venus in Cancer); another T-square is mutable (Jupiter in Sagittarius

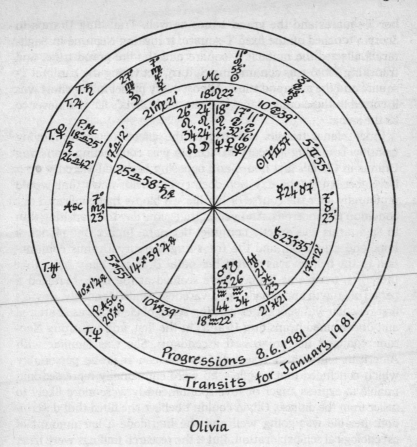

Olivia

Fig. 2

opposing the Sun in Gemini, squared by Uranus in Pisces), while the
third is fixed (the Moon conjunct Nepture in Leo opposing Mars in
Aquarius, squared by Mercury in Taurus). The chart also shows two
grand trines – one involving Sun, Saturn and Mars in air signs and
the other in fire involving Moon-Neptune, Jupiter and Chiron. From
the time of the diagnosis of her illness through to her recovery in
1982, transiting Uranus, Neptune and Pluto were triggering each of

her T-squares and the grand trines as well. Transiting Uranus in Scorpio touched off the fixed T-square; transiting Neptune in Sagittarius affected the mutable T-square and the fire grand trine; and transiting Pluto was conjuncting Saturn, activating the cardinal T-square and the air grand trine. Almost every planet in her chart was involved in these outer planet transits, and Olivia's life was never to be the same.

Inner planet transits can trigger the effects of slower-moving transits. Transiting Mercury in Scorpio was conjuncting transiting Uranus in Olivia's first house and opposing her natal Mercury on 7 December 1979, the day her doctor rang with news that would profoundly alter the course of her life – a biopsy had confirmed her condition as cancerous. And yet on that same day the transiting Sun in Sagittarius was exactly conjunct her natal Jupiter, the planet of hope and expansion, and the transiting Mercury–Uranus conjunction in the heaven was *trining* her natal Uranus – early hints that the crisis, terrible as it may have seemed at the time, heralded a period of growth and broadened awareness. Understandably, Olivia's first reaction was shock: her existing sense of identity was shattered and undermined (transiting Uranus in the first, and transiting Neptune conjunct her progressed ascendant). She was familiar with American and British research into the cancer-prone personality which concluded that people who were emotionally repressed and unable to express anger or love spontaneously were more likely to suffer from the disease. Olivia couldn't believe she fitted that description: her life was going well and she had done a fair amount of psychological self-exploration. But if the research findings were true, it meant that she was still not entirely open or receptive to the full range of her emotions. Transiting Uranus in the strongly emotional sign of Scorpio squared to her Moon–Mars opposition and trine to natal Uranus initiated a period in Olivia's life which would awaken feelings more powerful and deep than she had ever before experienced.

Although an operation in December 1979 had supposedly cured her of the cancer, she felt depressed and uneasy for some months after. As a result she sought the help of a psychotherapist in spring 1980, and through the work they did together, she discovered a host of denied emotions inside her. During this period, transiting Pluto was moving through the twelfth, arousing unconscious responses, and the Moon – the planet associated with feelings – was squared by transiting Uranus, trined by transiting Neptune and sextiled by transiting Pluto. In other words, the Moon was under the scrutiny of all three outer planets. These transits exposed losses, disappointments and broken dreams from earlier times in her life. However, Olivia was frightened by the depth of depair she had discovered in herself – part of her wanted to continue delving into her psyche, but another part was afraid she couldn't cope with the drastic changes and upheaval this might bring. Thinking that she needed time to assimilate what the therapy had brought to the surface so far, she chose not to continue with the sessions. By terminating counselling, she was trying to avoid the difficult emotional journey into the darkest regions of her psyche that her eighth house Sun, Scorpio ascendant, and twelfth house transiting Pluto were asking her to make. But it wouldn't be long before renewed attempts to heal her physical body would force her to follow that Scorpionic route.

In December 1980, a secondary cancer was diagnosed. The consultant who had performed the surgery the year before encouraged her to undergo a second operation. Olivia described this time as the bleakest period in the whole saga, 'like thinking you are in your own home and shelter, and then all of a sudden, the shelter moves away and you are left in the middle of an Arctic night in December'. Let down by the medical 'expert' who had led her to believe her first operation was all that would be needed, she had never felt so betrayed and so alone. Transiting Pluto was nearly stationary in the heaven at that time, stuck in 24 degrees of Libra in her twelfth house, 1 degree away from her Saturn. All her unconscious defences (Saturn) were under siege by Pluto, and she had to confront head-on life's most basic existential concerns. Not only was she confronting death (transiting Neptune and Pluto were both inconjuncting Mercury ruling the eighth house), but she also had to face the anxiety of being totally responsible for her life – no one could decide the next move for her. She could agree to another operation, but the thought of further surgical mutilation was abhorrent, and apparently it had a less than 60 per cent chance of curing the cancer. She could try an alternative therapy she had read about – a strict and demanding regime involving a major change in diet and lifestyle which, if unsuccessful, would amount to nothing but a very unpleasant and dull way of spending the last months of her life. Or she could forget about any kind of treatment and live out her remaining time engaged in activities she would enjoy – for instance, making a pilgrimage to various places in the world she longed to visit. The third option, that of forgoing any form of treatment and making the most of her last months as best she could, was very tempting. But in the end she chose to fight the cancer. This decision was reflected by transiting Pluto trining her fourth-house Mars and sextiling her Moon, and transiting Neptune sextiling the Mars and trining the Moon and Chiron. Somewhere from deep inside herself, she found the will (Mars) and inspiration (Moon) to battle for life.

Intuition guided her to undertake the alternative cancer therapy, which involved a strict vegan diet, vast amounts of freshly made raw fruit and vegetable juice, and a drastic programme of detoxification. Its premise was simple: if the body – damaged by environmental pollution and debilitated by over-processed foods – could be restored to a normal healthy functioning, it would destroy and eliminate the disease as a matter of course. Success in this therapy depended on strict adherence to its rules. Transiting Pluto in the twelfth was conjuncting Saturn and forcing Olivia to find from within herself a greater degree of discipline, commitment and consistency than she had ever before exercised. She wanted to learn the diet and routine properly, and decided to spend time at a clinic abroad specializing in the technique (the Moon, ruler of her ninth house of long journeys was sextiled by transiting Pluto and trined by transiting Neptune). The night she made up her mind to attend the clinic, she had a vivid dream. In it, the zodiacal symbol of Scorpio and the symbol of Cancer were stalking and circling each other on a deserted, rocky shore. They watched each other's every movement, poised to fight a duel to the death. She couldn't remember how the dream ended, but she had a sense of what it was trying to tell her. Over the last few years, she had neglected the Scorpionic side of her nature – qualities of endurance, tenacity and fierce determination had been absent from her life. From the dream she knew the time had come to reclaim these characteristics in herself. The cost of the clinic and the journey there would drain her savings (transiting Neptune in Sagittarius in the second inconjuncting natal Mercury, ruling her eighth house Gemini Sun), but that represented only a fraction of the price she would have to pay and the sacrifices she would have to make in the process of being healed and reborn.

Olivia stayed at the clinic from late January to April 1981. Transiting Pluto and Neptune – the two most potent gods of change – were aspecting her natal Moon, Mercury, Mars, Saturn, Chiron and Uranus during that period. The most important secondary progressions were the progressed Sun semi-sextile to natal Pluto, the progressed ascendant trine to natal Neptune and squared natal Uranus, and the progressed midheaven sextile to Neptune. Although many of these transits and progressions were trines and sextiles and therefore promised the hope of renewal, the fact that they also involved Pluto and Neptune meant that Olivia still felt stripped of her old persona. The cancer therapy forbade the use of anything artificial such as make-up or hair-colouring, and Olivia had to relinquish feminine vanities to which she had previously been attached (transiting Pluto and Neptune hitting the Moon). She was robbed of her professional identity, forced by her illness and the therapy to abandon her career (transiting Pluto conjunct Saturn and opposing Chiron in the sixth, transiting Pluto sextile to the Moon in the tenth, and transiting Neptune trining the Moon and Chiron). The stay at the clinic also meant she was separated from her close friends and loved ones (transiting Neptune and Pluto both inconjuncting her seventh-house Mercury which rules the eleventh, and transiting Saturn in the eleventh). The living accommodation at the clinic offered no real privacy, and although she made some new friends there (transiting Jupiter in the eleventh), much of the time she felt terribly alone among strangers (transiting Saturn in the eleventh). She also felt stripped of her options – she had no guarantee of a future, no plans or prospects she could make or rely on (transiting Pluto and Neptune inconjuncting Mercury ruling the eleventh house of goals and objectives).

Transiting Pluto and Neptune were aspecting Mars which ruled

Aries on the cusp of her sixth house of health, and the therapy required Olivia to assume an active (Mars) part in her body's healing process: every hour she had to drink a freshly made raw fruit or vegetable juice, and she alone was responsible for taking in the right order and at the right time each day the 30 tablets, capsules and pills which had been prescribed to her as part of the treatment. Because of the detoxifying nature of the diet, the body casts off poisons and toxins in order to heal itself, resulting in what are known as 'flare-ups' – periods of headaches, pain, sickness, irritability or depression. This dramatic process of detoxification was closely aligned with an inner process that released deep residues of poisonous emotion and negative feelings which were polluting her psyche, and Olivia experienced her most intense flare-ups in the form of anger: a dark, murderous rage which overwhelmed her usual self-control and destroyed her existing self-image: 'A lot of nastiness came out of me – I was a really horrible woman ... the meanness and the pettiness which came up was astounding. But at least I did most of my raging in private [natal Mars in the fourth], I'll say that for myself. But I got so angry over the most stupid, childish things. Part of me stood by and didn't believe what was going on.'

Olivia recalls a time in childhood when she saw her mother in a terrible state of anger. Her mother looked so fierce and dangerous that Olivia made a vow to herself – from that day on, she would always keep her own temper in check. Her innate discomfort with aggression is described by the natal T-square involving Mars: the Moon opposing Mars square to Mercury suggests that she too has something of her mother's angry nature. However, with natal Neptune conjuncting the Moon and opposing Mars, Olivia tried to conceal and rise above anger for much of her life. Because Mars rules Aries on the sixth-house cusp, there is a connection between aggression, health and the body. In other words, long-festering and unexpressed hostility was a contributing psychological factor to her illness. The flare-ups were purifying (transiting Pluto and Neptune in harmonious aspect to Mars): they brought her deeply guarded rage to the surface where it could be released from her system. Moreover, in denying anger, she had put the lid on a whole range of other emotions as well. Lifting the ban on Mars would ultimately enrich and enliven her entire feeling nature (transiting Pluto and Neptune had a cleansing effect not only on Mars but also on the Moon during this period). And by reconnecting to Mars she would also, from then on, gain a greater ability to direct and steer the course of her life.

In April 1981 she left the clinic and returned to her home in Scotland. For the next year, enormous amounts of will and discipline were needed to follow the health programme on her own. Throughout this period, Pluto was still conjuncting her twelfth-house Saturn, and transiting Saturn was approaching its second return – a thoroughly twelfth-house experience which Olivia compared to a lonely desert crossing, a slow trek through a wilderness, a monotonous and isolated incarceration. Olivia recalls one day during this period when she was strongly tempted to abandon the restrictions of the diet and indulge in a rich and sumptuous Indian meal. But that night she had a dream of a scorpion clinging to a rock in the midst of a violent tempest, and this image of indestructibility gave her the inspiration to carry on. Her dedication was not in vain and Saturn rewarded her justly: by the summer of 1982 she was not only rid of the cancer, but also declared cured of diabetes and incipient osteoarthritis, two other illnesses that had been diagnosed the previous year. Her physical recovery was only a part of the reward – as a result of the whole experience, Olivia underwent a major inner transformation. She had freed herself from old fears (transiting Pluto in the twelfth) and outworn values (transiting Neptune in the second) and was left with a new sense of freedom and wholeness (transiting Uranus in the first). Physically and psychologically healthier than she had been at any other time in her life, she was able to come off the strict diet and rigorous treatment just as Pluto completed its passage over her Saturn, and transiting Jupiter in Scorpio jubilantly appeared over her ascendant. She had travelled to the edge of death and returned to life again – a life more precious and abundant than she had ever known. And like many people who have made that journey, Olivia currently spends much of her time as a counsellor and therapist specializing in the care and support of cancer patients, where she has the opportunity to help others through the kinds of difficulties and crises she herself has known. In a recent conversation I had with Olivia, she reflected on what she had been through:

My illness made such a difference in my life. Now I can speak to people who are very ill, and I can talk to them about death without any hesitation or euphemisms. I also can talk about the alternatives to death. I don't push alternatives at them, but more often than not people can accept what I have to say. For many years I've been attached to a short poem, the gist of which, in free translation, goes:

> He who wants to learn to play the bagpipes
> has to go to the bottom of hell,
> and that is how he learns to play the bagpipes.

I guess I had to do that with my 8th house Sun.

Craig

Just to look at Craig, most people find it hard to believe he is ill. Attractive, intelligent and articulate, he exudes the natural 'fire', spirit and warmth you would expect from a Sagittarius with the Moon in Aries. He doesn't look like a sick person. But Craig, like hundreds of thousands of other people throughout the world, lives with a time-bomb ticking away inside him. He lives with AIDS.

In January 1985, Craig noticed a purple spot on his arm, and a biopsy in late February confirmed it was Kaposi's sarcoma, one of the opportunistic diseases associated with Acquired Immune Deficiency Syndrome. Even before the diagnosis, Craig was already beginning to question and re-evaluate his life. AIDS, however, has dramatically fuelled and accelerated this process. The transits and progressions from 1985 to the present reveal the nature of Craig's metamorphosis; but to appreciate more fully how confronting a life-threatening illness has changed him, we need to look further back into his personal history.

In the 1970s, Craig lived in Boston, where he earned a Bachelor's degree in journalism and a Master's degree in counselling; later he started a Ph.D. programme in psychology, but abandoned this in 1975. From then onward, he was caught up in what he now describes as the 'mainstream gay hedonistic scene', a lifestyle involving a fair amount of drinking, drug-taking, and many sexual encounters. Scraping together a living through various jobs caring for disabled children, Craig admits that he was more interested in his social and sexual life than in the serious pursuit of a career. He was born with Neptune rising in Libra (see fig. 3), and in the late 1970s transiting Pluto was conjuncting his natal Neptune at the same time as transiting Neptune was passing over his Mercury–Sun conjunc-

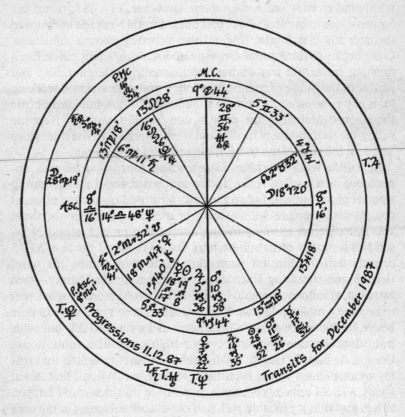

Craig

Fig. 3

tion in Sagittarius. In other words, during this phase of his life, Craig was mainly expressing the 'Neptunian' side of his nature – working with the disabled, but mostly drifting, 'boozing', experimenting with drugs, and indulging in the kind of Dionysian abandonment associated with Neptune.

In 1980 he moved to Houston, where he lived for three years. At first his life in Texas, as in Boston, revolved primarily around a social whirlwind of bar- and bed-hopping. However, in 1981, transiting Saturn came to his ascendant, conjuncted natal Neptune and moved through his first house. Under these sobering Saturn influences, Craig began to think more seriously about establishing himself in a fulfilling career. He was drawn into journalism (Mercury, Sun and Jupiter in the house of communications), and after a period working for a gay newspaper he became the editor of a hospital journal (the third-house Mercury–Sun conjunction sextiles angular Neptune ruling the sixth house of health and work; Mercury in the third rules Virgo on the cusp of the twelfth, the house of institutions).

In 1982, while working as a medical journalist, he was approached by a leading Texan doctor concerned about the increasing number of gay patients turning up with strange illnesses and physical complaints. Together with a team of medical professionals, Craig was instrumental in inaugurating a screening project to take blood samples from gay men, and he later helped to found the first AIDS organization in Houston (transiting Pluto was trining his natal Uranus and transiting Uranus was conjuncting his Chiron – two astrological influences signifying an early involvement in what was to become a major collective health crisis). Three years were to pass before he himself would be diagnosed as having AIDS, but with transiting Neptune opposing Craig's highly intuitive ninth-house Uranus, he already had an unshakeable, disturbing feeling that this mysterious illness would eventually strike him: 'When I first heard about AIDS I remember feeling deep inside that this could happen to me, and that it probably will . . . I remember shivering in my core – I knew I would get it. It didn't paralyze me, but it stayed in the back of my mind.'

In April 1983, with transiting Jupiter and Uranus moving together through the third house (writing and short journeys), Craig left

Houston for New York City, where he had a job working for the cancer information service at the Memorial Sloan-Kettering Cancer Center. Soon after, however, both these planets retrograded to square his natal Saturn, and Craig felt restless and disappointed not only with his new post, but also with life in New York – he had no close friends or ties in the city and hated the neighbourhood where he lived. To fill the emptiness he went to bars, drank and slept around, but without the same fervour as he had back in Houston and Boston. His old lifestyle and usual ploys to make himself feel better were no longer working (transiting Uranus in square to natal Saturn ruling the IC). With natal Uranus opposed by transiting Neptune and trined by transiting Pluto, and with transiting Saturn approaching his progressed ascendant in Scorpio, Craig was feeling the need to make some fundamental changes in his life:

> I was becoming conscious of how self-destructive I was. I always had been aware of it, but not in a way that was strong enough to make me want to change. I was still going to bars and drinking too much, but not with the regularity that I had done in the past. I had it in my mind that I wanted to get my career more together. I was beginning to get offers to work as a correspondent for different papers, especially for articles to do with AIDS and other gay issues. Instead of working full-time for one hospital or organization, I saw the possibility of establishing myself as a freelance writer.

Transiting Jupiter conjuncted Craig's natal Jupiter and passed over his IC and Mars, giving him the incentive in April 1984 to leave the job at Sloan-Kettering. Craig felt good about his decision to pursue a freelance career in journalism, but his new-found enthusiasm was shortlived. In September, when transiting Saturn passed over his Venus and triggered the natal square to Pluto, he became involved in a complicated, draining relationship that consumed much of his time and energy. The disappointing affair ended badly in December (transiting Jupiter square natal Neptune in Libra), and it was at this time that Craig began to feel very low, both psychologically and physically. Depressed and suffering from insomnia, he went into what he described as a tailspin – 'sleepless,

crazed and over-the-edge'. In January 1985, in an effort to resto
balance to his life, he began psychotherapy. This was also the mon..
when he noticed the foreboding purple spot on his arm. At first, he
chose to ignore it; but in late February a biopsy confirmed his worst
fears. He had been feeling empty and lost, and now AIDS had come
to fill that void.

During this period, transiting Pluto in Scorpio was passing over
his south node and approaching a conjunction with his progressed
ascendant. Pluto had brought the lurking illness out of hiding, and
with it came the need to deal not only with his initial reactions of
shock and depression, but also to explore and sort through deep-
seated emotions and ingrained patterns of behaviour (the south
node in Scorpio). Two years before, when transiting Saturn had
passed over his progressed ascendant, Craig had felt he wanted to
break free of self-destructive patterns and to build his life on a new
foundation, but, in spite of these urges, he hadn't made much
progress in this direction. Now with transiting Pluto reaching this
point, the need to change could no longer be avoided. By June of
1985, he found a new psychotherapist who was already working
with a number of AIDS patients. Faced with the possibility of
death, Craig chose to look more deeply into himself than ever before,
and attended therapy three times a week. As reflected by the transits
and progressions involving Pluto and Scorpio, Craig's inner explo-
rations brought him into contact with intense feelings of anger,
bitterness, grief and fear:

> Through the therapy, I looked at my anger towards my parents,
> and old feelings associated with the sudden death of my father
> when I was two. I also had to face how incredibly irritated I was
> with almost everyone around me. If I was at the grocery store and
> someone was complaining about having to wait too long in the
> check-out line, I wanted to slug that person in the face. What right
> did others have to complain and moan? Their problems were
> nothing compared to mine. I was going to die!

From the time of the diagnosis in early 1985 through to the end
of 1986, transiting Uranus was passing over Craig's natal Mercury–
Sun conjunction in Sagittarius and triggering the grand trine with

the Moon in Aries and Pluto in Leo. I was surprised to find the onset of full-blown AIDS coinciding with a major transit activating a grand trine, which, traditionally, is meant to be a benefic aspect, bringing blessings and good fortune into one's life. However, the fact that Craig's natal grand trine involves Pluto suggests that a crisis, breakdown, or major challenge may have been needed to help him realize the promise of this configuration and the unfolding of his life's quest or purpose. The fiery grand trine in air houses bestows Craig with a natural warmth, charm, intelligence, extroversion and adventurous spirit – qualities that had nearly always made it easy for him to 'get by' in life. But during this period, with transiting Uranus awakening the grand trine, he was presented with a crisis that would challenge him to mobilize many more of his untapped resources and strengths. The grand trine is also part of a Kite Formation: a planetary pattern which involves a fourth planet in opposition to one of the corners of the trine and sextile to the other ends. In his book *The Horoscope, The Road and Its Travelers*, Alan Oken writes that the Kite is a 'more stable and powerful configuration than the Grand Trine, as the opposition gives a definite focal point for the direction of the abundant energy contained within this planetary picture'.[1] In Craig's case, Neptune opposes his Moon, one of the ends of the grand trine, and sextiles the other two ends (the Sun and Mercury in Sagittarius and his Pluto in Leo). In other words, his first-house Neptune forms the focal point of the Kite and also rules his sixth-house of health. A 'Neptunian' illness could have turned Craig into a helpless victim. Instead, with Uranus transiting in aspect to all the planets involved in the Kite, AIDS activated Craig's fiery grand trine in a way it had never been used before: he discovered the initiator, the crusader and the fighter in himself.

Shortly after his diagnosis, Craig heard reports about ribaviron, a drug that reputedly could inhibit the virus from replicating itself, thereby holding the disease in check. Ribaviron, as yet untested by the American Medical Association, wasn't legal in the States. None the less, in September 1985 Craig arranged a trip to Mexico where it could easily be obtained. He brought a large supply back to New York, and began using it under the guidance of a consenting doctor. At this time, transiting Uranus (the planet associated with rebellion and defiance) was moving direct after a station in close sextile to his natal Neptune (the focal point of his Kite and the planet associated with drugs). Defying the medical establishment's position and obtaining the ribaviron was a turning-point for Craig; from then on, he felt more in control of his illness and his life: 'I had been in despair and had felt hopeless. But now I was feeling more powerful, and more determined to show the world I could tackle this disease. Getting hold of the ribaviron was the first step.'

Craig's therapist wanted him to join a group for people with AIDS. Craig, however, took this a step further. In January 1986 (with transiting Uranus conjuncting his Sun, ruling Leo on the cusp of his eleventh house of groups), instead of joining somebody else's group, he started his own. With so much diverse information coming from so many sources about how to treat AIDS, Craig felt that he and other people in the same situation as himself would benefit from pooling their experiences. The group he formed eventually became known as the 'Cure of the Week Club'; members met once a week for a year to support each other and to exchange information about any new treatments they had come across or tried. The group – *his* group – provided Craig with a purpose, a structure into which to channel effectively the rebellious energy activated by transiting Uranus. In addition, during much of this period, transiting Jupiter – the planet of hope and expansion – was moving through his sixth house of work and health. The weekly meetings kept Craig abreast of the latest information about AIDS, and in this way he became a personal clearing house of medical knowledge of the illness. What he learned then would later prove invaluable in furthering his writing career.

It was also through the group that Craig became friendly with a man who owned a huge mansion on Long Island. Invited to use the mansion as much as he pleased, Craig spent the summer of 1986 there, an idyllic location where he took advantage of an opportunity to co-author a novel with a writer friend (transiting Uranus over his third-house Sun ruling Leo on the cusp of the eleventh). The outside help he received during this period deepened Craig's appreciation of friendship and gave him a renewed sense of hope and well-being (transiting Neptune trine and transiting Pluto sextile natal Saturn in the eleventh which rules the fourth):

I was getting nurturing, and it made me feel good to be out of the dump I was living in – to be in a beautiful place in the country, like a glorious situation in the middle of the Titanic sinking. I started to feel alive again. My network of friends expanded and I was meeting new kinds of people – all kinds ... gay, straight, semi-celebrities. I realized then, more than ever, that I couldn't deal with my crisis alone. I needed an elaborate support system.

In 1986 and through much of 1987, transiting Pluto was sextiling Craig's Jupiter at the same time as transiting Neptune was approaching a conjunction with natal Jupiter. Jupiter rules his Sun, and any transit to it will have a powerful effect on his sense of identity. These transits to Jupiter correlated with a change in the way he was expressing the Sagittarian side of his nature. In his twenties and for much of his thirties, Craig mostly lived out the wilder side of Sagittarius – the hedonistic party-goer, coasting through life, drinking, playing, enjoying himself without too many strings attached. But with transiting Uranus over his Sun, and transiting Neptune and Pluto aspecting Jupiter (his Sun-ruler) in Capricorn, Craig shifted into a deeper level of Sagittarius – that of the wise, philosophical centaur:

Even when I was at my most hedonistic, I questioned why I was acting like a lunatic. One half of me is a monk on a hill and the other half of me is wild. I was always caught between these two parts – a divided self. Before I got sick, the wild part of me won out. I acted it out compulsively. AIDS was the vehicle to change that in me. I had to cut out the paganism and partying, and invest more in analyzing and understanding myself. AIDS pulled me out of the lunacy stuff and plugged me into a more sane part of myself. In a way it helped me to heal a split within myself. Before I was trapped by my wild side. I had been filling up empty holes in my life with various anaesthetics like alcohol and sex. When I stopped drinking and going to bars so much, I had to face the emptiness inside me. I spent more time alone at home. That was hard – without my addictions, I was left with a depression I had to face. And yet, having gone through that, I feel better off. I still have moments of real agony, but on the whole I feel more calm in myself, better balanced, and much more centred.

In the summer of 1987, Craig was asked to prepare a paper on his experience with AIDS, to be published as part of an anthology for a health conference in Boston (transiting Saturn passing over his third-house Mercury–Sun conjunction and triggering his grand trine/Kite at the same time as his progressed MC was conjuncting natal Pluto in the eleventh). At first Craig was afraid that he wouldn't be able to produce anything worthwhile. However, as transiting Jupiter in Aries was sextiling his natal Uranus in the ninth, he was invited on holiday to Italy. Typical of his Sagittarian nature, travelling gave him a needed distance and objectivity, and when he returned to America he successfully completed the article. In doing so, he realized he had much more to say than the length of the paper allowed. It was then that he decided to write a book, a guide offering to others the kinds of insights he had gained into living and coping with AIDS. By May 1988, he had secured a contract for his book; with Saturn and Uranus moving through his third house and opposing natal Uranus ruling his fifth house of creativity, he confronts the task of putting his vision into words:

> Getting a book contract was amazing. Just a couple of years ago, the idea of my writing a book about AIDS was so far-fetched, and now it is a reality. This is one of the payoffs to having to go through the nightmare I have been facing. My career is taking shape, and I believe in myself as a writer. I used to throw myself into self-defeating love affairs . . . I used up most of my time that way. Now I am freer to put my energy into other, more constructive things. Hopefully people can benefit from my perspective, from what I have gone through. I feel I have something to say – something to share with people who have AIDS, and something to say to those who know people with AIDS.

Transiting Uranus opposing Uranus is traditionally associated with the mid-life crisis, a period of self-examination and re-definition. Under this transit, we become more aware of our mortality, and as a result we may choose to make profound changes in how we conduct our lives. Facing his illness and the loss, through AIDS, of many of his close friends, Craig's recognition of his own mortality is far from theoretical. A very real spectre of death hovers over him, compounding and intensifying his mid-life issues, impelling him to cast aside superficial or destructive behaviour in favour of that which is positive and life-supporting.

At the same time as transiting Uranus is opposing his Uranus, transiting Neptune is now crossing Craig's IC and conjuncting his Mars, bringing out his natal Mars–Neptune square. This transit describes a time when Craig, a long-term AIDS survivor, has to live with constant uncertainty, with the possibility that his weakened immune system will no longer be able to ward off further infection and death. A Neptune–Mars conjunction can rob us of physical drive and energy, but it can also give rise to inspired action, great compassion and the desire to help other people. And now, more than ever before in his life, Craig can use his wise third-house Sun and Mercury in Sagittarius and his pragmatic Jupiter in Capricorn to teach, guide and inspire others with what he has so far learned:

> The explosive irony is that in the face of a nightmare that breathes death, we must develop a philosophy of living – *a strategy* – as our defense . . . Of all the traumas and issues associated with AIDS, I try to separate them into two categories – those that are in my control and those that are not. On a day-to-day basis, I find that it helps to ignore the issues over which I have no control and focus on those I *can* affect. The tendency to lean toward hope*ful*ness or hope*less*ness is largely dependent on this. Choice is a large part of control and I choose hopefulness . . . By taking charge of things that are at least partially controllable, a self-empowering energy emerges and coping becomes pro- gressively easier . . . Compared to the alternative – passive de- pression – is there really a choice?[2]

Craig has Mars conjunct Jupiter at the very bottom of his chart. Underneath it all, he is a fighter, determined to find meaning in what he is going through and to hold on to whatever power he has in his war against AIDS.

> If I had the chance to start all over again from square one, I wouldn't choose to go through this. But why not get what we can out of what is inescapable? I'm battle-scarred and battle-wounded,

but I have found a new kind of inner strength. It's the curious side of this business, that there is something to be found . . . that even with all the pain and misery, there is a light in the tunnel.

Notes

INTRODUCTION

1   Assagioli cited in Piero Ferrucci, *What We May Be* (Wellingborough, UK: Turnstone Press, 1982), p. 113.
2   Dane Rudhyar, *The Astrology of Self-Actualization and The New Morality* (Lakemont, Georgia: CSA Press, 1970), p. 27.
3   Although Chiron often appears as a major astrological factor in times of pain and crisis, I don't have enough experience of working with this planet to write at length about it and therefore have not dealt with transits to or from Chiron in this book (except briefly in the case histories in ch. 10). For an in-depth discussion of this planet, the reader is referred to Melanie Reinhart's insightful book, *Chiron and the Healing Journey: An Astrological and Psychological Perspective* (forthcoming, also part of the Arkana Contemporary Astrology series).
4   When referring to clients, names have been changed to ensure confidentiality.

CHAPTER 1:   The Search for Meaning

1   Viktor Frankl, *Man's Search for Meaning* (New York: Washington Square Press, 1984).
2   Ibid., p. 95.
3   Ibid., p. 98.
4   Piero Ferrucci, *What We May Be* (Wellingborough, UK: Turnstone Press, 1982), p. 163.
5   Robert Hand, *Planets in Transit* (Gloucester, Mass.: Para Research Inc., 1976), p. 5.
6   Liz Greene, *The Astrology of Fate* (London: George Allen and Unwin, 1984), p. 8.
7   Hand, *Planets*, p. 5.

379

8   Ibid., p. 6.
9   Greene, *Astrology*, p. 8.
10 Cited in Ferrucci, *What We May Be*, p. 163.
11 Frankl, *Man's Search*, p. 140.
12 Beata Bishop, 'Mapping the Psyche: The Use of Astrology in Psychotherapy', lecture given to Astrological Association of Great Britain, 21 June 1986.

CHAPTER 2:   Breaking Down to Break Through
1   Ken Wilber, *No Boundary* (Boulder, Col., and London: New Science Library, Shambhala, 1981), p. 4.
2   Ibid., pp. 5–14.
3   Marilyn Ferguson, *The Aquarian Conspiracy* (London: Granada, 1981), pp. 176–83.
4   Sallie Nichols, *Jung and the Tarot* (York Beach, Maine: Samuel Weiser Inc., 1980), p. 52.
5   Elisabeth Kübler-Ross, *On Death and Dying* (New York: Macmillan, 1969).
6   James Hillman, 'Betrayal', *Spring* 1965, Zurich and New York (Spring Publications), pp. 57–76.
7   Ferguson, *Aquarian Conspiracy*, p. 80.

CHAPTER 3:   Interpreting Transits: Some Practical Guidelines
1   Betty Lundsted, *Transits: The Time of Your Life* (York Beach, Maine: Samuel Weiser Inc., 1980), p. 10.
2   Tracy Marks, *The Astrology of Self-Discovery* (Reno, Nev.: CRCS Publications, 1985), p. 124.
3   Robert Hand, *Planets in Transit* (Gloucester, Mass.: Para Research Inc., 1976).
4   For more on midpoints the reader is referred to an excellent new book by Mike Harding and Charles Harvey, *Working with Astrology*: A psychological guide to midpoints, harmonics, and astro-cartography (London: Arkana, forthcoming in January 1990).

CHAPTER 4:   Uranian Crises
1   Rudhyar, cited in Arroyo, *Astrology, Karma, and Transformation* (Reno, Nev.: CRCS Publications, 1978), p. 41.
2   Fritjof Capra, *The Turning Point* (London: Fontana, 1982), p. 70.
3   Teilhard de Chardin, cited in Marilyn Ferguson, *The Aquarian Conspiracy* (London: Granada, 1981), p. 52.
4   Rupert Sheldrake, *A New Science of Life: The Hypothesis of Formative Causation* (London: Blond and Briggs, 1981).

CHAPTER 5:   The Transits of Uranus to the Planets and Through the Houses

1   Gail Sheehy, *Passages* (New York: Bantam Books, 1972).
2   Gail Sheehy, *Pathfinders* (New York: Bantam Books, 1981), p. 65.
3   Sheehy, *Pathfinders*, p. 37.
4   Ibid., p. 314.
5   Some astrologers attribute the fourth house to mother and the tenth to father, while other astrologers attribute the fourth to father and the tenth to mother. I believe that the 'shaping parent' – the one with whom the child spends the most time and who usually has the task of adapting the child to society – fits best with the tenth house; and the 'hidden parent' – the one who is with the child less and who may be more of a mystery or unknown quantity to the child – should be connected to the fourth house. Generally, the mother is the shaping parent, and for this reason, I assign her to the tenth house; while the father is often the more hidden or less well-known parent and therefore I associate him with the fourth. In actual practice, through talking with a client I can formulate which parent fits better with which house. (For a further discussion on this topic, see my book *The Twelve Houses* (Wellingborough, UK: Aquarian Press, 1985), pp. 56–7.)

CHAPTER 6:   Neptunian Crises

1   Alan Watts, *The Book on the Taboo Against Knowing Who You Are* (London: Abacus, 1977).
2   Paraphrased in Peter Russell, *The Awakening Earth* (London: Routledge and Kegan Paul, 1982), p. 127.
3.   Ibid., p. 127.
4   Ken Wilber, *No Boundary* (Boulder, Col., and London: New Science Library, Shambhala, 1981), p. 37.
5   Robert Bly (ed.), *The Kabir Book: Forty-Four of the Ecstatic Poems of Kabir* (Boston: The Seventies Press, 1977), p. 9.
6   Sallie Nichols, *Jung and the Tarot* (York Beach, Maine: Samuel Weiser Inc., 1980), p. 222.
7   T. S. Eliot, 'East Coker', in *Four Quartets* (London: Faber and Faber, 1959), p. 28.

CHAPTER 7: The Transits of Neptune to the Planets and Through the Houses

1   Robert Hand, *Planets in Transit* (Gloucester, Mass.: Para Research Inc., 1976), p. 443.
2   Gail Sheehy, *Pathfinders* (New York: Bantam Books, 1981), p. 294.

3 Erik Erikson, *Childhood and Society* (London: Triad Palladin, 1963), p. 241.
4 Ibid., p. 222.
5 Bernie Siegal, *Love, Medicine and Miracles* (New York: Harper and Row, 1986).
6 Hand, *Planets in Transit*, p. 430.
7 Elisabeth Kübler-Ross, *On Death and Dying* (New York: Macmillan, 1969).
8 For a fuller discussion of these issues, the reader is referred to Adolf Guggenbuhl-Craig, *Power and the Helping Professions* (Zurich: Spring Publications, 1978).
9 Einstein cited in Russell, *The Awakening Earth* (London: Routledge and Kegan Paul, 1982).
10 Will Durant, *On the Meaning of Life* (New York: Kay Long and Richard Smith, 1932), p. 128.
11 Judith Viorst, *Necessary Losses* (New York: Simon and Schuster, 1986), ch. 2.

CHAPTER 8:   Plutonian Crises
1 Melanie Klein, *Love, Guilt and Reparation and Other Works 1921–1945* (London: Hogarth Press, 1985).
2 Alice Bailey, *The Labours of Hercules* (London: Lucis Press, 1977), p. 67.
3 Rainer Maria Rilke, *Letters to a Young Poet*, trans. M. D. Herter (New York: W. & W. Norton, 1934), p. 69.
4 Rilke (Letter 74, *Briefe aus den Jahren 1907 bis 1914*) cited in Rollo May, *Love and Will* (London: Collins, 1969), p. 122.
5 For further elaboration on this myth, the reader is referred to Diane Wolkstein and Samuel Noah Kramer, *Inanna, Queen of Heaven and Earth* (London: Rider, 1984); and Sylvia Brinton Perera, *Descent to the Goddess* (Toronto: Inner City Books, 1981).
6 Irvin Yalom, *Existential Psychotherapy* (New York: Basic Books, 1980), p. 9.
7 Abraham Maslow, *The Farther Reaches of Human Nature* (New York: Penguin Books, 1985), p. 34.
8 See note 6.
9 Erich Fromm, *Escape from Freedom* (New York: Holt, Rinehart and Winston, 1941).
10 Yalom, *Existential Psychotherapy*, p. 423.

CHAPTER 9:   Transits of Pluto to the Planets and Through the Houses
1 Donna Cunningham, *Healing Pluto Problems* (York Beach, Maine: Samuel Weiser Inc., 1986), p. 148.

2 Irvin Yalom, *Existential Psychotherapy* (New York: Basic Books, 1980), p. 263.

3 See Cunningham, *Healing Pluto Problems*, section entitled 'Pluto and the Pregnancy Trap', p. 168.

4 Schweitzer, cited in Piero Ferrucci, *What We May Be* (Wellingborough, UK: Turnstone Press, 1982), p. 105.

5 Paraphrased in Peter Russell, *The Awakening Earth* (London: Routledge and Kegan Paul, 1982), p. 125.

6 Epictetus, cited in Ferrucci, *What We May Be*, p. 105.

7 For further information and advice on this subject, see Cunningham, *Healing Pluto Problems*, ch. 5.

8 Marilyn Ferguson, *The Aquarian Conspiracy* (London: Granada, 1981), p. 93.

9 Charles Harvey, 'John M. Addey', *Astrological Journal*, Astrological Association of Great Britain (Urania Trust Centre, 396 Caledonian Rd., London N1), Summer 1982, p. 136.

10 Erik Erikson, *Childhood and Society* (London: Triad Palladin, 1963), p. 226.

11 Robert Hand, *Planets in Transit* (Gloucester, Mass.: Para Research Inc., 1976), p. 482.

12 For an interesting study of the near-death experience, the reader is referred to Margot Grey, *Return from Death: An Exploration of the Near-Death Experience* (London: Arkana, 1985).

13 Hand, *Planets in Transit*, p. 485.

14 Betty Lundsted, *Transits: The Time of Your Life* (York Beach, Maine: Samuel Weiser Inc., 1980), p. 10.

15 Ferguson, *The Aquarian Conspiracy*, p. 93.

CHAPTER 10:   Three Case Histories

1 Alan Oken, *The Horoscope, The Road and Its Travelers* (New York: Bantam, 1974), p. 274.

2 Craig Rowland, 'A View from the Moon', published July 1988 in an anthology released at a conference called 'The Second International Lesbian and Gay Health Conference and AIDS Forum' in Boston, Massachusetts. The conference was sponsored by the National Lesbian and Gay Health Foundation.

Suggested Reading

Astrology

The following astrology books are recommended for their insights into the outer planets, transits and the creative use of pain and crisis.

Arroyo, Stephen, *Astrology, Karma, and Transformation* (Reno, Nev.: CRCS Publications, 1978).

Cunningham, Donna, *Healing Pluto Problems* (York Beach, Maine: Samuel Weiser Inc., 1986).

Freeman, Martin, *Forecasting by Astrology* (Wellingborough, UK: Aquarian Press, 1982).

Green, Jeff, *Pluto: The Evolutionary Journey of the Soul*, Volume 1 (St Paul, Min.: Llewellyn Publications, 1986).

Green, Jeff, *Uranus: Freedom from the Known* (St Paul, Minn.: Llewellyn Publications, 1988).

Greene, Liz, *Relating* (Wellingborough, UK: Thorsons, 1978).

Greene, Liz, *The Outer Planets and Their Cycles* (Reno, Nev.: CRCS Publications, 1983).

Greene, Liz, *The Astrology of Fate* (London: George Allen and Unwin, 1984).

Greene, Liz, *Neptune: The Inmost Light* (London: Penguin Arkana, forthcoming).

Greene, Liz, and Sasportas, Howard, *The Development of the Personality* (York Beach, Maine: Samuel Weiser Inc.; London: Routledge and Kegan Paul, 1987).

Greene, Liz, and Sasportas, Howard, *The Dynamics of the Unconscious* (York Beach, Maine: Samuel Weiser Inc., 1988).

Hand, Robert, *Planets in Transit* (Gloucester, Mass., Para Research Inc., 1976).

Lundsted, Betty, *Transits: The Time of Your Life* (York Beach, Maine: Samuel Weiser Inc., 1980).

Lundsted, Betty, *Planetary Cycles: Astrological Indicators of Crises and Change* (York Beach, Maine: Samuel Weiser Inc., 1984).

Marks, Tracy, *The Astrology of Self-Discovery* (Reno, Nev.: CRCS Publications, 1985).

Morimando, Patricia, *The Neptune Effect* (York Beach, Maine: Samuel Weiser Inc., 1979).

Reinhart, Melanie, *Chiron and the Healing Journey: An Astrological and Psychological Perspective* (London: Arkana, 1989).

Ruperti, Alexander, *Cycles of Becoming* (Reno, Nev.: CRCS Publications, 1977).

Stone, Pauline, *The Astrology of Karma* (Wellingborough, UK: Aquarian Press, 1988).

Psychology

Frankl, Viktor, *Man's Search for Meaning* (New York: Washington Square Press, 1984).

Friday, Nancy, *Jealousy* (London: Fontana/Collins, 1987). An exploration of jealousy, envy, and related emotional complexes.

Missildine, Hugh, *Your Inner Child of the Past* (New York: Pocket Books, 1982). How our experiences as a child affect our adult life.

Peck, M. Scott, *The Road Less Travelled: A New Psychology of Love, Traditional Values and Spiritual Growth* (London: Rider, 1985). Written by a practising psychiatrist, this book explores how facing pain and crisis can lead to a higher level of self-understanding.

Rowe, Dorothy, *Depression: The Way Out of Your Prison* (London: Routledge and Kegan Paul, 1983).

Scarf, Maggie, *Unfinished Business: Pressure Points in the Lives of Women* (New York: Doubleday, 1980). An investigation into the kinds of physical and psychological issues that women confront in different phases of their lives.

Scarf, Maggie, *Intimate Partners: Patterns in Love and Marriage* (London: Century, 1987). A fascinating study of problems in relationships and marriage, and how unresolved dilemmas from early life and the past affect later partnerships.

Sheehy, Gail, *Passages: Predictable Crises of Adult Life* (New York: Bantam, 1977). A road map of life exploring the kinds of changes we face in our twenties, thirties, forties and fifties.

Sheehy, Gail, *Pathfinders: Overcoming Crises of Adult Life and Finding your Own Path to Well-Being* (New York: Bantam, 1982). Sheehy explores such issues as the mid-life crisis, retirement and old age, and why some people overcome life's crises while others do not.

Viorst, Judith, *Necessary Losses: The Loves, Illusions, Dependencies and Impossible Expectations that All of Us Have to Give Up in Order to Grow* (New York: Simon and Schuster, 1986). Highly recommended as a readable, insightful study into the kinds of losses we experience in the process of living, revealing the inextricable link between loss and growth.

Death, Loss, and the Grieving Process

Kübler-Ross, Elisabeth, *On Death and Dying* (New York: Macmillan, 1969).

Levine, Stephen, *Who Dies? An Investigation of Conscious Living and Conscious Dying* (New York: Anchor Press, 1982).

Lewis, C. S., *A Grief Observed* (London and Boston, Mass.: Faber and Faber, 1961). One man's reflection on grief, written after death of his wife.

Pincus, Lily, *Death and the Family: The Importance of Mourning* (London and Boston, Mass.: Faber and Faber, 1974).

Stearns, Ann Kaiser, *Living Through Personal Crisis* (London: Sheldon Press, 1984).

Insights into Illness

McCormick, Elizabeth Wilde, *Nervous Breakdown: A Positive Guide to Coping, Healing and Rebuilding* (London: Unwin Paperbacks, 1988).

Siegel, Bernie, *Love, Medicine and Miracles: Lessons Learned about Self-Healing from a Surgeon's Experience with Exceptional Patients* (New York: Harper and Row, 1986).

Simonton, Carl, Stephanie Simonton and James Creighton, *Getting Well Again* (Toronto: Bantam Books, 1981).

PENGUIN

ARKANA

NEW AGE BOOKS FOR MIND, BODY & SPIRIT

CONTEMPORARY ASTROLOGY

Series Editor: Erin Sullivan

The ancient science of astrology, founded on the correlation between celestial movements and terrestrial events, recognizes the universe as an indivisible whole in which all parts are interconnected. Mirroring this perception of the unity of life, modern physics has revealed the web of relationships underlying everything in existence. Despite the inevitable backlash as old paradigms expire, we are now entering an age in which scientific explanations and models of the cosmos are in accord with basic astrological principles and beliefs. In such a climate, astrology is poised to emerge once again as a serious tool for a greater understanding of our true nature. In readable books written by experts, Arkana's *Contemporary Astrology* series offers all the insight and practical wisdom of the newest vanguard of astrological thought.

Titles already published or in preparation:

The Gods of Change: Pain, Crisis and the Transits of Uranus, Neptune and Pluto Howard Sasportas

Character and Fate: The Psychology of the Birthchart Katharine Merlin

Chiron and the Healing Journey: An Astrological and Psychological Perspective Melanie Reinhart

Working With Astrology Michael Harding and Charles Harvey

Saturn: A New Look at an Old Devil Liz Greene

The Karmic Journey Judy Hall

Neo-Astrology: A Copernican Revolution Michel Gauquelin

Saturn in Transit Erin Sullivan

PENGUIN

ARKANA

NEW AGE BOOKS FOR MIND, BODY & SPIRIT

With over 200 titles currently in print, Arkana is the leading name in quality books for mind, body and spirit. Arkana encompasses the spirituality of both East and West, ancient and new. A vast range of interests is covered, including Psychology and Transformation, Health, Science and Mysticism, Women's Spirituality, Zen, Western Traditions and Astrology.

If you would like a catalogue of Arkana books, please write to:

Sales Dept. – Arkana
Penguin Books USA Inc.
375 Hudson Street
New York, NY 10014

Arkana Marketing Department
Penguin Books Ltd
27 Wrights Lane
London W8 5TZ